The Middle-Income Trap

A World Bank Group Flagship Report

WORLD DEVELOPMENT REPORT 2024

The Middle-Income Trap

© 2024 International Bank for Reconstruction and Development / The World Bank
1818 H Street NW, Washington, DC 20433
Telephone: 202-473-1000; Internet: www.worldbank.org

Some rights reserved

1 2 3 4 27 26 25 24

This work is a product of the staff of The World Bank with external contributions. The findings, interpretations, and conclusions expressed in this work do not necessarily reflect the views of The World Bank, its Board of Executive Directors, or the governments they represent.

The World Bank does not guarantee the accuracy, completeness, or currency of the data included in this work and does not assume responsibility for any errors, omissions, or discrepancies in the information, or liability with respect to the use of or failure to use the information, methods, processes, or conclusions set forth. The boundaries, colors, denominations, links/footnotes, and other information shown in this work do not imply any judgment on the part of The World Bank concerning the legal status of any territory or the endorsement or acceptance of such boundaries. The citation of works authored by others does not mean The World Bank endorses the views expressed by those authors or the content of their works.

Nothing herein shall constitute or be construed or considered to be a limitation upon or waiver of the privileges and immunities of The World Bank, all of which are specifically reserved.

Rights and Permissions

This work is available under the Creative Commons Attribution 3.0 IGO license (CC BY 3.0 IGO) http://creativecommons.org/licenses/by/3.0/igo. Under the Creative Commons Attribution license, you are free to copy, distribute, transmit, and adapt this work, including for commercial purposes, under the following conditions:

Attribution—Please cite the work as follows: World Bank. 2024. *World Development Report 2024: The Middle-Income Trap*. Washington, DC: World Bank. doi:10.1596/978-1-4648-2078-6. License: Creative Commons Attribution CC BY 3.0 IGO

Translations—If you create a translation of this work, please add the following disclaimer along with the attribution: *This translation was not created by The World Bank and should not be considered an official World Bank translation. The World Bank shall not be liable for any content or error in this translation.*

Adaptations—If you create an adaptation of this work, please add the following disclaimer along with the attribution: *This is an adaptation of an original work by The World Bank. Views and opinions expressed in the adaptation are the sole responsibility of the author or authors of the adaptation and are not endorsed by The World Bank.*

Third-party content—The World Bank does not necessarily own each component of the content contained within the work. The World Bank therefore does not warrant that the use of any third-party-owned individual component or part contained in the work will not infringe on the rights of those third parties. The risk of claims resulting from such infringement rests solely with you. If you wish to reuse a component of the work, it is your responsibility to determine whether permission is needed for that reuse and to obtain permission from the copyright owner. Examples of components can include, but are not limited to, tables, figures, or images.

All queries on rights and licenses should be addressed to World Bank Publications, The World Bank, 1818 H Street NW, Washington, DC 20433, USA; e-mail: pubrights@worldbank.org.

ISSN, ISBN, e-ISBN, and DOI:

Softcover
ISSN: 0163-5085
ISBN: 978-1-4648-2078-6
e-ISBN: 978-1-4648-2096-0
DOI: 10.1596/978-1-4648-2078-6

Hardcover
ISSN: 0163-5085
ISBN: 978-1-4648-2097-7
DOI: 10.1596/978-1-4648-2097-7

Cover and interior design: Creative Services, Global Corporate Solutions, World Bank.
Library of Congress Control Number: 2024941787

Contents

xv   *Foreword*
xvii   *Acknowledgments*
xxi   *Summary*
xxv   *Glossary*
xxix   *Abbreviations*

1   Overview: Making a Miracle
1   In brief
2   'To get rich is glorious'
4   One trap or two?
5   Investment, infusion, and innovation—additively and progressively
10   The economics of creative destruction
17   Striking the right balance
26   The road ahead
28   Notes
28   References

31   Part 1: Middle-Income Transitions

33   Chapter 1: Slowing Growth
33   Key messages
33   Introduction
34   Growth in middle-income countries
37   Measuring progress through the middle stages of development
40   Growth in middle-income countries is slower
45   Notes
45   References

47   Spotlight

53   Chapter 2: Structural Stasis
53   Key messages
53   Introduction
55   Economic development = structural change
56   Infuse first, then innovate
67   Notes
67   References

69 Chapter 3: Shrinking Spaces
69 Key messages
69 Introduction
72 Fragmenting international trade
73 Elevated debt
75 Climate action
78 Notes
78 References

81 Part 2: Creative Destruction

85 Chapter 4: Creation
85 Key messages
85 Creation: The protagonist of economic growth, where incumbents create value alongside entrants
88 Creative destruction: Three decades of increasingly refined analysis
91 In middle-income countries, too few small entrants disrupt, and too few large incumbents innovate or infuse global technologies
96 How governments stifle firms' incentives to grow, infuse global technologies, and innovate
104 Modernizing data and diagnostic tools to understand and regulate creative destruction—from X-rays to MRIs
106 Notes
106 References

109 Chapter 5: Preservation
109 Key messages
109 Preservation is an antagonist of creation because it is also an antagonist of destruction
111 Talent drives economic progress, but social immobility holds back the development of talent
115 Elite pacts perpetuate social immobility and preserve the status quo
123 Patriarchal gender norms hold back a large proportion of the population
127 The cost of social immobility and preservation: Holding back the energies that drive creation
129 Notes
130 References

135 Chapter 6: Destruction
135 Key messages
135 Destruction: To be expected, managed, and mitigated
137 The climate and energy crises could trigger restructuring and reallocation
151 Destruction without creation: The risks of becoming stranded nations
155 Notes
156 References

159 Part 3: Making Miracles
161 Chapter 7: Disciplining Incumbency
161 Key messages
161 Balancing incumbents' innovation and abuse of dominance
163 Updating institutions to weaken the forces of preservation
172 Incentives for incumbents to strengthen creation
179 Interventions to correct errant behavior by incumbents
183 Notes
184 References

189 Chapter 8: Rewarding Merit
189 Key messages
189 Moving forward by promoting merit activities
190 The economic and social mobility of people
198 The value added by firms
207 Reducing an economy's greenhouse gas emissions
213 Notes
214 References

221 Chapter 9: Capitalizing on Crises
221 Key messages
221 Using crises to destroy outdated arrangements
222 Globalizing decarbonization
228 Expanding low-carbon infrastructure
232 Decoupling economic growth and emissions
239 Notes
240 References

Boxes

12	O.1	Who and what are incumbents? Leading firms, technologies, nations, elites—and men	65	2.3	The magic of investment accelerations
			70	3.1	Graying growth
			82	P2.1	Joseph Schumpeter and creative destruction
37	1.1	Misunderstanding through misclassification	93	4.1	Vibrant corporate R&D, connected places, mobile people, and successful markets for patents: How the United States nurtured an innovation ecosystem
41	1.2	A growth superstar: How the Republic of Korea leveraged foreign ideas and innovation			
42	1.3	Identifying growth slowdowns			
60	2.1	The Meiji Restoration reconnected Japan with global knowledge	97	4.2	Examples of size-dependent policies
61	2.2	Three ways to evade the middle-income trap: Swiftly (Estonia), steadily (Poland), or slowly (Bulgaria)	100	4.3	The productivity effects of credit misallocation and capital market underdevelopment

113	5.1	Firms with better-educated managers adopt more technology
120	5.2	Living in *favelas* makes it more difficult to get a job
128	5.3	Global Gender Distortions Index: Measuring economic growth lost to gendered barriers
138	6.1	The diffusion of low-carbon technologies as defined and measured in this chapter
172	7.1	A digital tool helps female entrepreneurs obtain capital and training in rural Mexico
174	7.2	Technology for market access
175	7.3	Supplier development programs to connect small firms with large firms
177	7.4	Turning brain drain into brain gain
179	7.5	Tackling anticompetitive practices increases incumbents' innovation incentives
192	8.1	Developing foundational skills: Learning from Finland and Chile
195	8.2	Promoting better student choices with digital tools
196	8.3	Improving students' test scores by using online studying assistance from the Khan Academy
203	8.4	Catching up by opening up and modernizing firms: The Spanish growth miracle
207	8.5	Productivity growth can slow deforestation in Brazil
212	8.6	Correcting abuses of dominance in electricity markets
237	9.1	Technologies that can act as "stabilizers" of energy supply

Figures

3	O.1	Income per capita of middle-income countries relative to that of the United States has been stagnant for decades
5	O.2	If capital accumulation were enough, work in middle-income countries would be nearly three-quarters as rewarding as in the United States, not just one-fifth
6	O.3	Economies become more sophisticated as they transition from middle-income to high-income status
7	O.4	Middle-income countries must engineer two successive transitions to move to high-income status
8	O.5	In the Republic of Korea, Poland, and Chile, the rapid growth from middle- to high-income status has been interspersed with economic crises
9	O.6	From infusion to innovation in the Republic of Korea
11	O.7	Over the last four decades, as the Republic of Korea's labor productivity relative to that of the United States continued to climb, Brazil's peaked—and then sagged
12	O.8	Three views of creative destruction
14	O.9	Creation is a weak force in middle-income countries, where it is characterized by a rampant misallocation of resources
17	O.10	Middle-income countries have to strike a balance among creation, preservation, and destruction
21	O.11	In emerging market and developing economies, few companies are funded by venture capital or private equity

Page	No.	Title
23	O.12	Countries with large, successful diasporas have the highest potential for knowledge transfers
26	O.13	In low- and middle-income countries, the cost of capital for renewables is high
35	1.1	A handful of economies have transitioned from middle-income to high-income status over the last three decades
36	1.2	Income per capita of middle-income countries relative to that of the United States has been stagnant for decades
40	1.3	Sustained growth periods are short-lived, even in rapidly growing economies
43	1.4	Growth slowdowns are most frequent when countries' GDP per capita is less than one-fourth of the United States'
44	1.5	Growth is expected to slow down as countries approach the economic frontier (United States)
44	1.6	Weak institutions hasten and worsen growth slowdowns
55	2.1	As economies develop, capital accumulation brings diminishing returns
56	2.2	A middle-income country will need to engineer two successive transitions to achieve high-income status: Infusion, followed by innovation
58	2.3	The demand for highly skilled workers increases in middle-income countries
59	2.4	STEM graduates are increasingly concentrated in middle-income countries, thereby increasing opportunities for technology infusion
60	2.5	Calibrating policies to a country's stage of development: From imitation to innovation in the Republic of Korea
64	2.6	The innovation gap between high-income countries and others is substantial
64	2.7	Middle-income countries significantly lag behind high-income countries in research capacity
66	B2.3.1	Investment growth accelerations: Colombia, Republic of Korea, and Türkiye
70	B3.1.1	Today's middle-income countries are aging more rapidly than high-income countries did in the past
72	3.1	Globally, harmful trade policies outnumber helpful trade policies
73	3.2	Harmful interventions in the global semiconductor trade have skyrocketed since 2019
74	3.3	Most developing economies are more severely indebted than ever
75	3.4	Debt service payments in emerging markets and middle-income countries may skyrocket as the cost of borrowing soars
76	3.5	In middle-income countries, the energy intensity and carbon intensity of energy consumption are quite high
77	3.6	In middle-income countries, the weighted average cost of capital for utility-scale solar power projects is substantially higher than the cost in high-income countries
78	3.7	Low- and middle-income countries are exposed to similar levels of risk from climate change, and they have less adaptive capacity

Page	No.	Title
83	P2.1	Rebalancing the forces of creation, preservation, and destruction to advance infusion and innovation
86	4.1	Both entrants and incumbents create value and reinforce one another's growth through competition in India's computing services industry
87	4.2	The interactions between entrants and incumbents set the pace of creative destruction
88	4.3	Entrants drive growth: Insights from Aghion and Howitt's seminal paper on creative destruction
89	4.4	Entrants and incumbents drive growth through turnover and upgrading: Insights from Akcigit and Kerr's refined approach to creative destruction
90	4.5	Contrasting examples of innovation: Growth is driven by entrants in the United States and by incumbents in Germany
91	4.6	Entrants and incumbents can reinforce one another's growth: The case of the US business services industry
92	4.7	A cartelized industry suppresses innovation and dynamism: Evidence from the Japanese auto parts sector
93	B4.1.1	The number of patents filed by corporations with the US Patent and Trademark Office has skyrocketed since 1880
95	4.8	In middle-income countries, the growth rate of firms across their life cycles is much lower than in the United States
96	4.9	Microenterprises dominate firm size distributions in India, Mexico, and Peru
97	4.10	Young firms—not small firms—create the most jobs (net) in the United States
100	B4.3.1	Productivity-dependent financial distortions, by GDP per capita
101	4.11	Productivity-dependent distortions are more severe in low- and middle-income countries
102	4.12	Management practices are worse in economies with more policy distortions
112	5.1	The share of skilled workers in large firms increases with GDP per capita
113	B5.1.1	Better-educated managers are more likely to adopt technology in middle-income countries
114	5.2	Higher inequality is associated with higher intergenerational immobility
115	5.3	Intergenerational mobility of skilled workers matters more for middle-income countries than for low-income countries
118	5.4	High inequality within cities is associated with low social mobility from one generation to the next
120	B5.2.1	Slum residents in Rio de Janeiro identified their residence in a *favela* as the largest impediment to getting a job
121	5.5	In many middle-income countries, movement of workers from one part of the country to another is more limited than in high-income countries such as France and the United States
122	5.6	In many middle-income countries, migration costs are higher for individuals without high levels of education

124	5.7	There is a substantial gap between low- and high-income countries in female educational attainment	162	7.1	In Italy, market leaders increase their political connections while reducing innovation
124	5.8	Female labor force participation is low in the Middle East and North Africa and in South Asia	163	7.2	Promoting contestability through institutions, incentives, and interventions
125	5.9	Female labor force participation has evolved differently across countries	164	7.3	In many middle-income countries, markets are dominated by a few business groups, as a survey suggests
125	5.10	The share of female professionals has risen in some countries but not others	165	7.4	In middle-income countries, restrictive product market regulations are pervasive
126	5.11	Globally, women own a smaller share of firms than men	166	7.5	In middle-income countries, both economywide and sectoral input and product market regulations are more restrictive than in high-income countries
127	5.12	Women lag behind men in having financial accounts			
139	6.1	Learning by doing in the manufacture of key low-carbon technologies has resulted in rapid cost declines	167	7.6	The BRICS and large middle-income countries have a significant presence of publicly owned enterprises and governance frameworks that stifle competition
140	6.2	The diffusion of low-carbon technologies is rapidly accelerating			
142	6.3	Low-carbon innovation is driving the emergence of new spatial clusters, start-ups, and financing	168	7.7	A state presence has important effects on firm entry, market concentration, and preferential treatment
145	6.4	The rate of adoption of clean energy technologies is growing more rapidly in middle-income countries than in high-income countries, but the level of adoption is lower	169	7.8	State-owned enterprises dominate coal power generation, while the private sector leads in modern renewable energy
			169	7.9	In low- and middle-income countries, state-owned enterprises are the largest investors in fossil fuel energy generation
147	6.5	Clean energy technology value chains are still dominated by high-income countries and China			
148	6.6	Costa Rica and China are the global front-runners in jobs related to low-carbon technologies	173	7.10	Foreign technology licensing is limited among middle-income country firms
153	6.7	Most of the countries currently "locked in" to declining brown industries are middle-income countries	178	B7.4.1	Some countries are strongly positioned to benefit from knowledge spillovers from their diaspora

180	B7.5.1	In Colombia, after a cartel is sanctioned, market outcomes improve through the entry and growth of previously lagging firms	223	9.1	Use of globalized value chains for solar panels results in faster learning and lower global prices
180	B7.5.2	In Colombia, after an abuse of dominance case, positive market outcomes are driven by improvements in leading firms	224	9.2	Middle-income countries can support global decarbonization by becoming global suppliers of "granular" (type 1 and type 2) energy technologies
181	7.11	Competition authorities in middle-income countries need more capacity to deal with sophisticated policy problems	225	9.3	Extraction and processing of critical minerals for the clean energy transition remain highly concentrated in certain countries
191	8.1	Middle-income countries that transitioned to high-income status first focused on foundational skills	226	9.4	Many middle-income countries have untapped potential to manufacture green products
200	8.2	Countries at lower levels of development have more opportunities for potentially productivity-enhancing job reallocation	227	9.5	All industrial policy implementation and green industrial policy implementation are correlated with GDP per capita
201	8.3	The number of countries creating special enforcement units for large taxpayers has increased	229	9.6	Countries must clear hurdles for both efficient domestic investment and foreign investment in renewable energy
202	8.4	Improvements in allocative efficiency in Chile, China, and India have been driven by reducing productivity-dependent distortions	230	9.7	In many middle-income countries, it is economically efficient to expand renewable energy
206	8.5	In emerging market and developing economies, few companies are funded through venture capital or private equity	231	9.8	In low- and middle-income countries, the cost of capital for renewables is high
208	B8.5.1	Amazon deforestation falls when Brazilian productivity rises	232	9.9	Today's upper-middle-income countries are more energy efficient than upper-middle-income countries in the past
209	8.6	Indirect carbon pricing such as energy taxes is the strongest price signal	233	9.10	Carbon emissions per unit of GDP have been declining worldwide
211	8.7	In some middle-income countries, the prices of renewable energy through competitive auctions have reached record lows	234	9.11	High-income countries have succeeded in reducing overall emissions by curbing energy intensity
			235	9.12	The world is slowly transitioning away from fossil fuels

Maps

141	6.1	In 2022, one-third of online job postings related to low-carbon technologies were in middle-income countries
150	6.2	Limited or outdated electricity transmission networks serve as barriers to the entry of renewable sources
154	6.3	Low-carbon technology jobs in China are growing in manufacturing hubs on the southeast coast, whereas fossil fuel jobs are close to coal mines

Tables

4	O.1	World Bank country classifications and selected global indicators, 2022
7	O.2	To achieve high-income status, countries will need to recalibrate their mix of investment, infusion, and innovation
27	O.3	The *3i* strategy: What countries should do at different stages of development
31	P1.1	World Bank country classifications and selected global indicators, 2022
49	S.1	Suggested indicators provide a clear picture of the underlying structure of an economy
54	2.1	Middle-income countries will need to engineer two successive transitions to develop economic structures that can sustain high-income status
103	4.1	Examples of possible effects of market power on development outcomes

Foreword

In 2007 the World Bank published *An East Asian Renaissance: Ideas for Economic Growth*—the report that coined the phrase "middle-income trap." This was during a decade of booming growth and poverty reduction in developing countries. Yet it was clear by then that many economies—particularly in Latin America and the Middle East—had remained stuck for decades, despite their efforts to rise to high-income status. "Middle-income trap" is now a popular phrase: it results in tens of thousands of Google search references. And it is frequently on the tongues of academics and politicians from developing countries—in Latin America and South Asia and just about every place in between.

A decade ago, in "The Middle-Income Trap Turns Ten," Brookings Institution economist Homi Kharas and I reviewed the burgeoning literature that *An East Asian Renaissance* had inspired. We found that economists had yet to provide a reliable theory of growth to help policy makers navigate the transition from middle- to high-income status. Some had attempted to develop models, but they were poor substitutes for a well-constructed growth framework on which policy makers could build effective development strategies. Meanwhile, the ranks of middle-income countries continued to grow. Five years later, in "Growth Strategies to Avoid the Middle-Income Trap," we proposed that Schumpeterian growth models emphasizing creative destruction and institutional change had the potential to provide the analytical foundations for a fuller understanding of middle-income economies. But to be useful they had to be made a lot more accessible to policy makers.

This is what *World Development Report 2024* sets out to do: provide a simple but reliable growth framework for avoiding or escaping the trap. It identifies lessons from more than 50 years of successes and failures among developing countries while they were climbing the income ladder. Based on these ideas and evidence, it proposes a sequenced, three-pronged approach for today's 100-odd middle-income countries: first *investment*, then *infusion* of new technology from around the world, and then *innovation*. Each shift requires a new mix of policies that, if implemented reasonably well, result in increasingly dynamic enterprises, an increasingly productive workforce, and an increasingly energy-efficient economy. It is an approach that can benefit all countries—low-, middle-, and high-income—seeking high-quality growth.

We are not naive enough to think this will be easy. Middle-income countries will have to work miracles—not only to lift themselves up to high-income status but also to shift away from carbon-intensive growth paths that will lead to environmental ruin. Income levels in Sub-Saharan Africa, where more than half the population lives in middle-income countries, are the same as they were a decade ago. Economic growth rates in middle-income countries have been falling and are expected to average just 4 percent in the 2020s, down from 5 percent in the 2010s and more than 6 percent in the 2000s.

This has implications for the whole world. Middle-income countries are home to three out of every four people—and nearly two-thirds of those who struggle in extreme poverty. They are responsible for 40 percent of the world's total economic output—and nearly two-thirds of global carbon emissions. In short, the global effort to end extreme poverty and spread prosperity and livability will largely be won or lost in these countries.

The road ahead has even stiffer challenges than those seen in the past: rapidly aging populations and burgeoning debt, fierce geopolitical and trade frictions, and the growing difficulty of speeding up economic progress without fouling the environment. Yet many middle-income countries still use a playbook from the last century, relying mainly on policies designed to expand investment. That is like driving a car just in first gear and trying to make it go faster. If they stick with the old playbook, most developing countries will lose the race to create reasonably prosperous societies by the middle of this century. At current trends, it will take China more than 10 years just to reach one-quarter of US income per capita, Indonesia nearly 70 years, and India 75 years.

The team that has written this report hopes to radically alter this arithmetic. Our hope is that *World Development Report 2024* will, in short order, make the expression "middle-income trap" completely obsolete.

Indermit Gill
Chief Economist of the World Bank Group and
Senior Vice President for Development Economics

Acknowledgments

World Development Report 2024 was prepared by a World Bank team led by Somik V. Lall. Ufuk Akcigit served as the Academic Lead, and Joyce Antone Ibrahim was the Report Manager. Overall guidance was provided by Indermit Gill, Senior Vice President and Chief Economist. The Report was sponsored by the Development Economics Vice Presidency.

The core team comprised Roberto Fattal Jaef, Maria Marta Ferreyra, Kenan Karakülah, Tatjana Kleineberg, Mathilde Lebrand, Martha Martinez Licetti, Dino Merotto, Forhad Shilpi, Katherine Stapleton, Maria Vagliasindi, and Ekaterina Vostroknutova.

Victor Ajayi, Deniz Aycan, Narcisse Cha'ngom, Dong Phuong Dao, Matteo Gasparini, Juan Holguín Posada, Karry Jiao, Yonatan Litwin, Theodore Naff, Juan Porras Lopez, Mariana Santi, Zeki Berkay Saygin, Karthik Sridhar, Gabriel Suárez Obando, Adesola Sunmoni, Facundo Ulivarri, and Natalia Valdebenito Contreras were research analysts.

Selome Missael Paulos provided the team with administrative support through May 2023, and Sandi Soe Lwin provided administrative support to the team beginning in May 2023.

Pia Andres, Oya Pinar Ardic Alper, Sina Ates, Christopher Bataille, Tania Begazo Gomez, Bhavna Bhatia, Tanuj Bhojwani, Julia Bird, Craig Chikis, Xavier Cirera, Fernando Dancausa Diaz, Yuheng Ding, Maciej Drozd, Alice Evans, Nisan Gorgulu, Soulange Gramegna Mesa, Rogelio Granguillhome Ochoa, Michael Grubb, Federico Haslop, Sheirin Iravantchi, Gautam Jain, Aidara Janulaityte, Noah Kaufman, Joohyun Lee, Munseob Lee, Ming Lu, Antonio Martins Neto, Penelope Mealy, Nandan Nilekani, Stefanie Onder, Paul Phumpiu Chang, Denisse Pierola Castro, Brian Pinto, Laurent Porte, Gaël Raballand, Ana Belen Ruival, Sagatom Saha, Yongseok Shin, Hassan Soumya, Sowjanya, Yana R. Ukhaneva, Harald Walkate, Diane Zovighian, and María Pluvia Zúñiga Lara provided inputs to the report at various stages.

Nicolas Moschovakis, Bruce Ross-Larson, and Timothy Taylor provided developmental guidance in drafting the Report. Anthony Venables was a member of the extended team.

Anwar Aridi and Hoon Sahib Soh contributed to box 1.2 on the Republic of Korea. Karsten Staehr and Sebastian Stolorz authored box 2.2 on Bulgaria, Estonia, and Poland. Tristan Reed and Kersten Stamm authored box 2.3 on investment accelerations. Pinelopi Goldberg, Michael Peters, and Aishwarya Ratan authored box 5.3 on the gendered barriers to growth. Oscar Calvo-González authored box 8.4 on the Spanish growth miracle. Marek Hanusch authored box 8.5 on Brazil.

Nurana Ahmadova, Narcisse Cha'ngom, Karry Jiao, Gabriel Suárez Obando, and Renato Schwambach Vieira assisted with the reviews of translations.

The communications and engagement strategy was led by a team comprising Chisako Fukuda, Kristen Milhollin, Karolina Ordon, Joseph Rebello, Mikael (Kelly) Reventar, Shane Romig, and Mariana Teixeira. Roula Yazigi provided web and online services.

Special thanks are extended to Mark McClure, who coordinated and oversaw formal production of the Report, and to the World Bank's Formal Publishing Program, including Cindy Fisher and Patricia Katayama. Mary C. Fisk facilitated the multiple translations of the overview and main messages by the Translations and Interpretation team, coordinated by Bouchra Belfqih. Yaneisy Martinez and Orlando Mota managed the printing and electronic conversions of the Report and the many ancillary products.

The Report was edited by Sabra Ledent and Nancy Morrison and proofread by Gwenda Larsen and Catherine Farley. Robert Zimmermann verified the Report's extensive citations and assisted with the copyediting. The design team of the World Bank's Global Corporate Solutions unit designed the cover and the interior layout. Bill Pragluski of Critical Stages designed some of the Report's figures and infographics. Datapage supplied typesetting services.

Dayana Leguizamon provided the team with resource management support. The team would also like to thank colleagues at various World Bank country offices who assisted with logistics and stakeholder engagements. Special thanks to Marcelo Buitron, Gabriela Calderon Motta, and Grace Soko for their help with coordination and high-level engagement strategies.

The team is grateful for the guidance, comments, and inputs provided by other World Bank Group colleagues, particularly those with the Development Economics Vice Presidency; East Asia and Pacific Region; Eastern and Southern Africa Region; Economics and Private Sector Development Vice Presidency (International Finance Corporation); Education Global Practice; Environment, Natural Resources, and Blue Economy Global Practice; Equitable Growth, Finance, and Institutions Vice Presidency; Europe and Central Asia Region; External and Corporate Relations; Gender Group; Human Development Vice Presidency; Independent Evaluation Group; Infrastructure Vice Presidency; Latin America and the Caribbean Region; Middle East and North Africa Region; Poverty and Equity Global Practice; South Asia Region; Sustainable Development Vice Presidency; and Western and Central Africa Region. The team thanks the many World Bank colleagues who offered written comments during the formal Bankwide review process. These comments provided invaluable guidance at a crucial stage in the production of the Report.

The team gratefully received suggestions and guidance from a High-Level Advisory Panel: Masood Ahmed, President, Center for Global Development; Ann Bernstein, Executive Director, Centre for Development and Enterprise (South Africa); Poonam Gupta, Director General, National Council of Applied Economic Research, and member of the Economic Advisory Council to the Prime Minister of India; Homi Kharas, Senior Fellow–Global Economy and Development, Center for Sustainable Development, Brookings Institution; Mario Marcel Cullell, Minister of Finance, Chile; Mustapha Kamel Nabli, former Minister of Economic Development and Minister of Planning and Regional Development and former Central Bank Governor, Tunisia; Njuguna Ndung'u, Minister of Finance, Kenya; José Antonio Ocampo, former Minister of Finance, Colombia; Normunds Popens, Acting Director General, Directorate-General for Regional and Urban Policy (DG REGIO), European Commission (through January 2024); and Omar Razzaz, former Minister of Education and former Prime Minister, Jordan.

The team received suggestions and inputs from an Academic Advisory Committee: Daron Acemoglu (Massachusetts Institute of Technology), Philippe Aghion (Collège de France, INSEAD, London School of Economics and Political Science), Gerardo Esquivel (El Colegio de México), Ricardo Hausmann (Harvard Kennedy School), Robert Pindyck (Sloan School of Management, Massachusetts Institute of Technology), Danny Quah (Lee Kuan Yew School of Public Policy, National University of Singapore), Jahen F. Rezki (Universitas Indonesia), Qiyuan Xu (Institute of World Economy and Politics, Chinese Academy of Social Sciences), and Fabrizio Zilibotti (Yale University). The team consulted other academics, including Manuel Agosin (Universidad de Chile), Belinda Archibong (Barnard College, Columbia University), Iwan Azis (Cornell University and Universitas Indonesia), Nicolas Bottan (Cornell University), Andrea Bubula (Columbia University), John Carruthers (Cornell University), Julieta Caunedo (Cornell University), Nancy Chau (Cornell University), Abigayle Davidson (Aspen Institute), Jan Eeckhout (Pompeu Fabra University), Gary Fields (Cornell University), Caroline Flammer (Columbia University), Rodrigo Fuentes (Pontificia Universidad Católica de Chile), Alvaro Garcia-Marin (Universidad de los Andes), Ravi Kanbur (Cornell University), David Kohn (Central Bank of Chile and Pontificia Universidad Católica de Chile), Saurabh Lall (University of Glasgow), Patricia Mosser (Columbia University), Cristian Pop-Eleches (Columbia University), Jan Svejnar (Columbia University), and Eric Verhoogen (Columbia University).

Thanks are due to the following academics who participated with presentations during a series of seminars hosted by the *World Development Report 2024* team: Craig Chikis (University of Chicago), Sebastián Gallegos (Business School, Universidad Adolfo Ibáñez, Santiago, Chile), Pulak Ghosh (Indian Institute of Management, Bangalore), Munseob Lee (University of California, San Diego), Ming Li (Chinese University of Hong Kong, Shenzhen), Javier Miranda (Halle Institute for Economic Research, Halle, Germany), Ricardo Paredes (former President of Duoc and current Minister, Free Trade Special Court, Santiago, Chile), Marta Prato (Bocconi University, Milan), Younghun Shim (International Monetary Fund), and María Pluvia Zúñiga Lara (United Nations University–Maastricht Economic and Social Research Institute on Innovation and Technology, Maastricht, the Netherlands).

The team thanks the Chinese Academy of Social Sciences (China), Columbia University (United States), Cornell University (United States), Fudan University (China), the National Council of Applied Economic Research (India), Políticas Públicas (Colombia), Shanghai Institute for International Studies (China), and Shenzhen Finance Institute (Chinese University of Hong Kong) (China) for organizing and hosting a roundtable discussion with academics.

The team conducted a series of bilateral consultations and field visits with several governments, including Brazil, Chile, China, Colombia, the European Commission, India, Italy, Kenya, Mexico, Morocco, and the United Kingdom.

The team benefited from the inputs of several think tanks, research institutes, academic institutions, civil society organizations, private sector organizations, and other organizations, including Accenture, African Centre for Economic Transformation, African Economic Research Consortium, ANT Group, Banco de Crédito e Inversiones S.A., Betterfly, Boston Consulting Group, Celulosa Arauco y Constitución, Center for Advanced Economic Studies, Center for International Knowledge on Development, Centre for Social and Economic Progress, China Academy of Information and Communications Technology, China Center for International Economic Exchanges, China Center for Macroeconomic Research, China International Capital Corporation, China Pacific Insurance Company, Chinese Academy of Social Sciences, Chinese University of Hong Kong, Economic Commission for Latin America and the Caribbean, Einaudi Institute for Economics and Finance, Empresas Copec, Enel, Essence Securities Company, Fudan University, Fundación Chile, Haitong International Securities Group Limited, Harvard Growth Lab, Huatai Securities, Inria, Institute for World Economy Studies Shanghai, Institute of Comparative Politics and Public Policy of Shanghai University, Institute of Economy Pontificia Universidad Católica de Chile, Institute of Quantitative and Technical Economics, Institute of Statistics and Applied Economics, International Centre for China Development Studies, Inversiones SB, Lal Bahadur Shastri National Academy of Administration, National Council of Applied Economic Research, National Evaluation and Productivity Commission, NTT Data Chile, Pan American Association of Student Loan Institutions, Peking University, Renmin University of China, Shanghai Artificial Intelligence Laboratory, Shanghai Institutes for International Studies, Shanghai Jiao Tong University, Sky Airlines, Sonda S.A., Songhe Chuangzhi Venture Capital Investment Partnership Enterprise, Tencent Research Institute, Thomas B. Fordham Institute, Tsinghua University, UBS Wealth Management, United Nations (Morocco), Universidad Andrés Bello, Universidad de Chile School of Economic Sciences and Business, Universidad de los Andes, Universidad del Desarrollo, and VIDA Security.

The team apologizes to any individuals or organizations inadvertently omitted from this list. It is grateful for the help received from all who contributed to this Report, including those whose names may not appear here. Team members would also like to thank their families for their support throughout the preparation of this Report.

Summary

Part 1: Middle-Income Transitions

Chapter 1: Slowing Growth

Is growth in middle-income countries *slower* than that in countries at other income levels?

- Yes. Growth slowdowns occur more frequently in middle-income countries than in low- or high-income countries.
- Development strategies that served countries well in their low-income phase—capital investment, in particular—yield diminishing returns.
- Countries with weaker institutions—and especially those with lower levels of economic and political freedom—are susceptible to slowdowns at even lower levels of income.

Chapter 2: Structural Stasis

Is growth in middle-income countries *different* from that in countries at other income levels?

- Yes. Successful middle-income countries will have to engineer two successive transitions to develop economic structures that can eventually sustain high-income levels.
- The first transition is from a 1*i* strategy for accelerating *investment* to a 2*i* strategy focusing on both *investment* and *infusion* in which a country brings technologies from abroad and diffuses them domestically—a process broadly applicable to lower-middle-income countries.
- The second transition is to switch to a 3*i* strategy, which entails paying more attention to *innovation*—a process more applicable to upper-middle-income countries.

Chapter 3: Shrinking Spaces

Is growth in middle-income countries now *harder* to achieve?

- Yes. Foreign trade and investment are in danger of becoming constricted by geopolitical tensions, and populism is shrinking the room for governments to act.
- Rising debt and adverse demographics are crowding out private investors and reducing public investment.
- Accelerating climate action will require large investments in infrastructure and regulatory reforms that may stall productivity.

Part 2: Creative Destruction

Chapter 4: Creation

Who creates value?

- Both incumbents and entrants can create value. *Incumbents bring scale.* They can compete with entrants in the market to jointly expand a country's technological capabilities, thereby moving the country closer to the global frontier. *Entrants bring change*—enterprises with new products or production processes, workers with new skills and ideas, or energy sources such as renewables that embody new technologies. By doing so, they expand a country's technology frontier.

What is the implication of having both incumbents and entrants as value creators?

- Policy makers will have to stop relying on superficial measures of structural efficiency such as firm size, income inequality, and energy sources. The imperative for today's middle-income economies is "efficiency"—in the use of capital, labor, and energy. Policy makers will need to heed the value added of firms, social mobility, and emissions intensity. They are more reliable and more realistic metrics for policy making, but they also require collecting more information.

Chapter 5: Preservation

How do incumbents preserve the status quo?

- Incumbents' dominance can buy economic, social, and political power. By capturing political and social institutions, incumbents have an outsize say in who learns where and what, who gets a sought-after job and what they are paid, and who gets to start a business.

How do discrimination and patriarchal gender norms hold back the potential of women?

- Patriarchal norms and systems of belief that give men greater status and authority and define strict gender roles and responsibilities hold back women from benefiting from attractive educational and job opportunities. Discrimination can be pervasive, affecting the businesses women own, the jobs they get, the pay they receive, what their families spend on educating them, and their ability to manage financial accounts.

Chapter 6: Destruction

Why is destruction important for structural change?

- The destruction of outdated arrangements—enterprises, jobs, technologies, private contracts, policies, and public institutions—is essential to creating value through infusion and innovation.

Who are the antagonists blocking creative destruction in response to today's energy crisis?

- Incumbents, usually state-owned enterprises, have the strongest incentive to maintain the status quo and limit competition from low-carbon energy providers.
- Many G20 economies are introducing incentives for producing and deploying low-carbon technologies. Some measures may unintentionally preserve enterprises in advanced economies and destroy them in middle-income countries.

Part 3: Making Miracles

Chapter 7: Disciplining Incumbency

How can middle-income countries weaken the forces of preservation that protect incumbents from healthy competition?

- By promoting contestable markets, middle-income countries can strike a balance between supporting incumbents and ensuring that they do not abuse their market power.

- Institutional arrangements that promote contestability include retracting protection of incumbents such as market leaders and state-owned enterprises and norms that work against women.
- Openness to foreign trade, investment, and talent helps with technological upgrading.
- Interventions that target errant incumbents to destroy harmful arrangements include adopting competition laws and ensuring the effectiveness of competition authorities, as well as using fiscal policy to make elites contestable.

Chapter 8: Rewarding Merit

How can middle-income countries strengthen the forces of creation by rewarding merit—that is, those forces that aid in the efficient use of talent, capital, and energy?

- To reward merit, middle-income countries can upgrade their talent pools, select efficient learners, and tap the productive power of women.
- To efficiently use capital, middle-income countries can move away from coddling small firms or vilifying large firms, let go of unproductive firms, modernize the management of firms, and connect entrepreneurs with mentors and markets.
- To decouple carbon emissions from a growing economy, middle-income countries can effectively price carbon emissions and scale up deployment of low-carbon energy by respecting the merit order—the sequence followed by grid operators selling power to the market.

Chapter 9: Capitalizing on Crises

How can middle-income countries capitalize on crises to destroy outdated arrangements and make way for creation?

- Because middle-income countries need to recalibrate their mix of investment, infusion, and innovation, crises can become a necessary evil because they provide the momentum to weaken the status quo.
- To capitalize on today's climate and energy crises, middle-income countries can support global decarbonization by infusing global technologies domestically to join low-carbon value chains for global markets. They can also invest in deploying low-carbon energy if it reaps economic returns.
- Middle-income countries face critical needs: growth, decarbonization, and energy security. Solutions will require decoupling emissions from a growing economy while extending affordable, secure energy to all firms and families.

Glossary

The following general descriptions of the terms and phrases commonly used in this Report reflect their context in the Report.

brain drain The movement of educated or professional people from one place or profession to another to gain better pay or living conditions.

brain gain An increase in the number of highly trained foreign-born professionals entering a country to live and work and benefit from the greater opportunities offered.

business of the state (BOS) An enterprise with majority or minority state shareholdings.

capital accumulation An increase in assets from investments or profits.

capitalizing on crises The process of using a crisis as an opportunity to implement major reforms that otherwise would have been blocked.

carbon capture and storage (CCS) A process in which a relatively pure stream of carbon dioxide from industrial sources is separated, treated, and transported to a long-term storage location.

carbon capture, utilization, and storage (CCUS) An advanced iteration of the traditional carbon capture and storage (CCS) technology. CCS focuses mainly on the capture and sequestration of carbon dioxide to mitigate emissions, and CCUS takes it one step further by finding practical applications for the captured carbon.

carbon intensity A measure of carbon dioxide and other greenhouse gases emitted per unit of activity.

contestability An environment in which incumbents feel pressure to compete and upgrade because their products and processes could be displaced by technologically sophisticated producers in their own country or from other countries.

creative destruction A concept introduced by economist Joseph Schumpeter that refers to the process of innovation and technological change that leads to the destruction of existing economic structures such as industries, firms, and jobs. This destruction paves the way for new structures to emerge, thereby creating long-term economic growth and progress.

decoupling growth from emissions A process that culminates in economic growth no longer strongly associated with carbon emissions.

disciplining incumbents A process in which policies or actions are aimed at limiting the power of incumbents to capture institutions or block competitors.

Economic Complexity Index (ECI) A ranking of countries based on the diversity and complexity of their export basket. High-complexity countries are home to a range of sophisticated, specialized capabilities and are therefore able to produce a highly diversified set of complex products.

energy intensity A measure of the energy use of an economy, calculated as units of energy per unit of gross domestic product (GDP) or another measure of economic output.

entrant An entity that enters an industry with a capacity to produce goods or services that can compete with those of existing entities in order to earn profits.

feed-in tariff A policy designed to support the development of renewable energy sources by providing a guaranteed, above-market price for producers.

incumbent An established entity in society, public office, or the market. This term is often used to describe the existing firms in the market, typically the leading firms, as well as the prevailing technology, social elites, or technologically advanced nations with an established presence in the production of certain goods or services.

industrial policy A policy that directs state support toward specific technologies, sectors, industries, or firms.

infusion A process in which countries focus on imitating and diffusing modern technologies and business models from more advanced economies and applying this knowledge at scale in their domestic economy, thereby enabling home industries to become global suppliers of goods and services.

innovation A process in which countries focus on building home country capabilities to add value to global technologies so that domestic firms can become global knowledge creators.

investment A process in which countries focus on increasing physical capital, such as machinery, equipment, and infrastructure, as well as improving human capital, such as education, training, and better health.

leapfrogging The process by which economies attempt to become "knowledge economies" before putting in place the institutional infrastructure and developing requisite capabilities.

Long Term Growth Model (LTGM) A spreadsheet-based tool to analyze future long-term growth scenarios in developing countries, building on the celebrated Solow-Swan growth model. The LTGM aggregates assumptions about growth fundamentals—such as investment, education, and productivity—to produce a trajectory for future growth. The drivers of growth are savings, investment, and productivity, but the model also analyzes human capital, demographics, the external sector (external debt, foreign direct investment, and current account balance), and labor force participation by gender.

low-carbon technologies Technologies or applications intended to counter the effects of climate change.

merit A person's possession of required skills or qualifications.

merit order The sequence followed by grid operators selling power to the market. The starting point is the cheapest offer, made by the power station with the lowest operating costs, which determines the wholesale market prices. Any provider that can offer renewable energy at zero marginal cost—that is, with insignificant operating costs—should have priority in meeting demand.

middle-income trap A situation in which a middle-income country experiences systematic growth slowdowns as it is unable to take on the new economic structures needed to sustain high-income levels.

Successful middle-income countries will have to engineer two successive transitions to develop such economic structures. The first transition is from a 1*i* strategy for accelerating *investment* to a 2*i* strategy focusing on both *investment* and *infusion*. In the latter, a country brings technologies from abroad and diffuses them domestically. Once a country has succeeded in the first transition, the second transition consists of switching to a 3*i* strategy, which entails paying more attention to *innovation*.

net zero The balance between the amount of greenhouse gas produced and the amount removed from the atmosphere. It can be achieved through a combination of emissions reduction and emissions removal measures.

power purchase agreement (PPA) A long-term agreement to purchase energy from a specific asset at a predetermined price between an electricity generator and a consumer—generally a utility—or between a developer and a supplier, which then resells the energy.

productivity-dependent distortion A policy distortion related to firm size that can discourage growth, innovation, and technology adoption.

proximity to the frontier A measure used in this Report to clarify the distribution of growth slowdowns along the national income spectrum around the world, defined as the ratio of a country's GDP per capita to that of the frontier country each year (not adjusted for differences in purchasing power parity). The frontier represents the growth leader—the country with the most advanced combination of economic production, innovation, and workforce—which is proxied by the United States in this Report.

resource curse The phenomenon of countries with an abundance of natural resources (such as fossil fuels and certain minerals) having lower economic growth, less democracy, or worse development outcomes than countries with fewer natural resources.

rewarding merit The act of policies, institutions, and other government structures aiding in the efficient utilization of talent, capital, and energy.

size-dependent policies Policies that, by design, stipulate different treatment of firms of different sizes.

social immobility A feature of a society with fixed social norms or a rigid class system so that movement from one social class, social or economic status, or social role to another is constrained.

social mobility A change in a person's socioeconomic situation either in relation to their parents (intergenerational mobility) or throughout their lifetime (intragenerational mobility).

state-owned enterprise (SOE) A legal entity created by a government to partake in commercial activities on the government's behalf.

stranded assets Assets that lose value or turn into liabilities before the end of their expected economic life. In the context of fossil fuels, this term refers to those fuels that will not be burned and thus remain in the ground.

total factor productivity (TFP) A measure of the efficiency with which all inputs (labor, capital, and so forth) are used in the production process. It represents the portion of output not explained by the amount of inputs used in production.

Abbreviations

AA	Account Aggregator
BECCS	bioenergy with carbon capture and storage
BOS	business of the state
CCAS	centralized choice and admission system
CCS	carbon capture and storage
CCUS	carbon capture, utilization, and storage
CO_2	carbon dioxide
COVID-19	coronavirus disease 2019
DACCS	direct air capture with carbon storage
ECI	Economic Complexity Index
EMDEs	emerging market and developing economies
ETS	emissions trading system
EU	European Union
EV	electric vehicle
FAT	Firm-level Adoption of Technology
FDI	foreign direct investment
FiT	feed-in tariff
G20	Group of Twenty
GATT	General Agreement on Tariffs and Trade
GDP	gross domestic product
GHG	greenhouse gas
GNI	gross national income
IBRD	International Bank for Reconstruction and Development
ICE	internal combustion engine
ICT	information and communication technology
IDA	International Development Association
IEA	International Energy Agency
IITs	Indian Institutes of Technology
IRA	Inflation Reduction Act
IRENA	International Renewable Energy Agency
LEED	Leadership in Energy and Environmental Design
LTGM	Long Term Growth Model
MIT	Massachusetts Institute of Technology
MNC	multinational corporation
NIPO	New Industrial Policy Observer
NTM	nontariff measure

OECD	Organisation for Economic Co-operation and Development
PMR	product market regulation
PPA	power purchase agreement
PPI	Private Participation in Infrastructure
PPP	purchasing power parity
PV	photovoltaic
R&D	research and development
RISE	Regulatory Indicators for Sustainable Energy
SAR	special administrative region
SDGs	Sustainable Development Goals
SMEs	small and medium enterprises
SOE	state-owned enterprise
STEM	science, technology, engineering, and mathematics
TCP	total carbon price
TCS	Tata Consultancy Services
TFP	total factor productivity
TVET	technical and vocational education and training
UNESCO	United Nations Educational, Scientific, and Cultural Organization
UPI	Unified Payments Interface
WDR	*World Development Report*
WTO	World Trade Organization

Overview: Making a Miracle

In brief

Middle-income countries are in a race against time. Since the 1990s, many of them have done well enough to escape low-income levels and eradicate extreme poverty, leading to the general perception that the last three decades have been great for development. But this is because of abysmally low expectations—remnants from a period when more than two-thirds of the world lived on less than a dollar a day. The ambition of the 108 middle-income countries with incomes per capita of between US$1,136 and US$13,845 is to reach high-income status within the next two or three decades. When assessed against this goal, the record is dismal: the total population of the 34 middle-income economies that transitioned to high-income status since 1990 is less than 250 million, the population of Pakistan.

During the last decade their prospects have worsened. With rising debt and aging populations at home, growing protectionism in advanced economies, and escalating pressures to speed up the energy transition, today's middle-income economies are growing into ever-tighter spaces. The odds that the 6 billion people in today's middle-income countries will see their countries grow to high-income status within a generation or two were never that good. Now they are decidedly daunting.

Drawing upon the development experience since the 1950s and advances in economic analysis by Schumpeterian economists, World Development Report 2024 (WDR 2024) *identifies pathways for emerging market economies to avoid what has become known and feared as the "middle-income trap." The Report points to the need for not one but two transitions during middle-income. The first is to transition from a 1i strategy for accelerating investment to a 2i strategy that emphasizes both investment and infusion in which a country brings technologies from abroad and diffuses them domestically. Governments in lower-middle-income countries must add to investment-driven strategies measures to infuse modern technologies and successful business processes from around the world into their national economies. This requires reshaping large swaths of domestic industry as global suppliers of goods and services.*

Once a country has succeeded in doing this, it can switch to a 3i strategy where it increases attention to innovation. Upper-middle-income countries that have mastered infusion can complement investment and infusion with innovation—beginning not just to borrow ideas from the global frontiers of technology but also to push the frontiers outward. This requires restructuring enterprise, work, and energy use once again, with an even greater emphasis on economic freedom, social mobility, and political contestability.

Transitions across growth strategies are not automatic. Success depends on how well societies juggle the forces of creation, preservation, and destruction. They can do this by disciplining incumbency, rewarding merit, and capitalizing on crises. Incumbents—large corporations, state-owned enterprises, and powerful citizens—can add immense value, but they can just as easily reduce it. Governments must devise mechanisms to discipline incumbents through competition regimes that encourage new entrants without either coddling small and medium-size enterprises or vilifying big corporations. Middle-income countries have smaller reservoirs of skilled talent than advanced economies and are less efficient in utilizing them, so they will have to become better at both accumulating and allocating talent. Cheap and reliable energy has been a cornerstone of rapid economic development, but prospering while keeping the planet livable will now require much more attention to energy efficiency and emissions intensity. Exigencies such as the rise of populism and climate change provide opportunities to dismantle outdated arrangements and make room for new ones; crises are painful, but in democracies they can help forge the consensus needed for tough policy reforms.

The handful of economies that have made speedy transitions from middle- to high-income have encouraged enterprise by disciplining powerful incumbents, developed talent by rewarding merit, and capitalized on crises to alter policies and institutions that no longer suit the purposes they were designed to serve. Today's middle-income countries will have to do the same. The question is how. Given the complex problems they will have to deal with to prosper, the imperative for today's middle-income economies is surprisingly simple: they will have to become efficient—in the use of capital, labor, and energy. This is easier said than done, but advances in economic analysis during the last three decades provide useful pointers.

Readers might immediately recognize the problem with equating a country's development with its income per capita. In fact, development practitioners have been using a raft of similarly superficial indicators to assess the structural strength of an economy and its disaggregates such as industry, society, and ecology. We have become accustomed to using the size distribution of firms in an industry to measure its productive efficiency, household income distributions to assess social durability, and the distribution of energy sources to approximate ecological sustainability. But as economic structures become more complex, these measures have become increasingly inaccurate and progressively poorer guides for making policy.

WDR 2024 is premised on the conjecture that, relative to the complexity of their economic structures, middle-income countries have more serious information deficits than either low-income countries or advanced economies. As a result, they suffer more than the others the consequences of policies predicated on superficial measures of economic efficiency, making them especially prone to premature slowdowns in development. This pathology was nicknamed the "middle-income trap" by World Bank economists, and strategies to avoid it are the subject of this Report.

In implementing these strategies, the Report recommends against using relatively superficial measures like firm size, income inequality, and energy sources to make policy, relying instead on unconditionally reliable measures such as value added, socioeconomic mobility, and emissions intensity. The latter are more realistic metrics for policy making, but they are also more demanding. Policy makers will have to be more willing to make public sensitive data, to openly debate policy, and take any opportunity to destroy outdated arrangements. This requires information that is harder to get, but it is essential. Without it, middle-income countries will be sailing blind into ever-stormier seas.

Since the 1970s, income per capita in the median middle-income country has stayed below a tenth of the US level. Growing geopolitical, demographic, and environmental complications will make economic growth harder in the years ahead. To become advanced economies despite these headwinds, middle-income countries will have to make miracles.

'To get rich is glorious'

You are a policy maker in one of the world's 108 middle-income countries. You have learned the importance of creating a credible, solid macroeconomic foundation for private investment, domestic and foreign, supported by strong institutions and clean governance. And, like Deng Xiaoping nearly 50 years ago, quoted here, you have big plans.

If your country is China, your 14th Five-Year Plan envisions reaching the median gross domestic product (GDP) per capita of developed nations by 2035, thereby greatly expanding your middle class. If it is India, your prime minister's vision is to turn the nation into a developed economy by 2047, the centennial of independence. If it is Viet Nam, your Socio-Economic Development Strategy 2021–2030 outlines a strategy for sustained GDP per capita growth of 7 percent through this decade, with a transition to high-income status by 2045. And if it is South Africa, your 2030 National Development Plan sets a goal of raising the income per capita from US$2,800 in

2010 to US$7,000 by 2030. Other middle-income countries have similar aspirations.

If these plans succeed, your country will reach high-income status in less than one generation, or in one or two. Your firms will be earning like never before. Your people will be consuming like never before. Far fewer people will be poor, with none desperately poor. In the halls of government, these plans generate tremendous optimism.

But there is a problem.

According to widely used measures such as the World Bank's World Development Indicators, you see that economic growth in middle-income countries—including your own—is *not* accelerating. If anything, it is slowing down as incomes increase—and even more so every decade.

Moreover, your country is not catching up with the income levels in advanced economies. Among those economies, the United States is still considered the world's economic leader; people living in countries with incomes higher than those of Americans add up to fewer than 25 million. Since 1970 the mean income per capita of middle-income countries has never risen above one-tenth that of the United States (figure O.1).

Compared with the United States, middle-income countries seem trapped at modest income levels.

The observed rates of economic growth in middle-income countries do not exceed those in high-income countries by the margins needed to catch up in one generation—or even two or three. Estimates using the World Bank's Long Term Growth Model, which is based on the celebrated Solow-Swan growth model, suggest that if the drivers of economic growth—investments in human capital, total factor productivity, labor force participation, and the shares of economic

Figure O.1 Income per capita of middle-income countries relative to that of the United States has been stagnant for decades

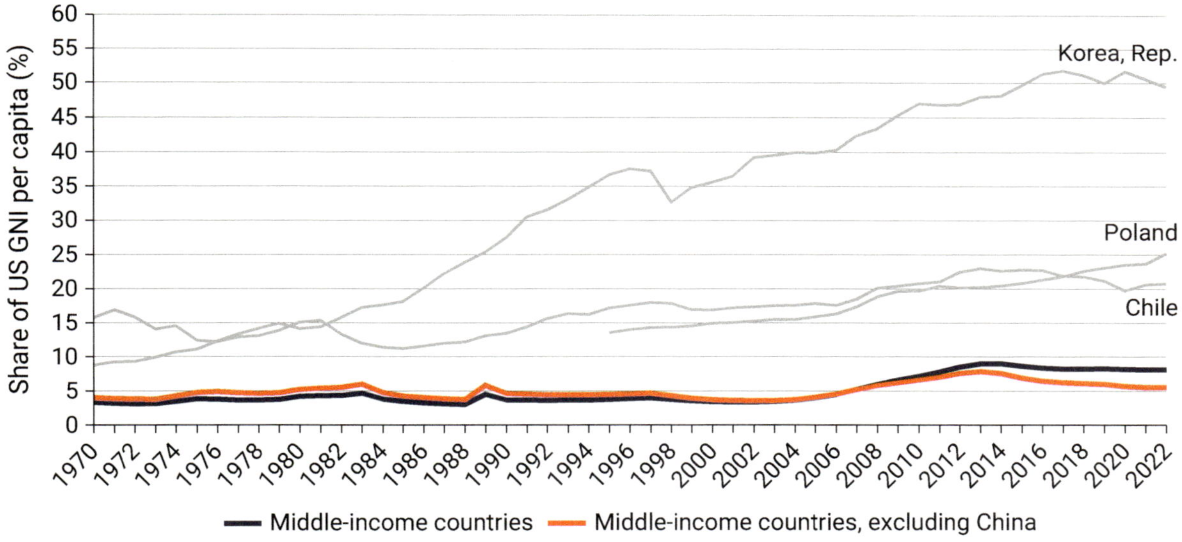

Source: WDR 2024 team using data from WDI (World Development Indicators) (Data Catalog), World Bank, Washington, DC, https://datacatalog.worldbank.org/search/dataset/0037712.

Note: The plotted lines indicate the trend of average income per capita in middle-income countries and in middle-income countries, excluding China, relative to income per capita of the United States (considered the economic frontier country). Country definitions are based on the first *World Development Report* (World Bank 1978), in which low-income countries have gross national income (GNI) per capita of US$250 or less; middle-income countries have GNI per capita of more than US$250; and industrialized (high-income) countries consist of member countries of the Organisation for Economic Co-operation and Development, except for Greece, Portugal, Spain, and Türkiye, which are classified as middle-income countries.

output devoted to public and private investment—follow recent and historic trends, most middle-income countries are likely to experience significant slowdowns between 2024 and 2100. Countries such as Brazil and Mexico are likely to be even further behind the United States in 2100 than they are today.

One trap or two?

The World Bank presently classifies 108 countries as "middle-income"—that is, those with annual income per capita ranging from US$1,136 to US$13,845.[1] These countries are critical to long-term global prosperity. They account for nearly 40 percent of global economic activity, more than 60 percent of people living in extreme poverty, and more than 60 percent of global carbon dioxide (CO_2) emissions (table O.1).

Developing economies change in structure as they increase in size, which means that changes in the pace of growth stem from factors that are new to them. Although these imperatives can vary across countries, economic expansion, on average, begins to decelerate and often reaches a plateau in income per capita growth, typically at about 11 percent of US GDP per capita. Today, this figure would be about US$8,000, or around the level at which countries are firmly considered upper-middle-income. A systematic slowdown in growth then occurs. Development strategies relying largely on capital accumulation that served these countries well in their low-income phase, for many even during their lower-middle-income phase between US$1,136 and US$4,465—begin to yield diminishing returns. Strategies based on factor accumulation alone are likely to steadily worsen results—a natural occurrence as the marginal productivity of capital declines.

To see why, consider this: if capital endowments were the only economically relevant difference between middle-income and high-income countries today, the GDP per capita of a typical middle-income country would have been nearly three-quarters of that of the United States in 2019 (figure O.2). In fact, it is about one-fifth that of the United States. Its growth prospects now depend increasingly on its ability to boost the sophistication of its production methods.

Since 2007, the World Bank has called this dependence the "middle-income trap."[2] And over the last 34 years, only 34 economies have succeeded in breaking out of it.

To achieve high-income status, a middle-income country needs to ramp up the sophistication of its economic structure. Using the

Table O.1 World Bank country classifications and selected global indicators, 2022

INCOME CLASSIFICATION	SHARE OF GLOBAL POPULATION (%)	SHARE OF GLOBAL GDP (%)	SHARE OF PEOPLE IN EXTREME POVERTY GLOBALLY (%)	SHARE OF GLOBAL CARBON DIOXIDE (CO_2) EMISSIONS (%)
Low-income	8.9	0.6	36.5	0.5
Lower-middle-income	40.3	8.3	55.4	15.7
Upper-middle-income	35.1	30.3	7.1	48.6
High-income	15.7	60.8	1.0	35.2

Sources: Population shares and global GDP shares computed from WDI (World Development Indicators) (Data Catalog), World Bank, Washington, DC, https://datacatalog.worldbank.org/search/dataset/0037712; extreme poverty shares from PIP (Poverty and Inequality Platform) (dashboard), World Bank, Washington, DC, https://pip.worldbank.org/home; carbon dioxide emissions data (2022) from Climate Watch (dashboard), World Resources Institute, Washington, DC, https://www.climatewatchdata.org/.

Note: The World Bank currently recognizes 26 economies as low-income (GNI per capita, calculated using the World Bank Atlas method, of US$1,135 or less in 2022); 54 as lower-middle-income (GNI per capita of between US$1,136 and US$4,465); 54 as upper-middle-income (GNI per capita of between US$4,466 and US$13,845); and 83 as high-income (GNI per capita of US$13,846 or more). GDP = gross domestic product; GNI = gross national income.

Figure O.2 If capital accumulation were enough, work in middle-income countries would be nearly three-quarters as rewarding as in the United States, not just one-fifth

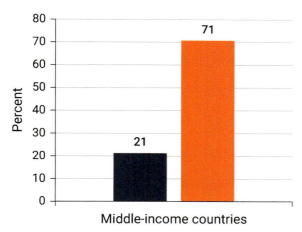

Source: WDR 2024 team using data from PWT (Penn World Table) (database version 10.1), Groningen Growth and Development Centre, Faculty of Economics and Business, University of Groningen, Groningen, the Netherlands, https://www.rug.nl/ggdc/productivity/pwt/.

Note: The bars show the simple average for middle-income countries in 2019. The data are calculated using the methodology outlined in Jones (2016). Following Jones (2016), the figure is based on Hicks-neutral and a constant labor share of two-thirds. GDP = gross domestic product.

economic complexity of a country's export basket—a measure of sophistication—there is a rising relationship between sophistication and income for all economies that transitioned from a GDP per capita of less than US$13,000 to more than US$31,000, regardless of whether their export baskets became more or less diversified (figure O.3).

However, the pace of progress in middle-income countries is slowing. Average annual income growth in these countries slipped by nearly one-third in the first two decades of this century—from 5 percent in the 2000s to 3.5 percent in the 2010s.[3] A turnaround is not likely soon because middle-income countries are facing ever-stronger headwinds. They are contending with rising geopolitical tensions and protectionism that can slow the diffusion of knowledge to middle-income countries,[4] difficulties in servicing debt obligations, and the additional economic and financial costs of climate change and climate action.

Investment, infusion, and innovation—additively and progressively

To achieve more sophisticated economies, middle-income countries need two successive transitions, not one. In the first, investment is complemented with infusion, so that countries (primarily lower-middle-income countries) focus on imitating and diffusing modern technologies. In the second, innovation is added to the investment and infusion mix, so that countries (primarily upper-middle-income countries) focus on building domestic capabilities to add value to global technologies, ultimately becoming innovators themselves. In general, middle-income countries need to recalibrate the mix of the three drivers of economic growth—*investment, infusion,* and *innovation*—as they move through middle-income status (table O.2).

What makes the move from middle-income status to high-income status so difficult? One reason is that as they move through middle-income status, countries cannot leap all at once from investment-driven growth to innovation-driven growth. Infusion of technology comes first and then innovation.

Infusion first

Economic success in lower-income countries stems largely from accelerating investment. As these economies move to middle-income status, continued progress requires complementing a good investment climate with measures deliberately designed to bring new ideas from abroad and diffuse them across the economy—so-called infusion.

Figure O.3 Economies become more sophisticated as they transition from middle-income to high-income status

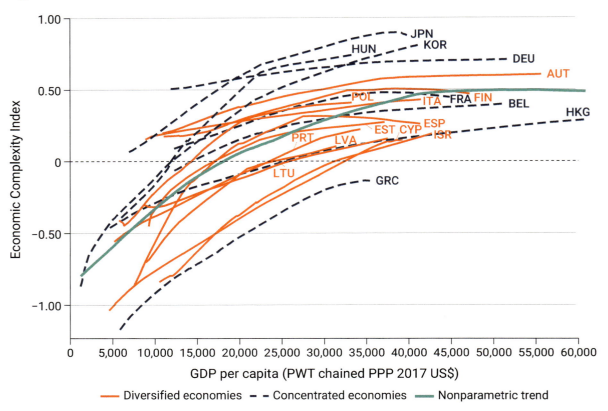

Source: Bahar, Bustos, and Yıldırım (2024) using PWT (Penn World Table) (database version 10.1), Groningen Growth and Development Centre, Faculty of Economics and Business, University of Groningen, Groningen, the Netherlands, https://www.rug.nl/ggdc/productivity/pwt/.

Note: The figure plots for each economy that transitioned from GDP per capita of less than US$13,000 to more than US$31,000 (50th and 75th percentile, respectively, in 2019) the relationship between GDP per capita and sophistication of its exports. Sophistication is measured as the weighted average of the Economic Complexity Index. The figure shows the sample of economies that diversified (orange solid line)—that is, an economy's final trend is more diversified than its starting point—and those whose production became more concentrated (dark blue dashed line). For country abbreviations, see International Organization for Standardization (ISO), https://www.iso.org/obp/ui/#search. GDP = gross domestic product; PPP = purchasing power parity.

To intentionally import state-of-the-art technology, knowledge of market potential, and business practices from abroad, as well as expedite their diffusion at home (figure O.4), newly minted middle-income economies have to change tack. Policy makers must support firms that are ready and able to incorporate global technologies into production. For firms to make the most of new technologies, they need technically skilled workers in large numbers and a sufficient supply of engineers, scientists, managers, and other highly skilled professionals. Countries that are relatively open to economic ideas from abroad and have instituted strong secondary education and vocational training programs at home tend to perform better than those that have not.

The experiences of three economies that have grown quickly from the lower-middle-income to high-income levels in recent decades—Chile,

Table O.2 To achieve high-income status, countries will need to recalibrate their mix of investment, infusion, and innovation

INCOME CLASSIFICATION	INVESTMENT	INFUSION	INNOVATION
Low-income	Higher priority	Lower priority	Lower priority
Lower-middle-income	Higher priority	Higher priority	Lower priority
Upper-middle-income	Higher priority	Higher priority	Higher priority

Source: WDR 2024 team.
Note: The orange dials indicate a strategy that is a priority for that particular income group. The blue dials indicate a strategy that is less of a priority for that particular income group until the priority strategy is successfully achieved.

Figure O.4 Middle-income countries must engineer two successive transitions to move to high-income status

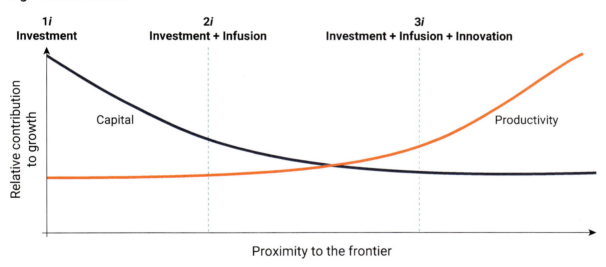

Source: WDR 2024 team.
Note: The curves illustrate the relative contributions of capital and productivity to economic growth (y-axis), according to countries' proximity to the frontier (represented by the leading economies). Countries farther out on the x-axis are closer to the frontier.

the Republic of Korea, and Poland—illustrate these ideas (figure O.5).

Korea's success may be the best support for the argument that sustaining high growth requires adding infusion to accelerations of investment, and then again augmenting the 2*i* mix with innovation policies. Korea was among the least developed countries globally in the early 1960s, with income per capita of less than US$1,200 in 1960. By 2023, after an unparalleled five-decade run of high output growth, Korea's income per capita had risen to about US$33,000.

Figure O.5 In the Republic of Korea, Poland, and Chile, the rapid growth from middle- to high-income status has been interspersed with economic crises

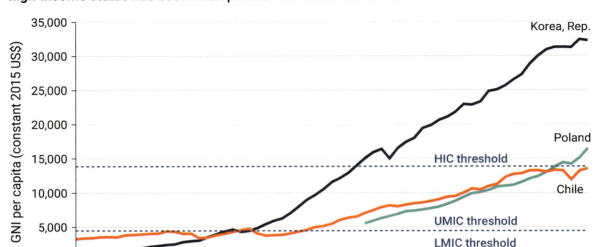

Source: WDR 2024 team using WDI (World Development Indicators) (Data Catalog), World Bank, Washington, DC, https://datacatalog.worldbank.org/search/dataset/0037712.
Note: GNI = gross national income; HIC = high-income country; LMIC = lower-middle-income country; UMIC = upper-middle-income country.

In the 1960s, a combination of measures to increase public investment and encourage private investment kick-started growth.[5] In the 1970s and 1980s, Korea's growth was powered by a potent mix of high investment rates and infusion, aided by an industrial policy that encouraged firms to adopt foreign technologies (figure O.6). Firms received tax credits for royalty payments, and family-owned conglomerates, or *chaebols*, took the lead in copying technologies from abroad—primarily Japan. As Korean conglomerates caught up with foreign firms and encountered resistance from their erstwhile benefactors, industrial policy shifted toward a 3*i* strategy supporting innovation. Then, as Korean firms became more sophisticated in what they produced, they needed workers with specialized engineering and management skills. The Ministry of Education, through public universities and the regulation of private institutions, did its part, setting targets, increasing budgets, and monitoring the development of these skills. These firms also required more specialized capital: for a growing middle-income economy, investment remained important.

Poland's case is different because of both its socialist past and its membership in the European Union (EU), the most powerful association of economies ever assembled. But its rapid increase in income is well known, and a Korea-like 1*i* to 2*i* to 3*i* transition is still discernible.

In the early 1990s, Poland underwent a transition from a planned economy to a market economy. It has since boosted its income per capita from 20 percent of the average for the European Union to 50 percent. What is Poland's winning strategy? It began by disciplining the large state-owned enterprises (SOEs). It hardened their budget constraints by cutting subsidies, tightening

Figure O.6 From infusion to innovation in the Republic of Korea

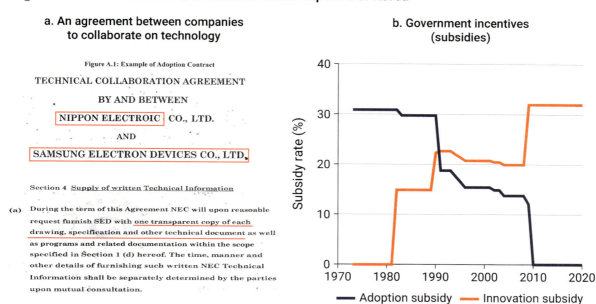

Sources: Panel a: National Archives of Korea, https://www.archives.go.kr/english/index.jsp. Panel b: Choi and Shim 2024.
Note: Panel b shows the adoption subsidy rate alongside the innovation (R&D) subsidy rate, calculated using the tax credit rate and the corporate tax rate. For example, a 30 percent subsidy rate indicates that firms can receive a reimbursement equivalent to 30 percent of their expenditures on adoption fees or R&D. R&D = research and development.

bank loans, and liberalizing import competition—including at the iconic Stocznia Gdańsk shipyard, where the Solidarność (Solidarity) movement began. This discipline paved the way for comprehensive reform. In Polish SOEs, managers shifted their focus from production targets to profitability and market share, and they upgraded firms' capabilities to prepare for privatization.[6] Poland then built on this foundation to attract investment, focus on infusion next, and turn to innovation last. It followed this sequence largely by raising productivity with technologies infused from Western Europe—a process accelerated in the 2000s by its entry into the EU common market, which spurred foreign direct investment. Poland also increased tertiary education rates from 15 percent in 2000 to 42 percent in 2012. Educated Poles put their skills to work across the European Union, opening another channel to infusing global knowledge into the Polish economy.

Chile's success has similar features. In 2012, Chile became the first Latin American country to reach high-income status, just two years after joining the Organisation for Economic Co-operation and Development (OECD). Chile has grown and diversified its exports since the 1960s, when mining made up about four-fifths of its exports. This share is now about half. Knowledge transfers from advanced economies have been supported by both public and private institutions. The public Chilean Agency for Exports Promotion (ProChile) has bolstered small and medium enterprises (SMEs), which over 2013–16 contributed one-third of export value added—the other two-thirds being contributed by large domestic exporters.[7] And Fundación Chile, a private nonprofit created in 1976, promotes technology transfer for domestic ventures. One example is the adaptation of Norwegian salmon farming technologies to local conditions, making Chile a leading world exporter of salmon.

Innovation next

Once a middle-income country has begun to exhaust the potential of infusion in the most promising parts of its economy—running out of technologies to learn and adopt—it should expand its efforts to become an innovation economy. But this transition is as or more daunting than the preceding one.[8] Infusion is powered mainly by the technology transfers embodied in flows of physical and financial capital.

Although innovation requires both of these flows, it also needs increasingly vigorous exchanges of human capital—often triggered by a reengagement with the emigrant diaspora, but also creating the conditions cherished by innovators such as freer economies, human rights, and livable cities. Moreover, to enable firms to innovate, governments must have done a lot during the infusion phase to reform and strengthen institutions. Weak institutions are as debilitating as premature attempts to leapfrog from investment to innovation. In some cases, ignoring the imperative of infusion to quicken innovation can even worsen the investment climate, setting middle-income economies back years if not decades. Latin America, ground zero for the middle-income trap, provides a cautionary example.

After reaching middle-income status in the 1970s, Brazil veered in the wrong direction. Its policy makers attempted to encourage firms to innovate by bypassing the infusion of foreign technologies. In 2001, the government implemented an innovation-driven economic growth strategy, driven in part by fears that foreign technology would exacerbate domestic inequality and lead to dependence on the more advanced economies in the North Atlantic. Notably, it imposed a 10 percent marginal tax rate on payments for international intellectual property. These tax revenues were used to subsidize innovation in targeted sectors, including biotechnology, aviation, health, and agriculture.[9]

One study found that the subsidies stimulated a rapid rise in applications at the Brazilian patent office, but the patents turned out to be of low quality and lacked any relevance to global markets. Moreover, as the share of firms that applied for patents within the economy increased, the wage premium for skilled workers declined, as did the value added.[10]

While Brazil was stumbling at home, Korea was racing around the world, making the infusion of foreign technology the cornerstone of domestic innovation. In 1980, the average productivity of a worker in Korea was just 20 percent that of the average US worker. By 2019, it had tripled to more than 60 percent (figure O.7). By contrast, Brazilian workers, who had been 40 percent as productive as their US counterparts in 1980, were just 25 percent as productive by 2018.

There are no shortcuts to innovation. It is unlikely that industrial policy will enable countries to leapfrog from an investment- and manufacturing export–driven model to an innovation-oriented model or services-led model of economic growth. The development literature is littered with reports recommending a leap from investment to innovation, skipping the stage of painful reforms to attract foreign investment and ideas. However, middle-income governments that have tried to spare their citizenry the pains associated with reforms and openness have also kept from them the gains that come from sustained growth.

The economics of creative destruction

The shifts from 1*i* to 2*i* to 3*i* strategies are neither smooth nor linear. They require a mix of economic, social, and political change that Karl Marx and other philosophers considered impossible under capitalism. They reasoned instead that market-based economies would be riddled with a growing concentration of wealth and wracked by crises until capitalism was replaced by communism. Joseph Schumpeter changed this debate with his 1942 treatise *Capitalism, Socialism and Democracy* and the phenomenon of "creative

Figure O.7 Over the last four decades, as the Republic of Korea's labor productivity relative to that of the United States continued to climb, Brazil's peaked—and then sagged

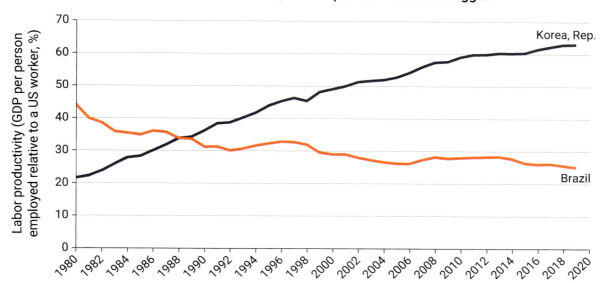

Source: WDR 2024 team using data from PWT (Penn World Table) (database version 10.1), Groningen Growth and Development Centre, Faculty of Economics and Business, University of Groningen, Groningen, the Netherlands, https://www.rug.nl/ggdc/productivity/pwt/.
Note: GDP = gross domestic product.

destruction."[11] For Schumpeter, the crises in capitalist economies could be simultaneously painful and restorative.

Nearly a century later, many of Schumpeter's insights appear to have been confirmed. Indeed, his admonitions and insights have been used by modern Schumpeterian theorists—most notably, Aghion and Howitt (1992) and Akcigit and Kerr (2018)—to construct formal frameworks. These advances in growth theory are useful in helping solve the hardest problem facing the global economy today: how should the 108 middle-income countries with 75 percent of the world's people, 60 percent of global emissions, but just 40 percent of global output correct these imbalances while converging toward the living standards of advanced economies?

Schumpeterian ideas provide helpful clues. Success seems to come most quickly to societies that balance the economic forces of *creation, preservation,* and *destruction.*

Energy: Incumbents can collude (Schumpeter's view)

Joseph Schumpeter (1942) wrote that society benefits when entrepreneurs with talent and vision introduce new products and technologies, displacing old products and business models and generating ever-higher productivity and growth. Often, however, incumbents collude to preserve the status quo (figure O.8, panel a). In today's environment, Schumpeter's view is perhaps best reflected in the contest between high- and low-carbon energy. High-carbon energy, particularly coal, has been an incumbent technology for over 300 years (box O.1). Technical progress has followed a path over which the efficiency with which fossil fuels are extracted and burned has increased, urban infrastructure has been built around the private motor vehicle, social attitudes and personal preferences are supportive of high carbon consumption, and political pressure groups represent carbon-intensive interests.

Figure O.8 Three views of creative destruction

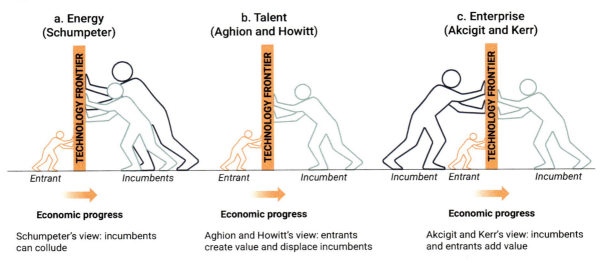

Source: WDR 2024 team based on Schumpeter (1942); Aghion and Howitt (1992); Akcigit and Kerr (2018).

Box O.1 Who and what are incumbents? Leading firms, technologies, nations, elites—and men

Incumbents are firms that usually have well-established brand names recognized and trusted by consumers. They often have better access to financial resources, such as capital for investment and technological infusion, and human resources, such as experienced employees. They also may have established relationships with suppliers and distributors, which can be leveraged to maintain a competitive edge. And they have resources to invest in research and development and to invent products and processes they can protect with patents.

Incumbents are well-established energy sources such as fossil fuels. Since 1709 when Abraham Darby, a British ironmaster, first smelted iron ore with coke, coal has been the fuel of choice around the world. In the more than 300 years since Darby's innovation, coal has become the largest source of electricity generation worldwide, producing more than one-third of global electricity in 2022.[a] Cities and economies have been built on cheap coal-powered energy, fueling their prosperity. However, the widespread use of coal generates the highest energy-related carbon dioxide emissions—15.5 gigatons—representing 42 percent of total emissions in 2022.

Incumbents are technologically advanced nations. They can share technologies with emerging economies through investing in, licensing, training, and hosting foreign students. For decades, they were instrumental in supporting the growth of emerging economies. But today, they are erecting walls to subsidize their domestic firms, blocking others from joining their value chains.

(Box continues next page)

> **Box O.1 Who and what are incumbents? Leading firms, technologies, nations, elites—and men** *(continued)*
>
> Finally, *incumbents are elites in society.* They are always powerful, generally wealthy, and—in middle-income economies—mostly men. But they are not all against progress. Elites can have the education and resources to accelerate growth by infusing their economies with global technologies. For a middle-income country seeking to infuse and innovate, elites may serve as the go-to pool of trained professionals, managers, entrepreneurs, and innovators. Men are also incumbents, for centuries enjoying better education and job opportunities than women and defining laws and institutions, often to buy social, economic, and political power. Such power has given them an outsize say in deciding who studies where and what, who gets a well-paid job, and who gets to start a business. Meanwhile, misogyny may keep women out of the market or at least the most desired jobs and business opportunities.
>
> Large firms, social elites, powerful men, and advanced economies have, however, also helped new entrants. The size and ownership of enterprises and the socioeconomic status and gender of individuals are not reliable attributes on which to base policy.
>
> a. IEA (2023).

The result is that the returns to investing in high-carbon activities are large because of all the complementary high-carbon investments that have been made.

In many middle-income countries, power markets are still a monopoly: an SOE operating under a vertically integrated utility remains in charge of generation, transmission, distribution, and the retail supply. This arrangement hinders competition and results in the inefficient use of resources. In addition, in many middle-income countries the first generators dispatched are often not those with the lower marginal prices (that is, power dispatch often does not follow merit order), serving as a barrier to the expansion of renewables with rapidly declining costs. In countries that include Pakistan, Poland, South Africa, and Türkiye, SOEs account for 84 percent of total installed capacity. By contrast, the private sector owns about an equal share (80 percent) of the installed capacity of renewable energy.[12]

Although advances in low-carbon energy can help to decouple economic growth from carbon emissions, the diffusion of low-carbon technologies in middle-income countries is patchy, reflecting a landscape of legacy policies that preserve a high-carbon economy. Middle-income countries have a greenhouse gas (GHG) intensity of GDP that is 3.5 times higher than that of high-income countries. This difference reflects both the misallocation in the use of energy (with the energy intensity of GDP also 2.5 times higher than in high-income countries) and the lower diffusion of low-carbon energy technologies (figure O.9, panel a).

Talent: Entrants create value and displace incumbents (Aghion and Howitt's view)

Schumpeter's ideas on creative destruction served as the inspiration for one of the most influential papers in economics that emerged from a fortuitous collaboration between two economists. In the summer of 1987, Philippe Aghion, a new professor at the Massachusetts Institute of Technology (MIT), and Peter Howitt, a Canadian economist, formalized a theory of creative destruction in which economies expand mainly through innovation by entrants.[13] Entrants challenge incumbents and become the protagonists of economic growth (figure O.8, panel b).

This formulation of creative destruction emphasizes the importance of both creating ever-larger reservoirs of talent and improving the allocation of talent to tasks. Not investing in the talents of women and minorities, keeping them out of the most rewarding activities, and adopting unfair compensation practices are surely the most self-defeating attributes of middle-income economies, where skills are already scarce. When these practices are discouraged, the payoff can be immense. In the United States between 1960 and 2010, the decline in gender and racial discrimination in education and work explains up to 40 percent of the observed growth during that period.[14]

As they grow, middle-income countries will need skilled workers such as engineers, technicians, and managers, but they have smaller reservoirs of skilled talent than advanced economies. And yet preservation forces discourage the acquisition of talent. Talent is wasted wherever that acquired through education, training, and work experience is allocated not by merit, but according to other factors outside the control of individuals. Gender, family background, ethnic and cultural identity—none of these factors should matter for school enrollment or career prospects in a country aspiring to grow rapidly through infusion and innovation. But for the average child in a middle-income country today, they matter all too much.

Economically and socially mobile societies are better at developing skills and utilizing talent, but social mobility in middle-income countries is about 40 percent lower than that in advanced economies.[15] Middle-income countries will need to ensure that more individuals, regardless of their parents' circumstances, have better opportunities to become skilled workers. And social mobility matters much more in middle-income countries than in low-income countries simply because the former need more skilled workers to invest, infuse, innovate, and grow (figure O.9, panel b).

Figure O.9 Creation is a weak force in middle-income countries, where it is characterized by a rampant misallocation of resources

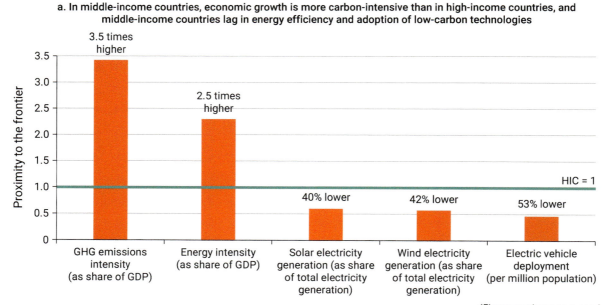

(Figure continues next page)

Figure O.9 Creation is a weak force in middle-income countries, where it is characterized by a rampant misallocation of resources *(continued)*

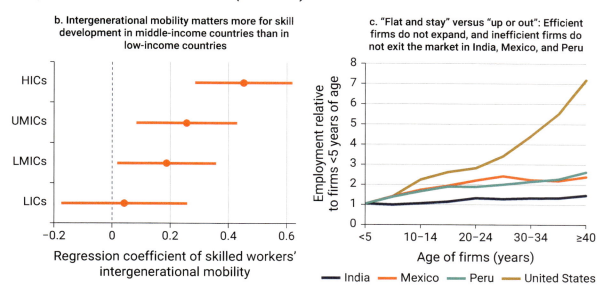

Sources: Panel a: Chepeliev and Corong 2022; Energy Institute 2023; Statistics Data (portal), International Renewable Energy Agency, Abu Dhabi, United Arab Emirates, https://www.irena.org/Data; WDI (World Development Indicators) (Data Catalog), World Bank, Washington, DC, https://datacatalog.worldbank.org/search/dataset/0037712. Panel b: WDR 2024 team estimates based on GDIM (Global Database on Intergenerational Mobility) (dashboard), Data Catalog, World Bank, Washington, DC, https://datacatalog.worldbank.org/search/dataset/0050771/global-database-on-intergenerational-mobility. Panel c: India, Mexico, and the United States: Hsieh and Klenow 2014; Peru: World Bank 2015.

Note: Panel a displays for middle-income countries compared with an index of 1, representing the high-income country (HIC) frontier, the greenhouse gas (GHG) emissions intensity of the gross domestic product (GDP), the energy intensity of GDP, the share of solar and wind energy in total electricity generation, as well as the battery electric vehicles per million population. Panel b plots regression coefficients of intergenerational mobility (which is equal to 1 minus the intergenerational relative mobility) for different country groups at the 95 percent confidence interval. The dependent variable in the regression is the share of skilled workers ("Legislators, sr. officials, managers"; "Professionals"; "Technicians and associate professionals"). The regression controls for the log of GDP per capita when the 1980s birth cohort was growing up. Intergenerational mobility estimates are for educational mobility of the 1980s cohort from the World Bank's GDIM. HICs = high-income countries; LICs = low-income countries; LMICs = lower-middle-income countries; UMICs = upper-middle-income countries. Panel c illustrates the average employment across a cohort of firms of different ages in the cross-section of firms. The number of employees serves as a proxy for firm size. The y-axis axis reports the average employment of each cohort relative to the average employment across firms under five years of age.

Why do preservation forces persist in constraining the opportunities for so many people? Part of the answer is that preservation insulates members of social elites from the forces of destruction that, in a more open society with meritocratic institutions, might dissipate their advantages in wealth and privilege. The same forces ensure that, beyond elites, few children will get the chance to climb to a higher rung on a country's income ladder than that occupied by their parents. So, income inequality remains high and social mobility remains low, transmitting inequality across generations, exacerbating the inequality of opportunity.

Three kinds of preservation forces perpetuate social immobility in middle-income countries, shutting out talent from economic creation. The first force is *norms*—biases that foreclose or limit opportunity for women and other members of marginalized groups. Next are *networks*—above all, family connections. And the last force is *neighborhoods*—regional and local disparities in access to education and jobs. Although all three factors can have positive impacts on talent creation—filling voids left by missing markets and services—they become forces of preservation when they block the disadvantaged from accessing opportunity.

Enterprise: Incumbents and entrants add value (Akcigit and Kerr's view)

The original Schumpeterian premise that new entrants drive change and create new economic potential while incumbents are inert runs counter to the latest empirical evidence on enterprises. Globally, larger and more established firms are infusing new knowledge into their businesses at a higher rate than smaller firms. In middle-income countries, it is the large firms that are employing the majority of highly skilled workers.[16] Throughout the twentieth century, the United States effectively transitioned its innovation focus from individuals working in their garages to established firms, leveraging advantages such as risk management, market access, brand reputation, and collaboration. These firms now account for over 75 percent of patents filed at the United States Patent and Trademark Office.[17]

A third generation of Schumpeterian economists have formalized the idea that both incumbent enterprises and entrants can create value (figure O.8, panel c).[18] Market leaders—successful incumbents—can bring *scale* and advance domestic industry by investing in upgraded products and business practices, as well as technology for new markets. Scale allows for adopting modern management practices, for hiring and rewarding skilled workers, and for making the most productive use of large amounts of capital. In other words, scale gives incumbents the power to boost their efficiency, whether in the expectation of competition from other incumbents or from entrants or in response to it. Scale also allows incumbents to specialize in multiple product lines, changing course to parry the new offerings of competitors.

However, the forces of creation are weak in middle-income countries. In India, Mexico, and Peru, for example, if a firm operates for 40 years, it will roughly double in size. In the United States, the average firm that survives that long will grow sevenfold (figure O.9, panel c). For firms in middle-income countries, this implies a "flat and stay" dynamic: firms that fail to grow substantially can still survive for decades. By contrast, for US firms the dynamic is "up or out": facing intense competitive pressure, a few entrepreneurs will expand their businesses rapidly, while most others will exit quickly. Among the majority who exit the market, many will become wage earners at the most flourishing firms.

In keeping with the flat and stay dynamics, firms in India, Mexico, and Peru tend to remain microenterprises: nearly nine-tenths of firms have fewer than five employees, and only a tiny minority have 10 or more. The longevity of undersize firms—many of them informal—points to market distortions that keep enterprises small while keeping too many in business. For example, a high regulatory cost attached to formal business growth may inhibit an efficient firm from gaining market share and driving out inefficient competitors. Such policy-induced distortions in middle-income countries result in misallocated resources, hampering creation and infusion at scale.

Balancing the three forces

Looked at it this way, middle-income countries face common challenges in balancing the three forces:

- *Creation—the primary protagonist of economic growth—is a weak force in many middle-income countries.* Large incumbents are slow to develop new products and processes, and, although small firms are continually entering various markets, most of them do not create or disrupt. Periods of growth are also times of creation, and thus of structural change.
- *Preservation—the arch antagonist of creation—is the strongest force in middle-income countries.* The same market leaders who could enable middle-income countries to speed up the infusion of global

knowledge are too often slowing down the process. Incumbent firms and elites are often successful in keeping things as they are whether through market power and collusion, through capture of policies and regulations, or through education systems and labor markets that place more importance on socioeconomic status than on talent or merit.

- *Destruction—a necessary evil that clears the way for creation by freeing up misallocated resources and sweeping away outdated institutions—is kept weak in middle-income countries by opposition from those with market power or government influence.* A growing economy that requires new arrangements in capital, labor, and energy markets needs to release itself from less efficient ones. To the extent that weak institutions and policies preserve outdated arrangements, creative destruction is stifled. However, this opposition tends to weaken during crises—whether economic, political, or ecological. When crises place intense pressure on governments to act, a window opens for reforms.

Striking the right balance

Middle-income countries are hampered by an imbalance among the forces of creation, preservation, and destruction. The forces of creation are weak, the forces of preservation are strong, and destruction is held back by the forces of preservation. Middle-income countries must therefore balance these forces (figure O.10). That means

- *Disciplining incumbency* to weaken the forces of preservation
- *Rewarding merit activities*—those with positive effects on general well-being and that aid in the efficient use of talent, capital, and energy—to strengthen the forces of creation
- *Capitalizing on crises* to aid the destruction of outdated policies and institutions that are difficult to dislodge during boom times.

These principles can help middle-income countries calibrate the mix of their three *i*'s—*investment, infusion,* and *innovation*—as they plan to accelerate economic growth. Because both incumbent firms and entrants can add value,

Figure O.10 **Middle-income countries have to strike a balance among creation, preservation, and destruction**

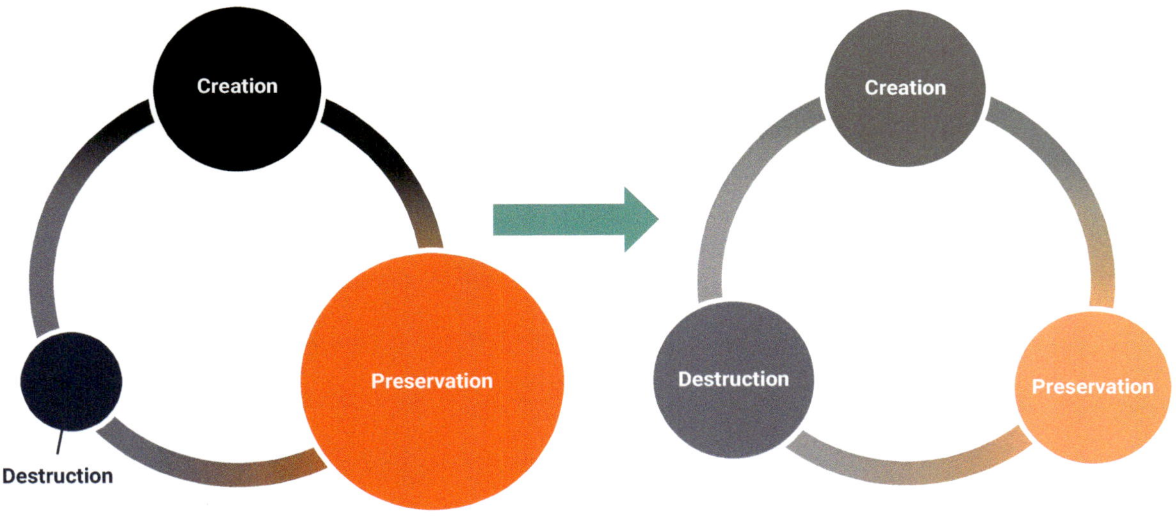

Source: WDR 2024 team.

industrial policies will need to focus on disciplining incumbency. And because the talent of women and disadvantaged groups is grossly underutilized, social policies will need to focus more on rewarding their merit and advancing social and economic mobility. And finally, because economic growth over the last three centuries has been emissions-intensive, middle-income countries will need to capitalize on today's energy crisis to cut emissions while balancing energy access and security.

Enterprise, openness, and reforms

Countries growing out of low-income status into middle-income status tend to have a 1*i* strategy for accelerating *investment*. Stronger institutions are needed to control inflation, ensure financial and macroeconomic stability, expand economic and political freedoms, and enforce the rule of law to encourage both domestic and foreign investment. Even if all middle-income countries enjoyed such enabling conditions, a 1*i* strategy would not be enough to support sustained growth and move these countries out of the middle-income level. Why? The returns from capital investment alone decline steadily. Growth in middle-income countries is boosted when economies take on new structures, enabled by a 2*i* strategy focusing on both investment and infusion. Institutions will need to create an environment conducive to integrating global technologies into the domestic economy.

Make markets globally contestable

Contestable markets—and the institutions that enable them—are vital for middle-income countries that aim to become a global supplier and sustain rapid economic growth through sophistication and scale.

Contestability is not chaos: it does not mean that firms in middle-income countries cannot earn comfortable market positions, becoming established and relatively difficult to displace. However, contestability does mean that firms feel pressure to compete because their current products and processes can be displaced by technologically sophisticated producers from other countries. Such contestability is central to creative destruction.

A key part of contestability is openness to foreign investors and global value chains that give domestic firms access to larger markets, technology, and know-how and allows them to add value and grow. And they are encouraged to make use of that access, thereby exposing domestic firms to competition, but also inspiration, from international firms that operate at or near the global technology frontier. Firms at home can seize the opportunity to infuse technology, increase the sophistication of their operations, and scale up, or they can keep doing business as usual and be eased out.

For example, in Chile imports of Chinese products rose at an average pace of 27 percent a year from 2001 to 2007, and large Chilean incumbent firms, or market leaders, boosted their product innovation by 15 percent and their product quality by 22 percent.[19] In Argentina, after MERCOSUR (Southern Common Market) was established, domestic firms in sectors facing export tariff reductions began to invest more in computing technology and in technology transfers and patents.[20] Again, in 12 European countries over 2000–2007 more than 15 percent of the increase in patenting, information technology intensity, and productivity was driven by import competition from China—and successful European firms boosted management quality while increasing research and development (R&D) and adding new skills.[21]

Connect local firms with market leaders

Because local firms often do not have information on specific technologies and the know-how to adopt them, consultants and advisory firms founded by experts can provide expertise and advice on technology adoption and implementation. Market leaders—especially multinationals—are often vanguards in technology and technical capabilities and can be some of the best partners for local firms, working together to deploy new technologies. The government can help make the relevant connections. For example, in Chile the Supplier Development Program, which offers large domestic buying firms an incentive to connect with suppliers that are SMEs, increased the suppliers' sales by 16 percent and their employment by 8 percent. It also boosted the sales of large sponsor firms by 19 percent.[22] Governments can also provide firms with information on market opportunities, enabling them to access finance and strengthen their capabilities, as well as to recognize opportunity and mobilize themselves to take advantage of it.[23]

Reduce factor and product market regulations

Reforms that roll back protection for specific activities, enterprises, families, or industries reinforce the gains from openness. However, today middle-income countries are slow to combine investment with infusion and innovation, stymied by the powerful institutional and regulatory forces of preservation. Especially binding are product market regulations. Besides imposing constraints on international trade and investment, these regulations prop up state control of business and impose legal and administrative barriers to entrepreneurship, thereby hobbling investment and infusion at scale.

Move away from coddling small firms or vilifying large firms

Small and medium-size enterprises are widespread in middle-income countries. Ideally, subsidies would help SMEs grow into larger, more productive companies that pay higher wages and adapt knowledge. But the same support also strengthens the forces of preservation by reducing incentives for a productive firm to expand, deterring it from scaling up production. Many firms in middle-income countries remain small even when long established; they simply do not aspire to grow.[24] The abundance of small firms in middle-income countries does not solely mirror the challenges they face. Instead, it indicates a deficiency in competition, originating from larger firms that would have displaced them in the market if they had expanded.[25] Blanket support for small firms can curtail the exit of unproductive small businesses, perpetuate smallness, crowd out other firms, and misallocate resources.[26] In countries that include Japan, Mexico, and Viet Nam, public support for small firms—not necessarily young firms—reduced productivity and increased resource misallocation.[27]

Even where tax codes do not create explicit provisions based on firm size, middle-income countries may be creating a practical subsidy to SMEs through size-dependent tax enforcement—that is, governments with weak tax collection capacity may concentrate enforcement on larger firms.[28] In Mexico, eliminating distortions created by size-dependent taxation policies favoring small firms could boost output by 9 percent.[29] In Chile, China, and India, reductions in distortions helped these economies close the gap between actual and potential productivity by 10 percent.

Let go of unproductive firms

Letting inefficient firms and business models fail is a core principle of creative destruction. Studies of firm exit—stemming from seminal work by Hopenhayn (1992)—have revealed that the exit of less productive firms contributes substantially to raising aggregate productivity. In many countries, during periods of trade liberalization the exit of the least productive firms has boosted growth.[30] In middle-income countries, however, bureaucratic frictions prolong the survival of zombie firms—inefficient, debt-ridden companies that crowd out investment by productive firms.[31] Reforms of bankruptcy laws should focus on enabling failed businesses to exit swiftly and predictably and on allowing viable businesses to restructure.

Strengthen competition agencies

As segments of an economy master infusion, they will need to adopt a 3*i* strategy. Institutions can foster the development of new technologies and ensure that entrants—new entrepreneurs—are not blocked by established incumbents, regulatory barriers, and entrenched industry practices. Antitrust laws can help prevent abuse of dominance by established incumbents. As economies (or sectors) move closer to the technology frontier, competition agencies will need to consider a possible trade-off between innovation incentives and market power.[32] Although market power enables investment in R&D to bring new ideas to market, firms may resort to anticompetitive behavior. Thus, competition and innovation policies need coordination, alongside developing independent, capable competition authorities.

For upper-middle-income countries shifting to a 3*i* strategy, a special concern is the containment of killer acquisitions—that is, when incumbents acquire innovative firms specifically to kill future competing products and technologies.[33] But not all acquisitions are deadly: many young entrepreneurs make a deliberate effort to be acquired by an incumbent, producing complementary innovations that an incumbent can scale up.

Deepen capital markets

Switching from a 2*i* to a 3*i* strategy also has implications for how firms access finance. Equity markets can be instrumental in supporting innovative activities, especially in private firms, which typically face larger financing gaps than publicly listed firms. However, private markets for equity financing lack depth and access in emerging economies (figure O.11). Start-up incubators and accelerators can be particularly helpful, providing mentorship, resources, networking opportunities, and sometimes funding to help start-ups grow and compete.

Education, social mobility, and entrepreneurship

As more parts of an economy shift from 1*i* to 2*i* and 3*i* strategies, demand increases for highly skilled workers—technicians, managers, scientists, and other professionals. This demand can increase income inequality. But, if it is accompanied by policies that expand access to higher education and reduce barriers for women and other disadvantaged groups so that they are now rewarded for their skills and able to create new businesses, it also generates greater social mobility.[34] Such conditions can provide both social stability and economic dynamism, which are equally necessary for middle-income countries to grow to high-income status. In fact, barriers to social mobility can derail a country's plans for moving beyond a 1*i* strategy.

Discipline, not vilify, elites

Social and economic elites can be either creative or inimical to creation. For a middle-income country seeking rapidly to enrich its talent pool, it would be self-defeating to lower elites' ambitions. Elites are most able to invest in their children's education—and larger investments, and better investment choices, yield increasing returns to parental background.[35] Elites are also best connected for job searches and placements. And elite women can most readily become role models for other women through education and professional work. However, elites—like large incumbent firms—need to be disciplined because of their power to capture institutions. If elites hog education, jobs, capital, and assets for themselves, thereby limiting access to outsiders, a middle-income country is suffering from elite capture: by preserving privilege, it is stymying creation.

Invest in talent and reward merit

People who are not only talented, but also—crucially—educated and have access to labor markets, enterprise opportunities, and business financing are key to the 2*i* and 3*i* strategies. Policy makers should especially consider initiatives to educate women, along with other excluded and marginalized groups, and to let families become more socially and economically mobile with each succeeding generation.

From the successes of former middle-income countries that have attained high income, three simple lessons emerge for education reform:

- *Broaden access to foundational skills.* Graduate more students from high school, broadening and deepening the talent pool.

Figure O.11 In emerging market and developing economies, few companies are funded by venture capital or private equity

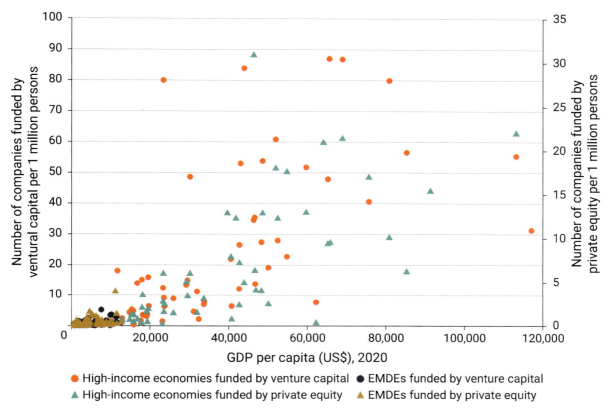

Source: Didier and Chelva 2023.
Note: The figure displays the number of companies funded by venture capital (left axis) and private equity (right axis) from deals concluded 2018–19. Economies are classified according to the World Bank's income classification as of June 2020 (Serajuddin and Hamadeh 2020). EMDEs = emerging market and developing economies; GDP = gross domestic product.

- *Monitor learning outcomes using student assessments.* Gauge progress toward explicit policy goals.
- *Embed educational reforms in a national economic growth strategy.* For example, in the early 1970s, as Finland's economy became less resource-dependent and agrarian and more urban and industrial, the country reformed education to meet the demands of firms and of a growing middle class.

Growing the talent pool takes time, and past mistakes can impede countries for decades. Although many middle-income countries have expanded tertiary education, a critical difference between those that graduated to high-income status and those that did not is that the former never wavered in their commitment to foundational skills, thereby developing a large pipeline of talent. Missing the opportunity to learn while in school is largely irreversible for children; they may not have a chance to study later in life. Strengthening foundational skills requires efficient and effective spending on education because spending by itself is not a guarantee of better learning outcomes.[36] Countries may consider adopting the "progressive universalism" principle: add incrementally to higher education investments as the quality at lower schooling levels rises to include more students.

Meanwhile, middle-income countries are not only talent-scarce relative to advanced economies, but also not nearly as effective in allocating the existing talent to tasks. For example, these countries do not fully reward the talents of women and people from less privileged families, while simultaneously protecting less able people from privileged families from competition in education.

Policies to ensure equal opportunities for women, minorities, and other disadvantaged groups whose talents have been undeveloped or unrewarded are likely to increase both economic efficiency and equity. However, in many countries patriarchal gender norms are part of a deeply entrenched system of preservation, limiting women's earning power and social and economic mobility across occupations and generations. Where economic and social rights favor men, middle-income countries that aspire to grow quickly must work hard to grant the same opportunities to women. Institutions and policies are needed to counter the exclusion of women—among others—from education, employment, enterprise financing, and contracting and to provide policies such as childcare support or flexible work for both men and women.

In education, policies that support girls who stay in school longer by offering them scholarships or conditional cash transfers can improve outcomes for women.[37] To boost female students' interest in science, technology, engineering, and mathematics (STEM), mentoring and information interventions have proven to be among the most effective methods.[38] However, because women face social, family, and logistical constraints—including household and childcare responsibilities—educating women is most effective when complemented by other interventions to address these constraints.

Leverage digital technologies

Digital technologies—such as the internet, mobile phones, social media, and web-based information systems—can promote both social mobility and talent development. When Nandan Nilekani, one of India's leading technology entrepreneurs, was tasked with developing Aadhar (the country's digital identification system) in 2009, he paved the way for Indians to accumulate digital capital (digital footprints of online activity and digital payments). Digital footprints become digital capital, which individuals own and can choose to make available to lenders when getting access to credit. Digital data on payments, receipts, taxes, and loan repayments all make it possible to assess financial credibility. According to a recent study, digital capital has increased entrepreneurship and business income in India and has favored small-scale vendors and economically lagging districts.[39] By delivering instructional material, digital technologies also provide students from disadvantaged backgrounds with opportunities to learn.

Reward innovators and scientists to match brain drain with brain gain

Investing in advanced skills is costly. Individuals invest in these skills with the expectation that their talent and acquired ability will be rewarded.[40] However, these rewards are often found on foreign shores. *World Development Report 2023* reported that in middle-income countries, 10 percent of highly skilled workers emigrate, with high-level skills in greater demand in Western Europe and North America.[41] To counter the brain drain, the report recommended that origin countries expand their capacity for training highly skilled workers because greater capacity increases the likelihood that a sufficient number of highly skilled workers will stay even when others migrate.

As countries adopt a *3i* strategy, they will need to tap into the knowledge and know-how of a country's diaspora. The emigration of highly skilled individuals can serve as an opportunity for the origin country if emigrants remain connected to the origin country—or even return. This is particularly relevant in conflict-affected countries such as Ukraine that have experienced a large outflow of highly skilled individuals. When the demand for advanced skills increases, the diaspora becomes an important talent pool to germinate innovation at home.

As migrants acquire skills abroad, migration may drive a brain gain in the sending country. Whether the sending country experiences brain drain or brain gain varies across countries, depending largely on how the sending country's policies address emigration. The most likely migrant to be exposed to modern production processes and technologies and to transmit valuable knowledge back to the origin country is highly skilled, moves to an advanced economy, and works there in a leading occupation as a manager, professional, or technician (figure O.12).

Building and expanding high-quality universities—institutions that can train top talent and contribute to innovation—require an efficient system of public funding for research, along with fluid university-industry connections

Figure O.12 Countries with large, successful diasporas have the highest potential for knowledge transfers

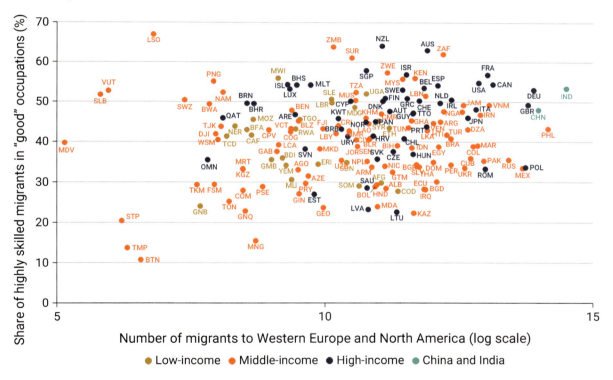

Source: WDR 2024 team.

Note: Data on migration flows by skill and current occupation are from OECD DIOC 2010–11, which covers migration flows from 200 origins to 34 OECD (Organisation for Economic Co-operation and Development) country destinations. Each scatter point represents an origin (or birth) country. For each birth country, the x-axis shows the number of migrants over 15 years of age who had completed tertiary education and were living in destination countries in Western Europe or North America (AUT, BEL, FRA, DEU, NLD, CHE, USA, GBR, IRL, CAN, ESP, ITA, DNK, NOR, SWE; in logs), and the y-axis the share of these tertiary-educated migrants working as managers, professionals, or technicians ("good" occupations) in the destination country. For country abbreviations, see International Organization for Standardization (ISO), https://www.iso.org/obp/ui/#search.

to promote exchange of knowledge. Most efficient for middle-income countries is to focus public funding on a few strategic research areas, such as STEM, health, and energy transition, with funds allocated competitively and based on performance. Partnerships with world-class universities can be a strategy for developing a research base.

To encourage knowledge exchanges between universities and industries, countries could grant R&D funding for such partnerships. Governments could also offer firms tax incentives for collaborating with universities. Establishing a regulatory framework for knowledge exchange is key—especially to define the government's intellectual property rights to knowledge produced by universities with public resources. One desirable outcome of university-industry collaboration is venture creation by university faculty, staff, students, and postdoctoral fellows, with private investors serving as venture capitalists. Universities can also form partnerships to provide services to local companies.

Energy, emissions, and crisis management

The destruction of outdated arrangements—enterprises, jobs, technologies, private contracts, policies, and public institutions—is essential for an economy to ensure that it has the appropriate balance of investment, infusion, and innovation. But in many countries the forces of destruction are weak during boom times, whereas crises often play an outsize role in weakening the forces of preservation, making way for the forces of creation.

In the context of energy, the oil price shocks in the 1980s increased the relative cost of fossil fuels and played a major role in accelerating investments in energy efficiency and the development of cleaner energy technologies.[42] The global financial crisis of 2007–09 coincided with a significant increase in the uptake of renewables.[43] Renewable energy use grew rapidly in the United States, China, and Germany in part because of the stimulus programs governments enacted to address the crisis. Today, two crises—the climate crisis and the global energy crisis—are combining to drive rapid progress in low-carbon technologies, defined as technologies or applications that counter the effects of climate change.

Discipline advanced economies to reduce the cost of global decarbonization
As middle-income countries move to a 2i strategy, they will have opportunities to join globalized supply chains for low-carbon products and reduce the cost of decarbonization worldwide. However, their success will depend on advanced economies easing up on protectionism in trade policy. Protectionist measures in advanced economies could prove to be the bane of the global energy transition.

Previous waves of middle-income countries have transitioned to high-income status with the help of coordinated trade policies in a globally integrated economy. By contrast, today's middle-income countries are navigating a hazier trade landscape. Countries have not yet agreed on the key rules for low-carbon energy product supply chains. And "make local" subsidies will likely do a lot to relocate production—to the United States, to the European Union, and to a growing number of other economies that are embracing "reshoring" efforts and enacting local content requirements. For example, initial modeling suggests that the US Inflation Reduction Act will substantially attract industry toward the United States, Mexico, and Canada and away from other major producers.[44] In effect, these subsidies and protectionist measures in high-income countries threaten to lock middle-income countries out of low-carbon value chains.

To be clear, subsidies have a role to play in a global transition to low-carbon energy sources in view of the positive externalities of such a transition and the extent of today's market failures. But they should not distinguish between domestic and foreign suppliers. Each segment of the value chain should be located where a product can be made at the lowest cost, averting a risk of protectionist retaliation and a race to the bottom (the most distorted and least efficient market structure). But such globally rational thinking is rarely favored by leaders with domestic politics on their minds. They are unlikely to enact subsidies consistent with a globally integrated economy because such subsidies would allow gains from supply chain reallocation to accrue to firms based in other countries.

Faced with this conundrum, policy makers in advanced economies should consider that the energy transition to low-carbon energy sources has many benefits, not just through its effects on the climate, but also through its implications for the economic development of middle-income countries. To lock middle-income countries out of global value chains with protectionist measures is to deny firms and industries in those countries the benefits of learning-by-doing spillovers.

To accommodate middle-income countries and support a global transition to low-carbon energy, policy makers in advanced economies will need to update trade policy rules by limiting green subsidies, export controls, and import controls and using clear language to define their appropriate use. One option is to modify existing agreements with supplementary clauses, much in the same way that Articles 20 and 21 of the General Agreement on Tariffs and Trade (GATT) were used to carve out exceptions. Such clauses can transparently acknowledge that all countries need to nurture emerging domestic industries if they are to achieve a just transition with energy security. But the use of subsidies should also be restricted to specific circumstances, such as the need for public support to develop and commercialize innovative low-carbon technologies.

Decouple emissions from economic growth

Rising incomes increase the demand for energy—even as they tend to intensify public concern about the environment and awareness that carbon emissions drive climate change. Furthermore, as middle-income countries ramp up the sophistication of their economies by switching to 2*i* and 3*i* strategies and expand their use of artificial intelligence and machine learning, their demand for energy will rise dramatically. In fact, the International Energy Agency (IEA) has predicted that the electricity demand by global data centers will more than double from 2022 to 2026, with artificial intelligence playing a major role in that increase.[45]

Middle-income countries will need to decide how best to reduce the carbon emissions of their growing economies—a combination of energy intensity (energy consumed per US dollar of GDP) and carbon intensity (carbon emissions per unit of energy). Today, emissions from a growing economy outweigh the reductions in emissions from lowering energy intensity and carbon intensity. To decouple emissions from economic growth, governments will need to discipline incumbency, reward merit, and derisk investments in low-carbon energy:

- *Disciplining incumbency.* Disciplining the incumbency advantage is especially important for increasing energy efficiency and decoupling emissions from economic growth. Market contestability, as well as opportunities for value-adding firms to grow, spurs the adoption of energy-saving technologies. In Georgia, for example, markets with a higher concentration have lower energy efficiency. In Argentina, firms with a higher share of skilled workers are better able to adopt advanced green technologies.[46] Exporters also tend to have lower emissions intensity than nonexporters.[47] If incumbents are disciplined, energy price increases hold considerable potential for firms to reduce energy intensity. In the longer term, increases in energy prices tend to be fully compensated for by higher efficiency.[48] A major challenge is that energy prices do not reflect costs—economic or ecological. Estimates suggest that middle-income countries account for 93 percent of explicit fossil fuel subsidies.[49] A promising approach is to consider the concept of total carbon price (TCP) to assess the price signal from a combination of direct and indirect carbon pricing instruments, including energy excise taxes and fuel subsidies.[50]

The incumbency advantage also should be disciplined in the electricity industry, where incumbent SOEs dominate fossil fuel power generation and block the entry of new players.

- *Rewarding merit.* The most efficient way to scale up the efficient provision of low-carbon energy is to respect the *merit order*: the sequence followed by grid operators selling power to the market. The starting point is set by the cheapest offer, made by the power station with the lowest running costs, which determines wholesale market prices. Any provider who can offer renewable energy at zero marginal cost—that is, with insignificant operating costs—should have priority in meeting demand. When the merit order functions as designed, it shifts prices along the supply curve, which energy economics calls the "merit order curve."[51]
- *Derisking investment.* The cost of capital for low-carbon energy such as solar photovoltaic and wind in middle-income countries is twice that in high-income countries, averaging 3.8 percent in high-income countries, but 7.2 percent in upper-middle-income countries and more than 8.5 percent in lower-middle-income countries (figure O.13).[52] Addressing technology risk, development risk, and pricing risk can help incentivize investors—utilities, banks, or other institutions—to invest in low-carbon energy. Derisking requires a whole-of-economy approach. It depends on licensing, policy stability, and social acceptance, along with reducing technical, market, and regulatory risks.[53] Derisking will make renewable energy projects less expensive, as well as reduce the public finance needed to support these projects.

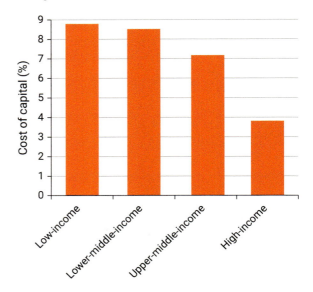

Figure O.13 **In low- and middle-income countries, the cost of capital for renewables is high**

Source: IRENA 2023.
Note: Data are for 2021 and 2022.

The road ahead

Three decades ago, Professor Robert Lucas, Jr., likened the development strategies that led to spectacular economic growth in Korea to the making of a "miracle."[54] *Given the changes in the global economy since the time that Korea was a middle-income economy, it would be fair to conclude that it would be a miracle if today's middle-income economies manage to do in 50 years what Korea did in just 25. It might even be miraculous if they replicated the impressive achievements of other successful countries such as Chile and Poland. But that is exactly what governments in Bangladesh, Brazil, China, India, Indonesia, Mexico, Morocco, South Africa, Türkiye, Viet Nam, among others, hope to accomplish.*

To do this, these countries will have to become more disciplined. They will have to time the shift from simpler investment-led growth strategies (1i) that worked well in the early stages of development to augmenting investment accelerations with intentional policies that aid the infusion of know-how from abroad (2i), and only then expend sizable resources on innovation (3i). Put another way, they will have to become more efficient in their use of capital—both financial and human—and labor and energy.

To do this, they will have to shed long-held prejudices about enterprise, talent, and energy. They will have to appreciate the importance of reliable information to shape and quicken the structural transformations that must accompany any durable increase in incomes and living standards. Depending on their special circumstance and the stage of development they have reached, they will need to adopt a sequenced and progressively more sophisticated mix of policies (table O.3). Low-income countries can focus solely on policies designed to increase investment—the 1i approach. Once they attain lower-middle-income status, they will need to shift gears and expand the policy mix to 2i, investment + infusion. At the upper-middle-income level, countries will have to shift gears again to 3i: investment + infusion + innovation. Middle-income countries will need progressively greater economic freedom, more open and informed debates, and—frequently—the political courage to change stubborn institutions and long-standing arrangements.

Table O.3 The 3*i* strategy: What countries should do at different stages of development

	LOW-INCOME COUNTRIES **1*i*: Investment**	**LOWER-MIDDLE-INCOME COUNTRIES** **2*i*: Investment + Infusion**	**UPPER-MIDDLE-INCOME COUNTRIES** **3*i*: Investment + Infusion + Innovation**
Enterprise	• Improve the investment climate to increase domestic and foreign investment.	• Discipline market leaders through integration into globally contestable markets. • Diffuse global technologies with fluid factor and product markets. • Reward value-adding firms to stimulate business dynamism.	• Deepen capital markets and expand equity financing. • Strengthen antitrust regulation and competition agencies. • Protect intellectual property rights.
Talent	• Invest in human capital by broadening foundational skills and improving learning outcomes.	• Discipline elites by providing equal opportunities for women, minorities, and disadvantaged groups. • Improve allocation of talent to task. • Develop links among local and globally leading universities. • Allow emigration of educated workers whose skills are not valued in domestic markets.	• Strengthen industry-academia links domestically. • Expand programs to connect with diaspora in advanced economies. • Enhance economic and political freedoms.
Energy	• Increase investment in expanding access and grid networks. • Reform regulatory frameworks to attract private investment and ensure fair competition.	• Discipline SOEs by hardening budget constraints. • Use international coalitions to encourage advanced economies to ease protection of domestic incumbents. • Aid adoption of energy-efficient practices. • Enhance economic efficiency by reflecting environmental costs in energy prices.	• Lower the cost of capital for low-carbon energy by reducing risks involving technology, markets, and policy. • Increase multilateral finance for very long-term investments.

Source: WDR 2024 team.
Note: SOEs = state-owned enterprises.

Notes

1. Throughout this Report, data on GDP and income per capita are as of July 1, 2023.
2. Gill and Kharas (2007).
3. Kose and Ohnsorge (2024).
4. Melitz and Redding (2021).
5. Soh, Koh, and Aridi (2023).
6. Pinto (2014).
7. Marcel and Vivanco (2021).
8. Lucas (1988); Romer (1990).
9. de Souza (2022).
10. de Souza (2022, 2023).
11. Schumpeter (1942).
12. Vagliasindi (2023).
13. Aghion and Howitt (1992).
14. Hsieh et al. (2019).
15. van der Weide et al. (2021).
16. Gottlieb, Poschke, and Tueting (2024).
17. Akcigit, Grigsby, and Nicholas (2017).
18. Akcigit and Kerr (2018).
19. Cusolito, Garcia-Marin, and Maloney (2023).
20. Bustos (2011).
21. Bloom, Draca, and Van Reenen (2016).
22. Arráiz, Henríquez, and Stucchi (2011).
23. Cirera and Maloney (2017).
24. Eslava and Haltiwanger (2020); Hsieh and Olken (2014).
25. Akcigit, Alp, and Peters (2021).
26. Bertoni, Colombo, and Quas (2023); Kersten et al. (2017).
27. Aivazian and Santor (2008); López and Torres (2020); Tsuruta (2020); Vu and Tran (2021).
28. Bachas, Fattal Jaef, and Jensen (2019).
29. López and Torres (2020).
30. Melitz (2003).
31. Didier and Cusolito (2024).
32. Cheng (2021); Gal et al. (2019).
33. Cunningham, Ederer, and Ma (2021).
34. *Social mobility* is intergenerational movement up or down a country's income ladder, allowing children to move away from their parents' position relative to generational peers.
35. Becker et al. (2018).
36. Angrist et al. (2023); World Bank (2018).
37. Chaudhury and Parajuli (2010).
38. Muñoz-Boudet et al. (2021).
39. Dubey and Purnanandam (2023).
40. Akcigit, Baslandze, and Stantcheva (2016).
41. World Bank (2023).
42. Peters et al. (2012).
43. UNEP (2009).
44. Baqaee and Farhi (2023).
45. https://time.com/6987773/ai-data-centers-energy-usage-climate-change/.
46. Albornoz et al. (2009).
47. Holladay (2016); Richter and Schiersch (2017).
48. Bashmakov (2007); Bashmakov et al. (2023).
49. Black et al. (2023).
50. Agnolucci, Gencer, and Heine (2024). TCP components labeled "energy taxes" and "energy subsidies" are based on "net" computed values (as proxies for the actual values of energy taxes and subsidies) due to data limitations. Energy taxes and subsidies are estimated based on the "price gap" between retail prices and supply costs for a particular energy carrier used in a specific sector in a jurisdiction in a given year. The net energy taxes and subsidies are then aggregated across sectors, fuels, and countries to yield a global value. More details on this methodology are provided in Agnolucci, Gencer, and Heine (2024).
51. Acemoglu, Kakhbod, and Ozdaglar (2017).
52. Estimates of the cost of capital are based on the cost of debt and the cost of equity. The cost of debt is the cost to finance a loan for a renewable energy asset. The cost of equity is the return on equity required by the project developer (IRENA 2023).
53. Noothout et al. (2016).
54. Lucas (1988).

References

Acemoglu, Daron, Ali Kakhbod, and Asuman Ozdaglar. 2017. "Competition in Electricity Markets with Renewable Energy Sources." *Energy Journal* 38 (1): 137–55.

Aghion, Philippe, and Peter Howitt. 1992. "A Model of Growth through Creative Destruction." *Econometrica* 60 (2): 323–51.

Agnolucci, Paolo, Defne Gencer, and Dirk Heine. 2024. "Total Carbon Pricing for Energy Consumption: The Importance of Energy Taxes and Subsidies." ESMAP Technical Report, Energy Subsidy Reform in Action Series, World Bank, Washington, DC.

Aivazian, Varouj Aram, and Eric Santor. 2008. "Financial Constraints and Investment: Assessing the Impact of a World Bank Credit Program on Small and Medium Enterprises in Sri Lanka." *Canadian Journal of Economics* 41 (2): 475–500.

Akcigit, Ufuk, Harun Alp, and Michael Peters. 2021. "Lack of Selection and Limits to Delegation: Firm Dynamics in Developing Countries." *American Economic Review* 111 (1): 231–75.

Akcigit, Ufuk, Salomé Baslandze, and Stefanie Stantcheva. 2016. "Taxation and the International Mobility of Inventors." *American Economic Review* 106 (10): 2930–81.

Akcigit, Ufuk, John Grigsby, and Tom Nicholas. 2017. "The Rise of American Ingenuity: Innovation and Inventors of the Golden Age." NBER Working Paper 23047 (January), National Bureau of Economic Research, Cambridge, MA.

Akcigit, Ufuk, and William R. Kerr. 2018. "Growth through Heterogeneous Innovations." *Journal of Political Economy* 126 (4): 1374–443.

Albornoz, Facundo, Matthew A. Cole, Robert J. R. Elliott, and Marco G. Ercolani. 2009. "In Search of Environmental Spillovers." *World Economy* 32 (1): 136–63.

Angrist, Noam, Elisabetta Aurino, Harry A. Patrinos, George Psacharopoulos, Emiliana Vegas, Ralph Nordjo, and Brad Wong. 2023. "Improving Learning in Low- and Lower-Middle-Income Countries." *Journal of Benefit-Cost Analysis* 14 (S1): 55–80.

Arráiz, Irani, Francisca Henríquez, and Rodolfo Stucchi. 2011. "Impact of the Chilean Supplier Development Program on the Performance of SMEs and Their Large Firm Customers." OVE Working Paper OVE/WP-04/11 (May), Office of Evaluation and Oversight, Inter-American Development Bank, Washington, DC.

Bachas, Pierre, Roberto N. Fattal Jaef, and Anders Jensen. 2019. "Size-Dependent Tax Enforcement and Compliance: Global Evidence and Aggregate Implications." *Journal of Development Economics* 140 (September): 203–22.

Bahar, Dany, Sebastian Bustos, and Muhammed A. Yıldırım. 2024. "Stages of Diversification Revisited." Background paper prepared for *World Development Report 2024*, World Bank, Washington, DC.

Baqaee, David Rezza, and Emmanuel Farhi. 2023. "Networks, Barriers, and Trade." NBER Working Paper 26108 rev. (February), National Bureau of Economic Research, Cambridge, MA.

Bashmakov, Igor. 2007. "Three Laws of Energy Transitions." *Energy Policy* 35 (7): 3583–94.

Bashmakov, Igor, Michael Grubb, Paul Drummond, Robert Lowe, Anna Myshak, and Ben Hinder. 2023. "'Minus 1' and Energy Costs Constants: Empirical Evidence, Theory, and Policy Implications." SSRN Preprint (March 30), Social Science Research Network, Rochester, NY. https://papers.ssrn.com/sol3/papers.cfm?abstract_id=4401851.

Becker, Gary Stanley, Scott Duke Kominers, Kevin M. Murphy, and Jörg L. Spenkuch. 2018. "A Theory of Intergenerational Mobility." *Journal of Political Economy* 126 (S1): S7–S25.

Bertoni, Fabio, Massimo G. Colombo, and Anita Quas. 2023. "The Long-Term Effects of Loan Guarantees on SME Performance." *Journal of Corporate Finance* 80 (June): 102408.

Black, Simon, Antung A. Liu, Ian W. H. Parry, and Nate Vernon. 2023. "IMF Fossil Fuel Subsidies Data: 2023 Update." IMF Working Paper WP/23/169 (August), International Monetary Fund, Washington, DC.

Bloom, Nicholas, Mirko Draca, and John Van Reenen. 2016. "Trade Induced Technical Change? The Impact of Chinese Imports on Innovation, IT and Productivity." *Review of Economic Studies* 83 (January): 87–117.

Bustos, Paula. 2011. "Trade Liberalization, Exports, and Technology Upgrading: Evidence on the Impact of MERCOSUR on Argentinian Firms." *American Economic Review* 101 (1): 304–40.

Chaudhury, Nazmul, and Dilip Parajuli. 2010. "Conditional Cash Transfers and Female Schooling: The Impact of the Female School Stipend Programme on Public School Enrolments in Punjab, Pakistan." *Applied Economics* 42 (28): 3565–83.

Cheng, Thomas K. 2021. *The Patent-Competition Interface in Developing Countries*. Oxford, UK: Oxford University Press.

Chepeliev, Maksym, and Erwin Corong. 2022. "Revisiting the Environmental Bias of Trade Policies Based on an Environmentally Extended GTAP MRIO Data Base." Paper presented at the virtual 25th Annual Conference, Global Economic Analysis, Center for Global Trade Analysis, Department of Agricultural Economics, Purdue University, West Lafayette, IN, June 8–10, 2022. https://www.gtap.agecon.purdue.edu/resources/res_display.asp?RecordID=6548.

Choi, Jaedo, and Younghun Shim. 2024. "From Adoption to Innovation: State-Dependent Technology Policy in Developing Countries." STEG Working Paper WP091 (March), Structural Transformation and Economic Growth, Centre for Economic Policy Research, London.

Cirera, Xavier, and William F. Maloney. 2017. *The Innovation Paradox: Developing-Country Capabilities and the Unrealized Promise of Technological Catch-Up*. Washington, DC: World Bank.

Cunningham, Colleen, Florian Ederer, and Song Ma. 2021. "Killer Acquisitions." *Journal of Political Economy* 129 (3): 649–702.

Cusolito, Ana Paula, Alvaro Garcia-Marin, and William F. Maloney. 2023. "Proximity to the Frontier, Markups, and the Response of Innovation to Foreign Competition: Evidence from Matched Production-Innovation Surveys in Chile." *American Economic Review: Insights* 5 (1): 35–54.

de Souza, Gustavo. 2022. "The Labor Market Consequences of Appropriate Technology." Working Paper WP 2022-53 (September 6), Federal Reserve Bank of Chicago, Chicago.

de Souza, Gustavo. 2023. "R&D Subsidy and Import Substitution: Growing in the Shadow of Protection." Working Paper WP 2023-37 rev. (October 5), Federal Reserve Bank of Chicago, Chicago.

Didier, Tatiana, and Beulah Chelva. 2023. "Private Equity Markets in EMDEs." World Bank, Washington, DC.

Didier, Tatiana, and Ana Paula Cusolito. 2024. *Unleashing Productivity through Firm Financing*. Washington, DC: World Bank.

Dubey, Tamanna Singh, and Amiyatosh Purnanandam. 2023. "Can Cashless Payments Spur Economic Growth?" Presentation at the National Bureau of Economic Research's Summer Institute 2023, "Macro, Money, and Financial Frictions." Cambridge, MA, July 12–13, 2023.

Energy Institute. 2023. "Statistical Review of World Energy 2023." June, Energy Institute, London.

Eslava, Marcela, and John C. Haltiwanger. 2020. "The Life-Cycle Growth of Plants: The Role of Productivity, Demand and Wedges." NBER Working Paper 27184 (May), National Bureau of Economic Research, Cambridge, MA.

Gal, Peter, Giuseppe Nicoletti, Theodore Renault, Stéphane Sorbe, and Christina Timilioti. 2019. "Digitalisation and Productivity: In Search of the Holy Grail; Firm-Level Empirical Evidence from EU Countries." OECD Economics Department Working Paper 1533 (February 6), Organisation for Economic Co-operation and Development, Paris.

Gill, Indermit Singh, and Homi Kharas. 2007. *An East Asian Renaissance: Ideas for Economic Growth*. With Deepak Bhattasali, Milan Brahmbhatt, Gaurav Datt, Mona Haddad, Edward Mountfield, Radu Tatucu, and Ekaterina Vostroknutova. Washington, DC: World Bank.

Gottlieb, Charles, Markus Poschke, and Michael Tueting. 2024. "Skill Supply, Firm Size, and Economic Development." Background paper prepared for *World Development Report 2024,* World Bank, Washington, DC.

Holladay, J. Scott. 2016. "Exporters and the Environment." *Canadian Journal of Economics* 49 (1): 147–72.

Hopenhayn, Hugo A. 1992. "Entry, Exit, and Firm Dynamics in Long-Run Equilibrium." *Econometrica* 60 (5): 1127–50.

Hsieh, Chang-Tai, Erik Hurst, Charles I. Jones, and Peter J. Klenow. 2019. "The Allocation of Talent and U.S. Economic Growth." *Econometrica* 87 (5): 1439–74.

Hsieh, Chang-Tai, and Peter J. Klenow. 2014. "The Life Cycle of Plants in India and Mexico." *Quarterly Journal of Economics* 129 (3): 1035–84.

Hsieh, Chang-Tai, and Benjamin A. Olken. 2014. "The Missing 'Missing Middle'." *Journal of Economic Perspectives* 28 (3): 89–108.

IEA (International Energy Agency). 2023. *World Energy Outlook 2023*. Paris: IEA.

IRENA (International Renewable Energy Agency). 2023. "The Cost of Financing for Renewable Power." IRENA, Abu Dhabi, United Arab Emirates.

Jones, Charles I. 2016. "The Facts of Economic Growth." In *The Handbook of Macroeconomics*, vol. 2A, edited by John B. Taylor and Harald Uhlig, 3–69. Amsterdam: Elsevier.

Kersten, Renate, Job Harms, Kellie Liket, and Karen Maas. 2017. "Small Firms, Large Impact? A Systematic Review of the SME Finance Literature." *World Development* 97 (September): 330–48.

Kose, M. Ayhan, and Franziska Ohnsorge, eds. 2024. *Falling Long-Term Growth Prospects: Trends, Expectations, and Policies*. Washington, DC: World Bank.

López, José Joaquín, and Jesica Torres. 2020. "Size-Dependent Policies, Talent Misallocation, and the Return to Skill." *Review of Economic Dynamics* 38 (October): 59–93.

Lucas, Robert B., Jr. 1988. "On the Mechanics of Economic Development." *Journal of Monetary Economics* 22 (1): 3–42.

Marcel, Mario, and Diego Vivanco. 2021. "Measuring Small and Medium-Size Enterprises' Contribution to Trade in Value Added: The Case of Chile 2013–2016." Working Paper of the Central Bank of Chile 914 (April), Central Bank of Chile, Santiago.

Melitz, Marc J. 2003. "The Impact of Trade on Intra-Industry Reallocations and Aggregate Industry Productivity." *Econometrica* 71 (6): 1695–725.

Melitz, Marc J., and Stephen J. Redding. 2021. "Trade and Innovation." NBER Working Paper 28945 (June), National Bureau of Economic Research, Cambridge, MA.

Muñoz-Boudet, Ana María, Lourdes Rodríguez-Chamussy, Cristina Chiarella, and Isil Oral Savonitto. 2021. "Women and STEM in Europe and Central Asia." Report AUS0002179, World Bank, Washington, DC.

Noothout, Paul, David de Jager, Lucie Tesnière, Sascha van Rooijen, Nikolaos Karypidis, Robert Brückmann, Filip Jirouš, et al. 2016. *The Impact of Risks in Renewable Energy Investments and the Role of Smart Policies: Final Report*. Karlsruhe, Germany: Fraunhofer Institute for Systems and Innovation Research.

Peters, Glen P., Gregg Marland, Corinne Le Quéré, Thomas Boden, Josep G. Canadell, and Michael R. Raupach. 2012. "Rapid Growth in CO_2 Emissions after the 2008–2009 Global Financial Crisis." *Nature Climate Change* 2: 2–4.

Pinto, Brian. 2014. "Why Poland Beat the Odds." Chapter 4 in *How Does My Country Grow? Economic Advice through Story-Telling*, 55–76. New York: Oxford University Press.

Richter, Philipp M., and Alexander Schiersch. 2017. "CO_2 Emission Intensity and Exporting: Evidence from Firm-Level Data." *European Economic Review* 98 (September): 373–91.

Romer, Paul Michael. 1990. "Endogenous Technological Change." *Journal of Political Economy* 98 (5, Part 2): S71–S102.

Schumpeter, Joseph Alois. 1942. *Capitalism, Socialism and Democracy*. New York: Harper and Brothers.

Serajuddin, Umar, and Nada Hamadeh. 2020. "New World Bank Country Classifications by Income Level: 2020–2021." *Data Blog* (blog), July 1, 2020. https://blogs.worldbank.org/opendata/new-world-bank-country-classifications-income-level-2020-2021.

Soh, Hoon Sahib, Youngsun Koh, and Anwar Aridi, eds. 2023. *Innovative Korea: Leveraging Innovation and Technology for Development*. Washington, DC: World Bank.

Tsuruta, Daisuke. 2020. "SME Policies as a Barrier to Growth of SMEs." *Small Business Economics* 54 (4): 1067–106.

UNEP (United Nations Environment Programme). 2009. "The Global Financial Crisis and Its Impact on Renewable Energy Finance." Division of Technology, Industry, and Economics, UNEP, Nairobi, Kenya.

Vagliasindi, Maria. 2023. "The Role of SOEs in Climate Change." Background paper prepared for *The Business of the State*, World Bank, Washington, DC.

van der Weide, Roy, Christoph Lakner, Daniel Gerszon Mahler, Ambar Narayan, and Rakesh Ramasubbaiah. 2021. "Intergenerational Mobility around the World." Policy Research Working Paper 9707, World Bank, Washington, DC.

Vu, Quang, and Tuyen Quang Tran. 2021. "Government Financial Support and Firm Productivity in Vietnam." *Finance Research Letters* 40 (May): 101667.

World Bank. 1978. *World Development Report 1978*. Washington, DC: World Bank.

World Bank. 2015. *Peru: Building on Success: Boosting Productivity for Faster Growth*. Washington, DC: World Bank.

World Bank. 2018. *World Development Report 2018: Learning to Realize Education's Promise*. Washington, DC: World Bank.

World Bank. 2023. *World Development Report 2023: Migrants, Refugees, and Societies*. Washington, DC: World Bank.

Part 1
Middle-Income Transitions

The share of middle-income countries in the global economy is increasing—over half of countries today are middle-income. As classified by the World Bank, 108 countries qualify as middle-income. With about three-fourths of the world's population, these 108 middle-income countries account for nearly 40 percent of global economic activity. Of every five people in extreme poverty globally, more than three live in middle-income countries. And they generate well over 60 percent of all carbon dioxide emissions (table P1.1). Not surprisingly, they will play a central role in global development, and the difficulties they face should be of global concern. So where are these economies headed?

Notably, the progress of the middle-income countries has slowed in recent decades. The median middle-income economy has income per capita that is less than one-tenth that of the United States. More surprising, this figure has remained almost unchanged for 50 years. Meanwhile, the prospects for middle-income countries are not improving in view of the direction the global economy is going, from healthy to wobbling. Against these headwinds, today's middle-income countries need to make miracles to develop at the pace of the 34 economies that reached high-income status between 1990 and 2021. And even if these headwinds were not getting stronger, middle-income countries would still face long

Table P1.1 World Bank country classifications and selected global indicators, 2022

INCOME CLASSIFICATION	SHARE OF GLOBAL POPULATION (%)	SHARE OF GLOBAL GDP (%)	SHARE OF PEOPLE IN EXTREME POVERTY GLOBALLY (%)	SHARE OF GLOBAL CARBON DIOXIDE (CO_2) EMISSIONS (%)
Low-income	8.9	0.6	36.5	0.5
Lower-middle-income	40.3	8.3	55.4	15.7
Upper-middle-income	35.1	30.3	7.1	48.6
High-income	15.7	60.8	1.0	35.2

Sources: Population shares and global GDP shares computed from WDI (World Development Indicators) (Data Catalog), World Bank, Washington, DC, https://datacatalog.worldbank.org/search/dataset/0037712; extreme poverty shares from PIP (Poverty and Inequality Platform) (dashboard), World Bank, Washington, DC, https://pip.worldbank.org/home; carbon dioxide emissions data (2022) from Climate Watch (dashboard), World Resources Institute, Washington, DC, https://www.climatewatchdata.org/.

Note: The World Bank currently recognizes 26 economies as low-income (GNI per capita, calculated using the World Bank Atlas method, of US$1,135 or less in 2022); 54 as lower-middle-income (GNI per capita of between US$1,136 and US$4,465); 54 as upper-middle-income (GNI per capita of between US$4,466 and US$13,845); and 83 as high-income (GNI per capita of US$13,846 or more). GDP = gross domestic product; GNI = gross national income.

odds of achieving high-income status because of growth trajectories suggestive of a "middle-income trap."

Part 1 of this Report examines the evidence for the middle-income trap and asks three questions. First, is growth in middle-income countries *slower*, with investment-led growth running out of steam (chapter 1, Slowing Growth)? Second, is growth in middle-income countries *different*, requiring a significant change in growth strategies (chapter 2, Structural Stasis)? And, third, is growth in middle-income countries now harder (chapter 3, Shrinking Spaces)?

Chapter 1 summarizes the evidence on growth slowdowns and highlights that in middle-income countries a majority of growth slowdowns take place as the returns from capital investment diminish sharply. The median growth slowdown episode occurs when a country reaches a little more than 11 percent of the gross domestic product (GDP) per capita level of the United States. Policy and institutional deficiencies exacerbate growth slowdowns; countries with weaker political institutions experience a growth slowdown much earlier, and at lower incomes, than countries with stronger institutions.

Chapter 2 identifies the two successive transitions that middle-income countries must undergo to achieve high-income status. Specifically, countries need to recalibrate their mix of investment, infusion, and innovation as they move through the middle-income status.

Pathways to high-income status can differ among countries sectorally and spatially. But they generally involve transitioning first from relying largely on *investment* in physical and human capital—the mainstay of successful growth at low-income levels of development—to combining investment with the *infusion* of global technologies and know-how, which applies largely to lower-middle-income countries. This transition is necessary, but it is not enough to move to the high-income level. The second transition involves adding an emphasis on *innovation* to the mix, which is more applicable to upper-middle-income countries. This mapping of transitions to income levels should be considered indicative. Strictly speaking, it is the structure of an economy that determines the timing of the shift, not its gross national income per capita.

Chapter 3 examines the forces that today are making growth harder to achieve. Foreign trade and investment channels are in danger of becoming constricted by geopolitical tensions. The room for governments to act has shrunk because of multiple crises and populist pressures. And in many middle-income countries, government debt—which is more expensive for this income group than for any other—is at an all-time high. Further complicating matters, fragility, conflict, and violence hamper development in some middle-income countries. And in every country, climate change is putting pressure on the government to rethink its growth strategies.

1
Slowing Growth

Key messages

- Today's 108 middle-income countries represent about 40 percent of the global economy, are home to about 75 percent of the world's population and more than 60 percent of the world's poor, and contribute nearly two-thirds of global carbon dioxide emissions.
- Middle-income countries are prone to systematic growth slowdowns—a concept termed the "middle-income trap." The median growth slowdown episode occurs when a country reaches about 11 percent of the gross domestic product per capita of the United States.
- Although income per capita is the metric most commonly used to measure the pace of economic development, measures of average income can differ greatly, depending on the measure.
- Countries with weaker institutions—and especially those with lower levels of economic and political freedom—are more susceptible to slowdowns at even lower levels of income.

Introduction

The problem of economic growth in middle-income economies has been a concern of development policy practitioners for at least five decades. In the first *World Development Report*, published in 1978, "middle-income" was an omnibus term applied to countries with diverse economic characteristics at various stages of development.[1] Middle-income countries were defined as those with annual income per capita of over US$250.[2] By that definition, 58 countries, home to about 900 million people, were designated middle-income. Despite the diversity, *World Development Report 1978* identified two characteristics that distinguished middle-income from low-income countries:

- Their growth prospects were more sensitive to economic conditions in the industrialized (high-income) countries, particularly the environment for trade and commercial capital flows.
- They had more resources available to raise the living standards of the poor.

The 1978 Report emphasized the central role of cultivating engineering talent to design products that change continually and rapidly, alongside better organizing workshops and other production facilities so they are made efficiently.[3]

Interest in the economic growth of middle-income countries rose over the last two decades, especially after a 2007 World Bank regional report on East Asia introduced the term "middle-income trap."[4] The term encapsulated the concern that middle-income countries are prone to systematic slowdowns in growth demonstrated, for example, by the economic stagnation in Latin America and the Middle East since the mid-1970s. This chapter assesses whether the experience of the developing world is consistent with this concern. It finds that the majority of growth slowdowns do take place in middle-income countries. The median growth slowdown episode occurs when a country reaches about 11 percent of the gross domestic product (GDP) per capita of the United States. This chapter also documents that countries with weaker institutions—and especially those with lower levels of economic and political freedom—are susceptible to slowdowns at even lower levels of income.

Chapter 2 explores a related but relatively qualitative question: Is economic growth during the middle-income stage systematically different from growth in low- and high-income countries? Chapter 3 examines the growing concern that rapidly changing economic conditions and policies in the advanced economies of the North Atlantic will make development in middle-income countries even more difficult.

Growth in middle-income countries

The share of middle-income countries in the global economy has increased rapidly since the 1990s, suggesting that it is easier to enter the middle-income stage than to exit it. According to the World Bank's 2023 income classifications, the 108 current middle-income countries are split evenly between lower- and upper-middle-income countries. Representing about 40 percent of the global economy, middle-income countries are home to about 75 percent of the world's population and more than 60 percent of the world's poor. In other words, more than 400 million of the extreme poor globally live in middle-income countries, a statistic that should concern wealthier countries. They also contribute nearly two-thirds of global carbon dioxide (CO_2) emissions (see table P1.1), a statistic that is of global concern.

Over the last three decades, the world's two most populous countries, China and India, joined the club of middle-income countries, in 1997 and 2007, respectively. It is not surprising, then, that growth in middle-income countries will play a pivotal role in international development.

Since 1990, 34 middle-income economies have transitioned to high-income status (figure 1.1).[5] Thirteen benefited from deep integration with the European Union (EU)—whose economic model features vigorous trade and capital flows, freer enterprise, free worker mobility, stronger institutions, and social inclusion—at a time of relatively rapid economic growth in Western Europe. They benefited greatly from institutional and regulatory reforms that enabled transitions to a market economy, incentivized emerging economies to attract foreign direct investment and infuse new technologies into their production structures while pushing advanced economies to innovate, and fostered an environment for developing a skilled workforce.

Among the other newcomers to high-income status, resource-rich economies such as Chile and Saudi Arabia benefited when they timed policy reforms to coincide with high commodity prices. East Asian economies such as the Republic of Korea and Taiwan, China,[6] stand out for following a path of high savings and investment, enlightened education policies, expansion of trade with export-oriented policies and technology adoption from more advanced economies, and a transition to local innovation well after closing the gaps with the global technology frontier.

For countries that are not fortunate enough to be in the European Union, are not endowed with abundant resources, or are not fiercely focused, progress through the middle-income stage has been slower. The average middle-income economy still has an income per capita less than one-tenth that of the United States (figure 1.2).

It is understandable why middle-income countries are not satisfied with the status quo and why most have plans for faster growth in living standards. China's 14th Five-Year Plan outlines a vision of achieving the median GDP per capita of developed nations by 2035, with a large increase in the middle class. The vision document also highlights that China's growth will be driven by major breakthroughs in key technologies, making it one of the most innovative nations in the world, buttressed by a modern economic system with digitalization, thriving cities, and modern agriculture. In India, the prime minister's vision is to transform

Figure 1.1 A handful of economies have transitioned from middle-income to high-income status over the last three decades

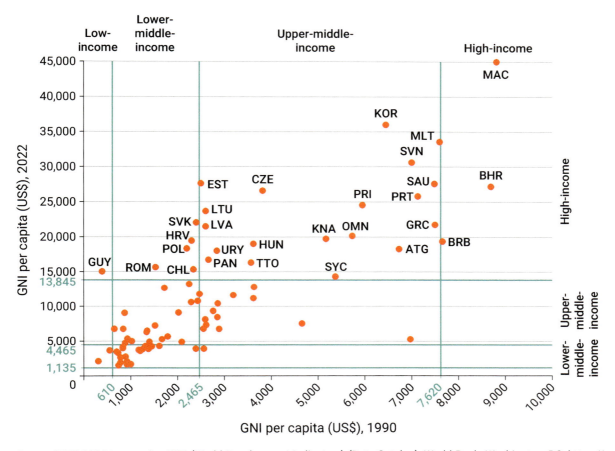

Source: WDR 2024 team using WDI (World Development Indicators) (Data Catalog), World Bank, Washington, DC, https://datacatalog.worldbank.org/search/dataset/0037712.

Note: Each scatter point indicates an economy's 1990 and 2022 gross national income (GNI) per capita in current US dollar terms (using the World Bank Atlas method). The blue vertical lines show thresholds to transition to lower-middle-income status, upper-middle-income status, and high-income status in 1990 (US$610, US$2,465, and US$7,620, respectively), while the blue horizontal lines show these thresholds in 2022 (US$1,135, US$4,465, and US$13,845, respectively) based on the World Bank income classifications (https://datahelpdesk.worldbank.org/knowledgebase/articles/906519-world-bank-country-and-lending-groups). The figure includes only economies at middle-income levels in 1990. For legibility, only economies that have transitioned to high-income status since 1990 are labeled (1990 data were unavailable for six economies). For country abbreviations, see International Organization for Standardization (ISO), https://www.iso.org/obp/ui/#search.

the nation into a developed economy by 2047— the hundredth year of independence. In Viet Nam, its Socio-Economic Development Strategy 2021–2030 outlines a plan to sustain GDP per capita growth of 7 percent through this decade, with a transition to high-income status by 2045. In South Africa, the 2030 National Development Plan has prioritized raising its income per capita from US$2,800 in 2010 to US$7,000 by 2030.

Other middle-income countries have similar aspirations.

But the growth prospects of middle-income countries are not improving. Over the last decade, the global economy has gone from healthy to hobbling and from largely integrated to increasingly fragmented.[7] Foreign trade and investment channels are also becoming more constricted—or at least encumbered—by geopolitical tensions.

Figure 1.2 Income per capita of middle-income countries relative to that of the United States has been stagnant for decades

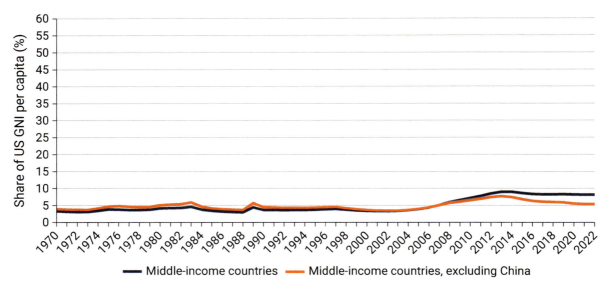

Source: WDR 2024 team using data from WDI (World Development Indicators) (Data Catalog), World Bank, Washington, DC, https://datacatalog.worldbank.org/search/dataset/0037712.

Note: The plotted lines indicate the trend of average income per capita in middle-income countries and in middle-income countries, excluding China, relative to income per capita in the United States (considered as the economic frontier country). Country definitions are based on the first *World Development Report* (World Bank 1978), in which low-income countries have gross national income (GNI) per capita of US$250 or less, and middle-income countries have GNI per capita of more than US$250; industrialized (high-income) countries consist of member countries of the Organisation for Economic Co-operation and Development (OECD), except for Greece, Portugal, Spain, and Türkiye, which are classified as middle-income countries.

Meanwhile, the room for governments to act is shrinking due to rapidly changing demographic trends (more rapid than countries had planned for), multiple crises, and populist pressures. In many middle-income countries, government debt—which is more expensive for this income group than for any other—is at an all-time high. And the belated efforts of advanced economies' central banks to normalize monetary policy and control inflation by raising interest rates has increased sovereign spreads (the difference between bond yields issued on international markets by the country in question versus those offered by governments with AAA ratings) and raised borrowing costs for emerging markets, in some cases to prohibitive levels. As a consequence, middle-income economies are being squeezed from several sides: tighter fiscal space reduces public investment and the cushion for structural reforms; higher public debt service crowds out private borrowing; and a higher risk of sovereign debt distress heightens policy uncertainty and dampens economic activity.

These difficulties are compounded by others. In some middle-income countries, fragility, conflict, and violence are hampering development. And in almost every country, climate change is putting pressure on the government to rethink its development strategy.

Given these headwinds, an economy at the middle-income stage will have to "make a miracle" to develop at the pace of the 34 economies that reached high-income status between 1990 and 2021.[8] That would require having a business sector that facilitates a radical transformation of enterprises, having a government that assuages the growing expectations of an increasingly restless middle class, and having a country transition sooner to less emissions-intensive ways of producing and consuming than those engineered by the middle-income economies of the 1990s.

Even without these headwinds, today's middle-income countries would still face long odds of achieving high-income status because of what the World Bank has called—since 2007—a "middle-income trap."[9] Although the term connotes inevitability, the original proposition was that getting mired in the middle stages of development is a possibility, not an inevitability. It would be inevitable only if countries did not adapt their policies and institutions to changing economic and structural needs. The three priorities for middle-income countries to evade the trap and maintain a growth momentum[10] could be summarized as:

- Increasing the sophistication of processes and products through integration into world markets, generally accompanied by the growing specialization of production
- Keeping up with changing education system priorities to help workers acquire skills that enable them to adjust to new technologies and shape new products and processes
- Quickening the pace of innovation by both fostering entrepreneurial activity and keeping markets open to competition.

These tasks have proved to be surprisingly difficult, and they are likely to become even harder.

Measuring progress through the middle stages of development

What indicates that an economy is developing? Income per capita is the most commonly used metric to measure the pace of economic development. But measures of average income can differ greatly, depending on the measure. For example, the World Bank, other international organizations, and bilateral aid agencies use GDP per capita at market exchange rates for analysis and lending (box 1.1). On the other hand, the use of GDP per capita based on adjustments for purchasing power parity (PPP, which reflects the purchasing power of a consumer for goods and services) can yield different results.[11]

A comparison of these two sets of measures for Türkiye and Chile illustrates the problem. According to World Bank estimates that use market exchange rates, Türkiye is a middle-income country, and Chile is a

Box 1.1 Misunderstanding through misclassification

The World Bank's income classification method for grouping countries was first presented in the 1978 *World Development Report*.[a] It introduced groupings of "low-income" and "middle-income" countries using a threshold of US$250 gross national income (GNI) per capita between the groups. The low-income threshold was set in keeping with the guidelines for procurement of goods and services for civil works projects for countries eligible for assistance from the International Development Association (IDA), the organization in the World Bank Group that supports the world's least developed countries. Specifically, the threshold was based on the "civil works preference" operational guideline for IDA countries.

The process of setting thresholds for income per capita began with finding a "stable relationship" between a summary measure of well-being such as poverty incidence and infant mortality, on the one hand, and economic variables, including GNI per capita estimated using the World Bank's Atlas method, on the other.[b] Based on such a relationship and the annual availability of the World Bank's resources, the original income per capita thresholds were established.[c] They were last updated in 1989, using GNI per capita valued

(Box continues next page)

Box 1.1 Misunderstanding through misclassification *(continued)*

annually in US dollars based on a three-year average exchange rate and were expanded to four categories:

- *Low-income.* The low-income threshold was officially set in 1988, still based on the value of the IDA's "civil works preference" and updated for inflation.[d]
- *Lower-middle-income.* The lower-middle-income threshold is based on the operational guidelines cutoff for determining access to 17-year repayment terms for loans through the World Bank Group's International Bank for Reconstruction and Development (IBRD), although these terms are no longer available. It appears to have first been introduced in the 1983 edition of the *World Development Report*.[e]
- *Upper-middle-income.* The upper-middle-income threshold is the range between lower-middle-income and high-income.
- *High-income.* The high-income threshold does not relate to a cutoff derived from the operational guidelines, but was set at GNI per capita of US$6,000 in 1987 prices in a paper presented to the World Bank's Board of Executive Directors in January 1989, which also reconfirmed the low- and lower-middle-income threshold levels.[f] The US$6,000 level has been updated over time for what is called "international inflation," defined as the average inflation rates of Japan, the United Kingdom, the United States, and the euro area. The choice of the high-income threshold was made to address anomalies in the classification of high-income and industrialized economies used in the World Bank's World Development Indicators prior to that point.

Under this current classification method, Zambia (with income per capita of US$1,170) and Bulgaria (with income per capita of US$13,250) are both middle-income economies. But few people would disagree with the observation that these countries have had vastly different development experiences and face vastly different growth challenges and trajectories. Yet these income classifications continue to be used widely in the development discourse[g] and in analyses of economic growth.[h] Moreover, although the World Bank may not use the income classifications for operational or lending purposes,[i] other international organizations and bilateral aid agencies do. Given its widespread use, many economists have called for a revision of the current income classification system.[j] The proposals include:

- *Reclassifying levels based on fiscal capacity.* Ravallion (2009) argues that levels of development should be assessed based on countries' internal capacities for redistribution (through taxes) in favor of their poorest citizens. Similarly, Ceriani and Verme (2014) propose a measure of a country's capacity to reduce its own poverty levels and show how these tools can be used to guide budget or aid allocations.
- *Reflecting the multidimensional nature of development.* Sumner and Vázquez (2012) use a set of indicators covering definitions of development from four conceptual frameworks (development as structural transformation; development as human development; development as democratic participation and good governance; and development as sustainability) to identify five types of developing countries. Similarly,

(Box continues next page)

Box 1.1 Misunderstanding through misclassification *(continued)*

Nielsen (2011) suggests the need to introduce a development taxonomy to classify countries based on a variety of existing development proxies (the Human Development Index, lifetime income measure, and so on) rather than income levels. Even the World Bank Group Strategy adopted in 2013 recognizes the need for an approach that pays more attention to the multiple facets and fragility across the development spectrum.[k]

a. World Bank (1978).
b. For more on the Atlas method, see World Bank Atlas Method: Detailed Methodology (Data Help Desk), Data, World Bank, Washington, DC, https://datahelpdesk.worldbank.org/knowledgebase/articles/378832-what-is-the-world-bank-atlas-method.
c. Ravallion (2013).
d. Ravallion (2012).
e. World Bank (1983).
f. World Bank (1989).
g. Dolan (2016).
h. Summers and Pritchett (2014).
i. Operationally, borrower countries are distinguished by their lending category within the World Bank: IDA-only; blend (both IDA and IBRD); and IBRD-only. IDA provides countries with the most difficulty borrowing externally with grants and concessional loans. IBRD offers nonconcessional loans to countries that it finds creditworthy. Because IBRD terms are "harder" (more market-based) than those of IDA, IBRD borrowers tend to be perceived as more developed than IDA borrowers. But graduating from low-income status is not the same as graduating from IDA. Eligibility for IDA benchmarks a country's income against different thresholds, while graduation from IDA takes into account factors other than income. See Dolan (2016) for more information.
j. Fantom and Serajuddin (2016).
k. World Bank (2015).

---

high-income country. Yet when adjusted for purchasing power, Türkiye's GDP per capita is higher than Chile's. The country for which both measures are defined as identical is the United States because purchasing power in any country is measured relative to what a dollar can buy in the United States. Türkiye's GDP per capita relative to that of the United States is nearly 50 percent when adjusted for PPP but less than 15 percent using market exchange rates. For Chile, the numbers are, respectively, 40 percent and 20 percent.

PPP adjustments have been criticized for their inability to reflect the complexity and diversity of economic production and capabilities in individual economies.[12] The adjustments do not consider quality or productivity differences among countries in the production of tradable as well as nontradable goods and services, including infrastructure, health care, and education.

However, recent assessments of PPPs appear to be highly correlated with economic activity. A comparison of countries using PPP adjustments could produce a better understanding of the distance to the technology frontier than gross national income. However, income or GDP per capita does not reflect the wide array of growth challenges that countries face. Two high-income countries provide an example. In 2022, Qatar's GDP per capita was US$88,046, driven mostly by exports of hydrocarbons from its abundant reserves of oil and natural gas. The same year, Denmark's GDP per capita was US$66,983, and its services sector employs about 80 percent of labor. Meanwhile, the countries vary significantly in their levels of technical sophistication; in 2021, Denmark was ranked twenty-fourth in the Economic Complexity Index and Qatar eighty-second.[13]

Growth in middle-income countries is slower

Economic growth is not a smooth process, and theory does not stipulate that it should be smooth.[14] Instead, economic growth tends to be highly volatile, and long-run growth averages tend to mask periods of success, struggle, and failure.[15] Growth in low- and middle-income countries is an "episodic" phenomenon, with countries experiencing distinct patterns of economic growth.[16] In fact, a key characteristic of economic growth in middle-income countries is its lack of persistence. The volatility of growth rates is even higher in those countries, with sustained growth periods that are typically short-lived, even in countries that historically have enjoyed high growth rates (figure 1.3).

The standout economy—the growth superstar even—is the Republic of Korea, and this Report prominently features its experiences. What was behind its success? As subsequent chapters explain, Korea's remarkable transformation from a postconflict country in the 1950s to an economy powered by the infusion of ideas from abroad to one that is transitioning to innovation at the global frontiers of technology makes its economic history required reading for policy makers in any middle-income country hoping to achieve high-income levels of living within their lifetimes (box 1.2; see chapter 2 for more information).

Growth slowdowns occur more frequently in middle-income countries than in low- or high-income countries (box 1.3). Research conducted for this Report uses a measure, *proximity to the economic frontier* (leading economies), to clarify

Figure 1.3 Sustained growth periods are short-lived, even in rapidly growing economies

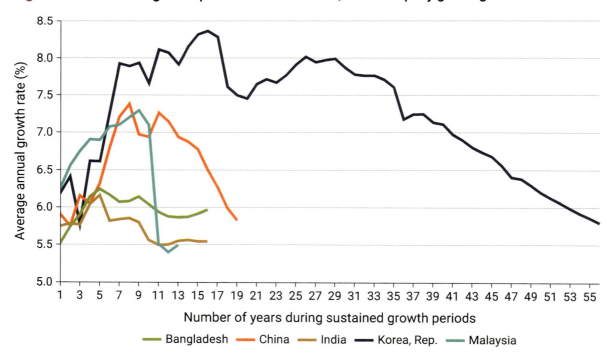

Source: WDR 2024 team using data from Maddison Project Database 2023, Groningen Growth and Development Centre, Faculty of Economics and Business, University of Groningen, Groningen, the Netherlands, https://www.rug.nl/ggdc/historicaldevelopment/maddison/releases/maddison-project-database-2023.

Note: The figure illustrates the growth paths of countries whose average gross domestic product (GDP) growth rate per capita is higher than 5 percent per year for at least eight years.

Box 1.2 A growth superstar: How the Republic of Korea leveraged foreign ideas and innovation

Over the last seven decades, Korea has engineered the most remarkable transformation in recorded economic history. It went from a war-torn, desperately poor country in the 1950s to one of the most prosperous, healthiest, and best-educated countries in the world today. With fewer than 50 million people, it is a global leader in innovation and technology and the tenth-largest economy. What was behind Korea's success?

First, Korea prioritized openness through export promotion and leveraged the international markets to expose domestic firms to competition. Over time, it reduced tariff barriers and loosened restrictions on foreign investors to open the domestic market to foreign competition. It also promoted private enterprises through policies that first favored the growth and expansion of large conglomerates (efficiency-driven) and then shifted to favor smaller firms and entrepreneurs (equity-driven). Investments in infrastructure helped its rapid economic growth, with physical capital accounting for about 60 percent of growth in the gross domestic product (GDP) between 1990 and 1997. Early investments in information and communication technology infrastructure, amounting to US$32.5 billion between 1995 and 2005 and an additional US$2.6 billion between 2005 and 2014, enabled Korea to leverage new sources of growth driven by digital and technology adoption.

Second, Korea devised public policies to ensure contestability. The government rewarded firms for investments in research and development (R&D) and exports through R&D; it promoted science, technology, and innovation policies; it offered tax incentives; and it adopted export facilitation measures. Korea's spending on R&D jumped from 0.5 percent of GDP in 1980 to 1.6 percent in 1990 when Korea was still an upper-middle-income country. Private R&D expenditures increased by an unprecedented 26 times from 1980 to 1990 and exceeded 80 percent of total R&D spending by the end of the 1990s. In parallel, Korea invested heavily in human capital and ensured that job creation was matched with the needed supply of skills at the different stages of development—vocational and technical secondary, STEM (science, technology, engineering, and mathematics) education, and R&D accelerators—which was carried out more effectively than by much richer countries.

Third, Korea got better at regulating the relationships among large, medium, and small firms. Initially, large firms were favored as the instrument for infusing new technologies into the economy. But by the mid-1990s the limits of this approach had become obvious, and yet powerful incumbents stymied the efforts of policy makers to change course. The 1997 Asian financial crisis changed the balance of power, and Korea established a new state–market relationship by adopting reforms to strengthen (1) financial market institutions with greater oversight and rules that diminished distortions; (2) competition policies that ended tacit government support for market collusion and concentration of market power; and (3) a pro-entrepreneurship policy regime with improved financing mechanisms for domestic technology ventures. The effectiveness of all of these policies was enhanced by stronger bureaucratic capacities, anticorruption initiatives, more transparent legal frameworks, better coordination mechanisms, and monitoring and evaluation systems.

Sources: Kim 2006; Soh, Koh, and Aridi 2023.

Box 1.3 Identifying growth slowdowns

Several studies have examined the reasons for growth slowdowns. Eichengreen, Park, and Shin (2011) identify frequent slowdowns in middle-income countries. They define a slowdown as a decline in the seven-year average growth rate of gross domestic product (GDP) per capita by at least 2 percentage points, with growth being higher than 3.5 percent in the preceding years. In addition, they limit slowdowns to cases in which GDP per capita is greater than US$10,000 in 2005 constant international prices adjusted for purchasing power parity (PPP). They discover slowdowns when GDP per capita reaches about US$16,540 (in 2005 constant international PPP prices). Extensions of the analysis indicate that growth in middle-income countries slows even at points early in the middle-income stage: specifically, in the range of US$10,000–US$11,000 GDP per capita (in 2005 constant prices) and in the range of US$15,000–US$16,000 (in 2005 constant prices).

Eichengreen, Park, and Shin (2011) find that slowdowns are driven largely by low productivity growth. They also find that the probability of middle-income traps is higher in countries with high investment rates, high old-age dependency ratios,[a] and undervalued real exchange rates that translate into a barrier to move up the technology ladder. In addition, they find that the level and structure of human capital, the level and structure of exports (specifically, the relative importance of low- and high-tech exports), financial and political stability, and external shocks are among the significant correlates of slowdowns.

Aiyar et al. (2013) define the middle-income trap as a special case of growth slowdowns. They distinguish between natural slowdowns in growth and unusually severe slowdowns. Although economies in all income groups experience growth slowdowns, based on their analysis covering 1960–2005 middle-income countries are especially vulnerable to growth slowdowns. They point to steep drops in the growth of total factor productivity (TFP)[b] as a key driver of such slowdowns. Spence (2011) also finds slowdowns clustering in a narrow band of countries with income per capita of between US$5,000 and US$10,000.

Im and Rosenblatt (2013) focus on the probability of a country transitioning to the next income category. They find that the transition from upper-middle- to high-income status is just as likely as the transition from lower-middle- to upper-middle-income status. They argue that income per capita relative to the frontier stagnates after reaching middle-income status (for both lower-middle- and upper-middle-income countries). Their analysis suggests that it will take a century or more for middle-income countries to catch up to high-income countries if middle-income economies grow by 3–4 percent in per capita terms, assuming that the growth rate of high-income countries proceeds at the world average, which is 1.8 percent.

Robertson and Ye (2013) identify the middle-income trap as an ailment in which a country's GDP per capita is time-invariant[c] and stays in the middle-income range, defined as between 8 percent and 36 percent of GDP per capita of the United States.

a. The old-age dependency ratio is the ratio of older dependents (age 65 and over) to the working-age population (ages 15–64).
b. Total factor productivity, a concept created by Robert Solow, is an equation used in economics to measure the impact of technological advancements and changes in worker knowledge. It attempts to measure the effects that these changes have on the long-term output of an economic system.
c. A time-invariant variable refers to a variable whose value does not change across time.

the distribution of growth slowdowns along the national income spectrum around the world. The frontier represents the growth leader: the country with the most advanced combination of economic production, innovation, and workforce. For this analysis, the United States is used as a proxy for the frontier. Technically, a growth slowdown is defined as a break in the time series of the growth rate of GDP per capita, whereby the growth following the break is distinctly lower than the growth preceding it.[17] Proximity to the frontier is the ratio of a country's GDP per capita to that of the frontier country (the United States) each year (not adjusted for differences in PPP).

Measured by their proximity to the frontier, the types of countries that experience growth slowdowns vary widely. When they enter a slowdown, their proximity to the frontier can range anywhere from just above 0 percent all the way to 150 percent. The median growth slowdown episode occurs in a country-year with just 11 percent proximity to the frontier, and the mean episode occurs at 21 percent proximity to the frontier—approximately the 75th percentile in the distribution. Together, these median and mean measures imply that a majority of growth slowdowns take place in middle-income countries (figure 1.4). In fact, a middle-income country is three times as likely to experience a growth slowdown compared with a high-income country.

Using the World Bank's Long Term Growth Model (LTGM),[18] figure 1.5 sheds more light on growth slowdowns in low- and middle-income countries. Assuming a "business as usual" baseline, where the growth drivers (ratios of public investment to GDP and private investment to GDP, total factor productivity, human capital, and labor force participation rates) follow their historical or recent trends,[19] most low- and middle-income countries are forecasted to experience significant slowdowns as they approach the economic frontier country (the United States) over 2023–2100. In addition, middle-income countries whose growth has already significantly slowed, such as Argentina, Bulgaria, and Mexico, are expected to diverge from the economic frontier over the next 70 years. This is an unfortunate outcome because the key drivers of growth—savings, investment,

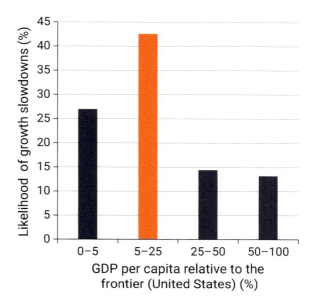

Figure 1.4 Growth slowdowns are most frequent when countries' GDP per capita is less than one-fourth of the United States'

Source: WDR 2024 team.
Note: GDP = gross domestic product.

productivity, human capital, and demographics—are already running out of steam.

Although researchers continue to debate the existence of a middle-income trap along the lines of that first flagged by the World Bank in the mid-2000s, policy makers in middle-income economies generally consider it a serious possibility. Their concerns are the motivation for this Report.

Developing countries should also seriously consider the close correlation between the quality of institutions and the probability of falling into the trap. Economists have conjectured that poor institutional quality discourages investment and innovation, distorts allocation, and lowers returns to entrepreneurship.[20] And policy and institutional deficiencies can put the brakes on and even derail development.[21] Research conducted for this Report reveals that countries with weaker political institutions—measured in many ways—experience growth slowdowns at lower levels of development than countries with stronger ones (figure 1.6). Panel a of figure 1.6 suggests that civil liberties may influence the overall conditions for investment, innovation, and growth.

Figure 1.5 Growth is expected to slow down as countries approach the economic frontier (United States)

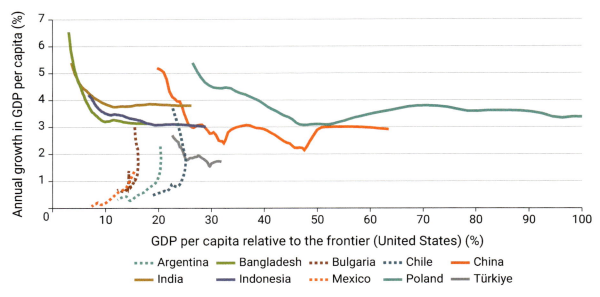

Source: WDR 2024 team.
Note: The dashed lines represent countries that will experience a divergence from the frontier over 2023–2100, although they were closer to the frontier in 2022. The solid lines indicate a convergence to the frontier over 2023–2100. These projections are based on extrapolation of recent historical trends using the World Bank's Long Term Growth Model. GDP = gross domestic product.

Figure 1.6 Weak institutions hasten and worsen growth slowdowns

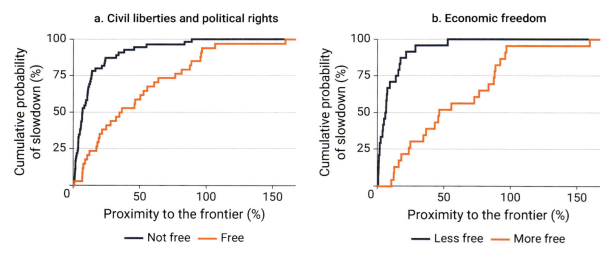

Source: Chikis 2024.
Note: The empirical distribution function for growth decelerations is as defined in Kar et al. (2013). Gross domestic product (GDP) is measured using market exchange rates. Proximity to the frontier indicates a country's GDP per capita relative to US GDP per capita. In panel a, political institutions are based on scores for "civil liberties" and "political rights" from Freedom House. In panel b, the plots of economic freedom use data from the Heritage Foundation Index of Economic Freedom. Countries with scores above the median are freer. That methodology identifies slowdowns in 69 countries between 1972 and 2010. See Countries and Territories (dashboard), Freedom House, Washington, DC, https://freedomhouse.org/countries/freedom-world/scores; Index of Economic Freedom, 30th Edition (dashboard), Heritage Foundation, Washington, DC, https://www.heritage.org/index/.

Countries with weaker economic freedoms also experience growth slowdowns while remaining far from the global frontier (figure 1.6, panel b). In other words, policy makers in middle-income countries should be mindful of the possibility that tighter economic restrictions may mean forgoing opportunities to close the gaps in living standards between their own economies and the more advanced economies in North America, Northeast Asia, Western Europe, and Oceania.

Notes

1. World Bank (1978).
2. Four member countries of the Organisation for Economic Co-operation and Development (OECD)—Greece, Portugal, Spain, and Türkiye—were included among the middle-income countries. The other OECD member countries were placed in the industrialized (high-income) group.
3. Engineering talent and organizational structure are central themes of this Report, which underpins an expansive economics literature on creative destruction (Aghion and Howitt 1992; Aghion et al. 2019; Grossman and Helpman 1991; Segerstrom, Anant, and Dinopoulos 1990). The central feature of the Industrial Revolution and its aftermath was the gradual shift from tacit knowledge (as embodied in craftsmanship and simple production techniques) to more formal knowledge created by mathematicians, physicists, chemists, medical doctors, and people schooled in engineering science (Mokyr 2023).
4. Gill and Kharas (2007).
5. The 34 economies that transitioned to high-income status since 1990 are American Samoa (United States); Antigua and Barbuda; Bahrain; Barbados; Chile; Croatia; Czechia; Estonia; Gibraltar; Greece; Guam; Guyana; Hungary; Isle of Man; the Republic of Korea; Latvia; Lithuania; Macao SAR, China; Malta; New Caledonia; Northern Mariana Islands; Oman; Panama; Poland; Portugal; Puerto Rico (United States); Romania; Saudi Arabia; the Seychelles; the Slovak Republic; Slovenia; St. Kitts and Nevis; Trinidad and Tobago; and Uruguay.
6. Taiwan, China, transitioned to high-income status before 1990.
7. Kose and Ohnsorge (2024).
8. Lucas (1993).
9. Gill and Kharas (2007).
10. Gill and Kharas (2007, 2015); Kharas and Gill (2020).
11. Hamadeh et al. (2022); World Bank (2020).
12. Almås (2012).
13. The Economic Complexity Index is a measure of a country's productive capabilities. It is defined as "the composition of a country's productive output, reflecting the structures able to hold and combine knowledge" (Hausmann et al. 2013, 18; see also Balland et al. 2022; Hidalgo and Hausmann 2009).
14. See, for example, Solow (1956); Mankiw, Romer, and Weil (1992).
15. Easterly et al. (1993); Jones and Olken (2008).
16. Pritchett et al. (2016).
17. Kar et al. (2013).
18. The Long Term Growth Model (LTGM) is a spreadsheet-based tool used to analyze future long-term growth scenarios in developing countries building on the celebrated Solow-Swan growth model. The LTGM aggregates assumptions about growth fundamentals—such as investment, education, and productivity—to produce a trajectory for future growth. The drivers of growth are savings, investment, and productivity, but the model also analyzes human capital, demographics, the external sector (external debt, foreign direct investment, current account balance), and labor force participation by gender.
19. The recent trend spans 2000–2019.
20. Aiyar et al. (2013).
21. Kharas and Gill (2020).

References

Aghion, Philippe, Ufuk Akcigit, Antonin Bergeaud, Richard Blundell, and David Hémous. 2019. "Innovation and Top Income Inequality." *Review of Economic Studies* 86 (1): 1–45.

Aghion, Philippe, and Peter Howitt. 1992. "A Model of Growth through Creative Destruction." *Econometrica* 60 (2): 323–51.

Aiyar, Shekhar S., Romain A. Duval, Damien Puy, Yiqun Wu, and Longmei Zhang. 2013. "Growth Slowdowns and the Middle-Income Trap." IMF Working Paper WP/13/71 (March), International Monetary Fund, Washington, DC.

Almås, Ingvild. 2012. "International Income Inequality: Measuring PPP Bias by Estimating Engel Curves for Food." *American Economic Review* 102 (2): 1093–117.

Balland, Pierre-Alexandre, Tom Broekel, Dario Diodato, Elisa Giuliani, Ricardo Hausmann, Neave O'Clery, and David Rigby. 2022. "The New Paradigm of Economic Complexity." *Research Policy* 51 (3): 104450.

Ceriani, Lidia, and Paolo Verme. 2014. "The Income Lever and the Allocation of Aid." *Journal of Development Studies* 50 (11): 1510–22.

Chikis, Craig. 2024. "The Developmental Trinity: Institutions, Infrastructure, and Technology." Background paper prepared for *World Development Report 2024*, World Bank, Washington, DC.

Dolan, Lindsay. 2016. "What's in a World Bank Income Classification?" *CGD Blog Post* (blog), July 11, 2016. https://www.cgdev.org/blog/whats-world-bank-income-classification.

Easterly, William Russell, Michael R. Kremer, Lant H. Pritchett, and Lawrence H. Summers. 1993. "Good Policy or Good Luck? Country Growth Performance and Temporary Shocks." *Journal of Monetary Economics* 32 (3): 459–83.

Eichengreen, Barry Julian, Donghyun Park, and Kwanho Shin. 2011. "When Fast Growing Economies Slow Down: International Evidence and Implications for China." NBER Working Paper 16919 (March), National Bureau of Economic Research, Cambridge, MA.

Fantom, Neil James, and Umar Serajuddin. 2016. "The World Bank's Classification of Countries by Income." Policy Research Working Paper 7528, World Bank, Washington, DC.

Gill, Indermit Singh, and Homi Kharas. 2007. *An East Asian Renaissance: Ideas for Economic Growth*. With Deepak Bhattasali, Milan Brahmbhatt, Gaurav Datt, Mona Haddad, Edward Mountfield, Radu Tatucu, and Ekaterina Vostroknutova. Washington, DC: World Bank.

Gill, Indermit Singh, and Homi Kharas. 2015. "The Middle-Income Trap Turns Ten." Policy Research Working Paper 7403, World Bank, Washington, DC.

Grossman, Gene M., and Elhanan Helpman. 1991. *Innovation and Growth in the Global Economy*. Cambridge, MA: MIT Press.

Hamadeh, Nada, Aart C. Kraay, Eric Metreau, Marko Rissanen, Giovanni Tonutti, Catherine Van Rompaey, Mizuku Yamanaka, and Kathryn Young. 2022. "Using Purchasing Power Parities in the World Bank's Classifications of Countries by Income Level." World Bank, Washington, DC.

Hausmann, Ricardo, César A. Hidalgo, Sebastián Bustos, Michele Coscia, Alexander James Gaspar Simoes, and Muhammed A. Yildirim. 2013. *The Atlas of Economic Complexity: Mapping Paths to Prosperity*. Cambridge, MA: MIT Press.

Hidalgo, César A., and Ricardo Hausmann. 2009. "The Building Blocks of Economic Complexity." *Proceedings of the National Academy of Sciences* 106 (26): 10570–75.

Im, Fernando Gabriel, and David Rosenblatt. 2013. "Middle-Income Traps: A Conceptual and Empirical Survey." Policy Research Working Paper 6594, World Bank, Washington, DC.

Jones, Benjamin F., and Benjamin A. Olken. 2008. "The Anatomy of Start-Stop Growth." *Review of Economics and Statistics* 90 (3): 582–87.

Kar, Sabyasachi, Lant H. Pritchett, Selim Raihan, and Kunal Sen. 2013. "Looking for a Break: Identifying Transitions in Growth Regimes." *Journal of Macroeconomics* 38 (Part B): 151–66.

Kharas, Homi, and Indermit Singh Gill. 2020. "Growth Strategies to Avoid the Middle-Income Trap." In *Trapped in the Middle? Developmental Challenges for Middle-Income Countries*, edited by José Antonio Alonso and José Antonio Ocampo, 24–47. Oxford, UK: Oxford University Press.

Kim, Kihwan. 2006. "The 1997–98 Korean Financial Crisis: Causes, Policy Response, and Lessons." Paper presented at the International Monetary Fund and Singapore government's High-Level Seminar on Crisis Prevention in Emerging Markets, Singapore, July 10–11, 2006. https://www.imf.org/external/np/seminars/eng/2006/cpem/pdf/kihwan.pdf.

Kose, M. Ayhan, and Franziska Ohnsorge, eds. 2024. *Falling Long-Term Growth Prospects: Trends, Expectations, and Policies*. Washington, DC: World Bank.

Lucas, Robert E. B., Jr. 1993. "Making a Miracle." *Econometrica* 61 (2): 251–72.

Mankiw, N. Gregory, David Romer, and David N. Weil. 1992. "A Contribution to the Empirics of Economic Growth." *Quarterly Journal of Economics* 107 (2): 407–37.

Mokyr, Joel. 2023. "The Industrial Revolution and the Origins of Modern Economic Growth: A New Look." Presentation at Tel Aviv University, Tel Aviv, Israel, May 1, 2023. https://en-social-sciences.tau.ac.il/sites/socsci-english.tau.ac.il/files/media_server/social/2023/Tel-Aviv-May'23.pdf.

Nielsen, Lynge. 2011. "Classifications of Countries Based on Their Level of Development: How It Is Done and How It Could Be Done." IMF Working Paper WP/11/31 (February), International Monetary Fund, Washington, DC.

Pritchett, Lant H., Kunal Sen, Sabyasachi Kar, and Selim Raihan. 2016. "Trillions Gained and Lost: Estimating the Magnitude of Growth Episodes." *Economic Modelling* 55 (June): 279–91.

Ravallion, Martin. 2009. "Do Poorer Countries Have Less Capacity for Redistribution?" Policy Research Working Paper 5046, World Bank, Washington, DC.

Ravallion, Martin. 2012. "Should We Care Equally about Poor People Wherever They May Live?" *Let's Talk Development* (blog), November 8, 2012. https://blogs.worldbank.org/en/developmenttalk/should-we-care-equally-about-poor-people-wherever-they-may-live.

Ravallion, Martin. 2013. "Why $12,616?" *CGD Blog Post* (blog), July 8, 2013. https://www.cgdev.org/blog/why-12616.

Robertson, Peter E., and Longfeng Ye. 2013. "On the Existence of a Middle Income Trap." Economics Discussion Paper 13-12 (February), Department of Economics, University of Western Australia, Perth.

Segerstrom, Paul S., T. C. A. Anant, and Elias Dinopoulos. 1990. "A Schumpeterian Model of the Product Life Cycle." *American Economic Review* 80 (5): 1077–91.

Soh, Hoon Sahib, Youngsun Koh, and Anwar Aridi, eds. 2023. *Innovative Korea: Leveraging Innovation and Technology for Development*. Washington, DC: World Bank.

Solow, Robert M. 1956. "A Contribution to the Theory of Economic Growth." *Quarterly Journal of Economics* 70 (1): 65–94.

Spence, Michael. 2011. *The Next Convergence: The Future of Economic Growth in a Multispeed World*. New York: Farrar, Straus and Giroux.

Summers, Lawrence H., and Lant H. Pritchett. 2014. "Growth Slowdowns: Middle-Income Trap vs. Regression to the Mean." *VoxEU Column: Development*, December 11, 2014. https://cepr.org/voxeu/columns/growth-slowdowns-middle-income-trap-vs-regression-mean#/.

Sumner, Andy, and Sergio Tezanos Vázquez. 2012. "Beyond Low- and Middle-Income Countries: What If There Were Five Clusters of Developing Countries?" IDS Working Paper 404, Institute of Development Studies, Brighton, UK.

World Bank. 1978. *World Development Report 1978*. Washington, DC: World Bank.

World Bank. 1983. *World Development Report 1983*. Washington, DC: World Bank; New York: Oxford University Press.

World Bank. 1989. "Per Capita Income." Board document SecM89-73 (January 17), World Bank, Washington, DC.

World Bank. 2015. *The World Bank Group: A to Z, 2015*. Washington, DC: World Bank.

World Bank. 2020. *Purchasing Power Parities and the Size of World Economies: Results from the 2017 International Comparison Program*. Washington, DC: World Bank.

Spotlight

From X-rays to MRIs: The need for a clear picture of economic structure

What indicates that a middle-income economy is advancing in its efforts to catch up with high-income economies?

The World Bank's income classification aims to reflect a country's level of development, drawing on Atlas gross national income (GNI) per capita as a broadly available indicator of economic capacity.[1] GNI per capita is a useful indicator that is often closely correlated with other, nonmonetary measures of quality of life. However, it does not directly measure a country's level of development or the welfare of its residents.[2] Moreover, measures of income per capita can reflect high levels of investment and consumption expenditure by governments—as well as good fortune in the area of natural resources.[3]

Because of these limitations, better indicators are needed to provide a clear picture of the underlying structure of an economy, much like an MRI provides three-dimensional images of the human body, going beyond the less-detailed view provided by an X-ray. To that end, the first step is to examine the dynamism of a country's enterprises, its talent, and its changing carbon emissions profile. The second step is to examine specific factors that drive progress and identify those that hold it back.

Enterprise

Middle-income growth requires a shift from investment in physical capital to infusion of technology and innovation. At this stage, countries need to improve their capabilities to produce a range of sophisticated products. The Economic Complexity Index (ECI) provides a measure of a country's productive capabilities based on the diversity and complexity of its export basket.

At this stage of growth, countries also need to improve the allocation of resources to their most productive firms. In fact, efficient allocation of the factors of production accounts for about 25 percent of productivity growth in developing countries.[4] Efficiency in allocating resources boosts job and output growth as well as creates positive spillovers for other businesses along the value chain.[5]

By reducing productivity-constraining distortions—defined as policy measures that curb the expansion and growth of productive firms—countries can encourage productive firms to infuse new technologies and grow. Finally, when countries focus on innovation, there is a rise in the number of their patents and the importance of these patents in the global production of knowledge.

Talent

Countries need a more skilled workforce as their production processes become more complex with infusion and innovation. Although low-skilled workers can fuel demand from firms at early stages, infusion and innovation require a shift toward workers with technical and professional skills.

Enrollment in formal schooling can signal a country's commitment to education—even if it may not reflect the actual skills and competencies being developed. The first step for countries, therefore, is to provide primary and secondary education to their youth.

The second step requires countries to improve social mobility—that is, to create better incentives for individuals to invest in their own skills development. With improved social mobility, they enjoy better opportunities to take advantage of their potential.

As countries improve their talent pools, innovation and infusion require countries to invest in their researchers, who contribute to the expansion of knowledge in various fields.

Energy

A reliable energy supply is vital for a country's economic prosperity and security. Unreliable supply disrupts production and creates additional pressures on firms to invest in alternate backup sources.

Further, growing energy use often exacerbates emissions. The ultimate impact of rising energy demand on carbon emissions will depend on the carbon intensity of production, reflecting both the energy mix and the energy intensity of production. Middle-income countries will need to enhance energy access and reliability while "decoupling" from their economic growth and carbon emissions.

The indicators suggested in table S.1 complement the use of GNI per capita to understand a country's economic structure. The selected countries in table S.1 account for 62 percent of the global population and 72 percent of global GDP. The proposed indicators can help policy makers gain a clearer and more complete picture of their countries' economic health. In the twenty-first century, business dynamism, the talent pool, and energy and carbon intensity are much more reliable indicators of the progress an economy is making toward reaching high-income status.

Table S.1 Suggested indicators provide a clear picture of the underlying structure of an economy

Country	Income group	GNI per capita, Atlas method (current US$, 2023)	Economic Complexity Index	Productivity-constraining distortions	Technology index	Upper-secondary completion rate (% of relevant age group)	Social mobility	Researchers per million inhabitants	Energy stability (% of firms identifying electricity as a major constraint)	Energy intensity (energy consumption/GDP, exajoules per trillion US$)	Carbon intensity of energy consumption (CO_2 emissions/energy consumption, Gt/exajoules)
Pakistan	LMIC	1,500	−0.6	0.47	0.0	23.25	0.23	394.9	24.20	9.57	0.12
India	LMIC	2,540	0.5	0.36	1.0	54.40	0.23	255.7	12.60	10.77	0.09
Viet Nam	LMIC	4,180	0.0	—	0.0	63.40	0.45	772.4	3.70	11.23	0.10
Indonesia	UMIC	4,870	−0.1	—	0.0	65.25	0.53	336.2	11.40	7.41	0.10
South Africa	UMIC	6,750	−0.1	—	0.2	53.20	0.77	491.7	19.40	11.87	0.10
Colombia	UMIC	6,870	−0.1	0.37	0.0	72.80	0.45	—	50.10	6.38	0.09
Brazil	UMIC	9,070	−0.2	—	0.3	69.00	0.57	—	46.00	6.98	0.08
Kazakhstan	UMIC	10,940	−0.5	—	0.0	98.00	0.65	658.2	21.90	14.15	0.09
Türkiye	UMIC	11,650	0.6	—	0.2	63.00	0.38	1,736.7	17.00	7.74	0.07
Malaysia	UMIC	11,970	0.9	0.25	0.4	—	0.69	1,433.0	22.20	11.90	0.06
Mexico	UMIC	12,100	1.1	—	0.2	58.25	0.55	348.7	46.70	6.17	0.07
Argentina	UMIC	12,520	−0.2	—	0.1	63.50	—	1,249.7	47.20	5.69	0.10
China	UMIC	13,400	1.3	—	13.1	73.50	0.44	1,523.5	1.80	8.87	0.08
Costa Rica	UMIC	13,850	0.4	—	0.1	62.20	—	369.6	63.20	—	—
Russian Federation	UMIC	14,250	0.2	—	4.6	90.40	0.58	2,727.0	7.70	12.90	0.08
Bulgaria	UMIC	14,460	0.6	0.31	0.2	86.00	0.35	2,354.6	12.70	9.37	0.06
Chile	HIC	15,820	−0.3	0.31	0.1	84.50	0.60	520.1	30.10	5.94	0.06
Romania	HIC	16,670	1.2	0.30	0.2	83.60	0.28	922.2	36.10	4.31	0.07
Hungary	HIC	19,820	1.5	0.25	0.5	85.60	0.36	4,156.8	12.40	5.35	0.06
Portugal	HIC	26,270	0.7	0.50	0.4	83.20	0.38	5,177.3	43.80	3.68	0.06

(Table continues next page)

Table S.1 Suggested indicators provide a clear picture of the underlying structure of an economy *(continued)*

Country	Income per capita		Enterprise			Talent			Energy		
	Income group	GNI per capita, Atlas method (current US$, 2023)	Economic Complexity Index	Productivity-constraining distortions	Technology index	Upper-secondary completion rate (% of relevant age group)	Social mobility	Researchers per million inhabitants	Energy stability (% of firms identifying electricity as a major constraint)	Energy intensity (energy consumption/GDP, exajoules per trillion US$)	Carbon intensity of energy consumption (CO₂ emissions/energy consumption, Gt/exajoules)
Korea, Rep.	HIC	35,490	2.0	—	92.5	98.75	0.79	8,483.2	—	7.63	0.05
Japan	HIC	39,030	2.3	—	50.1	95.50	0.65	5,476.3	—	4.22	0.06
France	HIC	45,070	1.3	0.11	11.5	88.40	0.72	4,947.1	40.20	3.01	0.04
United Kingdom	HIC	47,800	1.6	—	9.9	83.33	0.79	4,491.3	—	2.38	0.05
United Arab Emirates	HIC	53,290	0.1	—	0.2	—	—	2,582.8	—	9.95	0.05
Belgium	HIC	54,530	1.2	0.28	4.7	86.20	0.65	5,576.4	29.60	4.23	0.04
Qatar	HIC	70,070	−0.4	—	—	84.00	—	783.5	—	7.94	0.06
United States	HIC	80,300	1.4	0.00	100.0	94.00	0.66	4,340.9	—	3.77	0.06

Source: WDR 2024 team.

Note: Countries are listed within income groups from lowest to highest GNI per capita. The Economic Complexity Index is a ranking of countries based on the diversity and complexity of their export basket. Productivity-constraining distortions are estimates of a regression coefficient between the logarithm of idiosyncratic distortions and the logarithm of idiosyncratic physical productivity across firms, both computed as in Hsieh and Klenow (2009). The productivity-constraining distortions are reported relative to the level observed in the United States. The technology index is a composite index of patents per capita and the network centrality of the patents created by a country. Completion rate is the percentage of a cohort of children or young people three to five years older than the intended age for the last grade of each level of education (primary, lower secondary, or upper secondary) who have completed that level of education. Social mobility shows the intergenerational mobility between children (in the 1980s birth cohort) and parents' years of schooling. Social mobility is measured by 1 minus the intergenerational correlation in schooling. Energy stability is measured by the percentage of firms identifying electricity as a major constraint. Energy intensity is defined as the ratio of energy consumption to GDP (in exajoules per trillion US dollars). Carbon intensity of energy consumption is measured by carbon dioxide (CO₂) emissions per energy consumption (gigatons per exajoules). GDP = gross domestic product; GNI = gross national income; Gt = gigatons; HIC = high-income country; LMIC = lower-middle-income country; UMIC = upper-middle-income country; — = not available.

Notes

1. Hamadeh, Van Rompaey, and Metreau (2023).
2. Fantom and Serajuddin (2016).
3. World Bank (2020).
4. Cusolito and Maloney (2018).
5. Grover Goswami, Medvedev, and Olafsen (2019).

References

Cusolito, Ana Paula, and William F. Maloney. 2018. *Productivity Revisited: Shifting Paradigms in Analysis and Policy*. Washington, DC: World Bank.

Fantom, Neil James, and Umar Serajuddin. 2016. "The World Bank's Classification of Countries by Income." Policy Research Working Paper 7528, World Bank, Washington, DC.

Grover Goswami, Arti, Denis Medvedev, and Ellen Olafsen. 2019. *High-Growth Firms: Facts, Fiction, and Policy Options for Emerging Economies*. Washington, DC: World Bank.

Hamadeh, Nada, Catherine Van Rompaey, and Eric Metreau. 2023. "World Bank Group Country Classifications by Income Level for FY24 (July 1, 2023–June 30, 2024)." *Data Blog* (blog), June 30, 2023. https://blogs.worldbank.org/en/opendata/new-world-bank-group-country-classifications-income-level-fy24.

Hsieh, Chang-Tai, and Peter J. Klenow. 2009. "Misallocation and Manufacturing TFP in China and India." *Quarterly Journal of Economics* 124 (November): 1403–48.

World Bank. 2020. *Purchasing Power Parities and the Size of World Economies: Results from the 2017 International Comparison Program*. Washington, DC: World Bank.

2
Structural Stasis

Key messages

- Economic growth in middle-income countries is different than that for countries at other income levels. Capital returns diminish at later development stages, and therefore countries, to achieve sustained growth, need to also focus on technological progress and improved efficiency in converting capital and labor into goods and services.
- Successful middle-income countries will have to engineer two successive transitions to develop economic structures that can eventually sustain high-income levels.
- The first transition is from a 1*i* strategy for accelerating *investment* to a 2*i* strategy focusing on both *investment* and *infusion* in which a country brings technologies from abroad and diffuses them domestically. Policy makers in lower-middle-income countries will need to add to investment strategies to infuse modern technologies and business practices from global leaders into their own economies.
- Once a country has succeeded in the first transition, the second transition is to switch to a 3*i* strategy, which entails paying more attention to *innovation*. Upper-middle-income countries that have mastered infusion can complement investment and infusion with innovation, thereby developing industrial structures and technical competencies to add value to and advance the global technology frontier.

Introduction

In Brazil in the early 1970s, after several decades of impressive output growth, the average worker in the manufacturing sector was more than 40 percent as productive as his American counterpart. By 2008, this ratio had fallen to 17 percent. Up until about 1980, Brazil implemented protectionist policies from foreign competition and provided incentives to substitute imports by domestic manufacturers. Although all these policies were intended to make Brazil more competitive, they led to a decline in the productivity of Brazilian workers, and enterprises became less competitive than those in the United States.[1]

Meanwhile, in Northeast Asia something completely different was happening in the Republic of Korea and Taiwan, China. In the 1970s, the productivity of Korea's manufacturing workers was less than one-tenth of their American counterparts. By 2008, their productivity was greater than 70 percent that of the average American worker in the same sector.[2] Their enterprises became well known globally because their economies reinvented themselves after they had reached middle-income status—not once, but twice. Both economies grew rapidly to the upper-middle-income level, followed by the high-income level, and subsequently to levels of income and standards of living similar to those of advanced economies such as

Germany, Japan, the United Kingdom, and the United States.

What changed between the 1950s and 1960s (when Brazil was a low-income country), the 1970s (when Brazil achieved rapid growth), and the 1980s and 1990s (when Brazil—and its neighbors such as Argentina and Colombia—became both a middle-income economy and an also-ran)? How did the trajectory of economic development differ in Korea and its neighbors Japan and Taiwan, China?

This chapter explores whether economic growth in middle-income countries is different than that at other income levels. The simple logic is that if it is different, then these countries' development strategies cannot remain the same. The chapter points to evidence consistent with the hypothesis that successful middle-income countries have to engineer two successive transitions to develop economic structures that can eventually sustain high-income levels. The first is to transition from a 1*i* strategy for accelerating *investment* to a 2*i* strategy focusing on both *investment* and *infusion* in which a country brings technologies from abroad and diffuses them domestically (table 2.1). Policy makers in lower-middle-income countries will need to add to investment strategies to infuse modern technologies and business practices from global leaders into their own economies.

Once a country has succeeded in infusing global technologies and know-how in specific sectors or industries, it can switch to a 3*i* strategy by paying more attention to *innovation*. Upper-middle-income countries that have mastered infusion can complement investment and infusion with innovation, thereby developing industrial structures and technical competencies to add value to and advance the global technology frontier.

Infusion is powered mainly by technology transfers embodied in flows of *physical and financial capital,* while innovation requires both of these flows, as well as increasingly vigorous exchanges of *human capital* through engagement with the diaspora and the emigration of talented workers. However, these are not hard-and-fast rules. Some countries have succeeded in attaining high income levels without instituting the structural prerequisites needed to sustain them. They did so by getting rid of obsolete economic arrangements, by weakening the forces of preservation, and by creating the necessary new ones. However, it appears that these countries—such as Argentina and República Bolivariana de Venezuela—also find it difficult to ensure that their income gains are durable, and even more difficult to continue to close the gaps in living standards with economies at the global economic frontier.

Table 2.1 Middle-income countries will need to engineer two successive transitions to develop economic structures that can sustain high-income status

INCOME CLASSIFICATION	INVESTMENT	INFUSION	INNOVATION
Low-income	Higher priority	Lower priority	Lower priority
Lower-middle-income	Higher priority	Higher priority	Lower priority
Upper-middle-income	Higher priority	Higher priority	Higher priority

Source: WDR 2024 team.

Note: The orange dials indicate a strategy that is a priority for that particular income group. The blue dials indicate a strategy that is less of a priority for that particular income group until the priority strategy is successfully achieved.

Economic development = structural change

As described in chapter 1, the term "middle-income trap" refers to the risk of an economic slowdown or stagnation if a country fails to adapt its policies and institutions to changing economic and structural needs.[3] Strategies based on factor accumulation alone are likely to steadily worsen results—a natural occurrence as the marginal productivity of capital declines. Even if all middle-income countries enjoyed the enabling conditions of peace, freedom, factor mobility, and rule of law, the returns from capital investment alone would decline too sharply to support the countries' sustained and ongoing economic growth.[4]

If capital endowments were the only economically relevant difference between middle-income and high-income countries today, the gross national income (GNI) of a typical middle-income country would be about 75 percent that of the United States. In China, for example, its investment to gross domestic product (GDP) ratios have been stratospherically high for decades, but its GNI is less than 25 percent that of the United States. Another way to understand the problem is that, although there has been considerable convergence in capital to output ratios between low- and middle-income countries and high-income countries, income levels have not converged. And so other factors are clearly at work. A simple decomposition of factor endowments and total factor productivity (TFP) reveals that the contribution of physical capital per worker diminishes at later development stages (figure 2.1). What really matters for growth is TFP growth, which is clumsy longhand for the effects of technological progress and improved efficiency in converting capital and labor into goods and services. In fact, much of the growth in the United States between 1909 and 1949—when it was a middle-income country—stemmed from technical change, not an increase in capital per worker.[5]

If much of growth everywhere is the result of technical change, then conventional thinking would follow that every middle-income country needs to figure out how to quickly institute arrangements that foster technical progress, not only (or primarily) the accumulation of capital. But this interpretation is not helpful for policy making because of the ongoing importance of capital deepening across all categories

Figure 2.1 As economies develop, capital accumulation brings diminishing returns

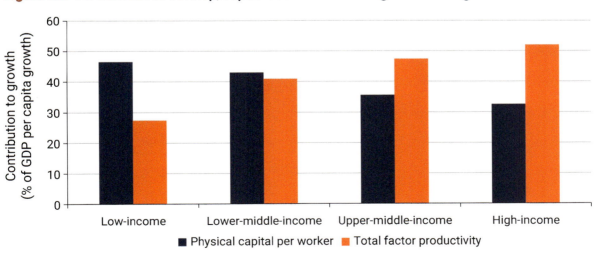

Source: WDR 2024 team using data from Lange, Wodon, and Carey (2018); PWT (Penn World Table) (database version 10.1), Groningen Growth and Development Centre, Faculty of Economics and Business, University of Groningen, Groningen, the Netherlands, https://www.rug.nl/ggdc/productivity/pwt/.

Note: GDP = gross domestic product.

of countries, but especially in middle-income economies.

In fact, the growth of middle-income countries depends on both capital accumulation and technical change, making the growth challenge twice as complex as it is for either low-income countries that primarily must focus on accumulation or high-income countries that must rely largely on technical change, even if a large part of it is in the form of new investment.

Infuse first, then innovate

How have the most successful middle-income countries engineered progress? Modern economic history provides one valuable lesson. Countries that have made technological advances and achieved high-income status did so through two successive transitions.

The first set of changes, described as *infusion* in this Report, dominates development strategies in rapidly growing lower-middle-income countries. Policy makers in these countries have emphasized importing modern technologies and business models from more advanced economies and diffusing this knowledge at scale in their domestic economy. These technologies and models have, often in short order, enabled enterprises to become regional and global suppliers of goods and services.

The second phase of structural change, commonly called *innovation,* occurs mainly in successful upper-middle-income economies. This transition involves a deliberate shift from imitating and adapting technologies used in advanced economies to building home country capabilities to change leading global technologies and products. An increasing number of domestic firms can become global knowledge creators and—eventually—leading innovators themselves.

The term *infusion* has been carefully chosen to connote both deliberately imitating technology and business practices from abroad and expediting their diffusion at home (figure 2.2). Not surprisingly, countries that have been relatively open to economic developments abroad *and* have been successful at instituting general secondary education and technical and vocational training programs at home have done better than those that failed to do one or both.

Figure 2.2 A middle-income country will need to engineer two successive transitions to achieve high-income status: Infusion, followed by innovation

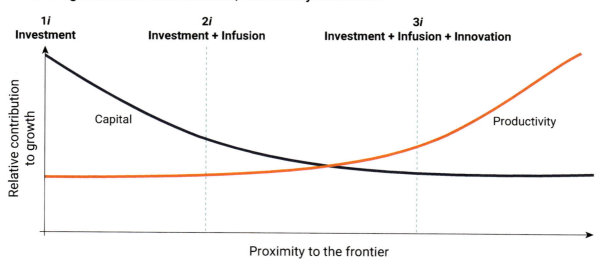

Source: WDR 2024 team.

Note: The curves illustrate the relative contributions of capital and productivity to economic growth (y-axis) according to countries' proximity to the frontier (represented by leading economies). Countries farther out on the x-axis are closer to the frontier.

The mechanics of the innovation stage of economic development are more difficult, and so this stage has received much attention.[6] Like others, this Report warns developing countries against attempts to "leapfrog" (that is, to prematurely attempt to transition) to the innovation stage (generally through the use of industrial policy interventions). What is more novel in this Report is its emphasis on the changing nature of knowledge exchanges and the successful impact of such exchanges on fostering development by benefiting from the international mobility, not only of capital and know-how but also of highly skilled people. The prerequisites needed to capitalize on the global nature of human capital—such as policies to attract entrepreneurs from the diaspora and ensure greater freedom of expression—are more difficult to institute and can stymie progress.

Successful infusion efforts have marked reversals of fortune in several parts of the world marred by war and violence:

- *Postwar Europe.* The onset of the European Golden Age was powered by infusion. The two world wars in the first half of the twentieth century destroyed much of Europe's capital stock and skills. And the exodus of talent in the interwar years meant that Europe lagged behind the United States in technology.[7] The Marshall Plan was developed to transfer technologies from the United States to Europe. European managers were sent to the United States to acquire skills, and businesses could obtain loans to purchase technologically advanced American capital goods under the US Productivity Program. As a result, Europe rapidly adopted modern technologies and best practices, allowing Western European countries to accomplish in 30 years what might otherwise have taken twice as long.[8]
- *Korea.* An important component of industrial policy in Korea was incentives for technological investment. In particular, Korea subsidized the adoption of foreign technologies and innovation through tax credits. Specifically, firms received tax credits for royalty payments or research and development (R&D) expenditures. The policy first subsidized technology adoption when the technology gap with foreign firms was large. But as Korean conglomerates caught up with foreign firms, the approach gradually shifted toward supporting innovation. Korean policy makers ensured that public support was monitored and evaluated, and data on innovation grants were made publicly available.
- *Malaysia.* Malaysia became a successful industrialized country through infusion-centered and export-oriented growth that replaced import substitution policies in the mid-1980s. Technology embodied in foreign direct investment (FDI) was important for developing and structuring the country's industrial base. Malaysia offered a spectrum of tax incentives to attract FDI through the Promotion of Investment Act in 1986.[9] Malaysia's growth in the 1980s was marked by large productivity gains from adopting and diffusing technology. But Malaysia did not perform as well as Singapore in attracting entrepreneurs of Malaysian origin living abroad.

As these examples show, *infusion*, tapping into global knowledge, and a country's institutional structure play a key role in supporting the economic growth of middle-income countries beyond just increasing a country's income per capita. And the key to infusion at scale is openness and exchange—through paths such as trade, FDI, pro-competition regulation, licensing, migration, and knowledge exchanges. A combination of investment and infusion can engineer high growth through investments in physical capital (infrastructure), structural change that improves the allocation of productive resources across firms and sectors, and technological convergence through the adoption and infusion of foreign technologies.[10]

Figure 2.3 The demand for highly skilled workers increases in middle-income countries

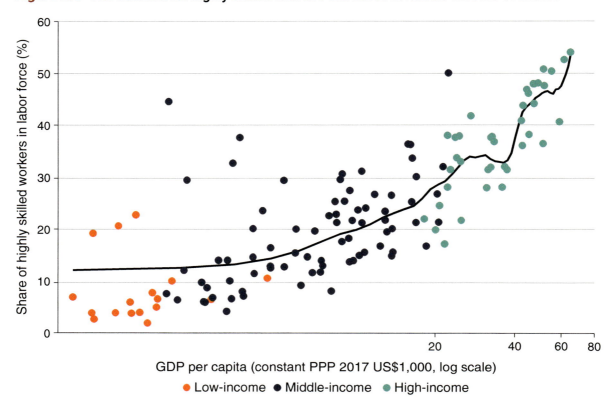

Source: WDR 2024 team using DataBank: Jobs, World Bank, Washington, DC, https://databank.worldbank.org/source/jobs; WDI (World Development Indicators) (Data Catalog), World Bank, Washington, DC, https://datacatalog.worldbank.org/search/dataset/0037712.

Note: Skilled workers consist of the top three International Standard Classification of Occupations (ISCO) codes ("Legislators, sr. officials, managers"; "Professionals"; "Technicians and associate professionals"). See ISCO (International Standard Classification of Occupations), International Labour Organization, Geneva, https://ilostat.ilo.org/methods/concepts-and-definitions/classification-occupation/. GDP = gross domestic product; PPP = purchasing power parity.

To undertake infusion at scale, however, countries need both globally competitive firms and specialized talent. As firms adopt newer technologies, their need for engineers, scientists, managers, and other highly skilled professionals increases. The variety and skill content of work also increase in middle-income countries (figure 2.3). In fact, the central feature of the Industrial Revolution and its aftermath was the slow shift from tacit knowledge that is not codified or easily expressed (as embodied in craftsmanship and simple production techniques) to more formal knowledge created by mathematicians, physicists, chemists, medical doctors, and people schooled in "engineering science."[11] Today, graduates from the science, technology, engineering, and mathematics (STEM) fields play a central role in generating and spreading ideas and technologies. Encouragingly, three-quarters of STEM graduates are now in middle-income countries, and Chinese and Indian STEM graduates make up about half of global STEM graduates (figure 2.4).

The example of Korea, the only country ever to sustain economic growth that averaged more than 5 percent for more than 50 years, is especially illustrative. How did Korean industry do it? Domestic firms such as Samsung embarked on a journey that began with infusion. By licensing technologies from Sanyo and NEC in Japan, Samsung transitioned from making noodles

Figure 2.4 STEM graduates are increasingly concentrated in middle-income countries, thereby increasing opportunities for technology infusion

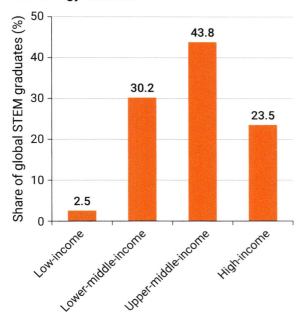

Source: WDR 2024 team.

Note: The primary data for the calculation of the percentage share of science, technology, engineering, and mathematics (STEM) graduates in tertiary education are from UIS.Stat (dashboard), Institute for Statistics, United Nations Educational, Scientific, and Cultural Organization, Montreal, http://data.uis.unesco.org/. The STEM data set covers 144 countries.

to manufacturing televisions for domestic and regional markets (figure 2.5, panel a).[12] This transition created a higher demand for engineers, managers, and skilled professionals that was monitored, and the targets were met by the Ministry of Education through both providing the needed education in public universities and regulating private institutions. Korea also generated a demand for more specialized capital: for economies at the infusion stage, investment remains important.

The first *World Development Report* (1978) highlighted the need to differentiate between strategies of imitation and innovation in driving growth in middle-income countries.[13] A large part of middle-income country growth happens through a combination of investment and imitation (see box 2.1 for a description of how Japan connected with global knowledge). But eventually the gains from imitation begin to subside. As an economy approaches the global technology frontier, policies that supported growth eventually become a burden for sustaining further development.[14] When Samsung reached that point, it moved toward innovation—nudged by support from the Korean government, which had calibrated its incentives to encourage imitation first and support innovation much later (figure 2.5, panel b). To nurture innovation, institutions must give inventors and entrepreneurs incentives and ensure that they can acquire the technical and financial resources to carry out their designs.[15]

Once a middle-income country has infused its economy with technology from global innovators and is sustaining rapid growth, it can aspire to converge to the global technology frontier by preparing to join those innovators—that is, to become an *innovation economy*. To reach this point, however, governments must have done everything possible in the infusion phase to not just prepare the economic structure for the different next stage, but also reform and strengthen supporting institutions. Those who falter in infusion or try to leapfrog will find it much more challenging to transition toward innovation.

A comparison of Estonia, Poland, and Bulgaria is illustrative. Transitioning from central planning, Estonia reached 80 percent of Western European income by 2021, Poland 75 percent, and Bulgaria 50 percent (box 2.2). Estonian independence in 1991 catalyzed a swift transition to high levels of innovation. By contrast, Bulgaria protected many incumbent state-owned enterprises (SOEs) from competition and stymied efficient resource allocation, preventing the contraction of low-productivity sectors. As for Poland, it privatized many of its SOEs and championed competition.

Middle-income countries lag noticeably behind high-income countries in terms of the "novelty" of their knowledge, as well as in producing new

Figure 2.5 Calibrating policies to a country's stage of development: From imitation to innovation in the Republic of Korea

a. An agreement between companies to collaborate on technology

b. Government incentives (subsidies)

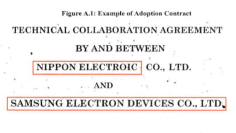

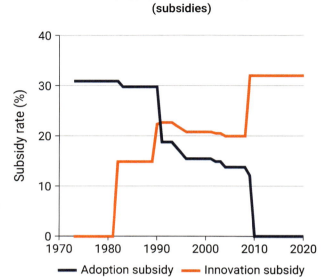

Sources: Panel a: National Archives of Korea, https://www.archives.go.kr/english/index.jsp. Panel b: Choi and Shim 2024.
Note: Panel b shows the adoption subsidy rate alongside the innovation (R&D) subsidy rate, calculated using the tax credit rate and the corporate tax rate. For example, a 30 percent subsidy rate indicates that firms can receive a reimbursement equivalent to 30 percent of their expenditures on adoption fees or R&D. R&D = research and development.

Box 2.1 The Meiji Restoration reconnected Japan with global knowledge

The turning point for Japan's rapid industrialization was the Meiji Restoration in the late 1800s. The government embarked on a project, Shokusan Kogyo (industrial development and promotion of industries).[a] Under it, Japan began investing in modernizing infrastructure (such as telegraph, rail, and electricity) and deploying demonstration factories to facilitate private sector learning and technological diffusion and to assume the first-mover risks of deploying technology. Trade flows were a critical factor in launching Japan toward the technological frontier.

Government-sponsored trips to the United States and Europe were also instrumental in acquiring technical expertise from frontier countries. The 1871–73 Iwakura Mission to both areas proved critical to facilitating the knowledge transfers needed to push Japan to the technology frontier. The statesmen and students who participated set out to study Western institutions, economic structures, educational systems, and industrial capabilities. Although German and English industry impressed senior diplomats,[b] Mission staff took an interest in US applications of new technologies and the productivity gains reaped from such innovations.[c]

(Box continues next page)

60 | WORLD DEVELOPMENT REPORT 2024

Box 2.1 The Meiji Restoration reconnected Japan with global knowledge *(continued)*

In 1888, engineers in the newly formed Ministry of Communications were dispatched to the United States, among other Western countries, to collect information on the state-of-the-art technology needed to construct the country's telecommunications network.[d] The ministry officials who attended this trip visited US telecommunications firms such as Western Electric, brought back equipment such as switchboards, and urged the Japanese government to implement Western Electric's systems for the country's network.[e] Foreign expertise was transmitted to Japanese students through foreign practitioners who taught in domestic technical schools (usually in English, indicating that some of the professors must have been American).[f] The government also sent engineering students to Western countries. By the end of the 1880s, one-quarter of the students who had traveled abroad had visited the United States.

a. Genther (2020); Odagiri and Goto (1996).
b. Beasley (1972).
c. Swale (2008).
d. Ohno (2019).
e. Mason (1992).
f. Ohno (2019).

Box 2.2 Three ways to evade the middle-income trap: Swiftly (Estonia), steadily (Poland), or slowly (Bulgaria)

Over the last three decades, Bulgaria, Estonia, and Poland have transitioned simultaneously from central planning to market economies, and Estonia and Poland have moved from middle-income to high-income status.[a] By 2021, Estonia had reached 80 percent of Western European income, Poland 75 percent, and Bulgaria 50 percent.[b] This remarkable leap from income per capita of between 20 and 30 percent of Western European levels in the early 1990s occurred at different speeds, which provides valuable policy insights.

Policy insight 1: Comprehensive reforms unlock productivity and prosperity

Structural reforms, specifically privatization and market liberalization, have played a crucial role in speeding up income convergence among Central and Eastern European economies, as documented in an extensive cross-country study by Matkowski, Prochniak, and Rapacki (2016). They find that the rate of convergence has significantly benefited from enhancements of institutions, economic freedom, and governance quality.

(Box continues next page)

Box 2.2 Three ways to evade the middle-income trap: Swiftly (Estonia), steadily (Poland), or slowly (Bulgaria) *(continued)*

Higher investment rates, a skilled labor force, low budget deficits, and lower tax burdens have been associated with accelerated economic growth.

Estonian independence in 1991 catalyzed a swift transition to high levels of productivity growth driven by a strategic divestment of public sector assets, trade liberalization, and a flat tax system. These policies opened up the market for new entrants, attracted a surge in foreign direct investment (FDI), and boosted private sector productivity. The magnitude of FDI inflows to Estonia during the 1990s was seven times that to Bulgaria and three times that to Poland.[c] Estonia maintained its status as a leading innovator in the region, with the highest research and development (R&D) intensity—1.75 percent of its gross domestic product (GDP) in 2021—and a high ranking in the Global Innovation Index (GII).[d]

As for Poland, early "big bang" reforms, trade competition, and hard budget constraints for state-owned enterprises (SOEs) systematically activated a cycle of creative destruction, closing the gap with advanced countries, as evidenced by an increase in R&D expenditure to 1.3 percent of GDP in 2021, as well as higher GII scores.

Policy insight 2: Incentives for incumbents to drive innovation are crucial

Productivity growth is a dominant driver of income convergence. Between 1996 and 2021, Estonia displayed robust annual productivity growth of 3.8 percent, followed by Poland at 2.6 percent and Bulgaria at 1.4 percent. Lowering barriers to entry and streamlining regulation—enhanced by accession to the European Union (EU)—have initiated a virtuous cycle that has sustained productivity growth. In this cycle, competition spurs innovation, which then fuels further competition, ultimately raising societal well-being.

During Bulgaria's initial phase of its transition, many incumbent SOEs were shielded by regulatory safeguards and anticompetitive practices. This environment hampered productivity growth by delaying the shift of resources toward more productive sectors. Throughout much of the period preceding EU accession, growth among Bulgaria's high-productivity industries was limited. At the same time, low-productivity sectors that relied on low-skilled labor—such as construction, retail, and ground transportation—continued to expand. Unlike Estonia and Poland, Bulgaria took nearly a decade longer to free up resources for more productive uses. Even now, some industries benefit from regulation that inhibits healthy competition.

Poland's mass privatization program is a compelling example of how to catalyze a virtuous cycle of competition and innovation, despite some challenges. By redistributing equity from more than 500 SOEs—which constituted up to 5 percent of the nation's wealth—to 27 million citizens, Poland created incentives for both new and established companies to champion competition. In Poland's early transition, the implementation of hard budget constraints, established so that SOEs would avoid reliance on unlimited government support, led to a monumental shift in attitude toward market competition. Even iconic SOEs such as the Stocznia Gdańsk shipyard, where Lech Walesa's Solidarność (Solidarity) movement began, triggering the collapse of communism in Central and Eastern Europe,

(Box continues next page)

Box 2.2 Three ways to evade the middle-income trap: Swiftly (Estonia), steadily (Poland), or slowly (Bulgaria) *(continued)*

were not bailed out. The alignment of managerial incentives—both explicit and implicit—propelled creative destruction. Managers at Polish SOEs shifted their attention from production targets to profitability and market share.[e] These managers became the primary agents of restructuring and innovation, facing both financial constraints and competition.

Policy insight 3: Skilled labor is essential for moving from infusion to innovation

As economies mature, the returns from capital become dependent on a supply of sophisticated workers. Continual enhancements in firm efficiency and workforce skills are vital to staying competitive in the rapidly changing productivity landscape.

The success stories of Estonia and Poland illustrate strategic ways to close the technology gap—initially by adopting existing technology and subsequently by developing innovative capacity. Poland narrowed its productivity gap primarily by adopting older technologies from more advanced economies rather than through the transfer of new, cutting-edge technologies.[f] Domestic investments in innovation further accelerated Poland's move toward the technology frontier, enhancing firms' ability to contribute to global technological progress. Labor also played a critical role in the transformation in Poland, according to a breakdown of the growth in total factor productivity.[g] A notable 20 percent of the contribution came from labor alone, a figure driven not by a reduction in workforce numbers but by the enhanced quality and diversity of the labor force. A significant rise in the proportion of individuals between the ages of 25 and 34 with a tertiary education, which increased from 15 percent to 42 percent between 2000 and 2012, had a significant impact on output growth.[h]

Bulgaria's experience illustrates how shortages of skilled labor can impede new investment and the growth of high-productivity ventures. The educational landscape in Bulgaria has lagged in quality, participation, equity, and intergenerational mobility. Certain segments of the population still struggle with the acquisition of basic skills, undermining their potential contribution to productivity. Prioritizing human capital development to take advantage of adoption and innovation is essential, especially in view of the demographic changes in many middle-income countries, which are at risk of "growing old before becoming rich," as the saying goes.

a. Gross national income (GNI) per capita and gross domestic product (GDP) per capita data in this report are as of July 2023. As of July 2023, Bulgaria was classified by the World Bank as an upper-middle-income country, with a GNI per capita (Atlas method, current US dollars) of US$13,350, short of crossing the high-income country threshold of US$13,846.
b. These figures are measured using purchasing power parity for the four largest EU economies.
c. These figures capture net FDI per capita accumulated by the end of 1999.
d. See GII (Global Innovation Index) (dashboard), World Intellectual Property Organization, Geneva, https://www.wipo.int/global_innovation_index/en/.
e. Pinto, Belka, and Krajewski (1993).
f. Kolasa (2008).
g. Gradzewicz et al. (2018).
h. Bukowski et al. (2006).

knowledge (figure 2.6). Innovation is concentrated in a handful of high-income economies: Germany; Japan; the Republic of Korea; Taiwan, China; and the United States. The magnitude and impact of new research in other countries is quite limited (figure 2.7).

To support innovation, countries will have to find ways to make existing firms (incumbents)—both industrial conglomerates and economic elites—innovative and more productive and to make way for newcomers. To be sure, the emerging markets are already hotbeds of entrepreneurial activity. Novel products are being used by millions, and new production methods are increasing consumer choices and lowering prices. Jack Ma, cofounder of China-based Alibaba, and Narayana Murthy, cofounder of India-based Infosys, have grown their enterprises to scale and created thousands of jobs by successfully competing in global markets and even pushing the technology frontier outward. Still, too many markets are hobbled by excessive business regulations, government patronage, and limited international competition. In such an environment, powerful owners and unproductive large firms can stifle growth, lobbying to protect their preferential access and monopoly rents when they could instead be investing in productivity-enhancing technology.

As policy makers shift their emphasis toward innovation, they should first combine a lot of investment with a lot of infusion (box 2.3).

Figure 2.6 The innovation gap between high-income countries and others is substantial

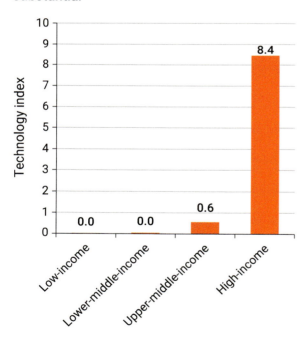

Source: WDR 2024 team.
Note: The technology index is constructed using the number of granted patents per capita and network centrality. Network centrality is calculated to measure a country's "frontierness" in technology and is defined by the citations in a country's patents of other countries' patents in a given period. Therefore, the technology index embeds both patent importance and scale.

Figure 2.7 Middle-income countries significantly lag behind high-income countries in research capacity

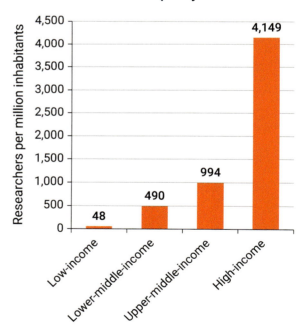

Source: WDR 2024 team.
Note: The primary data for number of researchers per million inhabitants are from UIS.Stat (dashboard), Institute for Statistics, United Nations Educational, Scientific, and Cultural Organization, Montreal, http://data.uis.unesco.org.

Box 2.3 The magic of investment accelerations

Investment is a fundamental pillar of economic progress. Not only does investment growth allow countries to enhance their stocks of physical capital such as factories, offices, roads, bridges, schools, and clinics, but it is also a necessary condition for infusing global technologies in domestic production possibilities. Because technology is embodied in capital, a country will find it challenging to advance technologically without scaling up investment.

Investors look for macroeconomic stability and ease of doing business in deciding where, in what, and how much to invest. The experiences of Colombia, Türkiye, and the Republic of Korea are examples. In 2001, Colombia implemented a comprehensive reform package to stabilize its economy by restraining public spending, increasing central bank independence, and introducing a floating exchange rate. Similarly, in the early 2000s Türkiye implemented a primary surplus target, the central bank became independent, and reforms to improve the business climate and liberalize the banking sector were adopted. Earlier, Korea implemented two rounds of reform packages. In the mid-1980s, Korea adopted a balanced budget, improved the business climate by promoting competition, and liberalized trade. A second round of reforms in the late 1990s improved the independence of the central bank, consolidated government finances, strengthened the financial sector, and liberalized the capital account.

Following these reform efforts, all three countries experienced investment accelerations: Colombia from 2001 to 2007, Türkiye from 2003 to 2008, and Korea in 1985–96 and from 1999 to 2007. Investment accelerations are periods with a sustained increase in investment growth. During these periods, investment as well as productivity grew much faster than in nonacceleration years (figure B2.3.1). More broadly, across a sample of 104 economies, including 69 emerging market and developing economies (EMDEs) and 35 advanced economies covering the years 1950 to 2022, 192 episodes of investment acceleration occurred in which per capita investment growth averaged at least 4 percent per year over at least six years.[a] On average, an EMDE has experienced about 1.7 investment accelerations. During these accelerations, investment growth more than tripled to 10 percent a year over that of nonacceleration years; output growth increased by 2 percentage points; and productivity growth quadrupled to 1.7 percent per year.

In the sample of 104 economies, 82 percent of the transitions from middle-income status to high-income status that occurred over the last three decades happened during or shortly after investment accelerations. Sectoral shifts gained momentum during investment accelerations because output grew substantially faster in the manufacturing and services sectors than before the acceleration. Accelerations were also often periods during which more progress was made in reducing poverty, living standards improved, and the pace of convergence to advanced economy income per capita levels increased.

(Box continues next page)

Box 2.3 The magic of investment accelerations *(continued)*

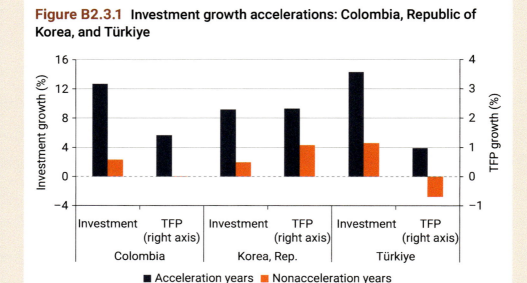

Figure B2.3.1 Investment growth accelerations: Colombia, Republic of Korea, and Türkiye

■ Acceleration years   ■ Nonacceleration years

Sources: Dieppe 2021; Feenstra, Inklaar, and Timmer 2015; World Bank 2024; Database Profiles (dashboard), Our Data, Haver Analytics, New York, https://www.haver.com/our-data; WDI (World Development Indicators) (Data Catalog), World Bank, Washington, DC, https://datacatalog.worldbank.org/search/dataset/0037712.

Note: Investment refers to gross fixed capital formation. The sample period is 1980–2022. Bars are simple averages of growth in investment and total factor productivity (TFP). Acceleration years cover the full duration of the episodes. Nonacceleration years exclude acceleration years that are not included in this box (see World Bank 2024, box 3.1).

a. World Bank 2024.

And they should not bet the farm—or even a field—on leapfrogging. Infusion is imperative. A review of the literature on middle-income traps highlights that countries often try to make premature leaps from investment to innovation. According to Gill and Kharas (2015, 28–29),

> [Some countries tried] to leapfrog prematurely into "knowledge economies," with none of the institutional infrastructure in place to accomplish this. Poor quality universities, low levels of human capital, limited venture capital, regulatory barriers and incomplete rule of law present significant barriers to becoming an innovation-driven economy. Middle-income countries that invest heavily and prematurely in trying to become "knowledge economies" can find low returns to such investments. The combination of wasted fiscal spending and a faulty growth diagnostic can lead to substandard performance—another example of the middle-income trap.

Notes

1. Nassif, Feijó, and Araújo (2015).
2. Branstetter and Kwon (2018).
3. Gill and Kharas (2007).
4. Mokyr (2018).
5. Solow (1957). *Technical change* is an economic term meaning a change in the amount of output produced from the same amount of inputs.
6. Lucas (1988); Romer (1990).
7. Toniolo (1998).
8. Fernández-Villaverde and Ohanian (2018). In the 1950s, for example, Italian firms benefited from sponsored training trips for their managers, enabling them to acquire modern management practices from firms in the United States. Some firms also received loans to procure modern machinery from the United States (technology transfer). Specifically, firms that engaged in both management and technology transfers witnessed the most substantial long-term productivity growth, highlighting the important role of infusion (Giorcelli 2019).
9. Chuah, Loayza, and Nguyen (2018).
10. Acemoglu, Aghion, and Zilibotti (2006); Gerschenkron (1962); König et al. (2022); Zilibotti (2017).
11. Mokyr (2023).
12. Choi and Shim (2023).
13. World Bank (1978).
14. Zilibotti (2017).
15. Mokyr (2023).

References

Acemoglu, Daron, Philippe Aghion, and Fabrizio Zilibotti. 2006. "Distance to Frontier, Selection, and Economic Growth." *Journal of the European Economic Association* 4 (1): 37–74.

Beasley, William G. 1972. *The Meiji Restoration*. Stanford, CA: Stanford University Press.

Branstetter, Lee G., and Namho Kwon. 2018. "South Korea's Transition from Imitator to Innovator: The Role of External Demand Shocks." *Journal of the Japanese and International Economies* 49 (September): 28–42.

Bukowski, Maciej, Iga Magda, Łukasz Marć, and Julian Zawistowski. 2006. "Źródła i perspektyw wzrostu produktywności pracy w Polsce" [Sources and prospects of productivity growth in Poland]. December, Instytut Badań Strukturalnych, Warsaw.

Choi, Jaedo, and Younghun Shim. 2023. "Technology Adoption and Late Industrialization." STEG Working Paper WP033 rev. (September), Structural Transformation and Economic Growth, Centre for Economic Policy Research, London.

Choi, Jaedo, and Younghun Shim. 2024. "From Adoption to Innovation: State-Dependent Technology Policy in Developing Countries." STEG Working Paper WP091 (March), Structural Transformation and Economic Growth, Centre for Economic Policy Research, London.

Chuah, Lay Lian, Norman V. Loayza, and Ha Nguyen. 2018. "Resource Misallocation and Productivity Gaps in Malaysia." Policy Research Working Paper 8368, World Bank, Washington, DC.

Dieppe, Alistair, ed. 2021. *Global Productivity: Trends, Drivers, and Policies*. Washington, DC: World Bank.

Feenstra, Robert C., Robert Inklaar, and Marcel Peter Timmer. 2015. "The Next Generation of the Penn World Table." *American Economic Review* 105 (10): 3150–82.

Fernández-Villaverde, Jesús, and Lee Edward Ohanian. 2018. "The Lack of European Productivity Growth: Causes and Lessons for the U.S." PIER Working Paper 18-024, Penn Institute for Economic Research, Department of Economics, University of Pennsylvania, Philadelphia.

Genther, Phyllis A. 2020. *A History of Japan's Government-Business Relationship: The Passenger Car Industry*. Michigan Papers in Japanese Studies Series. Ann Arbor: University of Michigan Press.

Gerschenkron, Alexander. 1962. *Economic Backwardness in Historical Perspective*. Cambridge, MA: Belknap Press.

Gill, Indermit Singh, and Homi Kharas. 2007. *An East Asian Renaissance: Ideas for Economic Growth*. With Deepak Bhattasali, Milan Brahmbhatt, Gaurav Datt, Mona Haddad, Edward Mountfield, Radu Tatucu, and Ekaterina Vostroknutova. Washington, DC: World Bank.

Gill, Indermit Singh, and Homi Kharas. 2015. "The Middle-Income Trap Turns Ten." Policy Research Working Paper 7403, World Bank, Washington, DC.

Giorcelli, Michela. 2019. "The Long-Term Effects of Management and Technology Transfers." *American Economic Review* 109 (1): 121–52.

Gradzewicz, Michał, Jakub Growiec, Marcin Kolasa, Łukasz Postek, and Paweł Strzelecki. 2018. "Poland's Uninterrupted Growth Performance: New Growth Accounting Evidence." *Post-Communist Economies* 30 (2): 238–72.

Kolasa, Marcin. 2008. "How Does FDI Inflow Affect Productivity of Domestic Firms? The Role of Horizontal and Vertical Spillovers, Absorptive Capacity and Competition." *Journal of International Trade and Economic Development* 17 (1): 155–73.

König, Michael, Kjetil Storesletten, Zheng Song, and Fabrizio Zilibotti. 2022. "From Imitation to Innovation: Where Is All That Chinese R&D Going?" *Econometrica* 90 (4): 1615–54.

Lange, Glenn-Marie, Quentin T. Wodon, and Kevin Carey, eds. 2018. *The Changing Wealth of Nations 2018: Building a Sustainable Future*. Washington, DC: World Bank.

Lucas, Robert E., Jr. 1988. "On the Mechanics of Economic Development." *Journal of Monetary Economics* 22 (1): 3–42.

Mason, Mark. 1992. *American Multinationals and Japan: The Political Economy of Japanese Capital Controls, 1899–1980*. Harvard East Asian Monographs Series, vol. 154. Cambridge, MA: Asia Center, Harvard University.

Matkowski, Zbigniew, Mariusz Prochniak, and Ryszard Rapacki. 2016. "Real Income Convergence between Central Eastern and Western Europe: Past, Present, and Prospects." Paper presented at the 33rd Centre for International Research on Economic Tendency Surveys' Conference on Economic Tendency Surveys and Economic Policy, Copenhagen, September 14–17, 2016. https://www.econstor.eu/handle/10419/146992.

Mokyr, Joel. 2018. "The Past and the Future of Innovation: Some Lessons from Economic History." *Explorations in Economic History* 69 (July): 13–26.

Mokyr, Joel. 2023. "Creative Destruction or Destructive Creation? A Prelude to the Industrial Revolution." In *The Economics of Creative Destruction: New Research on Themes from Aghion and Howitt,* edited by Ufuk Akcigit and John Michael Van Reenen, 714–35. Cambridge, MA: Harvard University Press.

Nassif, André, Carmem Feijó, and Eliane Araújo. 2015. "Structural Change and Economic Development: Is Brazil Catching Up or Falling Behind?" *Cambridge Journal of Economics* 39 (5): 1307–32.

Odagiri, Hiroyuki, and Akira Goto. 1996. *Technology and Industrial Development in Japan: Building Capabilities by Learning, Innovation, and Public Policy.* New York: Oxford University Press.

Ohno, Kenichi. 2019. "Meiji Japan: Progressive Learning of Western Technology." In *How Nations Learn: Technological Learning, Industrial Policy, and Catch-Up,* edited by Arkebe Oqubay and Kenichi Ohno, 85–106. New York: Oxford University Press.

Pinto, Brian, Marek Belka, and Stefan Krajewski. 1993. "Transforming State Enterprises in Poland: Evidence on Adjustment by Manufacturing Firms." *Brookings Papers on Economic Activity BPEA* 1993 (1): 213–70.

Romer, Paul Michael. 1990. "Endogenous Technological Change." *Journal of Political Economy* 98 (5, Part 2): S71–S102.

Solow, Robert M. 1957. "Technical Change and the Aggregate Production Function." *Review of Economics and Statistics* 39 (3): 312–20.

Swale, Alistair. 2008 "America, 15 January to 6 August 1872: The First Stage in the Quest for Enlightenment." In *The Iwakura Mission to America and Europe: A New Assessment,* edited by Ian Nish, 7–23. Meiji Japan Series, vol. 6. London: Routledge.

Toniolo, Gianni. 1998. "Europe's Golden Age, 1950–1973: Speculations from a Long-Run Perspective." *Economic History Review* 51 (2): 252–67.

World Bank. 1978. *World Development Report 1978.* Washington, DC: World Bank.

World Bank. 2024. *Global Economic Prospects, January 2024.* Washington, DC: World Bank.

Zilibotti, Fabrizio. 2017. "Growing and Slowing Down Like China." *Journal of the European Economic Association* 15 (5): 943–88.

3 Shrinking Spaces

Key messages

- The growth prospects of middle-income countries are becoming more problematic because of an increasingly fragmented global economy, rapidly changing demographic trends, multiple crises, populist pressures, rising government debt, and climate change pressures.
- Previous episodes of growth acceleration have been accompanied by trade integration, but rising geopolitical tensions have affected trade policy, and further protectionism can potentially worsen the diffusion of knowledge to low- and middle-income countries.
- Many middle-income countries are severely indebted in the aftermath of the COVID-19 pandemic, and monetary tightening in high-income countries risks compounding the burden of high debt.
- Middle-income countries will need significant resources to scale up reliable low-carbon energy. But many face the rising cost of borrowing, high up-front infrastructure requirements, and high capital costs, all of which could increase the cost of low-carbon technologies and delay the diffusion of low-carbon energy.

Introduction

Growing past middle-income status has never been easy—slowing growth (chapter 1) and structural stasis (chapter 2) dampen growth prospects. This chapter asks whether growth in middle-income countries is becoming harder. The answer: it is.

Two decades into the twenty-first century, the world is at a historic crossroads. Foreign trade and investment are in danger of becoming constricted by geopolitical tensions, and the room for governments to act is shrinking because of rising populism and public debt. As a result, economic growth in the remainder of this decade will likely be weaker than it was in the last two.[1]

For middle-income countries, this prospect means they are growing into shrinking spaces with the retrenchment of globalization (a force that has spurred *infusion* and *innovation*), difficulties in servicing debt obligations, and the additional economic and financial costs of climate change and climate action. On the latter, middle-income countries will need to build resilience to the shocks arising from a changing climate, as well as accelerate their energy transitions. Such challenges will have to be confronted against the backdrop of a rapidly aging world population and therefore waning demographic dividends (box 3.1). At the same time, middle-income countries need to ensure macroeconomic stability since it is essential for high and sustainable rates of growth. Macroeconomic instability will increase the cost of borrowing and keep both domestic and foreign investors away.

Box 3.1 Graying growth

Historically, demographic dividends have fostered economic growth in many countries. An increase in the working-age population and a consequent decrease in dependency ratios free up resources to be spent on education, health care, employment, and social protection schemes.[a] However, the world is aging rapidly and fertility rates are declining rapidly,[b] which will especially affect middle-income countries projected to face labor crunches in the coming decades. In fact, today's middle-income countries are aging more rapidly than high-income countries did in the past. Transitioning from an aging society to an aged society took about 61 years in today's high-income countries and as long as 69 years in the United States and 115 years in France.[c] By contrast, transitioning from an aging society to an aged society is estimated to take about 26 years for today's middle-income countries (figure B3.1.1).

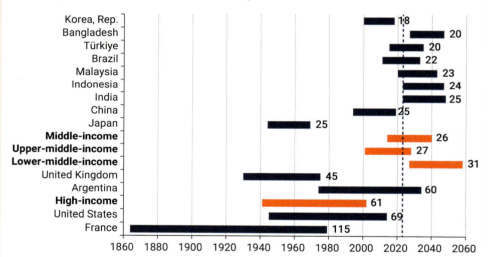

Figure B3.1.1 Today's middle-income countries are aging more rapidly than high-income countries did in the past

Sources: WDR 2024 team using data of World Population Prospects (dashboard), Population Division, Department of Economic and Social Affairs, United Nations, New York, https://population.un.org/wpp/; World Bank (2016).

Note: The bars indicate beginning and end years for transitioning from 7 percent (aging) to 14 percent (aged) of the population age 65 and older. The number corresponding to each bar shows total number of years to transition from aging to aged. Aging and aged thresholds are based on definitions by the Population Division of the United Nations Department of Economic and Social Affairs (UN DESA). Bars for income groups represent the averages of countries included in the corresponding income group. The dashed vertical line indicates the year 2023.

(Box continues next page)

Box 3.1 Graying growth *(continued)*

Working-age populations are already declining in middle-income countries in East Asia.[d] Latin America will retain a large workforce until the early 2040s, while the Middle East and North Africa and South and Central Asia regions will begin to lose working-age persons by 2045. As a result, middle-income countries can no longer rely on increasing employment as a primary source of output growth. This prospect of "growing old before becoming rich" makes escaping the middle-income trap more challenging and more urgent, including among the largest middle-income countries such as Brazil, China, Mexico, and Türkiye.

The demographic challenge has implications for public policy. Investments will be needed in infrastructure and technologies to support the elderly, in addition to expanding fiscal transfers for older persons. These measures will, in turn, necessitate policies that support savings among the working-age population. Meanwhile, countries will need to invest in upgrading skills of their workforce and ensuring that everyone's talent is used appropriately and efficiently. Furthermore, automation and other productivity-enhancing technologies to compensate for a shrinking workforce will have to be deployed and have been prioritized by aging countries such as Japan.[e] The path from imitative to innovative growth is the key for middle-income countries to address the needs of their aging populations.

Finally, the booming populations in low-income countries and lower-middle-income countries in Sub-Saharan Africa and elsewhere will need to be integrated into graying societies' labor markets (especially those in middle-income countries).[f] Canada has successfully relied on immigration as a strategy to manage its low fertility rates and labor shortages.[g] *World Development Report 2023: Migrants, Refugees, and Societies* argues that if managed effectively, migration could unlock further growth for destination countries.[h] And this migration need not be a brain drain imposed on lower-income countries with high population growth rates. For example, professional links established between expat scientists and those they leave behind may generate knowledge spillovers in their countries of origin.[i]

a. UN DESA (2022). *Dependency ratios* refer to the number of children (ages 0–14) and older persons (age 65 and over) to the working-age population (ages 15–64).
b. Lee and Mason (2006); UN DESA (2022).
c. Aging society and aged society thresholds are based on the definition of the Population Division of the United Nations Department of Economic and Social Affairs (UN DESA). According to the definition, the share of people age 65 and older exceeds 7 percent of the population in an aging society, and a country qualifies as an aged society if this share exceeds 14 percent.
d. UN DESA (2022).
e. Moss (2017).
f. Wakeman-Linn et al. (2015).
g. Green (2023).
h. World Bank (2023b).
i. Prato (2023).

Fragmenting international trade

Episodes of growth acceleration have been accompanied by trade integration.[2] The Republic of Korea's economic metamorphosis was underpinned by a licensing regime to import frontier technologies, followed by a shift toward promotion of research and development.[3] The Korean story suggests that catching up and eventually leading the pack requires trade liberalization to buy foreign technology and to sell a country's own inventions. More broadly, globalization has increased incentives to adopt foreign technologies by enhancing international competition.[4]

But the international trade architecture that allowed countries such as Korea to ascend is facing challenges. First, declining potential global output threatens trade flows, compounding the blows dealt by the global financial crisis and the COVID-19 pandemic.[5] Second, rising geopolitical tensions have affected trade policy,[6] and further protectionism could worsen the diffusion of knowledge to low- and middle-income countries.[7] Although there is limited evidence of widespread "friend-shoring" or realignment of trade along geopolitical lines beyond the United States–China decoupling, this situation could change in the near future if trade tensions continue to rise.[8] Many industries that use technology and innovation intensively will face extensive costs and risks if critical global links are reduced because these links are at the heart of technology-intensive industries such as information and communication technology (ICT) and smartphones.[9] Globally, since 2019 the number of harmful trade policies has exceeded the number of helpful trade policies, and the pace of their enactment is increasing: the number of new harmful trade measures enacted per year doubled over the last decade (figure 3.1).

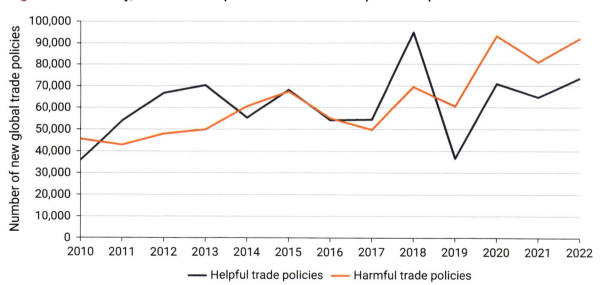

Figure 3.1 Globally, harmful trade policies outnumber helpful trade policies

Source: WDR 2024 team using the GTA (Global Trade Alert) database, St. Gallen Endowment for Prosperity through Trade, University of St. Gallen, St. Gallen, Switzerland, https://www.globaltradealert.org/data_extraction.

Note: Measuring trade policies is fraught with challenges, and the GTA database may overrepresent countries that issue a relatively high quantity of legislative documents or those with greater regulatory transparency. The plotted lines indicate global trade policies that were introduced in the corresponding year. Helpful trade policies include interventions that liberalize on a nondiscriminatory basis or improve the transparency of a relevant policy. Harmful trade policies include interventions that discriminate against foreign commercial interests. See Harmonized System (dashboard), World Customs Organization, Brussels, https://www.wcotradetools.org/en/harmonized-system.

Figure 3.2 Harmful interventions in the global semiconductor trade have skyrocketed since 2019

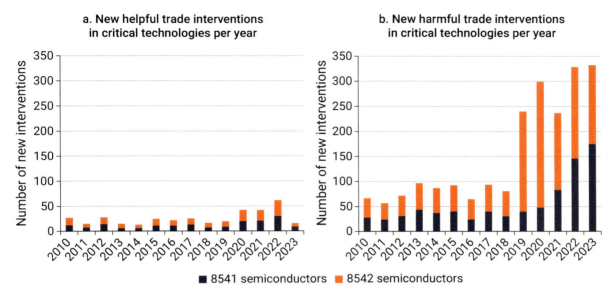

Source: WDR 2024 team using the GTA (Global Trade Alert) database, St. Gallen Endowment for Prosperity through Trade, University of St. Gallen, St. Gallen, Switzerland, https://www.globaltradealert.org/data_extraction.

Note: Measuring trade policies is fraught with challenges, and the GTA database may overrepresent countries that issue a relatively high quantity of legislative documents or those with greater regulatory transparency. The bars indicate global trade policies introduced in the corresponding year. Helpful trade policies include interventions that liberalize on a nondiscriminatory basis or improve the transparency of a relevant policy. Harmful trade policies include interventions that discriminate against foreign commercial interests. "8541" and "8542" refer to the four-digit Harmonized System codes for semiconductors. See Harmonized System (dashboard), World Customs Organization, Brussels, https://www.wcotradetools.org/en/harmonized-system.

Moreover, most high-income and large middle-income countries are now increasingly resorting to industrial policy and trade-related measures that may result in restrictions to trade flows.[10] For example, some of the largest trading nations have adopted a "friend-shoring" approach that concentrates their supply chain network among allies and friendly countries in response to rising tensions with the Russian Federation and China.[11] In addition, the costs associated with technological fragmentation are estimated to be as high as 5 percent of the gross domestic product (GDP) for many economies.[12] Compounding that are the high risks associated with disrupting critical industries and global supply chains. In a deglobalized scenario, some critical industries may be unable to function, or it would take decades for those industries to catch up their current levels of functionality because of their massively modular industrial organization.[13] Unfortunately, harmful interventions to block the trade of critical technologies have more than tripled since 2019 (figure 3.2).

Elevated debt

Global debt relative to GDP has remained stubbornly high in the aftermath of the COVID-19 pandemic (figure 3.3). Indeed, many middle-income countries are more severely indebted than ever before.[14] Postpandemic fiscal deficits in response to spikes in food and energy costs

Figure 3.3 Most developing economies are more severely indebted than ever

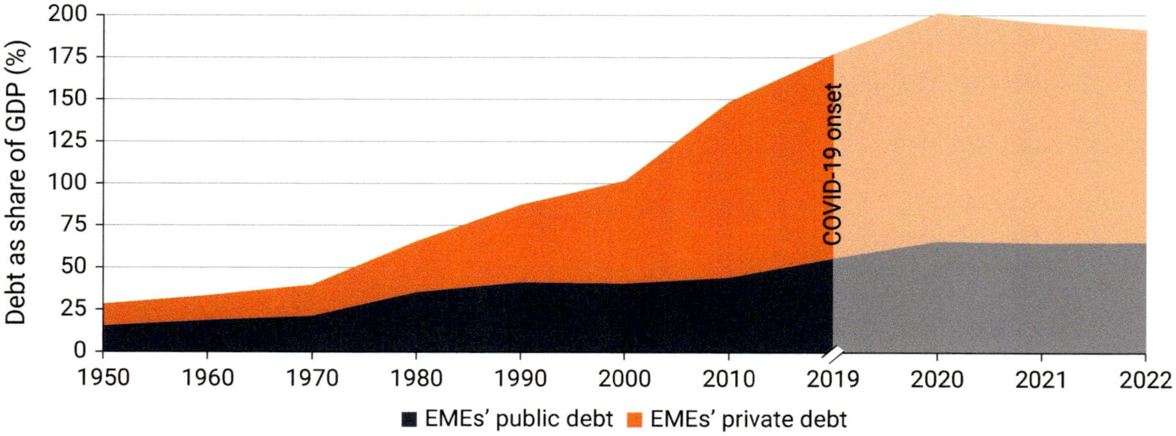

Source: WDR 2024 team based on IMF (2023b); Kose and Ohnsorge (2024).
Note: The figure shows the total debt of emerging market economies (EMEs) in terms of weighted averages broken down into public debt and private debt. GDP = gross domestic product.

have kept public debt levels elevated. Meanwhile, monetary tightening in high-income countries risks compounding the burden of high debt-to-GDP ratios for middle-income countries. About three-quarters of countries tightened both fiscal and monetary policy in 2022.[15] As interest rates have surged, government budgets have been squeezed. This squeeze has increased sovereign spreads and borrowing costs for many emerging and frontier markets. The resulting loss of market access for some of these countries and the lack of access to these avenues of relief are likely to result in a wave of uncoordinated defaults in middle-income countries over the medium term. Unfortunately, there is no sign of relief because high-income countries are likely to sustain high interest rates for the foreseeable future (figure 3.4). Many low- and middle-income countries now spend more on debt service payments than they do on health, education, and infrastructure. Because fiscal space is eroding due to costlier borrowing in low- and middle-income countries, new investment needs—including in the green transition, education, the capacity to innovate, and infrastructure—are likely to be put on hold.

Encouraging growth in low- and middle-income countries under the current circumstances will not be easy. Reducing debt vulnerabilities and reversing long-term debt trends should be at the core of these countries' agendas. In particular, the governments of middle-income countries urgently need to take steps to alleviate debt distress in the medium term. More broadly, reforms to improve debt transparency and strengthen debt management policies and frameworks are key to reducing the risks of debt distress. These reforms could also foster economic growth if they are coupled with reforms in labor markets and product markets. In addition, reducing debt burdens is crucial to creating the fiscal space for investments in health, education, and infrastructure. Middle-income countries can make quick progress in transitioning to higher-income status only if they achieve strong and sustained investment growth.

Figure 3.4 Debt service payments in emerging markets and middle-income countries may skyrocket as the cost of borrowing soars

Source: WDR 2024 team using data from Fiscal Monitor (dashboard), International Monetary Fund, Washington, DC, https://data.imf.org/?sk=4be0c9cb-272a-4667-8892-34b582b21ba6.
Note: GDP = gross domestic product.

Climate action

Fossil fuels—coal, oil, and natural gas—are the major contributors to global climate change, accounting for over three-fourths of total greenhouse gas emissions and about 90 percent of carbon dioxide (CO_2) emissions.[16] The International Energy Agency has announced that achieving net zero emissions by 2050 will require reducing between 2020 and 2050 the global demand for coal by 90 percent, oil by 75 percent, and natural gas by 55 percent.[17] Therefore, climate action—measures to mitigate climate change—requires changing the way energy is produced and consumed.

Because middle-income countries presently account for about two-thirds of global CO_2 emissions, their decarbonization is material to the world's ability to meet its climate goals. Today, both energy intensity and carbon intensity are quite high in middle-income countries (figure 3.5). Energy intensity (panel a) in middle-income countries is about double that in high-income countries, and the carbon intensity of their energy consumption (panel b) is also relatively inefficient.

At the same time, reliable cheap energy is critical to supporting industrial activities and powering businesses. It is also correlated with higher living standards. But over 300 million people in middle-income countries still lack access to electricity. Moreover, blackouts and brownouts are common in middle-income countries. As energy demand rises with income, expanding access to reliable energy will be as critical as transitioning to lower-carbon energy.[18]

Today, energy transition technologies constitute the largest investment gap. Significant resources are needed to scale up reliable, low-carbon energy. Low-carbon energy technologies

Figure 3.5 In middle-income countries, the energy intensity and carbon intensity of energy consumption are quite high

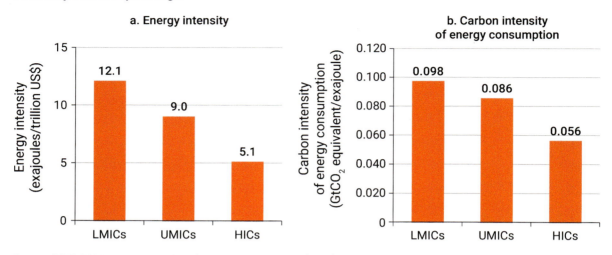

Source: WDR 2024 team using data from Energy Institute (2023); WDI (World Development Indicators) (Data Catalog), World Bank, Washington, DC, https://datacatalog.worldbank.org/search/dataset/0037712.
Note: Data for low-income countries are not available. GtCO$_2$ = gigatons of carbon dioxide; HICs = high-income countries; LMICs = lower-middle-income countries; UMICs = upper-middle-income countries.

require considerable up-front capital despite lower operating expenses.[19] Thus middle-income countries need access to low-cost capital to increase the affordability of low-carbon energy transitions because considerable improvement of capital-intensive clean energy assets—such as wind power, solar photovoltaic (PV), electric vehicles, and hydrogen electrolyzers—is required. The cost of capital is key because the weighted average cost of capital can account for 20–50 percent of the levelized cost of electricity from utility-scale solar PV projects.[20] And yet the cost of capital for utility-scale solar power projects in middle-income countries is significantly higher than that in the United States and Europe (figure 3.6).[21] High up-front infrastructure requirements and capital costs could potentially increase the cost of low-carbon technologies.

High borrowing costs make it more challenging for middle-income countries to finance green energy investments and to diffuse low-carbon energy. In addition, developing countries are currently spending more on interest payments than on climate investments even though they need to more than triple climate investments to meet the Paris Agreement targets.[22]

Meanwhile, middle-income countries are more exposed to risks from climate change than high-income countries and have less capacity to adapt to such risks (figure 3.7). They also face overwhelmingly high costs to finance climate adaptation. In 2030, annual adaptation costs are estimated to exceed 1 percent of GDP per year for some middle-income countries, while annual global adaptation needs will reach about 0.25 percent of global GDP.[23]

The room for governments to act in middle-income countries is shrinking because of rising debt and interest rates, and their feeble growth prospects stem from a weakening foreign trade and investment outlook. In addition, international

Figure 3.6 In middle-income countries, the weighted average cost of capital for utility-scale solar power projects is substantially higher than the cost in high-income countries

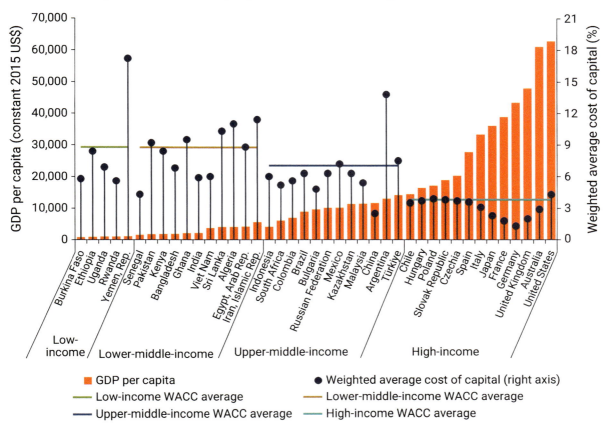

Source: WDR 2024 team using IRENA (2023); WDI (World Development Indicators) (Data Catalog), World Bank, Washington, DC, https://datacatalog.worldbank.org/search/dataset/0037712.
Note: GDP = gross domestic product; WACC = weighted average cost of capital.

pressures and domestic pledges for climate action will require these countries to allocate substantial investment to adaptation and mitigation. With many middle-income economies facing high debt and higher borrowing costs, a policy dilemma arises between achieving ambitious climate actions that pay off in the longer term and averting short-term macroeconomic imbalances.

The constraints facing middle-income countries and the extensive and frenetic pace of change required for them to transition to high-income status make policy making more challenging than at the low- or high-income stage. The chapters that follow focus on feasible steps that could aid this transition.

SHRINKING SPACES | 77

Figure 3.7 Low- and middle-income countries are exposed to similar levels of risk from climate change, and they have less adaptive capacity

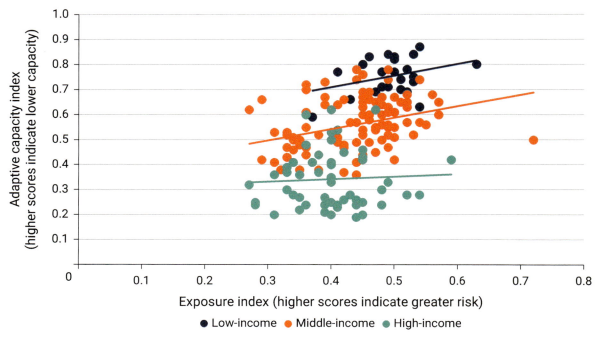

Source: WDR 2024 team using data from ND-GAIN Country Index (University of Notre Dame Global Adaptation Index) (dashboard), University of Notre Dame, Notre Dame, IN, https://gain.nd.edu/our-work/country-index/.
Note: The solid lines show the linear relationship for each country group.

Notes

1. World Bank (2023a).
2. Hausmann, Pritchett, and Rodrik (2005).
3. Choi and Shim (2024).
4. IMF (2018).
5. Goldberg and Reed (2023); Kose and Ohnsorge (2024).
6. Góes and Bekkers (2022); Goldberg and Reed (2023).
7. Melitz and Redding (2021).
8. Pierce and Yu (2023).
9. Thun et al. (2022).
10. Barattieri, Mattoo, and Taglioni (2024).
11. Gill (2023).
12. Cerdeiro et al. (2021).
13. Thun et al. (2022).
14. Kose and Ohnsorge (2024).
15. IMF (2023a).
16. UNEP (2023).
17. IEA (2021b).
18. Kahn and Lall (2022).
19. Erdogan and Arboleya Sarazola (2023).
20. IEA (2021a).
21. Steffen (2020); UNEP (2023).
22. UNCTAD (2024).
23. Aligishiev, Bellon, and Massetti (2022).

References

Aligishiev, Zamid, Matthieu Bellon, and Emanuele Massetti. 2022. "Macro-Fiscal Implications of Adaptation to Climate Change." IMF Staff Climate Note 2022/002 (March), International Monetary Fund, Washington, DC.

Barattieri, Alessandro Eugenio Maria, Aaditya Mattoo, and Daria Taglioni. 2024. "Trade Effects of Industrial Policies: Are Preferential Agreements a Shield?" Policy Research Working Paper 10806, World Bank, Washington, DC.

Cerdeiro, Diego A., Johannes Eugster, Rui C. Mano, Dirk Muir, and Shanaka J. Peiris. 2021. "Sizing Up the Effects of Technological Decoupling." IMF Working Paper WP/21/69 (March), International Monetary Fund, Washington, DC.

Choi, Jaedo, and Younghun Shim. 2024. "From Adoption to Innovation: State-Dependent Technology Policy in Developing Countries." STEG Working Paper WP091 (March), Structural Transformation and Economic Growth, Centre for Economic Policy Research, London.

Energy Institute. 2023. "Statistical Review of World Energy 2023." June, Energy Institute, London.

Erdogan, Musa, and Lucila Arboleya Sarazola. 2023. "Cost of Capital Survey Shows Investments in Solar PV Can Be Less Risky than Gas Power in Emerging and Developing Economies, though Values Remain High." *Commentary*, November 30, 2023. https://www.iea.org/commentaries/cost-of-capital-survey-shows-investments-in-solar-pv-can-be-less-risky-than-gas-power-in-emerging-and-developing-economies-though-values-remain-high.

Gill, Indermit Singh. 2023. "The New Threat to Prosperity Everywhere." *Paradigm Shifts* (blog), March 13, 2023. https://www.project-syndicate.org/magazine/deglobalization-new-fiscal-monetary-policy-norms-bad-for-economic-development-by-indermit-gill-2023-03.

Góes, Carlos, and Eddy Bekkers. 2022. "The Impact of Geopolitical Conflicts on Trade, Growth, and Innovation." WTO Staff Working Paper ERSD-2022-09 (July 4), Economic Research and Statistics Division, World Trade Organization, Geneva.

Goldberg, Pinelopi Koujianou, and Tristan Reed. 2023. "Is the Global Economy Deglobalizing? And If So, Why? And What Is Next?" *Brookings Papers on Economic Activity* BPEA 2023 (Spring): 347–96.

Green, Mark A. 2023. "Canada: Ageing Workforce, Boosting Immigration." *Stubborn Things* (blog), April 18, 2023. https://www.wilsoncenter.org/blog-post/canada-ageing-workforce-boosting-immigration.

Hausmann, Ricardo, Lant H. Pritchett, and Dani Rodrik. 2005. "Growth Accelerations." *Journal of Economic Growth* 10 (4): 303–29.

IEA (International Energy Agency). 2021a. "The Cost of Capital in Clean Energy Transitions." Report, December 17, IEA, Paris.

IEA (International Energy Agency). 2021b. *Net Zero by 2050: A Roadmap for the Global Energy Sector*. 4th rev. (October). Paris: IEA.

IMF (International Monetary Fund). 2018. *World Economic Outlook, April 2018: Cyclical Upswing, Structural Change*. Washington, DC: IMF.

IMF (International Monetary Fund). 2023a. *Fiscal Monitor: On the Path to Policy Normalization*. April. Washington, DC: IMF.

IMF (International Monetary Fund). 2023b. "2023 Global Debt Monitor." September, Fiscal Affairs Department, IMF, Washington, DC.

IRENA (International Renewable Energy Agency). 2023. *Renewable Power Generation Costs in 2022*. Abu Dhabi, United Arab Emirates: IRENA.

Kahn, Matthew E., and Somik Vinay Lall. 2022. "Will the Developing World's Growing Middle Class Support Low Carbon Policies?" NBER Working Paper 30238 (July), National Bureau of Economic Research, Cambridge, MA.

Kose, M. Ayhan, and Franziska Ohnsorge, eds. 2024. *Falling Long-Term Growth Prospects: Trends, Expectations, and Policies*. Washington, DC: World Bank.

Lee, Ronald Demos, and Andrew Mason. 2006. "What Is the Demographic Dividend?" *Finance and Development* 43 (3): 16–17.

Melitz, Marc J., and Stephen J. Redding. 2021. "Trade and Innovation." NBER Working Paper 28945 (June), National Bureau of Economic Research, Cambridge, MA.

Moss, Daniel. 2017. "Aging Japan Wants Automation, Not Immigration." *Bloomberg: Opinion*, August 22, 2017. https://www.bloomberg.com/view/articles/2017-08-22/aging-japan-wants-automation-not-immigration.

Pierce, Justin R., and David Yu. 2023. "Assessing the Extent of Trade Fragmentation." FEDS Notes. Board of Governors of the Federal Reserve System, Washington, DC. https://www.federalreserve.gov/econres/notes/feds-notes/assessing-the-extent-of-trade-fragmentation-20231103.html.

Prato, Marta. 2023. "The Global Race for Talent: Brain Drain, Knowledge Transfer, and Economic Growth." Working Paper, Ettore Bocconi Department of Economics, Bocconi University, Milan.

Steffen, Bjarne. 2020. "Estimating the Cost of Capital for Renewable Energy Projects." *Energy Economics* 88 (May): 104783.

Thun, Eric, Daria Taglioni, Timothy J. Sturgeon, and Mark P. Dallas. 2022. "Massive Modularity: Understanding Industry Organization in the Digital Age: The Case of Mobile Phone Handsets." Policy Research Working Paper 10164, World Bank, Washington, DC.

UN DESA (United Nations Department of Economic and Social Affairs). 2022. "World Population Prospects 2022: Summary of Results." Document UN DESA/POP/2021/TR/NO. 3, United Nations, New York. https://www.un.org/development/desa/pd/sites/www.un.org.development.desa.pd/files/wpp2022_summary_of_results.pdf.

UNCTAD (UN Trade and Development). 2024. *A World of Debt: A Growing Burden to Global Prosperity*. New York: United Nations.

UNEP (United Nations Environment Programme). 2023. *Broken Record: Temperatures Hit New Highs, Yet World Fails to Cut Emissions (Again)*. Emissions Gap Report 2023. Nairobi, Kenya: UNEP.

Wakeman-Linn, John, Rahul Anand, Paulo Drummond, Richard Erlebach, Francisco Roch, Vimal Thakoor, and Juan Treviño. 2015. "How Can Africa Harness the Demographic Dividend?" In *Sub-Saharan Africa: Navigating Headwinds*, 25–45. With research assistance of Idan Elmelech, Cleary Haines, and George Rooney. Regional Economic Outlook, April. World Economic and Financial Surveys Series. Washington, DC: International Monetary Fund.

World Bank. 2016. *Live Long and Prosper: Aging in East Asia and Pacific*. World Bank East Asia and Pacific Regional Report. Washington, DC: World Bank.

World Bank. 2023a. *Global Economic Prospects, January 2023*. Washington, DC: World Bank.

World Bank. 2023b. *World Development Report 2023: Migrants, Refugees, and Societies*. Washington, DC: World Bank.

Part 2
Creative Destruction

Part 1 of this Report highlights the need for middle-income countries to undergo not one but two transitions. In the first, these countries transition from a "1*i*" strategy for accelerating *investment* to a "2*i*" strategy focusing on both *investment* and *infusion* in which a country brings technologies from abroad and diffuses them domestically. Once a country has successfully undertaken this effort, it can switch to a "3*i*" strategy in which it pays greater attention to *innovation*—beginning to not just borrow ideas from the global frontiers of technology but also to push the frontiers outward. Part 2 of this Report provides a diagnostic framework based on advances in Schumpeterian economic theory to examine what hinders and what helps countries engineer shifts in growth strategies (box P2.1). Economic analysis using a Schumpeterian creative destruction framework provides more reliable diagnoses because it draws on the microeconomic foundations of growth. But like most new technologies, it requires greater expertise in assessing the evidence, higher-quality data for informing the analysis, and greater care in interpreting the results.

Underpinning the Schumpeterian framework are three sets of forces: creation, preservation, and destruction (figure P2.1). These unruly forces have to be domesticated. To advance technological progress, the forces of creation need to be amplified, the forces of preservation weakened, and the forces of destruction managed. Policy makers thus need to understand and account for

- *Creation.* Incumbents and entrants compete by creating economic value (see chapter 4). The forces of creation are strengthened by fostering openness in the exchange of goods, services, and ideas. The same forces are weakened by excessive government regulation and macroeconomic uncertainty.
- *Preservation.* Economic, social, and political structures are susceptible to being captured by powerful incumbents (see chapter 5). The forces of preservation must be reined in and prevented from smothering creation. Where institutions are weak, incumbents often capture them to preserve the status quo.
- *Destruction.* The forces of preservation are weakened only when crises arise (see chapter 6). The vital forces of destruction place tremendous pressure on governments to act because a growing economy needs to shed outdated arrangements (in capital, labor, and energy markets) as much as it needs to invent new ones. Where the forces of destruction are constrained by misguided policies, creation struggles and advances slowly.

Box P2.1 Joseph Schumpeter and creative destruction

The concept of *creative destruction* was featured in the early writings of many influential political economists such as Werner Sombart (1863–1941) and Friedrich von Wieser (1851–1926).[a] However, it became the trademark of Joseph A. Schumpeter (1883–1950), an Austrian economist, who widely popularized the term and made it accessible through his book *Capitalism, Socialism and Democracy*. Schumpeter's view was that *creative talents* with vision would create new products and technologies to change the way we live. According to Schumpeter, "Railroads did not emerge because some consumers took the initiative in displaying an effective demand for their service in preference to the services of mail coaches. Nor did consumers exhibit the wish to have electric lamps or rayon stockings, or to travel by motorcar or airplane, or to listen to radios, or to chew gum."[b] What leads to economic growth is the "change" that is ultimately generated by an entrepreneur's desire and leadership. Without change, a society is doomed.

Schumpeterian growth theory provides sharper instruments for diagnosing the economic health of economies because it features

- *Heterogeneous agents*. The theory is premised on differentiation among firms (such as small and large; new and old) and workers (such as unskilled and skilled; rural and urban). It can usefully be extended to distinguish between energy sources (such as renewable and carbon-intensive; reliable and risky).
- *Continuous dynamics*. The theory recognizes the importance of both creation (start-ups, investment, new skills, and innovation) and destruction (firm closures, skill obsolescence, and stranded assets) in the process of structural change and economic development.
- *Institutional inertia*. The theory provides insights into the forces of preservation of societal arrangements and status quo biases in industrial organization and public policy.
- *Constructive crises*. Related to inertia, the theory recognizes that economic and environmental crises present opportunities for improvements; with the right policies, creation can emerge from destruction.

a. Campagnolo and Vivel (2012); Reinert and Reinert (2006).
b. Schumpeter (1942, 73).

The forces of creation, preservation, and destruction appear in each transition of middle-income economic growth—first, in adding *infusion* to *investment,* and, second, in adding *innovation* to the mix.

Chapter 4 focuses on enterprise dynamics to illustrate the forces of creation, chapter 5 on talent to illustrate the forces of preservation, and chapter 6 on energy to highlight how new technologies and climate crises generate both the need and the potential to destroy current arrangements in energy markets. Firms, talent, and energy are closely connected, and their interactions shape the forces of creative destruction.

Figure P2.1 Rebalancing the forces of creation, preservation, and destruction to advance infusion and innovation

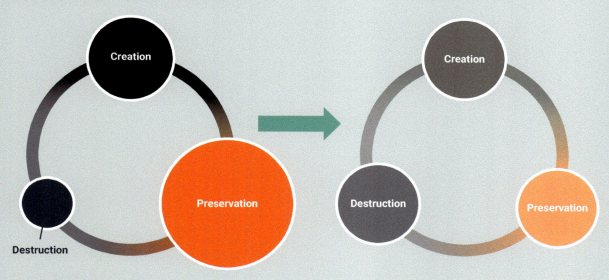

Source: WDR 2024 team.

References

Campagnolo, Gilles, and Christel Vivel. 2012. "Before Schumpeter: Forerunners of the Theory of the Entrepreneur in 1900s German Political Economy—Werner Sombart, Friedrich von Wieser." *European Journal of the History of Economic Thought* 19 (6): 908–43.

Reinert, Hugo, and Erik S. Reinert. 2006. "Creative Destruction in Economics: Nietzsche, Sombart, Schumpeter." In *Friedrich Nietzsche 1844–1900: Economy and Society*, edited by Jürgen G. Backhaus and Wolfgang Drechsler, 55–85. New York: Springer.

Schumpeter, Joseph Alois. 1942. *Capitalism, Socialism and Democracy.* New York: Harper and Brothers.

4 Creation

Key messages

- In an economy, both entrants and incumbents can add value. Entrants bring change in the form of enterprises with new products or production processes, workers with new skills and ideas, or energy sources such as renewables that embody new technologies. Incumbents bring scale—and can compete with entrants in the market to jointly expand a country's technological capabilities—moving the country closer to the global technology frontier.
- In most middle-income countries, too few entrants disrupt because the majority of entrepreneurs start businesses driven by necessity, not business opportunity. And too few incumbents infuse global technologies and know-how. Instead, they abuse their dominance to block entry, resist innovation, and capture political institutions.
- Government policies in middle-income countries are often based on the size of firms rather than their ability to create value. As a result, policies tend to favor small firms and reduce the incentives of firms to grow.
- Governments will need more reliable diagnostics to implement effective policies, including microlevel data on firms, a more comprehensive approach to examining business dynamism, and greater analytical expertise.

Creation: The protagonist of economic growth, where incumbents create value alongside entrants

In the 1960s, the Tata Business Group, a major conglomerate based in India, needed computers for its various businesses, but they were difficult to purchase and import because the government had enacted import restrictions to protect state-owned enterprises (SOEs). To allow foreign hardware to be imported, the government required Indian companies to commit to exporting products or services. This challenge inspired the conglomerate to create a new business, Tata Consultancy Services (TCS). Tapping into talent from its various businesses and India's elite technical institutions, TCS became the first Indian exporter of computing services to the United States. As part of a large conglomerate, TCS could have stifled creativity and misused its import allowance. In practice, however, TCS opened the world's eyes to the high-quality, lower-cost talent that India's software development had to offer. Many entrants took advantage of this opportunity. Among them, Infosys, a company founded by former IBM engineers and financed by their own savings, dramatically increasing the value it created, has become a global leader in information technology consulting (figure 4.1).

Figure 4.1 Both entrants and incumbents create value and reinforce one another's growth through competition in India's computing services industry

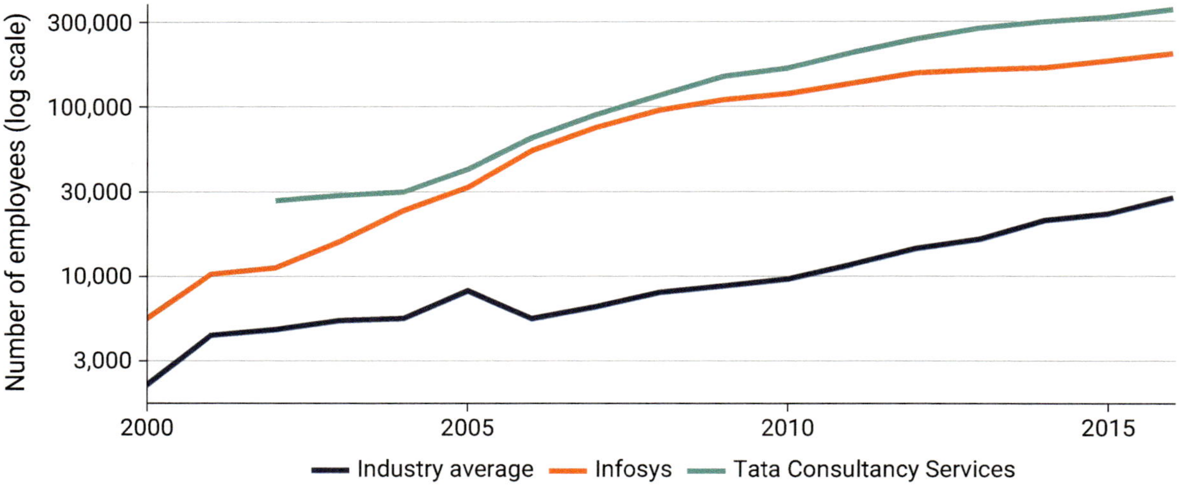

Source: Worldscope (database), Baker Library, Bloomberg Center, Harvard Business School, Boston, https://www.library.hbs.edu/find/databases/worldscope.

Note: The figure reports the number of employees in Infosys and Tata Consultancy Services and the average across firms listed in India's stock exchange in the same two-digit industry (Mean-Industry-India). "Two-digit" refers to NAICS (North American Industry Classification System) (database), US Census Bureau, Suitland, MD, https://www.census.gov/naics/.

The gales of *creative destruction* carry new ideas, products, processes, and practices to the shores of middle-income economies. The term *creative destruction* was popularized by Austrian economist Joseph A. Schumpeter in his book *Capitalism, Socialism and Democracy* (1942). Schumpeter was concerned by the growing concentration of wealth in market economies where dominant incumbents colluded to preserve the status quo. He argued that economic and social improvements arise from new products and technologies introduced by entrepreneurs with talent and vision.

The forces of creation, preservation, and destruction interact to shape the growth of nations through technological advancement. This chapter examines how the forces of creation play out in middle-income countries to create value. Chapters 5 and 6 examine the forces of preservation and destruction. To shed light on the potency of creation in middle-income countries, this chapter examines three questions:

1. *Who creates value?* Schumpeter highlighted that entrants bring change, and incumbents collude to preserve their dominance (figure 4.2, panel a) in the form of enterprises with new products or production processes, workers with new skills and ideas, or energy sources, such as renewables, that embody new technologies. In the process, they expand a country's technology frontier. Interactions among firms, workers, and energy/technology underpin creative destruction (see box P2.1). In the current environment, Schumpeter's view is reflected in the competition between high- and low-carbon energy. Fossil fuels have been the dominant incumbent technology for over 300 years. Technical progress, complementary public and private investment, individual preferences, and powerful interest groups interact to preserve a high-carbon status quo.

Schumpeter's ideas inspired the formal models of creative destruction developed by Philippe Aghion and Peter Howitt, who make a strong case that the entirety of growth stems from entrants and that incumbents assume the primary task of producing goods until they are replaced by these new players (figure 4.2, panel b). Their approach is particularly useful in highlighting the value added by investing in the talents of women and enabling women to seek the most rewarding opportunities.

But must a new entrant always drive creation and displace incumbents? Although Schumpeter and his immediate followers celebrated entrants and downplayed the role of incumbents, Tata Consultancy Services' journey reveals that incumbents can also create value (figure 4.2, panel c). Incumbents bring *scale*, which enables them to invest in upgrading products, hire and reward skilled workers, and effectively use large amounts of capital. They can compete with entrants in the market jointly to expand a country's technological capabilities, advancing the country closer to the global frontier.

The symbiotic view is most applicable to the modern enterprise. Regardless of whether they are entrants or established companies, firms that create value must be able to expand their operations, hire more workers, and displace enterprises that fail to generate additional value. This approach ensures that capital and labor are not held captive by unproductive firms but are utilized more efficiently by growing enterprises. In fact, 50–70 percent of productivity growth stems from successful resource reallocation among firms—whether incumbents or entrants.[1]

2. *Are entrants and incumbents creating value in middle-income countries?* Too few entrants disrupt, and too few incumbents infuse global technologies and know-how. The majority of entrepreneurs start businesses driven by necessity, not business opportunity. Incumbents that create value are unable to expand, limiting their potential for infusing technologies. Dominant incumbents can be vanguards for infusing global technologies and exporting globally. But, too often, they abuse their dominance to capture political institutions.

3. *Are middle-income country governments strengthening the forces of creation?* Governments often use outdated rules of

Figure 4.2 The interactions between entrants and incumbents set the pace of creative destruction

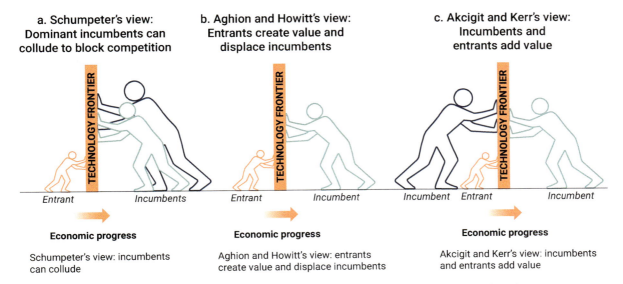

Source: WDR 2024 team based on Schumpeter (1942); Aghion and Howitt (1992); Akcigit and Kerr (2018).

thumb to regulate and lack the information and capabilities needed to identify key constraints impeding the growth of firms. Over the last three decades, economists have developed modern techniques to provide calibrated assessments of what is enabling or suppressing the growth of firms. These techniques include better measurement of business dynamics that includes market concentration, markups, productivity dispersion, firm entry and exit rates, and job reallocation.

This chapter examines the forces of creation from the perspective of firms with an emphasis on the process in middle-income countries. A broader treatment that includes talent and energy sources appears in part 3 of this Report.

Creative destruction: Three decades of increasingly refined analysis

A first look: Entrants create value

When Canadian economist Peter Howitt visited the Massachusetts Institute of Technology (MIT) in the summer of 1987, he crossed paths with Philippe Aghion, an assistant professor at MIT. Their collaboration gave birth to the formal theory of creative destruction, and their paper "A Model of Growth through Creative Destruction," published in *Econometrica* in 1992, became one of the most influential papers in economics.[2] Their main insight was that economies expand organically through innovation driven by *new entrants*. Aghion and Howitt attributed innovation and growth exclusively to newcomers (figure 4.3).

Such models of creative destruction, that is, quality ladder models, depict a hierarchical structure with multiple rungs in which each innovation adds a new rung to the ladder and elevates the prospects for all future producers—a phenomenon known as *intertemporal spillovers*. This hierarchy suggests that there may be *underinvestment* in innovation because innovators often fail to consider the height of each rung, which

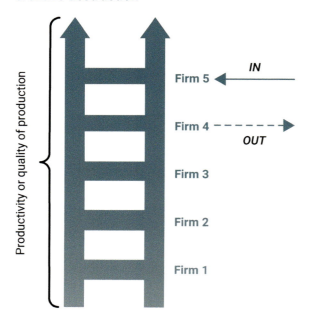

Figure 4.3 Entrants drive growth: Insights from Aghion and Howitt's seminal paper on creative destruction

Source: WDR 2024 team.
Note: The figure depicts a quality ladder based on the Aghion-Howitt model of creative destruction. *IN* represents a new firm entering the market and *OUT* represents a firm exiting the market. Each innovation adds a new rung to the ladder and elevates the prospects for all future producers. This hierarchy suggests that there may be underinvestment in innovation because innovators often fail to consider the height of each rung, which determines the long-term benefits of their creative endeavors for society. On the other hand, there may be an overinvestment in entry. Entrants primarily focus on displacing incumbents, so more entry is associated with shorter durations of monopoly for incumbents, discouraging innovations by future entrants.

determines the long-term benefits of their creative endeavors for society. On the other hand, there may be an *overinvestment* in entry. Entrants primarily focus on displacing incumbents, and so more entry is associated with shorter durations of monopoly for incumbents, discouraging innovations by future entrants. This motive—called "business stealing"—carries the risk that a society could end up *overinvesting* in research and development (R&D) and creating too much entry. Whether equilibrium results in an excess or deficiency of R&D depends on the varying magnitudes of spillovers and business stealing, which can differ significantly from one sector to another and from one country to another. This novel framework has opened the door to a more nuanced and realistic discourse on innovation policy.

A recent view: Incumbents also create value

Schumpeter's ideas, as well as the framework presented in Aghion and Howitt's seminal 1992 paper, focused predominantly on entrants and small businesses, downplaying the role of incumbents (often larger firms) in fostering infusion and innovation. In fact, the theory of creative destruction highlights an important tension between the incumbent currently in production and the new entrant that endeavors to replace the incumbent with a superior product or technology.

In 2004, Tor Klette and Sam Kortum refined the framework by reimagining each firm as a conglomerate of production units in different sectors.[3] Within this framework, firms are able to expand their products or services into new markets and compete with other incumbents, but not scale up their existing products or services. In essence, this framework indicated that, within each narrow sector, all innovations originate from external sources and never from incumbents within the production unit.

In 2018, Ufuk Akcigit and William Kerr further advanced the framework to enable a more accurate description of innovation and growth.[4] In their framework, incumbents not only expand into new markets through external R&D, but also enhance their existing products through internal R&D without directly displacing other producers. In fact, upon venturing into new markets, many established incumbents allocate a significant portion of their resources to refining and elevating their current products and technologies. The significant insight is that creative destruction can be instigated not only by entrants but also by incumbents. Moreover, not every innovation introduced by incumbents inevitably results in creative destruction through the dismantling of others in their "ecosystem" (figure 4.4).

The United States and Germany are contrasting cases of creative destruction. In Germany,

Figure 4.4 Entrants and incumbents drive growth through turnover and upgrading: Insights from Akcigit and Kerr's refined approach to creative destruction

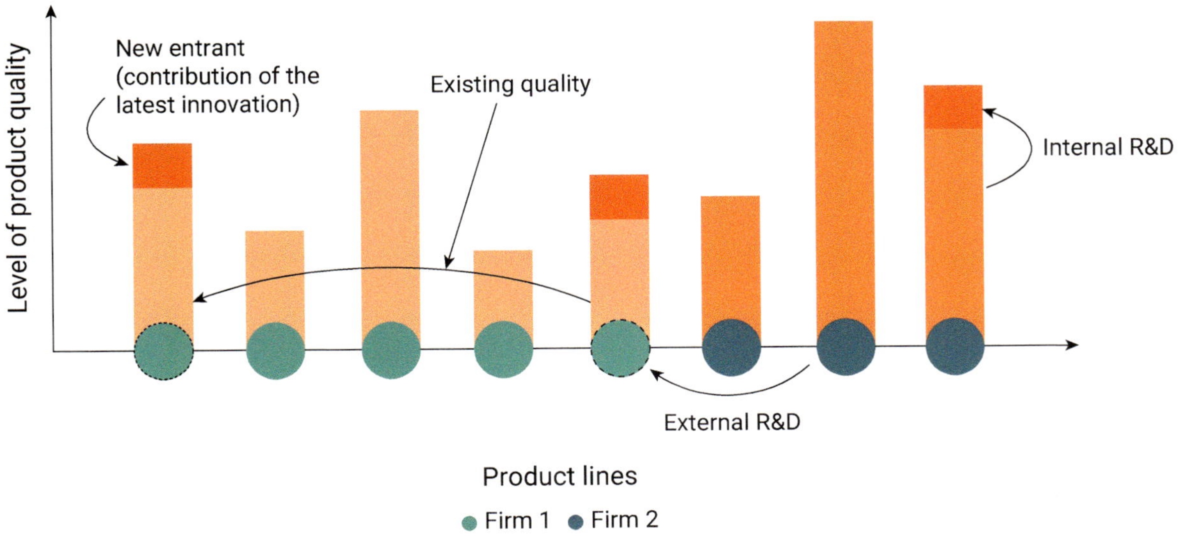

Source: Akcigit and Kerr 2018.
Note: R&D = research and development.

companies established before 1950 constitute a substantial 70 percent of publicly traded companies—a figure that diverges markedly from that for the United States, where the equivalent proportion is approximately 50 percent. Furthermore, although the annual rate of new firm creation is about 8 percent in the United States, it is 3 percent in Germany. Despite these pronounced disparities in terms of incumbent longevity and the pace of firm entry, there is a striking symmetry in the number of patents per capita between the two economies. This convergence in patent output underscores a noteworthy distinction: innovation in Germany is primarily championed by long-standing incumbents, whereas in the United States it is shouldered to a greater extent by emerging young entrants (figure 4.5).

A more nuanced view of incumbents: Incumbents' power can drive or suppress creation

The turn of the twentieth century witnessed a rapid transformation in the typical manufacturing enterprise in the United States. Characterized until the early 1900s by single-unit firms with one or a small number of owners, the modern multiunit enterprise, administered by salaried middle and top managers overseeing complex layers of production, became the typical business model by World War I. Recordkeeping, accounting, and inventory control were all tasks required by the "visible hand" managing a firm.[5]

This transformation of business proved to be fertile ground for the emergence of what became a powerhouse of corporate innovation, the Computing-Tabulating-Recording-Company, later IBM. In 1939, when William Hewlett and David Packard created their company in a rented garage in Palo Alto, California, IBM was already a well-established company with more than 10,000 employees. Herman Hollerith, founder of one of the companies consolidated into IBM in 1911, could not anticipate that his invention, the electromechanical tabulation of punched card data, would become the backbone of a computer hardware and software company.

Figure 4.5 Contrasting examples of innovation: Growth is driven by entrants in the United States and by incumbents in Germany

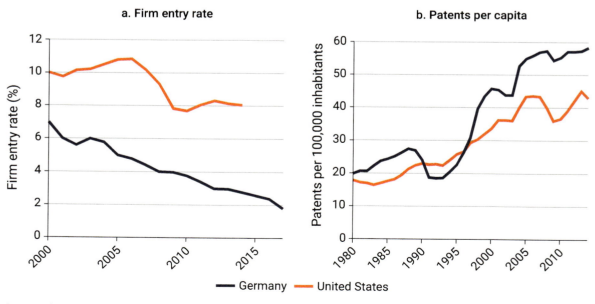

Source: Akcigit et al. 2024.

Similarly, Hewlett and Packard did not envision that their frequency oscillator would pave the way for their small firm to become a leading manufacturer of personal computers that would compete with a giant like IBM. Yet both companies found themselves competing against each other for decades. It was only later that many others, such as Dell and Microsoft, entered the market to compete.

On the surface, the forces of creation are more apparent than the forces of destruction in the Schumpeterian view of forces of innovation. In the US business services industry, as HP, Dell, Microsoft, and Oracle entered various branches of the hardware, software, and computing services markets, the pace of growth of IBM (as the incumbent) slowed—but not to the level of shutting down the company (figure 4.6). Destruction still occurs within firms as they replace older products and tap into newer markets.

But dominant firms can also use their incumbency advantage to block entry and resist innovation. They can collude, with the most significant players coordinating price-setting to outbid smaller competitors, while avoiding price wars against one another. For example, in 2013 the US Department of Justice uncovered a decade-long cartel of Japanese auto part makers conspiring against the United States car industry (figure 4.7). Mitsuba Corporation, a prominent cartel member, increased its sales relative to the average performance of publicly listed companies in the same industry. However, this growth was not fueled by innovation but rather by suppressing competition, partly reflected in the decline in the number of public firms in the same industry.

When incumbents respond to competition by upgrading technologies and business practices either to defend existing market positions or to tap into newer ones, they drive progress, as in the United States (box 4.1). When incumbents resist competition by enacting barriers to entry, it not only stalls infusion and innovation but also can entirely prevent them.

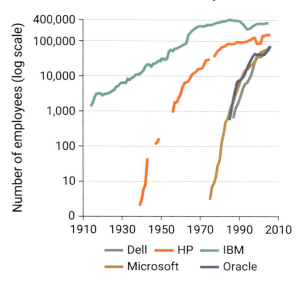

Figure 4.6 **Entrants and incumbents can reinforce one another's growth: The case of the US business services industry**

Source: Luttmer 2011.

Note: The figure reports the number of employees for a selected group of US business services firms: Dell, Hewlett Packard (HP), IBM, Microsoft, and Oracle.

In middle-income countries, too few small entrants disrupt, and too few large incumbents innovate or infuse global technologies

Although large incumbent firms can spur as well as block the forces of creation, large incumbents do not capture the broader economic landscape in middle-income countries. Most establishments are microenterprises that neither grow nor exit, and therefore they do not contribute to growth in productivity. Furthermore, many medium and large firms that have the potential to leverage the incumbency advantage to lead infusion and innovation often achieve scale by benefiting from distortions rather than from merit (see next section for that discussion).

"Flat and stay" and "up or out" describe entrepreneurial dynamics. One reason for the

Figure 4.7 A cartelized industry suppresses innovation and dynamism: Evidence from the Japanese auto parts sector

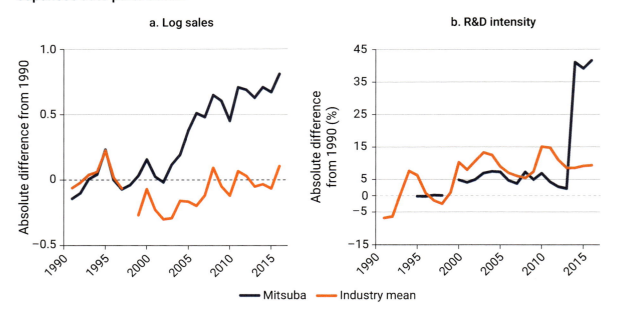

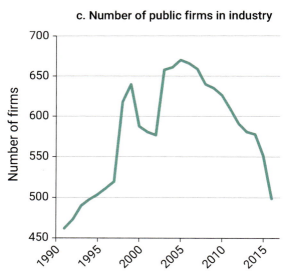

Source: WDR 2024 team based on Worldscope (database), Baker Library, Bloomberg Center, Harvard Business School, Boston, https://www.library.hbs.edu/find/databases/worldscope.

Note: The figure reports a series of sales (panel a) and shares of research and development (R&D) expenditures relative to total investment (panel b) for Mitsuba Corporation and the average across listed firms in Japan's stock exchange within the same two-digit industry. Panel c shows the number of listed companies in Japan's stock exchange in the same two-digit industry. Sales are presented in logarithms and reported as a difference from their value in 1990, the first year in the sample. The share of R&D expenditures to total investment, R&D intensity, is also reported as a difference from the share in 1990. "Two-digit" refers to NAICS (North American Industry Classification System) (database), US Census Bureau, Suitland, MD, https://www.census.gov/naics/.

Box 4.1 Vibrant corporate R&D, connected places, mobile people, and successful markets for patents: How the United States nurtured an innovation ecosystem

The US economy has fostered innovation for centuries, inspiring numerous inventors to generate brilliant ideas that have, subsequently, been harnessed by businesses to create consumer products or production technologies that have had a widespread impact. Four dimensions have been important:

- *Who "creates" has shifted from small, independent inventors to corporate research and development (R&D) and innovation.* Over the last 150 years, there has been a remarkable transition from the realm of "garage inventors" to the corporate R&D facilities of modern corporations (figure B4.1.1). The transition has coincided with the growing sophistication of the US economy.
- *Connected places are more inventive.* Connectivity enhances the market size for innovation and the flow of knowledge. Inventive activity in the early nineteenth century accelerated in US locations that were near navigable waterways and had developed railroads.[a]
- *The migration of people is critical to innovation.* Technology sectors in the United States with a higher concentration of immigrant inventors between 1880 and 1940 experienced accelerated growth from 1940 to 2000.[b] Furthermore, immigrant inventors exhibited greater productivity throughout their careers than their native-born counterparts. Unfortunately, despite their heightened productivity, immigrant innovators found that their earnings were much lower.

Figure B4.1.1 The number of patents filed by corporations with the US Patent and Trademark Office has skyrocketed since 1880

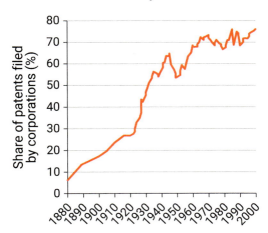

Source: Akcigit, Grigsby, and Nicholas 2017b.

(Box continues next page)

CREATION | 93

Box 4.1 Vibrant corporate R&D, connected places, mobile people, and successful markets for patents: How the United States nurtured an innovation ecosystem *(continued)*

- *The secondary market for innovations (such as patent resale or licensing) is as important as innovation itself.* This secondary market has played an outsize role in the United States. Between 1870 and 1910, inventors increasingly sought the services of the more than 500 specialized registered patent agents nationwide to navigate the intricacies of patent-related transactions. For example, Edward Van Winkle, a mechanical engineer who pursued a law degree via correspondence courses, possessed the ideal skill set to provide clients on both sides of the market with expert advice on the legal and technical aspects of inventions. He established a network of businessmen, inventors, and fellow lawyers to broker patent deals between buyers and sellers.[c]

a. For waterways, see Sokoloff (1988); for railroads, see Donaldson and Hornbeck (2016) and Perlman (2015).
b. Akcigit, Grigsby, and Nicholas (2017a).
c. For historical markets for technologies, see Lamoreaux and Sokoloff (2002). For more contemporary markets, see Akcigit, Celik, and Greenwood (2016).

lack of business dynamism in the economies of middle-income countries can be traced to the typical life cycle of a firm's growth (figure 4.8, panel a). In the United States, a celebrated feature of the economy is the selectivity of its markets. Start-ups and young businesses are confronted by pressure to move up or out. The average young US firm grows by a factor of 7 by age 40, assuming it is still in business. Failing entrepreneurs either move up to newer ventures, or out to find wage-earning opportunities by means of the rising labor demand in flourishing firms. By contrast, in middle-income countries flat and stay is a more accurate description of entrepreneurial dynamics. The growth rates of firms in India, Mexico, and Peru are far lower than those of firms in the United States, with firms expanding by less than a factor of 3 (figure 4.8, panel a). Conversely, when firms with growth potential lack dynamism, they fall short of displacing unproductive small firms from the market. This absence of creative destruction results in a stark contrast: although the share of small firms with at most four workers declines by 60 percent by the age of 25 in the United States, the decrease is only about 10 percent in India (figure 4.8, panel b). Consequently, the Indian economy lacks the mechanism for effective selection among firms, hindering the reallocation of resources to more productive users.

The life cycle dynamics of firms exhibits a similar flatness when expanding the sample to include a few East European and East Asian economies (figure 4.8, panel a). Serbia and Malaysia seem to have stabilized at a notably lower level of life cycle growth than the United States, comparable with the dynamics of the other middle-income economies in the figure. Viet Nam seems to be at a critical point at which it either continues its promising trend and accompanies a similar degree of dynamism as observed in the United States, or it succumbs to the lackluster performance characteristic of the middle-income trap.

The weakness of firm dynamics in middle-income countries translates into stark differences in the distribution of firms across sizes (figure 4.9).

Figure 4.8 In middle-income countries, the growth rate of firms across their life cycles is much lower than in the United States

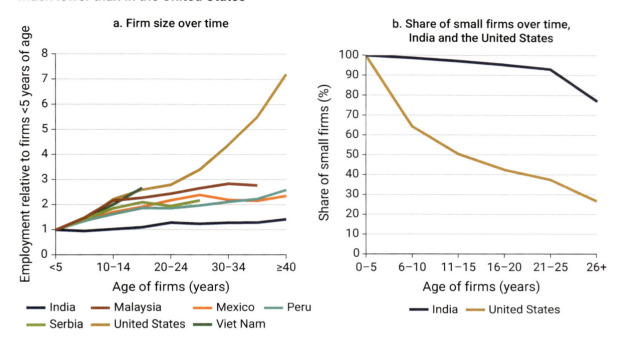

Sources: Panel a: India, Mexico, and the United States: Hsieh and Klenow 2014; Peru: World Bank 2015; Malaysia: de Nicola and Timmis, forthcoming; Serbia and Viet Nam: World Bank 2024b. Panel b: Akcigit, Alp, and Peters 2021.

Note: Panel a illustrates the average employment across a cohort of firms of different ages in the cross-section of firms. The number of employees serves as a proxy for firm size. The vertical axis reports the average employment of each cohort relative to the average employment across firms under five years of age.

In the United States, microenterprises are the dominant form of production in terms of share of firms, but firms are distributed more uniformly across the size spectrum. Start-ups enter small and proceed to grow up or get out, which explains the prominence of medium and large firms. In India, Mexico, and Peru, the flat and stay behavior translates into a market in which more than 80 percent of firms employ fewer than five workers each.

Informal establishments account for most of the microenterprises in the firm size distribution in India, Mexico, and many other countries.[6] Although informal entrepreneurs may have had greater success at growing and becoming formal if the costs of business entry were lower, attempts to reduce the costs of business entry for firms in developing countries have had modest results at best.[7] Instead, the large informal sectors in many middle-income countries reflect a misallocation in jobs whereby distortions in firm growth reduce wages and wage-earning opportunities in the formal sector. Such distortions misallocate resources from their best use and discourage incentives to adopt and innovate technologies. This vicious cycle, in turn, reduces higher-paying formal wage jobs and further fuels informality.

Middle-income countries are not benefiting from technological disruption by their smaller firms. This outcome challenges the commonly perceived notion that micro- and small enterprises are the drivers of job creation and economic dynamism. That misconception is compounded by the fact that start-ups are primarily small. However, age, not size, should be the measure used to assess dynamism. In fact, in the United States small firms are the net destroyers of jobs, except for start-ups

Figure 4.9 Microenterprises dominate firm size distributions in India, Mexico, and Peru

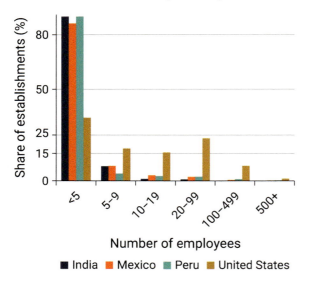

Sources: India: Sixth Economic Census 2013–14 (dashboard), National Data Archive, Ministry of Statistics and Programme Implementation, New Delhi, https://microdata.gov.in/nada43/index.php/catalog/47; Mexico: Iacovone et al. (2022), based on tabulations from Economic Censuses 2019 (dashboard), Instituto Nacional de Estadística y Geografía (National Institute of Statistics and Geography Mexico), Aguascalientes, Mexico, https://en.www.inegi.org.mx/programas/ce/2019/; Peru: IV Censo Nacional Económico 2008 (dashboard), Instituto Nacional de Estadística e Informática, Lima, Peru, http://censos1.inei.gob.pe/cenec2008/redatam_inei/; United States: 2019 data from BDS (Business Dynamics Statistics) (dashboard), US Census Bureau, Suitland, MD, https://www.census.gov/programs-surveys/bds.html.

Note: The figure reports the share of establishments of various size classes. Shares for India and the United States are for the manufacturing sector only.

younger than a year—they are not the net creators (figure 4.10).

How governments stifle firms' incentives to grow, infuse global technologies, and innovate

Most firms in middle-income countries are small, do not grow, and do not exit the economy. This lackluster performance is due, in large part, to government policies that interfere with the forces of creative destruction. Governments often use outdated rules of thumb to identify who creates value, and they lack the information and capabilities to identify key constraints to the growth of productive firms. When size is used to target larger firms to advance social objectives, the incentives to grow are dampened. As a consequence, an economy produces far below its potential.

Adopting and developing technologies are costly endeavors, and so entrepreneurs will incur these costs only if rewarded with a sufficient rate of return. When governments effectively lower the rate of return to adopting and developing technologies, they undermine the whole economy's production possibilities relative to the potential frontier, locally and globally.

Screening firms by size—not by their ability to create value—often ends up being misguided. Talented entrepreneurs are not able to attract more capital and labor, jobs shift from high-productivity firms to low-productivity ones, and value creation declines. Compounding this effect is the more consequential one of reduced upgrading, which lowers the number of firms that have the ability to grow.

Outdated rules of thumb stifle progress

The goals of protecting small businesses and preventing the concentration of economic power have motivated many countries to implement policies based on firm size (size-dependent policies). By using size to screen which firms should be protected and which firms should be penalized, policy makers end up taxing firms that create value (box 4.2). A firm that creates value attracts capital and workers—it grows in size. Thus a policy that screens by size is effectively a policy that curtails productivity and value creation. Such policies keep productive firms smaller and less productive firms larger than they should be based on their technical capabilities.

An example is the Small-Scale Reservation Laws implemented in India between the 1960s and early 2000s. The laws stipulated that most manufactured goods could be produced only by small-scale

Figure 4.10 Young firms—not small firms—create the most jobs (net) in the United States

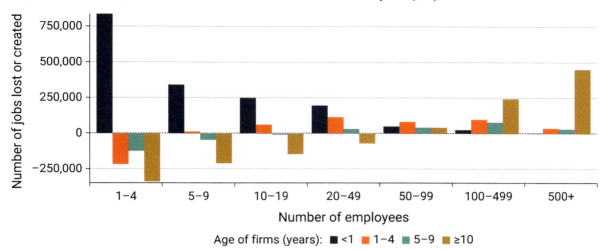

Source: 2019 data from Business Employment Dynamics (dashboard), Bureau of Labor Statistics, United States Department of Labor, Washington, DC, https://www.bls.gov/bdm/business-employment-dynamics-data-by-age-and-size.htm.
Note: The figure reports the net number of jobs created by firms of different sizes and ages in the United States.

Box 4.2 Examples of size-dependent policies

In some countries, smaller firms below a specific size are exempt from regulations or taxation. In other countries, once the firm exceeds a specified size threshold, it faces higher taxes and more regulations. In extreme versions, such policies restrict the production of certain items to firms of a given size.

Many other policies and market frictions may also result in a size-dependent distortion based on the abilities of firms of different sizes, productivity levels, and internal wealth to circumvent such policies. For example, stringent collateral requirements for business loans disproportionately affect young, productive firms with strong borrowing needs but little history of retaining enough earnings to accumulate internal wealth.

Some examples of explicit size-dependent policies in various middle- and high-income countries follow. Although individual policies like these, in isolation, may have only a minor effect on the full extent of misallocation and lack of innovation in middle-income economies, explicit size-dependent policies may interact with implicit size-dependent distortions and reinforce one another. For example, a regulation that increases the fixed and variable costs of labor for firms with 50 or more workers (an explicit size-dependent distortion) may coexist with a financial market that imposes tighter credit standards on young businesses and for loans aimed at financing intangible capital investments such as research and development (an implicit size-dependent distortion). The overall degree

(Box continues next page)

Box 4.2 Examples of size-dependent policies *(continued)*

of resource misallocation and underinvestment in innovation is the outcome of multiple distortions interacting and reinforcing one another.

Mexico. Mexico's income tax law created REPECO (Régimen de Pequeños Contribuyentes), a special provision for small businesses based on their level of sales. For ordinary firms whose sales exceed the threshold, the tax on capital income amounts to 38 percent (28 percent for the government and 10 percent for profit-sharing with employees). Firms with annual sales below US$163,000 (Mex$2 million) do not have to pay the capital tax, but instead pay a 2 percent sales tax, with 7.5 percent of the 2 percent sales tax directed to the profit-sharing scheme. Once the sales of a REPECO firm exceed the threshold, it cannot become a REPECO firm again.[a]

Türkiye. Türkiye's labor and safety laws impose several regulations that apply to firms above certain size thresholds. Firms employing more than 50 workers must establish a health and safety board; set up a health unit and hire physicians and other health staff; and employ disabled workers and formerly convicted workers.[b]

India. Small-Scale Reservation Laws in India are the poster child of a size-dependent policy that fosters misallocation and discourages innovation.[c] Since 1960, the government of India has "reserved" the production of many manufactured goods for small-scale industries only. The definition of a *small-scale industry* is based on an industry's cumulative investment in plant and machinery. Effectively, all establishments with plant and machinery below a specific limit have been considered small and allowed to produce the reserved goods. Although the number of products falling into the reserved category increased steadily between 1960 and 2002, the policy has been progressively dismantled, with only 20 products remaining under the reservation law in 2010.

Peru. Various labor laws in Peru are size-dependent. For example, a profit-sharing agreement applies to firms with more than 21 salaried workers. The fraction of profits to be distributed ranges from 10 percent in manufacturing to 8 percent in mining, retail, wholesale, and restaurants. Workers can join a firm-specific union of at least 20 members, exposing firms beyond this size to the unionization of their workforce. And firms exceeding 20 employees must set up a health and safety committee.[d]

Portugal. The average size of firms in Portugal fell sharply between the mid-1980s and mid-2000s. Size-dependent policies may have contributed to such a dramatic shift in the production structure.[e] Notably, firms with less than 50 workers are allowed to pay up to 50 percent less than the minimum wage, are subsidized in hiring young workers, and receive support for worker hiring. Firms with more than 50 workers must maintain a worker health protection system.

Italy. Italy's Employment Protection Legislation imposes a disproportionately higher cost on firms employing more than 15 workers to fire workers. Firms with fewer than 15 workers must pay a dismissal cost equivalent to between 2.5 and 6 months of salary in cases of unjustified firing. Firms with more than 15 workers must compensate workers for forgone wages between the time of dismissal and the court's sentence. Dismissal trials can last up to five years, and there is no upper limit on the amount of forgone wages.[f]

(Box continues next page)

Box 4.2 Examples of size-dependent policies *(continued)*

France. Labor laws in France apply special provisions to firms with more than 10, 11, 20, or 50 employees.[g] In particular, as a firm reaches 50 employees, a committee for hygiene, safety, and work conditions must be formed and trained; a works council must be formed and meet at least every other month; and a higher payroll tax rate, which goes from 0.9 percent to 1.5 percent, subsidizes worker training. In addition, if a firm fires more than nine workers for "economic reasons," it must follow a special legal process, which increases dismissal costs and creates legal uncertainty for the firm.

Republic of Korea. When a firm is classified as a small or medium enterprise (SME), it can receive about 160 benefits from the SME support policy. Benefits include differential corporate tax rates, tax relief benefits, and government-guaranteed loans for SMEs.[h]

a. Sánchez-Vela and Valero-Gil (2011).
b. Akcigit et al. (2023).
c. García-Santana and Pijoan-Mas (2014).
d. Dabla-Norris et al. (2018).
e. Braguinsky, Branstetter, and Regateiro (2011).
f. Schivardi and Torrini (2004).
g. Gourio and Roys (2014).
h. Jung and Jung (2022).

---

plants, defined as those whose capital stock did not exceed a government-set threshold.[8] This policy was complemented by several additional benefits for small-scale enterprises, such as the Private Sector Lending Program, in effect until the 1990s, which stipulated that commercial banks had to allocate up to 40 percent of their private credit at subsidized rates to small firms. In Peru, the constitution and legislation require firms with more than 21 workers to distribute a portion of their before-tax profits to their formal labor force.[9] And, in France, firms with more than 50 workers pay a higher payroll tax rate and must comply with additional regulations.[10] Such programs create perverse incentives in terms of resource allocation and innovation. They also contribute to increased informality in developing countries.[11]

Turnover taxes that tax intermediate and capital goods and corporate taxes, even when set at uniform rates, are also examples of size-dependent policies in the way in which they are enforced. Larger firms are more likely to face tax enforcement in low- and middle-income countries, whereas this practice is almost absent in advanced economies.[12]

In terms of credit, when contract enforcement is weak and secured transactions and bankruptcy laws are poorly designed and enforced, banks may demand higher interest rates, impose more stringent lending standards, and tighten their collateral requirements.[13] Some firms may have more collateral to pledge and thus may not be affected by the financial requirements. Others may have accumulated enough internal liquid funds to cope with the pressing needs of working and physical capital without financial intermediation. However, for many other firms credit is necessary. Tighter collateral constraints hamper these firms' abilities to scale up to the level merited by their capabilities. It is usually young entrepreneurs with innovative business ideas but without collateral they can pledge who are most negatively affected (box 4.3).[14]

Box 4.3 The productivity effects of credit misallocation and capital market underdevelopment

A concerning feature of credit markets is the misallocation of credit away from the most productive businesses in middle-income economies. More productive firms in these countries receive lower amounts of debt and equity financing than merited by their technical efficiency, a property that is less prevalent in high-income countries (figure B4.3.1). In Mexico, for example, access to finance across firms favors the least productive over the most productive firms.[a]

Another feature of developing economies is the underdevelopment of capital markets. Unlike bank-provided credit, debt and equity financing are associated with productive investments by firms, leading to expansions in infusion, innovation, and physical capital.[b] By excessively relying on banks for financial intermediation, middle-income countries are limiting their capable firms to access finance.

Figure B4.3.1 Productivity-dependent financial distortions, by GDP per capita

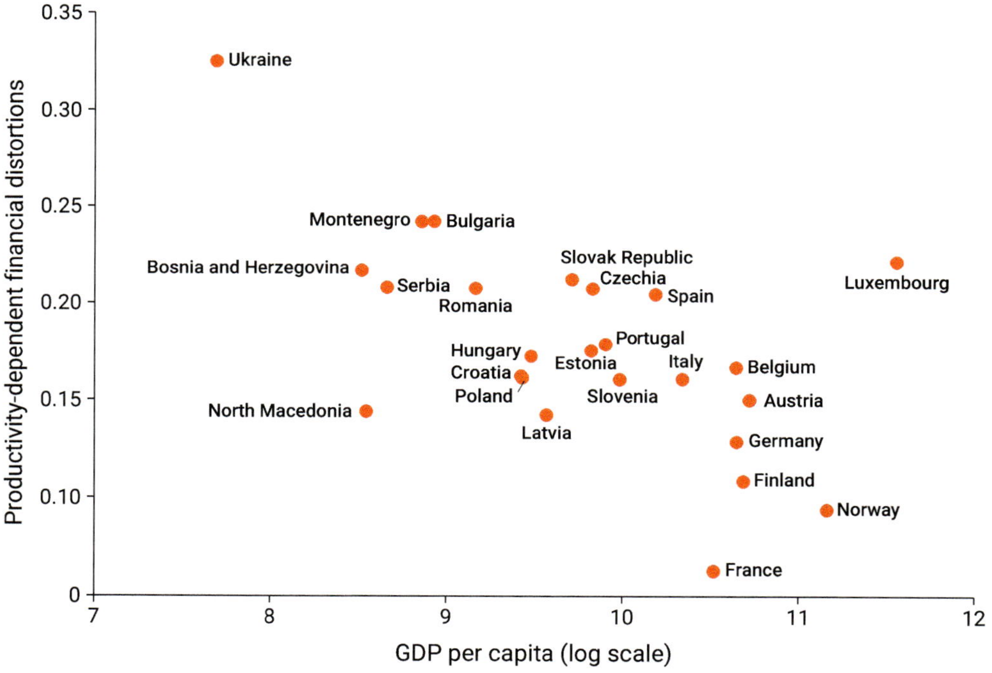

Source: Cusolito et al., forthcoming.

Note: The figure reports the estimate of a regression coefficient between the logarithm of idiosyncratic financial distortions and the logarithm of idiosyncratic physical productivity across firms, both computed as in Whited and Zhao (2021). A high value of the coefficient means that more productive firms face higher distortions in financial markets than less productive ones. Thus, there is a weaker relationship between a firm's productivity and its debt and equity financing compared with efficient allocation. GDP = gross domestic product.

(Box continues next page)

Box 4.3 The productivity effects of credit misallocation and capital market underdevelopment *(continued)*

Episodes of capital account liberalization, opening middle-income countries' economies to foreign capital financing, can reduce the misallocation of capital.[c] For example, India's capital market liberalization contributed to a more efficient allocation of resources across firms over the last 20 years.

a. Iacovone et al. (2022).
b. Didier et al. (2020).
c. Bau and Matray (2023).

Figure 4.11 Productivity-dependent distortions are more severe in low- and middle-income countries

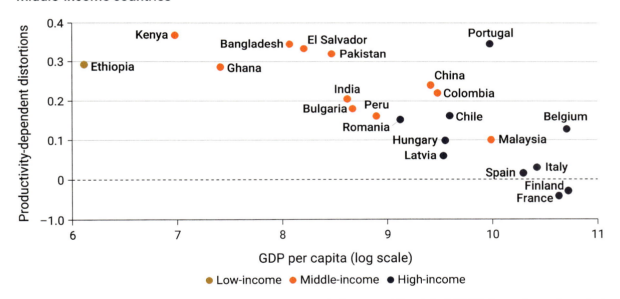

Sources: Productivity-dependent distortions: WDR 2024 team calculations and Fattal Jaef (2022). Gross domestic product (GDP) per capita: PWT (Penn World Table) (database version 9.0), Groningen Growth and Development Centre, Faculty of Economics and Business, University of Groningen, Groningen, the Netherlands, https://www.rug.nl/ggdc/productivity/pwt/pwt-releases/pwt9.0?lang=en.

Note: The figure reports the estimates of a regression coefficient between the logarithm of idiosyncratic distortions and the logarithm of idiosyncratic physical productivity across firms, both computed as in Hsieh and Klenow (2009). The corresponding estimate for the United States is subtracted from each country's estimate so that productivity-dependent distortions are reported relative to the level observed in the United States. A high value for this elasticity means that a productive firm confronts higher distortions than less productive ones, and thus there is a weaker relationship between firm productivity and firm size than the output-maximizing allocation would require.

More broadly, these rules of thumb impose a hefty tax on productive firms, a practice known as "taxing the good" (figure 4.11). By discouraging the expansion and growth of firms, these policies also discourage the adoption of modern management practices, a necessary condition for improving efficiency and adopting technologies.[15] Alfred D. Chandler, Jr., a renowned economic historian,

CREATION | 101

Figure 4.12 Management practices are worse in economies with more policy distortions

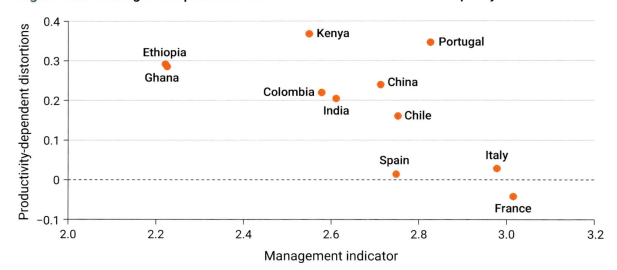

Sources: Productivity-dependent distortions: Fattal Jaef 2022; management indicator: WMS (World Management Survey) (dashboard), London School of Economics, London, https://worldmanagementsurvey.org (see Bloom and Van Reenen 2007).
Note: Productivity-dependent distortions refer to policy distortions related to firm size that can discourage innovation and technology adoption. The figure reports, on the y-axis, the estimates of a regression coefficient between the logarithm of idiosyncratic distortions and the logarithm of idiosyncratic productivity of the firms. The idiosyncratic distortion and the physical productivity are computed as in Hsieh and Klenow (2009). On the x-axis, the figure reports the management indicator across firms, as provided in the World Management Survey.

suggested that one of the critical transformations in the US economy between the mid-1880s and World War I was the replacement of the traditional family enterprise with the modern multiunit enterprise managed by a complex layer of top- and middle-management structures.[16]

Countries with a higher quality of management practices—as measured by the World Management Surveys—have lower productivity-dependent distortions (figure 4.12).[17] In the United States, a firm's managerial capabilities are central to its ability to grow and innovate. However, in most middle-income countries, managerial capabilities of firms are underdeveloped.[18] The exceptions are a handful of countries that have enjoyed sustained growth accelerations.

Benefits extended to state-owned enterprises hurt private enterprise

When countries are early in their development journey, the state favors its SOEs for undertaking ventures in the market. However, these preferences hurt private enterprise. Although SOEs benefit from lower costs of labor and capital, this benefit increases the cost of production for their private counterparts, which are often more productive. Benefits extended to SOEs not only misallocate resources away from more productive firms but also discourage the private sector from investing in costly initiatives (such as R&D) to become more innovative or produce more innovative goods or services.[19] SOEs in manufacturing and contestable service industries have become a source of resource misallocation.[20]

In the critical area of energy supply, electricity continues to be delivered primarily by SOEs. In 2020, 60 percent of 125 low- and middle-income countries still relied on a public distribution utility.[21] The role of SOEs in fossil fuel power investment increased from 43 percent to 50 percent from 2015 to 2019, notably due to the expansion of coal plants in India and South Africa and gas plants in the Middle East and North Africa.

Preferences for incumbents block progress

Large enterprises are important drivers of innovation and are able to imitate at scale. However, weak institutions may encourage these firms to protect their profitability by deterring competition rather than innovating their way out of competition. A firm's market power and incentives to abuse its dominance are shaped by features of the market, government interventions, and its strategic behavior.

The problem is not the market power of some firms per se, but the exercise of dominance that undermines effective competition, dampening innovation, harming consumers, and driving equally efficient competitors out of the market (table 4.1). Market leaders can also acquire smaller competitors to wind down the operations of potential competitors, such as in the pharmaceutical industry.[22] Market power becomes problematic under the following conditions:[23]

- *Market power is not the result of innovation.* For example, politically connected firms in Italy's local markets changed their behavior as they grew. Rather than innovating and competing with other firms, they brought local politicians onto their payroll.[24] At the same time, their innovation (measured in terms of numbers of patents) began to decline.

- *Market power is sustained over time by government interventions that protect a firm or provide it with specific advantages.* In Mexico, for example, although the telecommunications sector was open to competition in 1995 after 20 years of public monopoly, followed by five years of private monopoly,[25] it was not until 2014 that the government imposed the first obligations on Telmex and Telcel as operators with significant market power.[26] The inability of the sector regulator and the competition authority to impose such conditions in previous years made its owner, Carlos Slim, the richest man in the world between 2011 and 2013, according to *Forbes* magazine. Similarly, overly long concession contracts for limestone and restrictive standards for cement helped Aliko Dangote become the richest man in Africa.[27]

- *Market power is sustained over time by illegal strategic behavior,* such as when dominant firms exclude their rivals from the market or when a few firms agree to collude. Anticompetitive practices that close entry and place competitors at a disadvantage are common in digital platform markets.[28]

If large incumbent firms are not disciplined by means of regulations that promote competition or antitrust rules, firms with market power are more prone to abusive practices—such as predatory pricing, price squeezing, or denial to supply

Table 4.1 Examples of possible effects of market power on development outcomes

DEVELOPMENT OUTCOMES	PROS	CONS
Productivity	Mergers and acquisitions can lead to more efficiency.	Conglomerates can cross-subsidize unproductive firms, crowding out more productive competitors.
Consumer welfare	More efficient structures can lead to lower costs and therefore lower prices.	It is easier to form cartels when fewer players are in the market.
Innovation	Some firms acquire market power because they innovate and push the frontier.	There are fewer incentives to innovate, and firm entry is low.
Jobs	The demand for highly skilled workers grows.	Wages for lower-skilled workers are depressed, while the most talented workers are captured.

Source: World Bank 2024a.

other competitors—contributing to a decrease in competition. Although many competition authorities have the mandate to sanction anticompetitive practices, prevent anticompetitive mergers, and provide policy advice to eliminate regulatory restrictions to competition, not all competition authorities in middle-income countries have the resources needed to enforce their mandate. For example, although Brazil, China, India, Mexico, and South Africa have a wide range of resources such as enforcement tools, budget, and staff, authorities in Bangladesh, Malaysia, Morocco, and Nigeria have limited resources.[29]

Modernizing data and diagnostic tools to understand and regulate creative destruction—from X-rays to MRIs

Modern Schumpeterian thinking on creative destruction has the potential to provide much more reliable diagnostics than what analysts, researchers, and regulators have been using so far. No longer is it enough to decompose aggregate output growth into the growth of measurable production factors—physical and human capital and the residual, total factor productivity. Nor is it enough to rely solely on measures such as firm employment and size distribution to gauge an industry's health. These diagnostics are much like using two-dimensional images from X-ray machines to analyze economic structures. They are necessary but not sufficient.

A nuanced understanding of the process of creative destruction emphasizes the tensions that arise between entrants and incumbents, as well as among incumbents competing for market leadership. Diagnostics that examine these links need the latest instruments—akin to three-dimensional images from MRIs. As with MRIs, using these instruments also requires more skilled practitioners, more data, and more care.

New questions to answer. Moving beyond firm employment size, diagnostics will need to examine the following questions: Do firms grow from "within" by enhancing their existing product portfolio, or do they expand "across" the market by challenging other incumbents in different markets? If growth is from within, are gatekeepers hindering firms from developing new products for new markets? Examining the health of an economy and measuring its vital signs require a comprehensive approach to weighing its business dynamism, including responsiveness to productivity shocks, job creation and destruction rates, turnover among market leadership, entry and exit rates, life cycle (age and size) dynamics, R&D investment, and spending on technology licensing, among other things.

New sources of data and new opportunities for data-driven policy analysis. The creative destruction framework offers a distinctive advantage in understanding aggregate economies by addressing microlevel intricacies and frictions that combine to form the macroeconomy. Although certain underperforming countries may exhibit analogous macroeconomic trends in terms of investment dynamics and sluggish productivity growth, their microlevel challenges can vary significantly. For example, one economy may grapple with financial frictions affecting the "cost" of investment for firms, while another may contend with high market concentration hindering investment incentives by lowering "returns." Similarly, entrants may face obstacles in one economy, while incumbent firms encounter distinct challenges in others. A microlevel investigation, informed by reliable data on firms and individuals, is needed. The recent digital revolution facilitates not only the collection and organization of extensive firm-level data sets but also their processing through innovative techniques for data-driven policy analysis.

Several "must-have" data sets exist. One noteworthy example is the census of firms, a thorough and complete collection of information about all businesses or firms within a specific geographic area or industry. Many countries now grant experts access to their census of firms for research purposes. Unlike a sample survey, which gathers data from a subset of the population, a census aims to encompass every entity within the defined scope. Typically, census of firms data include details such as the number of firms, their size, location, ownership structure, industry, number of employees, revenue, and other pertinent information. This data collection method provides a detailed, accurate representation of the entire population of firms, enabling a comprehensive analysis of many measures of business dynamism.

The World Bank's Enterprise Surveys are the go-to resource for cross-country analysis of firm-level information about the business environment. More recently, the surveys have been expanded to include the informal sector. The World Bank also conducts the Firm-level Adoption of Technology (FAT) survey, collecting information on the adoption of general business functions and sector-specific technologies in 11 developing economies. Some commercial databases have also been widely used in the literature. Salient examples are the Orbis database, produced by Bureau van Dijk, and Worldscope, accessible via online platform.[30]

Social Security records are also widely utilized. These records often contain employment-related information, including earnings, work history, and contributions to social security programs. Experts can scrutinize labor market dynamics, employment patterns, and strategic hiring, even investigating "killer acquisitions" by examining which firms hire workers from their rivals to stifle competition. Emerging online platforms present invaluable opportunities for real-time tracking of businesses.[31] In middle-income countries, especially among small firms with limited internal resources, susceptibility to macroeconomic conditions has increased, underscoring the need for frequent real-time monitoring of the health of the small business sector. Meeting this need was previously challenging because of a lack of the appropriate data. However, the emergence of online cloud-based accounting software has bridged this gap. Many businesses now leverage these platforms for improved efficiency, accessibility, security, and flexibility in managing their financial processes. As a result, platform data can provide information, even on the smallest businesses, almost in real time, even when government statistics are unavailable.

Several additional "good-to-have" data sources are available for conducting in-depth firm-level investigations, including Orbis Europe,[32] Orbis M&A,[33] PitchBook,[34] and PATSTAT.[35] These data sets offer valuable insights into firm performance at the micro level.

Greater analytical expertise. As the sources and volume of data soar, avoiding misdirection and framing the appropriate questions become challenging. A starting point is to carefully investigate whether promising new firms can easily enter the economy or they face obstacles, be it from direct means such as licensing or indirectly from a significant presence of SOEs. Furthermore, a better understanding of the productivity dynamics among incumbent firms is needed. As firms expand, there is typically an upsurge in the concentration of economic activities. Market concentration can either signify "productive behavior" or be linked to rent-seeking and "strategic behavior." The challenge lies in distinguishing between the two. Analysts must therefore scrutinize whether growing firms are expanding due to enhanced productivity or are exhibiting strategic behavior without an actual improvement in productivity. Improving the analytic capabilities of analysis is just as important as improving the quality of data.

In conclusion, the forces of creation will need strengthening in middle-income countries. Both entrants and incumbents can create value—by infusing global technologies and by innovating. Outdated rules of thumb, a preference for SOEs, and political capture by large incumbents stymie the forces of creation. By modernizing data and diagnostics, governments can help in the modernization of productive firms, leading to better managers, better professionals, and better technologies. Governments can also discipline dominant incumbents.

Notes

1. Foster, Haltiwanger, and Krizan (2001); Lentz and Mortensen (2016).
2. Aghion and Howitt (1992).
3. Klette and Kortum (2004).
4. Akcigit and Kerr (2018).
5. Chandler (1977).
6. See, for example, Abreha et al. (2022) for a discussion of informality and the firm size distribution in Sub-Saharan Africa.
7. Bruhn and McKenzie (2014); Ulyssea (2020).
8. García-Santana and Pijoan-Mas (2014).
9. Dabla-Norris et al. (2018).
10. Gourio and Roys (2014).
11. Akcigit et al. (2023).
12. Bachas, Fattal Jaef, and Jensen (2019).
13. Rodano, Serrano-Velarde, and Tarantino (2016).
14. Buera, Kaboski, and Shin (2011); Midrigan and Xu (2014).
15. Cirera and Maloney (2017).
16. Chandler (1977, 123–26).
17. Bloom and Van Reenen (2007).
18. Bloom and Van Reenen (2010).
19. Akcigit and Cilasun (2023).
20. Brandt, Kambourov, and Storesletten (2020); Hsieh and Klenow (2009); Whited and Zhao (2021); World Bank (2023).
21. Küfeoğlu, Pollitt, and Anaya (2018).
22. Cunningham, Ederer, and Ma (2021).
23. World Bank (2024a).
24. Akcigit, Baslandze, and Lotti (2023).
25. OECD (2012).
26. OECD (2017).
27. *Economist* (2014).
28. World Bank (2021).
29. World Bank (2024a).
30. See Orbis (database), Baker Library, Bloomberg Center, Harvard Business School, Boston, https://www.library.hbs.edu/find/databases/orbis#:~:text=ORBIS%2C%20a%20global%20company%20database,company%20data%20including%20subsidiary%20locations; Worldscope (database), Baker Library, Bloomberg Center, Harvard Business School, Boston, https://www.library.hbs.edu/find/databases/worldscope.
31. Akcigit et al. (2024).
32. See https://www.eui.eu/Research/Library/ResearchGuides/Economics/Statistics/DataPortal/OrbisEurope.
33. See https://libguides.eur.nl/az.php?q=ZEPHYR.
34. PitchBook (portal), PitchBook, Seattle, https://pitchbook.com/.
35. PATSTAT (Patent Statistical Database), European Patent Office, Munich, https://www.epo.org/en/searching-for-patents/business/patstat#:~:text=PATSTAT%20contains%20bibliographical%20and%20legal,or%20can%20be%20consulted%20online.

References

Abreha, Kaleb Girma, Xavier Cirera, Elwyn Adriaan Robin Davies, Roberto N. Fattal Jaef, and Hibret Belete Maemir. 2022. "Deconstructing the Missing Middle: Informality and Growth of Firms in Sub-Saharan Africa." Policy Research Working Paper 10233, World Bank, Washington, DC.

Aghion, Philippe, and Peter Howitt. 1992. "A Model of Growth through Creative Destruction." *Econometrica* 60 (2): 323–51.

Akcigit, Ufuk, Yusuf Emre Akgündüz, Harun Alp, Seyit Mumin Cilasun, and Jose M. Quintero. 2023. "Good Firms, Bad Policies: The Dynamics of Informality and Industry Policy in Shaping Economic Growth." University of Chicago Working Paper, University of Chicago, Chicago.

Akcigit, Ufuk, Harun Alp, and Michael Peters. 2021. "Lack of Selection and Limits to Delegation: Firm Dynamics in Developing Countries." *American Economic Review* 111 (1): 231–75.

Akcigit, Ufuk, Sina T. Ates, André Diegmann, Furkan Kilic, and Steffen Müller. 2024. "Steadfast Germany, Dynamic USA: Incumbents and Entrants Shaping Economic Growth." Working paper, University of Chicago, Chicago; Halle Institute for Economic Research, Halle, Germany.

Akcigit, Ufuk, Salomé Baslandze, and Francesca Lotti. 2023. "Connecting to Power: Political Connections, Innovation, and Firm Dynamics." *Econometrica* 91 (2): 529–64.

Akcigit, Ufuk, Murat Alp Celik, and Jeremy Greenwood. 2016. "Buy, Keep or Sell: Economic Growth and the Market for Ideas." *Econometrica* 84 (3): 943–84.

Akcigit, Ufuk, and Seyit Mumin Cilasun. 2023. "A Brief Overview of State-Owned Enterprises in Türkiye." Background paper prepared for *The Business of the State* report, World Bank, Washington, DC.

Akcigit, Ufuk, John Grigsby, and Tom Nicholas. 2017a. "Immigration and the Rise of American Ingenuity: Innovation and Inventors of the Golden Age." *American Economic Review* 107 (5): 327–31.

Akcigit, Ufuk, John Grigsby, and Tom Nicholas. 2017b. "The Rise of American Ingenuity: Innovation and Inventors of the Golden Age." NBER Working Paper 23047 (January), National Bureau of Economic Research, Cambridge, MA.

Akcigit, Ufuk, and William R. Kerr. 2018. "Growth through Heterogeneous Innovations." *Journal of Political Economy* 126 (4): 1374–443.

Bachas, Pierre, Roberto N. Fattal Jaef, and Anders Jensen. 2019. "Size-Dependent Tax Enforcement and Compliance: Global Evidence and Aggregate Implications." *Journal of Development Economics* 140 (September): 203–22.

Bau, Natalie, and Adrien Matray. 2023. "Misallocation and Capital Market Integration: Evidence from India." *Econometrica* 91 (1): 67–106.

Bloom, Nicholas, and John Van Reenen. 2007. "Measuring and Explaining Management Practices across Firms and Countries." *Quarterly Journal of Economics* 122 (4): 1351–408.

Bloom, Nicholas, and John Van Reenen. 2010. "Why Do Management Practices Differ across Firms and Countries?" *Journal of Economic Perspectives* 24 (1): 203–24.

Braguinsky, Serguey, Lee G. Branstetter, and Andre Regateiro. 2011. "The Incredible Shrinking Portuguese Firm." NBER Working Paper 17265 (July), National Bureau of Economic Research, Cambridge, MA.

Brandt, Loren, Gueorgui Kambourov, and Kjetil Storesletten. 2020. "Barriers to Entry and Regional Economic Growth in China." Working Paper 652 (January 5), Department of Economics, University of Toronto, Toronto.

Bruhn, Miriam, and David J. McKenzie. 2014. "Entry Regulation and the Formalization of Microenterprises in Developing Countries." *World Bank Research Observer* 29 (2): 186–201.

Buera, Francisco Javier, Joseph P. Kaboski, and Yongseok Shin. 2011. "Finance and Development: A Tale of Two Sectors." *American Economic Review* 101 (5): 1964–2002.

Chandler, Alfred D., Jr. 1977. *The Visible Hand: The Managerial Revolution in American Business.* Cambridge, MA: Harvard University Press.

Cirera, Xavier, and William F. Maloney. 2017. *The Innovation Paradox: Developing-Country Capabilities and the Unrealized Promise of Technological Catch-Up.* Washington, DC: World Bank.

Cunningham, Colleen, Florian Ederer, and Song Ma. 2021. "Killer Acquisitions." *Journal of Political Economy* 129 (3): 649–702.

Cusolito, Ana Paula, Roberto Fattal Jaef, Davide Salvatore Mare, and Akshat Singh. Forthcoming. "From Financial to Real Misallocation: Evidence from a Global Sample." Policy Research Working Paper, World Bank, Washington, DC.

Dabla-Norris, Era, Laura Jaramillo Mayor, Frederico Lima, and Alexandre Sollaci. 2018. "Size-Dependent Policies, Informality, and Misallocation." IMF Working Paper WP/18/179 (August), International Monetary Fund, Washington, DC.

de Nicola, Francesca, and Jonathan D. Timmis. Forthcoming. "Firm Foundations: Digital Technologies and Productivity Growth in East Asia and Pacific." World Bank, Washington, DC.

Didier, Tatiana, Ross Eric Levine, Ruth Llovet Montanes, and Sergio Schmukler. 2020. "Capital Market Financing and Firm Growth." Policy Research Working Paper 9337, World Bank, Washington, DC. http://dx.doi.org/10.2139/ssrn.3666203.

Donaldson, Dave, and Richard Hornbeck. 2016. "Railroads and American Economic Growth: A 'Market Access' Approach." *Quarterly Journal of Economics* 131 (2): 799–858.

Economist. 2014. "Building on Concrete Foundations." *Business,* April 12, 2014. https://www.economist.com/business/2014/04/12/building-on-concrete-foundations.

Fattal Jaef, Roberto N. 2022. "Entry Barriers, Idiosyncratic Distortions, and the Firm Size Distribution." *American Economic Journal: Macroeconomics* 14 (2): 416–68.

Foster, Lucia, John C. Haltiwanger, and C. J. Krizan. 2001. "Aggregate Productivity Growth: Lessons from Microeconomic Evidence." In *New Developments in Productivity Analysis,* edited by Charles R. Hulten, Edwin R. Dean, and Michael J. Harper, 303–72. National Bureau of Economic Research Studies in Income and Wealth Series, vol. 63. Cambridge, MA: National Bureau of Economic Research; Chicago: University of Chicago Press.

García-Santana, Manuel, and Josep Pijoan-Mas. 2014. "The Reservation Laws in India and the Misallocation of Production Factors." *Journal of Monetary Economics* 66 (September): 193–209.

Gourio, François, and Nicholas A. Roys. 2014. "Size-Dependent Regulations, Firm Size Distribution, and Reallocation." *Quantitative Economics* 5 (2): 377–416.

Hsieh, Chang-Tai, and Peter J. Klenow. 2009. "Misallocation and Manufacturing TFP in China and India." *Quarterly Journal of Economics* 124 (4): 1403–48.

Hsieh, Chang-Tai, and Peter J. Klenow. 2014. "The Life Cycle of Plants in India and Mexico." *Quarterly Journal of Economics* 129 (3): 1035–84.

Iacovone, Leonardo, Rafael Muñoz Moreno, Eduardo Olaberria, and Mariana De La Paz Pereira López. 2022. *Productivity Growth in Mexico: Understanding Main Dynamics and Key Drivers.* Washington, DC: World Bank.

Jung, A-Reum, and Do-Jin Jung. 2022. "The Effects of Size-Dependent Policy on the Sales Distortion Reporting: Focusing on the Discretionary Sales Management of Korean SMEs." *Managerial and Decision Economics* 43 (2): 301–20.

Klette, Tor Jakob, and Samuel Kortum. 2004. "Innovating Firms and Aggregate Innovation." *Journal of Political Economy* 112 (5): 986–1018.

Küfeoğlu, Sinan, Michael Gerald Pollitt, and Karim L. Anaya. 2018. "Electric Power Distribution in the World: Today and Tomorrow." Cambridge Working Paper in Economics 1846 (August 16), University of Cambridge, Cambridge, UK.

Lamoreaux, Naomi R., and Kenneth L. Sokoloff. 2002. "Intermediaries in the U.S. Market for Technology, 1870–1920." NBER Working Paper 9017 (June), National Bureau of Economic Research, Cambridge, MA.

Lentz, Rasmus, and Dale T. Mortensen. 2016. "Optimal Growth through Product Innovation." *Review of Economic Dynamics* 19 (January): 4–19.

Luttmer, Erzo G. J. 2011. "On the Mechanics of Firm Growth." *Review of Economic Studies* 78 (3): 1042–68.

Midrigan, Virgiliu, and Daniel Yi Xu. 2014. "Finance and Misallocation: Evidence from Plant-Level Data." *American Economic Review* 104 (2): 422–58.

OECD (Organisation for Economic Co-operation and Development). 2012. *OECD Review of Telecommunication Policy and Regulation in Mexico.* Paris: OECD.

OECD (Organisation for Economic Co-operation and Development). 2017. *OECD Telecommunication and Broadcasting Review of Mexico 2017.* Paris: OECD.

Perlman, Elisabeth Ruth. 2015. "Dense Enough to Be Brilliant: Patents, Urbanization, and Transportation in Nineteenth Century America." CEH Discussion Paper 2015–06 (March), Centre for Economic History, Research School of Economics, Australian National University, Canberra.

Rodano, Giacomo, Nicolas Serrano-Velarde, and Emanuele Tarantino. 2016. "Bankruptcy Law and Bank Financing." *Journal of Financial Economics* 120 (2): 363–82.

Sánchez-Vela, Claudia, and Jorge N. Valero-Gil. 2011. "The Effect of Firm-Size Dependent Policies on the Economy: The Case of the Repecos Law in Mexico." IDB Working Paper IDB-WP-216 (February), Inter-American Development Bank, Washington, DC.

Schivardi, Fabiano, and Roberto Torrini. 2004. "Firm Size Distribution and Employment Protection Legislation in Italy." Temi di discussione (Economic Working Paper) 504, Economic Research and International Relations Area, Bank of Italy, Rome.

Schumpeter, Joseph Alois. 1942. *Capitalism, Socialism and Democracy*. New York: Harper and Brothers.

Sokoloff, Kenneth L. 1988. "Inventive Activity in Early Industrial America: Evidence from Patent Records, 1790–1846." NBER Working Paper 2707 (September), National Bureau of Economic Research, Cambridge, MA.

Ulyssea, Gabriel. 2020. "Informality: Causes and Consequences for Development." *Annual Review of Economics* 12 (1): 525–46.

Whited, Toni M., and Jake Zhao. 2021. "The Misallocation of Finance." *Journal of Finance* 76 (5): 2359–407.

World Bank. 2015. *Peru: Building on Success, Boosting Productivity for Faster Growth*. Washington, DC: World Bank.

World Bank. 2021. "Antitrust and Digital Platforms: An Analysis of Global Patterns and Approaches by Competition Authorities." Equitable Growth, Finance, and Institutions Insight. Trade, Investment, and Competitiveness, Levelling Up Series, World Bank, Washington, DC.

World Bank. 2023. *The Business of the State*. Washington, DC: World Bank.

World Bank. 2024a. *From Market Power to Powering Markets for Development*. Washington, DC: World Bank.

World Bank. 2024b. *Investment Climate Assessment 2.0 Diagnostic Manual*. Washington, DC: World Bank.

5 Preservation

Key messages

- Many middle-income countries have a shortage of talent, a key ingredient for bolstering the forces of creation. Yet the forces of preservation prevent talent from developing as well as waste the existing talent.
- Talent matters more in middle-income countries than in low-income countries because in middle-income countries skilled workers have become increasingly key to their economic, structural, and technological transformation.
- The opportunities for social mobility in middle-income countries are few due to three main forces of preservation: networks, neighborhoods, and norms.
- Networks, such as elite pacts, facilitate the formation of groups that can determine access to jobs, services, and policy making. As a result, they tend to keep in-groups in and out-groups out, devalue talent and merit, perpetuate inequities of opportunity, and depress expectations for upward mobility in middle-income countries.
- Neighborhoods shape the access of those who were born, grew up, and lived there to opportunities and aspirations. In many middle-income countries, neighborhoods keep people stuck in place, impede migration, hinder productive agglomeration, slow knowledge diffusion, and block the pathways to scale that efficient small enterprises need to become large productive and innovative firms.
- Norms—particularly patriarchal social norms—can hold back women and other marginalized communities from entering the labor force, as well as from benefiting from educational opportunities. In this way, norms prevent the development and growth of talent among half the population of middle-income countries.

Preservation is an antagonist of creation because it is also an antagonist of destruction

In 2005, the government of Indonesia attempted to implement reforms that would heighten students' achievement in elementary and lower secondary schools. One such reform included a rigorous teacher certification requirement in exchange for doubling teachers' salaries. Although the certification process was supposed to include high-quality external assessments of teachers' subject knowledge and pedagogical practice, the issue became highly politicized.

Consequently the intended competency tests were replaced with weak certification requirements, and the reform amounted to a 100 percent salary hike for all teachers. Despite its very high fiscal price tag, the reform yielded no improvement in student achievement,[1] although such a systemic improvement of teacher requirement may take a longer time to have a systemwide impact on learning.

As enterprises in middle-income countries infuse global technologies, they will need technical workers and specialized professionals to adopt and use technology as well as managers to run modern firms. Middle-income countries have a shortage of such talent, which is a key ingredient of efforts to bolster the forces of creation (see chapter 4). Yet the forces of preservation keep talent from developing as well as waste the existing talent, therefore reducing the incentives for many individuals to invest in developing their human capital. In many middle-income countries, access to opportunities is not based on merit, resulting in high income inequality and few opportunities for social mobility, thereby perpetuating "social immobility." The roots of social immobility can be traced to networks, neighborhoods, and norms:

- *Networks* keep in-groups in and out-groups out, devalue talent and merit, perpetuate inequities of opportunity, and depress expectations for upward mobility, all for the sake of preserving social elites—and, with them, inefficient incumbent firms.
- *Neighborhoods* keep people stuck in place, impeding migration, hindering productive agglomeration, slowing knowledge diffusion, and blocking the pathways to scale that efficient small enterprises need to become large productive firms—and to become the innovative incumbents of the future.
- *Norms* keep women and marginalized communities out of the labor force, out of education, out of skills, out of luck, and out of hope.

The first two forces of preservation emerge from elite pacts, keeping out-groups out. The third is a consequence of patriarchal social norms and a system of attitudes and beliefs. The result is that women have unequal access to resources and power, thereby holding back a large proportion of the population. To be sure, all three factors can be helpful in filling the gaps left by missing markets and missing services, but they also become sources of preservation when they restrict and ration access based on social status.

This chapter highlights how social immobility preserves the status quo, exacerbating the stunting and waste of talent in middle-income countries. Although the forces of preservation discussed here focus on talent for a growing middle-income economy, the principles broadly apply to enterprise and energy as well. For example, obstructions posed by incumbents, including state-owned enterprises, hobble the drive for a quick lower-carbon transition, mainly led by young firms in the private sector. Incumbents can cause significant delays by refusing network connection on shared assets ("deep connection"). Incumbents can also "curtail" the distribution of power generated by wind and solar energy—a persistent problem for renewable energy developers in several middle-income countries, despite a "must-run" assurance in regulations to deliver reliable energy supplies.

This chapter examines three questions:

- *How harmful are the forces of preservation in middle-income countries?* As countries transition from low-income to middle-income status, the demand for skilled workers such as technicians, professionals, and managers increases substantially. As income per capita increases, the share of workers employed in small firms declines, and the share of those employed in medium and large firms steadily increases. Countries with greater social mobility have more skills to draw on in the workforce. The forces of preservation, holding back social mobility, are much more harmful in middle-income countries than in low-income countries.

- *How do the economic and social "elite" preserve the status quo?* Although economic and social elites have the resources and the education to help accelerate growth through the infusion of global technologies, their dominance can also buy economic, social, and political power. By capturing political and social institutions, they have an outsize say in who studies where and what, who gets a sought-after job and what they are paid, and who gets to start a business. They also influence housing markets to determine who lives where and whether newcomers to a city or country are welcome. The status quo is preserved by keeping "others" out.

- *How does gender inequality hold back the potential of women?* In many middle-income countries, patriarchal gender norms hold back women from taking advantage of attractive opportunities in the labor market and for entrepreneurship. Discrimination, sexism, and misogyny occur in all walks of life, including the businesses women own, the jobs they get and the pay they receive; how much their families spend on educating them and for how long; and their ability to operate bank accounts. Unequal social norms and beliefs and the institutions that reinforce men's status advantage and access to more resources and power hold back nearly half a country's people, curtailing an economy's growth. It is of particular concern in graying middle-income countries projected to face labor crunches.

Talent drives economic progress, but social immobility holds back the development of talent

Fostering talent is a priority for middle-income countries

As economies grow, their production processes become more complex; they rely on a growing division of labor, and the need for new talents emerges. Agrarian societies need few skills, whereas high-income countries need many more for their high-end, sophisticated services. The share of skilled workers among the workforce is very low in low-income countries, but it increases steadily as countries move from lower-middle-income to upper-middle-income to high-income status (see chapter 2, figure 2.3). Pakistan would need to double its share of skilled workers to reach the level of Chile, and China would also need to increase its share substantially. In general, as middle-income countries grow—particularly as they approach high-income status and must innovate rather than simply adopt technologies—they require increasingly sophisticated talent. Such transformations in the economy make the development and efficient allocation of talent particularly important for middle-income countries and place social mobility and equitable access to opportunities at the forefront of policies to promote growth and social welfare.

Skilled workers are key to economic, structural, and technological transformation

Firms grow as skilled workers, such as managers and professionals, become more abundant. In lower-income countries with gross domestic product (GDP) per capita under US$3,000, most workers are unskilled and employed in small firms with fewer than 10 employees (figure 5.1). As GDP per capita increases, the share of workers employed in small firms declines, and the share of those employed in medium and large

Figure 5.1 The share of skilled workers in large firms increases with GDP per capita

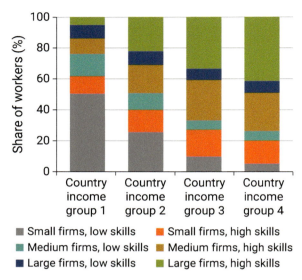

Source: Gottlieb, Poschke, and Tueting 2024.

Note: The figure shows the share of low-skilled and highly skilled workers who are employed in small, medium, and large firms across four country income categories, which correspond to gross domestic product (GDP) per capita levels of US$0–US$3,000 (group 1), US$3,000–US$10,000 (group 2), US$10,000–US$30,000 (group 3), and more than US$30,000 (group 4). Shares are computed from nationally representative labor force surveys from 76 countries covering 805 country-years. Small firms have fewer than 10 employees. Medium firms have 10–50 employees. Large firms have more than 50 employees. Workers are classified as low-skilled if they have less than nine years of formal education, and as highly skilled otherwise. For countries in each income group, the bars add up to 100 percent.

firms increases steadily. As economies transition to higher-income status, the demand for skilled workers such as technicians, professionals, and managers increases substantially. In turn, more educated managers are more likely to adopt technology for general and sector-specific business functions, thereby raising not only the productivity of their firm but also contributing to creation and economic progress for the economy as a whole (box 5.1).

Improving social mobility is a priority for middle-income countries

How do societies select who has access to education, employment, and finance? What prevents talent from being nurtured? A better-educated and wealthier parent has a greater capacity to finance investments and make better investment decisions, has better connections for job searches and placements, and can serve as a role model in terms of education and professional work. In a self-reinforcing cycle, greater investments—and better investment choices—yield increasing benefits to parental background: that is, they create increasing returns.[2] In particular, greater investments by parents in early childhood increase the returns on later investments.[3] This approach can lead to higher inequality and the development of a "human capital elite," where there is considerable mobility within a class boundary but not across classes.[4] A striking example is the intergenerational persistence among political elites (where the social and economic status of family members between generations stays the same). In many low-income and middle-income countries, the descendants of political elites also tend to be involved in and consolidate power and resources through politics.[5]

Countries characterized by higher income inequality are often those in which a significant portion of economic advantage is transmitted from parents to their children. The association between income inequality and intergenerational *immobility*—often referred to as the "Great Gatsby Curve"—is positive as more unequal countries are more socially immobile (figure 5.2).[6] This association is much stronger for middle-income countries than for high-income countries.

At one end of the income equality scale is Finland, where schooling is largely free at all levels and is of very high quality by international standards. There, 80 percent of children attain a level of social mobility that is not dependent on their parents' social status.[7] By contrast, in middle-income countries on average, intergenerational persistence is much higher (40 percent). Specifically, the share of individuals whose social and economic status is the same as that of the previous generation is more than twice as large as in Finland. Closing even a fraction of this gap means a great boost to acquisition and allocation of talent and to growth.

Box 5.1 Firms with better-educated managers adopt more technology

If technology is available, why don't more firms adopt it? Data from the World Bank's Firm-level Adoption of Technology (FAT) survey of 12,000 firms in 11 developing countries reveal that the average firm has adopted an intermediate level of technology, scoring 2.4 on the technology adoption index out of a possible 5.[a] The education level of managers is an important factor in the adoption of technology because better-educated managers are more likely to adopt technology (figure B5.1.1). A manager's education is particularly important to the adoption of advanced technologies such as enterprise resource planning for business administration, software-based statistical control or automated systems for quality control, and robots or additive manufacturing for advanced manufacturing.

The process may also work two ways: firms that adopt more technology hire more educated managers. But a considerable share of firms (more than 30 percent in Georgia, Ghana, India, Kenya, and Senegal) view the lack of capabilities—including managers' and workers' skills—as an important barrier to technology adoption, suggesting that having better-educated managers may be a prerequisite for greater technology adoption.

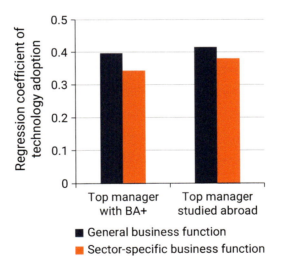

Figure B5.1.1 Better-educated managers are more likely to adopt technology in middle-income countries

Source: WDR 2024 team based on data from the Firm-level Adoption of Technology (FAT) survey.

Note: The figure shows coefficients from regressing a technology adoption index (extensive index, 1–5) on the independent variables shown in the figure, controlling for fixed effects by country, sector, and firm size (small/medium/large). The figure covers the following middle-income countries: Bangladesh, Brazil, Cambodia, Georgia, Ghana, India, Kenya, Senegal, and Viet Nam. BA = bachelor's degree.

a. The World Bank–administered FAT survey provides firm-level data on the adoption of more than 300 technologies across approximately 50 business functions. These include general business functions that are common to all firms and sectors, such as business administration, operations planning, sales, and quality control. They also include sector-specific business functions that vary across sectors. For food processing, for example, functions include input testing; mixing, blending, and cooking; antibacterial procedures; packaging; and storage. For further information, see Cirera, Comin, and Cruz (2022).

Figure 5.2 Higher inequality is associated with higher intergenerational immobility

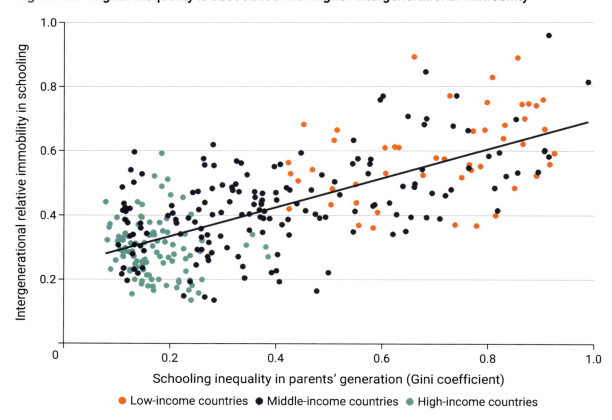

Source: WDR 204 team based on 2018 data from GDIM (Global Database on Intergenerational Mobility) (dashboard), Data Catalog, World Bank, Washington, DC, https://datacatalog.worldbank.org/search/dataset/0050771/global-database-on-intergenerational-mobility.

Note: The y-axis depicts the intergenerational relative immobility, which is the slope estimate from a regression of children's schooling on parents' schooling. The estimate shows the extent to which children can pull away from the shadow of their parents. The x-axis measures the Gini coefficient of years of schooling for the parents' generation.

Social mobility is key to enabling growth, particularly more equitable and inclusive growth. Countries with greater social mobility have more skilled workforces. Data reveal that if two countries have the same income per capita but one has more social mobility than the other from one generation to the next (intergenerational mobility), the country with greater intergenerational mobility has a higher share of skilled workers. This positive association between the share of skilled workers and social mobility arises because a country with higher mobility is able not only to produce more talent but also to generate more skilled jobs. More advanced economies are also better able to ensure that more individuals, regardless of their parents' circumstances, have better opportunities to become skilled workers. And social mobility matters much more in middle-income countries than in low-income countries simply because the former need more skilled workers to invest, infuse, innovate, and grow (figure 5.3).

Figure 5.3 Intergenerational mobility of skilled workers matters more for middle-income countries than for low-income countries

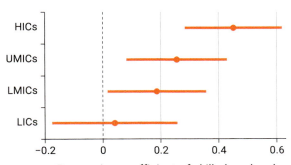

Regression coefficient of skilled workers' intergenerational mobility

Source: WDR 2024 team estimates based on GDIM (Global Database on Intergenerational Mobility) (dashboard), Data Catalog, World Bank, Washington, DC, https://datacatalog.worldbank.org/search/dataset/0050771/global-database-on-intergenerational-mobility; WDI (World Development Indicators) (DataBank), World Bank, Washington, DC, https://databank.worldbank.org/source/world-development-indicators.

Note: The figure plots regression coefficients of intergenerational mobility (which is equal to 1 minus the intergenerational relative mobility) for different country groups at the 95 percent confidence interval. The dependent variable in the regression is the share of skilled workers ("Legislators, sr. officials, managers"; "Professionals"; "Technicians and associate professionals"). The regression controls for the log of gross domestic product (GDP) per capita when the 1980s birth cohort was growing up. Intergenerational mobility estimates are for educational mobility of the 1980s cohort from the World Bank GDIM. HICs = high-income countries; LICs = low-income countries; LMICs = lower-middle-income countries; UMICs = upper-middle-income countries.

Elite pacts perpetuate social immobility and preserve the status quo

Creative destruction requires talent; individuals, in turn, need opportunities to develop their talents and an expectation that investing in such talent will improve their lives. In the early twentieth century, a high school or college degree held the greatest potential for fostering inventions.[8] However, in today's world marked by ever-advancing and complex technologies, the focus on innovation has moved toward even more specialized education, exemplified by the pursuit of advanced degrees such as PhDs.[9] When deciding how much to invest in their own human capital—or that of their children—individuals weigh the expected returns of those investments against their costs, largely based on societal norms and rules that determine an individual's access to the relevant markets and services.

When these norms and rules are biased—for example, in favor of the wealthy and the elite—they restrict access to opportunity. Inequitable access to opportunity exacerbates social immobility, which preserves the existing social hierarchy, perpetuating inequality. Social immobility, in the aggregate, holds back the energies that drive the forces of creation.

Elite pacts hinder learning, employment, and entrepreneurship

Networks facilitate the formation of groups that can determine access to jobs, services, and policy making. Better-educated and wealthier parents have broader social networks to assist in their child's job search.[10] Networks also matter for entrepreneurship. Because better-educated and wealthier entrepreneurs have access to wider and better social networks than others, they have greater access to opportunities and credit.

Networks keep outsiders out

Networks and group memberships based on parental and family ties can secure access to jobs, public services, and political power for individuals from wealthy and close-knit groups. Such tight social groups are common in many countries. Although these social relationships are often instrumental in building trust and facilitating business transactions, they also create unequal playing fields, limiting opportunities for those outside the network. And they keep outsiders out. In fact, the majority of people in many countries believe that social connections, mostly through family, are a key to success, as opposed to personal effort, grit, or talent.[11]

In the Middle East, an implicit social contract known as *wasta* obliges those within the group—typically a tribal group—to aid others from the group. The use of *wasta* is common when searching for a job, procuring a driver's license or business license, gaining admission to a university, and performing many other day-to-day transactions. Compared with other individuals, those who have access to a *wasta* obtain more favorable rulings from agencies and courts, are more likely to obtain government contracts, and benefit more from government rules that limit competition.[12] Other examples of such social contracts include *guanxixue* in China, *blat* in the Russian Federation, *compadrazgo* in Latin America, and the "old boys network" in Western countries.

A situation in which only well-connected individuals obtain rewarding jobs, irrespective of skills and talent, can have profound negative effects on the incentives for outsiders to attend school and even to perform well in school. Cronyism and corruption in education lead to lower academic achievement for a given level of public spending on education, thereby lowering the efficacy of such expenditures.[13]

Networks also facilitate the formation of interest groups, which block the entry of new actors. For example, in public school systems there is often a symbiotic relationship between teachers' unions and political leaders, which can hamper children's achievement. When in office, political leaders provide teachers with benefits such as higher salaries. Teachers then pay union fees from their salaries, and unions contribute a portion of this revenue to politicians' campaigns. Although replacing the lowest-performing teachers with more effective ones would improve children's achievement, the often politically powerful teachers' unions typically block efforts aimed at improving education quality.[14] This occurs in many middle-income countries, including Indonesia and Mexico.[15]

Connections in job recruitment and starting a business can worsen existing inequalities

Job-seekers and firms alike rely on social networks for recruitment. Social networks provide job-seekers with information about job opportunities, access to hiring managers, and other support. When official credentials (such as degrees) convey little information about a job candidate's skills and personal traits, recruitment through social networks helps employers lower the risk of choosing unqualified candidates. But because social networks are mostly defined by a person's socioeconomic background and where they grew up, they can worsen existing inequalities. Research shows that new technologies, particularly when introduced by entrants, can foster social mobility, although this effect diminishes in economies where incumbents spend more time and money on lobbying activities.[16]

In lower- and middle-income countries, between 40 and 80 percent of workers find jobs through social networks.[17] Hiring through social networks can lead to discrimination against individuals without access to high-quality networks. One reason is people's tendency to associate with others of similar backgrounds or characteristics.[18] In Malawi, for example, men systematically refer fewer women than men to jobs.[19]

Social connections matter to entrepreneurial success—and the connections that matter most are often parents and extended families. Social and ethnic networks help the next generation of entrepreneurs by facilitating access to credit.[20] They also help with enforcing contracts, providing operational support, and developing further connections. Because many entrepreneurs in developing countries lack a legal and institutional framework within which to operate, they rely instead on their kinship networks.

Developing social networks from scratch is costly for entrants to any circle, which strengthens the status quo—the forces of preservation—and leads to persistent social inequality. Furthermore, the persistence of social networks is resistant to shocks.

An inability to trust people and institutions beyond one's own family and social network can limit firm growth and productivity. In developing countries, firm owners generally make major management decisions themselves because they fear the consequences of delegating to their managers. But because their time and talent are limited, owners are compelled to manage firms through their children. Consequently, the number of male children emerges as one of the best predictors of firm size, thereby impeding the growth and profitability of their firm.[21] In India, for example, this factor underlies firms' inability to grow. Its effect is sizable; poor delegation of managerial responsibilities could account for 11 percent of the difference in income per capita between India and the United States.[22]

Insiders keep outsiders out of sight in distant and disadvantaged neighborhoods

Where a person is born, grows up, and lives shapes that person's access to opportunities and aspirations. In the United States, children of similar family incomes raised in nearby neighborhoods with different postal codes may have vastly different chances of succeeding as adults.[23] This is equally true in middle-income countries, where social mobility is typically limited to only some geographic areas. Individuals who live in areas with high levels of poverty fare much worse than others on a wide range of economic, health, and educational outcomes.[24]

In middle-income countries, income inequality is typically higher in urban areas than in rural areas because cities attract both highly skilled and unskilled workers. But cities also have higher social mobility because they offer more opportunities to develop talent than rural areas.[25] For example, since 1950 social mobility in Latin American cities has been higher for larger cities,[26] although not for all cities. In Brazil, dynamic cities such as São Paulo and Rio de Janeiro offer scant opportunities to poor children.[27] In India, social mobility has improved greatly in urban areas in recent decades,[28] and has delivered larger gains for the disadvantaged than in rural areas during the period following India's economic liberalization.

Cities can be formidable engines of social mobility, but cities in middle-income countries are less socially mobile than cities in high-income countries. Further, they have greater inequality (figure 5.4). For example, inequality between urban neighborhoods is high in Cape Town, and overall in South Africa, and mobility between generations is quite low. Cities where consumption is more unequal across neighborhoods—due, for example, to income differences across neighborhoods—are located in countries with fewer opportunities for social mobility.

By shaping the laws, regulations, and rules determining who lives where, the social elite keep outsiders out—relegated to rural areas or disadvantaged neighborhoods. A dominant mechanism is setting urban planning standards that are unaffordable for outsiders.[29] When the US city of Philadelphia was settled, for example, city authorities set a minimum lot size of about 30 square meters. By contrast, minimum lot sizes in Ethiopia range from 75 to 300 square meters.

Even in accessing finance for housing, there is a long history of discrimination. In the United States, the Home Owners Loan Corporation (HOLC) drew maps in the 1930s for more than 200 cities as part of its City Survey Program to document the relative riskiness of lending in neighborhoods. Risk factors included race, ethnicity, and immigration status. The lowest-rated neighborhoods, most of whose residents were African American, were drawn in red. Borrowers from these "redlined" neighborhoods were denied access to credit due to the demographic composition of their neighborhoods. For more than two decades, the redlining in effect barred African Americans from buying homes in attractive neighborhoods, even when they could afford them, and kept their home values low.

Although this discriminatory practice was banned by the Fair Housing Act in 1968, the effects still linger today. Neighborhoods that were formerly redlined fare worse in terms of housing value, homeownership rates, racial composition, and exposure to pollutants. The inability to own a home prevented those discriminated against from generating home equity, the main source of wealth for most American households and the major source of inherited (intergenerational) wealth.[30]

Figure 5.4 High inequality within cities is associated with low social mobility from one generation to the next

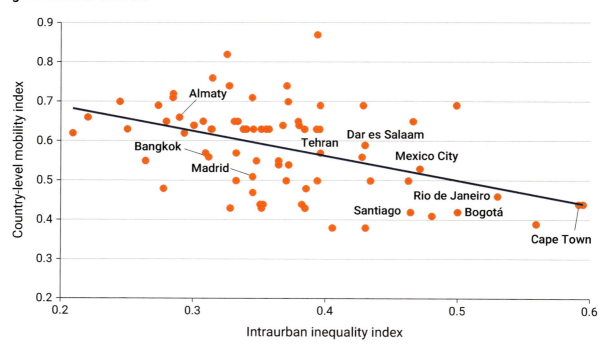

Sources: GDIM (Global Database on Intergenerational Mobility) (dashboard), Development Research Group, World Bank, Washington, DC, https://www.worldbank.org/en/topic/poverty/brief/what-is-the-global-database-on-intergenerational-mobility-gdim; Park et al. 2022.

Note: The mobility index is defined as 1 minus the correlation between parents' and children's years of schooling. The intraurban inequality index is defined as the Gini coefficient based on consumption data from the Global Monitor Database (GMD) surveys, matched with administrative area and GHS-Urban Center Database (GHS-UCDB) data. See Aron et al. 2023; GHSL (Global Human Settlement Layer) (dashboard), Joint Research Center, European Commission, Ispra, Italy, https://ghsl.jrc.ec.europa.eu/index.php.

Distant and disadvantaged neighborhoods restrict upward social mobility

Living in a disadvantaged neighborhood affects adults' outcomes and children's trajectories because residential segregation impairs schooling, health outcomes, intergenerational mobility, and the formation of social capital.[31]

Children who grow up in better neighborhoods have improved outcomes in their education and in the labor market.[32] These outcomes could result from being born into a family that would choose to live in these better neighborhoods (sorting) or could be attributable to the neighborhood itself. In developing countries, about one-third of these outcomes stem from the neighborhood itself (that is, living in certain neighborhoods).[33] The benefits of moving to a better neighborhood are larger for younger children because they are exposed to beneficial effects for a longer period.

Neighborhoods matter for children's life outcomes. First, richer neighborhoods tend to have higher school quality, a major determinant of upward social mobility.[34] Differences in neighborhood-level school quality can arise when schools are financed locally, which is more common in higher-income countries. In middle-income countries, central governments are responsible for the large part of the public expenditure on education, although in many countries provincial governments also contribute. In South Africa, for example, more school funding is allocated to poorer neighborhoods. Yet the quality of schools is lower in poorer neighborhoods in cities and in more remote rural areas, where schools struggle to attract and retain high-quality teachers, doctors, and other service providers because of poorer infrastructure, services, and amenities. Having high-quality teachers not only improves test scores but also can influence important noncognitive and behavioral attributes in positive ways. The absence of high-quality teachers contributes to the poor performance of schools in disadvantaged neighborhoods.[35]

Second, children find their peers and role models in their neighborhoods and form the social networks that can help them in their future job search. Better neighborhoods help in all these aspects.[36] For example, the probability of dropping out of school or committing crimes is similar among children who attend the same school or grow up in the same neighborhood (and are presumably peers). Similarly, children in poor neighborhoods may have strong ties with friends and neighbors, but these are of little use in searching for a job because they do not include contacts with people outside the community.[37]

Third, poor neighborhoods typically have poor infrastructure and services. Lack of sanitation and greater exposure to pollution are common in urban slums. As a result, children growing up in slums are more susceptible to diseases. All these factors have negative impacts on early-life health, human capital, and labor market outcomes.[38]

Fourth, poorer neighborhoods tend to have a high incidence of crime and violence. For example, young children growing up in one of the numerous slums (*favelas*) in Rio de Janeiro affected by conflicts between drug gangs perform significantly worse at school.[39] Between 2003 and 2009, at least one *favela* was in a drug-related conflict in Rio de Janeiro during four of those six years. Living in such poor neighborhoods in middle-income countries can carry a social stigma that affects life outcomes for the residents (box 5.2).

In addition, violence may disrupt school routines, increase teacher and student absenteeism, and cause major psychological distress that can lower test scores for students exposed to violence. In the United States, children who move to a county with lower crime rates, lower concentration of poverty, less income inequality, stronger schools, and a greater share of two-parent households experience better outcomes. For example, moving a child out of public housing in the United States to an area with a low poverty level when the child is young using a subsidized voucher has been estimated to increase the child's total lifetime earnings by about US$302,000.[40]

In disadvantaged neighborhoods, occupational choices are limited

Nearly one in six people around the world lives in urban slums, areas characterized by inadequate infrastructure and property status. The largest slums—Khayelitsha in Cape Town, Kibera in Nairobi, Dharavi in Mumbai, Ciudad Neza in Mexico City, and Orangi Town in Pakistan—are located in some of the largest cities in middle-income countries and form their own towns. Many migrants settle in slums in search of better economic opportunities and intend to stay there temporarily, yet often remain there for decades.[41] For some individuals, slums are a "social elevator"—a temporary stop before finding regular housing.[42] For others, slums are a poverty trap they cannot escape. Slum dwellers face risks from criminal gangs, contagious diseases, and pollution, and often struggle with long commutes and relatively high housing costs.

In urban slums in middle-income countries, children can often access education opportunities, but still have limited job opportunities. In the slums in Bangalore, India, parents' top priority has been investing in their children's education, which has led the children to have higher education levels than their parents.[43] Although most families experience gains in income and assets over time, longer-term residents (extending to a fourth generation) have not been able to move out. In the slums in Jakarta, Indonesia, intergenerational

Box 5.2 Living in *favelas* makes it more difficult to get a job

In her book *Favela: Four Decades of Living on the Edge in Rio de Janeiro,* Janice Perlman documented the experiences of families living in Brazilian slums (*favelas*) for more than 30 years.[a] The respondents were interviewed in 1969 and again in 2001, when the original interviewees and their children and grandchildren were asked for their perceptions about why they were the targets of discrimination. The reasons most frequently mentioned by the original interviewees and their children for not getting a job were their residence in *favelas*, followed by skin color, their appearance, and being a migrant (figure B5.2.1). Grandchildren, on the other hand, perceived less discrimination than their grandparents based on skin color or migrant status, although they perceived living in *favelas* and their own appearance as major impediments to obtaining jobs.

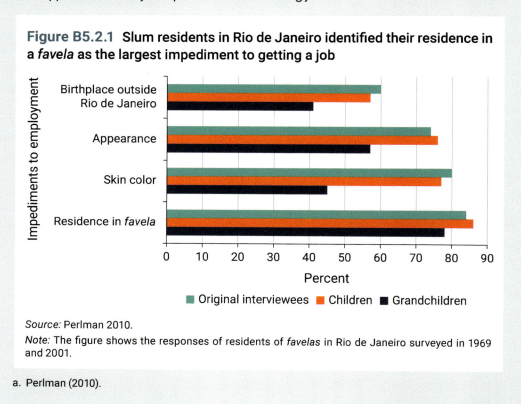

Figure B5.2.1 Slum residents in Rio de Janeiro identified their residence in a *favela* as the largest impediment to getting a job

Source: Perlman 2010.

Note: The figure shows the responses of residents of *favelas* in Rio de Janeiro surveyed in 1969 and 2001.

a. Perlman (2010).

---

mobility is higher among younger children than older children because they have benefitted from recent improvements in educational mobility.[44] Educational mobility is also relatively high in *favelas* in Rio de Janeiro, Brazil.[45] However, educational mobility does not translate into higher occupational mobility in any of these three cities.

Most slum residents—particularly women—work in the slums and cannot obtain formal jobs because of their lack of access to job networks and their isolation from city centers. Moreover, slum residents are highly vulnerable to adverse events such as spells of bad health.[46] Overall, residents in the Bangalore, Jakarta, and Rio de Janeiro slums are neither stuck in poverty traps nor are they on a steady trajectory toward the middle class.[47] Their main constraint is securing a better job, particularly outside of their own neighborhoods.

Keeping migrants out misallocates talent

Internal migration allows individuals to meet and learn from more productive people, sell their ideas in better markets, and expand job opportunities, thereby contributing to a more efficient allocation of workers across an economy.[48] By contrast, barriers to internal migration are costly for growth. The low internal migration rate in some middle-income countries suggests the presence of high mobility barriers, even among highly educated individuals (figure 5.5).

The lack of information or social networks in the destination, as well as market or policy distortions, can limit migration opportunities. Migration barriers can include caste boundaries in India; government regulations such as *hukou* in China and *propiska* in Central Asia; and welfare schemes tied to residence.[49] In China, the *hukou* system has historically imposed large costs on working and living outside of one's *hukou* location, primarily through restricted access to social services and limited employment rights.[50] In 2000, the average cost of moving from rural to urban areas within a Chinese province was equivalent to reducing one's real income by a factor of nearly 3; moves between provinces were even costlier.[51] Between 2000 and 2005, following a reform of the *hukou* system, migration costs declined by 18 percent on average and by about 40 percent for moves between provinces.

Location preferences or discrimination can also limit migration opportunities.[52] On average, individuals with a tertiary education (university or beyond) face much lower migration costs

Figure 5.5 In many middle-income countries, movement of workers from one part of the country to another is more limited than in high-income countries such as France and the United States

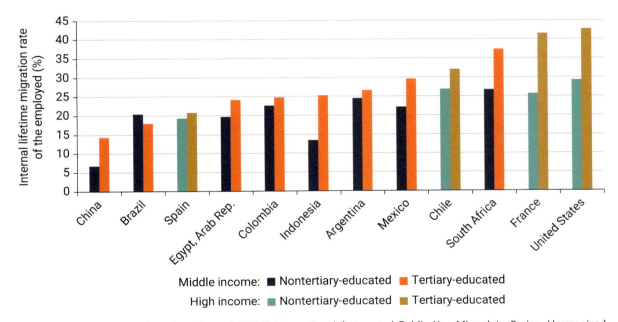

Source: WDR 2024 team based on data of IPUMS International (Integrated Public Use Microdata Series, Harmonized International Census Data for Social Science and Health Research) (dashboard), Minnesota Population Center, University of Minnesota, Minneapolis, https://international.ipums.org/international/.

Note: The sample includes China (2000), Brazil (2000), Spain (2001), the Arab Republic of Egypt (2006), Colombia (2005), Indonesia (2010), Argentina (2001), Mexico (2000), Chile (2002), South Africa (2001), France (1999), and the United States (2000). Internal lifetime migration is defined as current residence different from residence at birth within the same country. Tertiary education refers to schooling at the university level or beyond.

Figure 5.6 In many middle-income countries, migration costs are higher for individuals without high levels of education

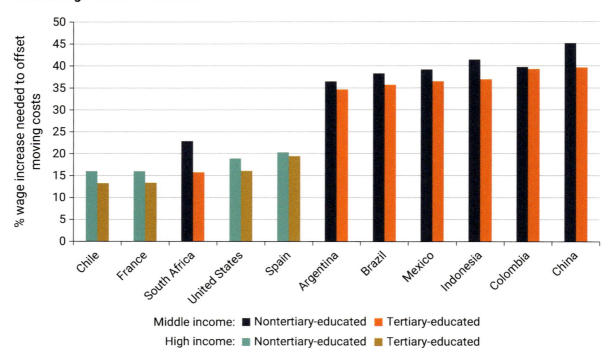

Source: Census data of IPUMS International (Integrated Public Use Microdata Series, Harmonized International Census Data for Social Science and Health Research) (dashboard), Minnesota Population Center, University of Minnesota, Minneapolis, https://international.ipums.org/international/.

Note: Moving costs refer to the percentage of wage increase at the destination needed to compensate for the cost of moving. The sample includes Chile (2002), France (1999), South Africa (2001), the United States (2000), Spain (2001), Argentina (2001), Brazil (2000), Mexico (2000), Indonesia (2010), Colombia (2006), and China (2000). Tertiary education refers to schooling at the university level or beyond.

than individuals with less education (figure 5.6). For example, on average, migrants with a tertiary education in China need a 39.5 percent wage increase to compensate for their moving costs, while migrants who lack a tertiary education need a 45.1 percent wage increase.[53]

A missing opportunity: Education

Although norms, networks, and neighborhoods contribute to preserving the status quo, policy can disrupt them and unleash creation and social mobility. A critical policy is expanding quality education, as it represents for many the best—and perhaps the only—hope to climb the social ladder. Education systems that promote human capital accumulation are therefore key to disrupting the status quo, and yet middle-income countries have largely failed at building those systems.

Learning poverty is alarmingly high in middle-income countries. In the median lower-middle-income country and upper-middle-income country, only 31 and 63 percent of children ages 10 or younger, respectively, are able to understand a text relative to 94 percent in the median high-income country.[54] Among 15-year-olds, only half of high school students are proficient in math, reading, and science in the median upper-middle-income country and 30 percent in the median lower-middle-income country, relative to 80 percent in the median high-income country.[55] Low shares of young people are enrolled in higher education (18 percent and 45 percent in the median lower-middle-income country and upper-middle-income country, respectively, relative to 70 percent in the median high-income country).[56] And even lower shares have graduated from higher education: 12 percent in the median lower-middle-income country, 28 percent in the median upper-middle-income country, and 43 percent in the median high-income country.[57]

The education system failures are particularly acute for disadvantaged students. Gender, location, and wealth create large and worrisome access and completion gaps in elementary and secondary education.[58] In higher education, the poorest students and those in rural areas are much less likely than others to complete at least two years of higher education.[59] These gaps are so large that the percentage of individuals who have completed at least two years would rise by about 30–40 percent if location gaps were eliminated and would double if wealth-related gaps were eliminated.[60]

Furthermore, higher education contributes to social mobility only if it provides skills that are effectively rewarded in the labor market. Educational institutions can identify and fulfill the skill needs of the economy by connecting with enterprises and the labor market, and yet this link is often broken in middle-income countries. In a World Economic Forum executive survey, when companies are asked to rank the skills of higher education graduates relative to their needs (on a scale of 1–7), the average score is 4.13 in the median middle-income country, well below 5.03 in the median high-income country. Moreover, higher education in middle-income countries produces relatively few graduates in fields typically supportive of infusion and innovation—engineering, information and communication technology, science, and health. Similarly, a low share of higher education students (15 percent in the median middle-income country) are enrolled in short-cycle programs (two or three years long), which provide the technical skills needed to engage in midlevel knowledge-intensive occupations.[61]

Patriarchal gender norms hold back a large proportion of the population

Norms are the unwritten rules and shared expectations that govern human behavior within societies. Patriarchal social norms perpetuate gender inequality. They hold back women—out of the labor force, out of education, out of skills, out of luck, and out of hope. Men, who benefit from more access to resources and opportunities, have the most incentives to protect the status quo. Other norms keep marginalized groups down—and are shaped by the social elite.

These unequal norms and beliefs can be deeply ingrained in a nation's social fabric and exert a powerful influence on individual actions. Norms can strongly influence the behaviors and choices of caregivers and parents—often not treating their daughters on a par with their sons. These norms define a child's access to education, liberty, employment, and entrepreneurship. Furthermore, parents pass on cultural norms to their children, perpetuating and reinforcing inequality, whether based on gender, race, ethnicity, or religion. These norms hold back a country's growth and development.

Girls: Starting to show up in school

Improving women's educational attainment ensures that economies can expand their talent pool. Therefore, expanding the middle class requires providing the needed skills and competencies to all members of society.

In the area of ensuring access to basic education, remarkable progress across the world during the past two decades has reduced (and in some countries, even eliminated) gender gaps in enrollment and educational attainment. In some countries, the higher educational attainment of women has resulted in an improvement in mobility from one generation to the next (intergenerational mobility)—that is, daughters can move up the educational ladder even if their mothers or parents were lower down that ladder.[62] Despite this improvement, in many countries higher educational attainment for successive generations is still lower for women and disadvantaged groups (figure 5.7),[63] although not in Sub-Saharan Africa and Latin America and the Caribbean.[64]

Figure 5.7 There is a substantial gap between low- and high-income countries in female educational attainment

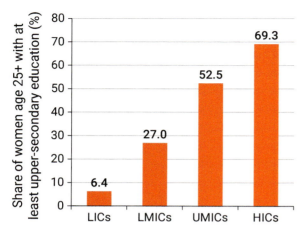

Source: WDR 2024 team.

Note: The figure illustrates educational attainment of women 25+ years of age for at least upper-secondary education. The data cover 141 countries. HICs = high-income countries; LICs = low-income countries; LMICs = lower-middle-income countries; UMICs = upper-middle-income countries.

Women: Missing at work

Female labor force participation is low in several middle-income countries, particularly in the Middle East and North Africa and in South Asia (figure 5.8). By contrast, female labor force participation has increased in many countries over the last decades (figure 5.9). In 1990, the Republic of Korea had the same level of GDP per capita (in terms of purchasing power parity, PPP) as India in 2020. However, the female labor force participation rate in Korea was about 51 percent in 1990, while India's was 30 percent in 2020 but has improved in recent years.[65] In the Arab Republic of Egypt, India, and Türkiye, female labor force participation is well below what would be expected given their levels of income per capita, whereas the rates are much higher in Indonesia and Malaysia.

Even when women are employed, they are more likely to work in lower-paid jobs or be self-employed (and thus have unpredictable incomes) than men in these types of jobs. They are much less likely than men to work in higher-paid jobs such as professional, managerial, and technical positions, which have high

Figure 5.8 Female labor force participation is low in the Middle East and North Africa and in South Asia

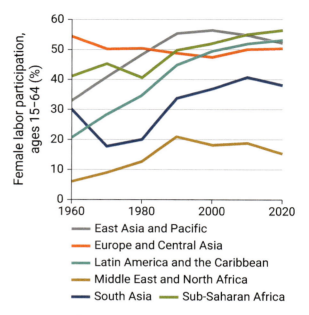

Source: WDI (World Development Indicators) (DataBank), World Bank, Washington, DC, https://databank.worldbank.org/source/world-development-indicators.

Note: Data are averages of national estimates for middle-income countries in each region.

returns to talent, education, and experience. Compounding the problem, fewer higher-skilled jobs are available in middle-income countries—for men and for women—than in high-income countries, and women in middle-income countries have relatively less access to them than women in high-income countries. However, in some middle-income countries such as Indonesia, the share of women in professional occupations has grown rapidly in recent decades (figure 5.10). In some lower-middle-income countries, such as Egypt, the share has grown as well but remains low, indicating a large talent misallocation.

In high-income countries and middle-income countries alike, women are less likely than men to enroll in science, technology, engineering, and mathematics (STEM) fields.[66] The share of women among STEM graduates is on average higher in India compared with even developed countries, and yet women's representation in prestigious colleges lags behind. In 2016, for example, only

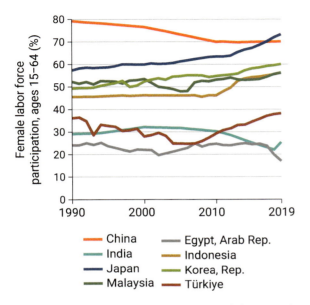

Figure 5.9 Female labor force participation has evolved differently across countries

Source: WDI (World Development Indicators) (DataBank), World Bank, Washington, DC, https://databank.worldbank.org/source/world-development-indicators.

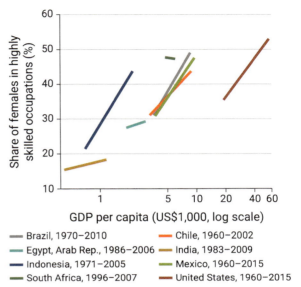

Figure 5.10 The share of female professionals has risen in some countries but not others

Source: WDR 2024 team based on census data of IPUMS International (Integrated Public Use Microdata Series, Harmonized International Census Data for Social Science and Health Research) (dashboard), Minnesota Population Center, University of Minnesota, Minneapolis, https://international.ipums.org/international/.

Note: Professional occupations combine the top three 1-digit International Standard Classification of Occupations (ISCO) occupation codes ("Legislators, sr. officials, managers"; "Professionals"; "Technicians and associate professionals"). GDP = gross domestic product.

about 8 percent of students admitted to India's prestigious Indian Institutes of Technology (IITs) were women, compared to 46 percent admitted to the Massachusetts Institute of Technology (MIT) in the United States. The IITs went on to establish a female enrollment target of 20 percent, which was achieved in the 2023 cohort.

Some middle-income countries educate relatively more females in STEM fields than high-income countries, and yet they employ relatively fewer.[67] Why would women pursue STEM fields but not work in them? Recent evidence suggests a possible driver: higher returns to a STEM education in the marriage market. In Pakistan, female physicians are considered "trophy brides" in the marriage market. More than 70 percent of graduates of medical school are women in Pakistan, and yet only 23 percent of them practice their profession after they graduate.[68] Similarly, in Egypt returns to higher education—not just in STEM fields—are much higher in marriage markets than in labor markets.[69]

Women: Missing independence in owning property, opening financial accounts, and running businesses

The gender gap extends to formal entrepreneurship. Women are more likely than men to work as subsistence microentrepreneurs and earn lower profits than male microentrepreneurs. Furthermore, women are less likely than men to work in formal firms. Globally, only 23 percent of businesses are female-owned, with large variation across sectors (figure 5.11). Female-owned businesses are more egalitarian employers: although male-owned firms employ few female employees (25 percent) and even fewer female managers (6 percent), female-owned firms tend to employ males and females equally.

PRESERVATION | 125

Figure 5.11 Globally, women own a smaller share of firms than men

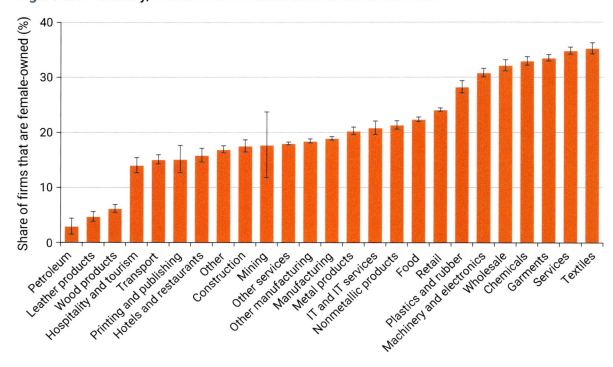

Sources: Chiplunkar and Goldberg 2021; WBES (World Bank Enterprise Surveys) (dashboard), World Bank, Washington, DC, https://www.enterprisesurveys.org/en/enterprisesurveys.
Note: The figure shows the share of female-owned firms across 25 sectors, as well as the confidence intervals for the 95th percentile. The WBES sample covers 141 countries across 13 years (2006–18). IT = information technology.

The gender gap in access to financial accounts (such as formal and mobile banking) is also still very large (figure 5.12). Even in countries such as Bangladesh and Nigeria, where mobile phone and mobile banking penetration have been impressive, there are still large gender gaps in financial inclusion. In Morocco, the gap is more than 25 percentage points, whereas the gap does not exist in Sweden.

Indeed, a 10 percent or higher gender gap in account ownership persists in 41 countries, and women are 37 percent less likely than men to have an account in fragile and conflict-affected situation countries.[70] Women are also less likely than men to own a debit or credit card, have borrowed from a formal financial institution, or have borrowed to support a farm or business.[71] It is thus not surprising that women-led businesses are more likely to identify access to finance as a major obstacle, and that there is an estimated US$1.7 trillion global financing gap.[72]

One barrier to women gaining expanded access to finance is the continued restrictions they face in asset ownership. The property rights of women and disadvantaged groups—manifested, for example, through property and inheritance laws—also vary. Across the world, 40 percent of economies still constrain women's property rights, denying them equal access to essential resources for financial security and economic independence.[73] Among middle-income economies, 14 percent do not grant women equal ownership of immovable property such as real estate or land; 24 percent have unequal inheritance rights that favor sons over daughters; 25 percent do not grant equal inheritance rights to male and female surviving spouses, further marginalizing women's and girls' economic empowerment and autonomy; and 34 percent still do not recognize

Figure 5.12 Women lag behind men in having financial accounts

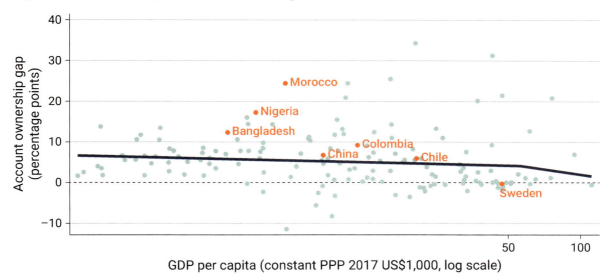

Sources: Global Findex (Global Financial Inclusion Database), World Bank, Washington, DC, https://globalfindex.worldbank.org/#data_sec_focus; WDI (World Development Indicators) (DataBank), World Bank, Washington, DC, https://databank.worldbank.org/source/world-development-indicators.

Note: The figure shows the absolute difference (in percentage points) in 157 countries between the share of men with a financial account and the share of women with a financial account. Accounts include those in financial institutions and mobile accounts. GDP = gross domestic product; PPP = purchasing power parity.

nonmonetary contributions, including caring for minor children or taking care of the family home, undermining women's crucial roles in caregiving and domestic responsibilities.[74]

Gender inequality is a major barrier to socioeconomic mobility and a growing middle class. Box 5.3 outlines a program of research to examine the economic growth lost to gendered barriers.

The cost of social immobility and preservation: Holding back the energies that drive creation

Elite pacts and patriarchal gender norms maintain the status quo, stunting and misallocating talent. These are costly missteps. In the United States, for example, the reduction of gender and racial barriers in educational and occupational choices between 1960 and 2010 explains 20–40 percent of the observed economic growth over that period.[75]

However, there is still room for progress: if the chance of becoming an innovator in the United States today were as high for women, minorities, and children from low-income families as for men from high-income families, innovation in the US economy would increase fourfold.[76]

The forgone growth in some middle-income countries is likely much larger than in the United States. For example, removing barriers to entrepreneurship for women in India would double female labor force participation and raise real income by 40 percent.[77] And globally, closing the gender gap in employment and entrepreneurship could raise the global GDP by more than 20 percent.[78] Eliminating the gender gap over the next decade would essentially double the current global economic growth rate.

High migration costs prevent workers from locating where they are most productive. In Indonesia, reducing migration costs to levels similar to those in the United States would lead to a 7.1 percent boost in productivity.[79] The reform of the Chinese *hukou* system in 2003 led to a 5 percent

Box 5.3 Global Gender Distortions Index: Measuring economic growth lost to gendered barriers

In the United States, policies that reduced labor market barriers and other forms of discrimination against women and African Americans contributed up to 30 percent of post–World War II economic growth. How can today's middle-income countries evaluate the economic dividends of progress toward equal opportunity and improved talent allocation? How can policy makers identify specific barriers within their labor markets that need to be addressed and given priority?

Researchers at Yale University's Economic Growth Center, working under the Gender and Growth Gaps project, are developing a Global Gender Distortions Index (GGDI) to measure the losses in global economic growth stemming from gender gaps in the labor market. The GGDI links changes in gender gaps in the labor market to productivity growth through improvements in the allocation of women's talent. Specifically, this index measures by how much the gross domestic product (GDP) of a country (or subnational unit) has grown, or could grow, from improvements in women's labor market opportunities.

The index highlights that women often do not choose the occupation in which they have a comparative advantage because of (1) labor demand distortions that lead to a wedge between wages and marginal products and (2) differences in occupational preferences that capture factors such as social norms and other labor supply distortions. The GGDI is computed by using observed differences in women's wages, labor supply, and employment across job type (formal versus informal) to derive an estimate of economywide productivity losses or gains. By quantifying growth losses stemming from gender inequality and distilling them into a single measure, the GGDI allows comparisons across time and locations that can inform policy decisions. It can also complement the World Bank's *Women, Business and the Law* (WBL) index by measuring the aggregate consequences of de facto labor market barriers, whereas the WBL measures de jure barriers.[a]

In a proof-of-concept exercise, the GGDI team uses a cross-sectional analysis across Indian states for 2018 and finds that labor demand distortions are negatively related to state-level economic development.[b] Poorer states such as Bihar gain 10 percent in state GDP from removal of labor demand distortions, whereas richer states such as Kerala gain 4 percent in GDP. By contrast, labor supply distortions are not related to state-level GDP.

The GGDI, which will be computed for 30 countries over the next 24 months, can act as a dynamic barometer for countries and regions, providing researchers and policy makers with a valuable new resource.

a. World Bank (2024).
b. Goldberg et al. (2024).

increase in labor productivity.[80] Furthermore, low mobility costs can mitigate the shocks inherent to creative destruction. During the nineteenth century, the US city of Detroit grew into a thriving hub of commerce and industry largely based on the auto industry. But when the industry contracted, low mobility costs allowed workers to relocate to other production hubs in the United States. In middle-income countries, in addition to high migration costs, the costs of ineffective education systems are high because they fail to develop talent and perpetuate existing inequalities.

The forces of preservation are holding middle-income countries back from creative destruction and growth. Creative destruction requires the development of talent, which individuals undertake when they expect economic returns and social mobility. Poor expectations of social mobility hamper talent development. Similarly, inequitable opportunities in markets and education hinder talent development and social mobility, producing a talent misallocation—a waste—with costly consequences for individuals and countries alike. These considerations suggest two main roles for policy in creative destruction: removing barriers to developing talent and actively promoting talent development (see chapter 8 for further details).

Notes

1. de Ree et al. (2018).
2. Becker et al. (2018).
3. This is due to the dynamic complementarities studied by García, Heckman, and Ronda (2023). Also see, Schady et al. (2023).
4. The term "human capital elite" is from Becker et al. (2018).
5. Stone (1990).
6. Social immobility is measured by intergenerational correlation between children's and parents' years of schooling. The correlation is the slope coefficient in the regression of children's schooling on parents' years of schooling. This measure is also known as the intergenerational relative mobility. Other measures of intergenerational mobility are available such as absolute mobility, which indicates whether the distribution of children's years of schooling moved relative to that of parents. A similar concept is upward mobility. These two measures relate to overall progress in schooling, not just whether a child's status depends on that of parents. This Report uses the relative mobility measure instead of the absolute mobility measure. Relative mobility also provides a direct estimate of inequality of opportunity. Social mobility is measured by 1 minus the intergenerational correlation in schooling. The correlation in schooling is used because of the lack of data to estimate intergenerational income mobility in developing countries where a large fraction of the population is self-employed.
7. Narayan et al. (2018); WEF (2020).
8. Akcigit, Grigsby, and Nicholas (2017).
9. Akcigit, Pearce, and Prato (2020).
10. Becker et al. (2018).
11. Coco and Lagravinese (2014).
12. Barnett, Yandle, and Naufal (2013).
13. Coco and Lagravinese (2014); Suryadarma (2012).
14. Zingales (2014).
15. See, for example, de Ree et al. (2018); Schneider (2022).
16. Aghion et al. (2019).
17. Beaman and Magruder (2012); Caria, Franklin, and Witte (2022); Gatti et al. (2014); Mani and Riley (2021); Nicodemo and García (2015).
18. Jackson (2021).
19. Beaman, Keleher, and Magruder (2018).
20. Blanchflower and Oswald (1998); Evans and Jovanovic (1989); Evans and Leighton (1989).
21. Bloom et al. (2010).
22. Akcigit, Alp, and Peters (2021).
23. Chetty et al. (2014); Chyn and Katz (2021).
24. Chyn and Katz (2021).
25. Lall et al. (2023).
26. Neidhöfer, Ciaschi, and Gasparini (2021).
27. Britto et al. (2022).
28. Emran, Jiang, and Shilpi (2021); Emran and Shilpi (2015).
29. Lall, Henderson, and Venables (2017).
30. Rothstein (2017).
31. Acevedo-Garcia et al. (2003); Alexander and Currie (2017); Baum-Snow and Lutz (2011); Chetty, Hendren, and Katz (2016); Chetty et al. (2022); Granovetter (1973).
32. Chetty and Hendren (2018); Chetty, Hendren, and Katz (2016); Chyn (2018); Deutscher (2020); Laliberté (2021); Nakamura, Sigurdsson, and Steinsson (2022).
33. Alesina et al. (2021).
34. Britto et al. (2022); Chetty et al. (2014).
35. Jackson (2021).
36. Bayer, Ross, and Topa (2008); Hellerstein, Kutzbach, and Neumark (2019); Hellerstein, McInerney, and Neumark (2011); Topa and Zenou (2015).
37. Chetty et al. (2022).
38. Chyn and Katz (2021).
39. Monteiro and Rocha (2017).
40. Chetty, Hendren, and Katz (2016), looking at the Moving to Opportunity system of subsidized vouchers.
41. Marx, Stoker, and Suri (2013).
42. Glaeser (2011).
43. Krishna (2013).

44. Bryan and Morten (2019).
45. Perlman (2010).
46. See Perlman (2006) for Brazil; Turok and Borel-Saladin (2018) for South Africa; Ziraba, Kyobutungi, and Zulu (2011) for Kenya.
47. Rains and Krishna (2020).
48. Akcigit et al. (2018, 2022); Lucas (2009); Lucas and Moll (2014); Perla and Tonetti (2014).
49. Grover, Lall, and Maloney (2022); Selod and Shilpi (2021).
50. *Hukou* is a system of household registration used in China. Under the system, each citizen is required to register in only one place of permanent residence. An individual's *hukou* status defines his or her rights and eligibility for social welfare and various services, including public education and housing, within a specific administrative unit.
51. Tombe and Zhu (2019).
52. D'Aoust, Galdo, and Ianchovichina (2023).
53. Wong (2019).
54. Based on the Learning Poverty Index, calculated by World Bank and UNESCO.
55. Based on the 2018 Programme for International Student Assessment (PISA), a study administered by the Organisation for Economic Co-operation and Development (OECD), and the 2019 Trends in International Mathematic and Science Study (TIMSS) administered by the International Association for the Evaluation of Educational Achievement (IEA).
56. UIS.Stat (dashboard), Institute for Statistics, United Nations Educational, Scientific, and Cultural Organization, Montreal, http://data.uis.unesco.org/. These figures correspond to the higher education gross enrollment ratio, defined as the number of individuals enrolled in higher education relative to all age-relevant individuals (18–24 years of age).
57. UIS.Stat (dashboard), Institute for Statistics, United Nations Educational, Scientific, and Cultural Organization, Montreal, http://data.uis.unesco.org/. These figures correspond to the gross graduation ratio, defined as the ratio between the number of graduates from bachelor's or graduate degree programs by the population of the theoretical graduation age of the most common bachelor's program.
58. World Bank (2018).
59. WDR 2024 team analysis using UNESCO Education Inequalities Database based on household surveys.
60. WDR 2024 team calculations based on UNESCO data.
61. Bianchi and Giorcelli (2020) show that greater access to science, technology, engineering, and mathematics (STEM) and vocational and technical programs in Italy in the 1960s led to an increase in patenting. For Finland, Toivanen and Väänänen (2016) find large effects of greater access to engineering master's programs on patenting.
62. Asher, Novosad, and Rafkin (2024); Emran and Shilpi (2015).
63. Asher, Novosad, and Rafkin (2024); Emran and Shilpi (2015).
64. Alesina et al. (2021); Neidhöfer, Ciaschi, and Gasparini (2021).
65. Estimates on India's female labor force participation rate vary. See, for example, India's Economic Survey for 2022–23, https://www.indiabudget.gov.in/economicsurvey/doc/eschapter/echap06.pdf.
66. Hammond et al. (2020).
67. Hammond et al. (2020).
68. Hammond et al. (2020).
69. In Egypt, it is common for the groom to transfer significant resources to the new household at the time of marriage. This is a direct and informative measure of the monetary gains women may obtain through the marriage market. Exploiting the staggered rollout of a school reform in Egypt that reduced the number of years required to complete primary education from six to five, Deng et al. (2023) find that the return to a bride's compulsory education is about 100 percent for the marital transfer, about 14 percent for the husband's wage at the time of marriage, and about 16 percent for a measure of the husband's permanent income. These returns to education in the marriage market are much higher than the returns to education that Egyptian women experience in the labor market.
70. Demirgüç-Kunt et al. (2022).
71. Demirgüç-Kunt et al. (2022).
72. IFC (2017).
73. World Bank (2024).
74. World Bank (2024).
75. Hsieh et al. (2019).
76. Bell et al. (2019).
77. Chiplunkar and Goldberg (2021).
78. Pennings (2022).
79. Bryan and Morten (2019).
80. Tombe and Zhu (2019).

References

Acevedo-Garcia, Dolores, Kimberly A. Lochner, Theresa L. Osypuk, and S. V. Subramanian. 2003. "Future Directions in Residential Segregation and Health Research: A Multilevel Approach." *American Journal of Public Health* 93 (2): 215–21.

Aghion, Philippe, Ufuk Akcigit, Antonin Bergeaud, Richard Blundell, and David Hemous. 2019. "Innovation and Top Income Inequality." *Review of Economic Studies* 86 (1): 1–45.

Akcigit, Ufuk, Harun Alp, and Michael Peters. 2021. "Lack of Selection and Limits to Delegation: Firm Dynamics in Developing Countries." *American Economic Review* 111 (1): 231–75.

Akcigit, Ufuk, Santiago Caicedo, Ernest Miguelez, Stefanie Stantcheva, and Valerio Sterzi. 2018. "Dancing with the Stars: Innovation through Interactions." NBER Working Paper 24466 (March), National Bureau of Economic Research, Cambridge, MA.

Akcigit, Ufuk, John Grigsby, and Tom Nicholas. 2017. "The Rise of American Ingenuity: Innovation and Inventors of the Golden Age." NBER Working Paper 23047 (January), National Bureau of Economic Research, Cambridge, MA.

Akcigit, Ufuk, John Grigsby, Tom Nicholas, and Stefanie Stantcheva. 2022. "Taxation and Innovation in the Twentieth Century." *Quarterly Journal of Economics* 137 (1): 329–85.

Akcigit, Ufuk, Jeremy G. Pearce, and Marta Prato. 2020. "Tapping into Talent: Coupling Education and Innovation Policies for Economic Growth." NBER Working Paper 27862 (September), National Bureau of Economic Research, Cambridge, MA.

Alesina, Alberto Francesco, Sebastian Hohmann, Stelios Michalopoulos, and Elias Papaioannou. 2021. "Intergenerational Mobility in Africa." *Econometrica* 89 (1): 1–35.

Alexander, Diane, and Janet Currie. 2017. "Is It Who You Are or Where You Live? Residential Segregation and Racial Gaps in Childhood Asthma." *Journal of Health Economics* 55 (September): 186–200.

Aron, Danielle Victoria, R. Andres Castaneda Aguilar, Carolina Diaz-Bonilla, Maria Gabriela Farfan Betran, Elizabeth Mary Foster, Tony Henri Mathias Jany Fujs, Dean Mitchell Jolliffe, et al. 2023. "September 2023 Update to the Poverty and Inequality Platform (PIP): What's New." Global Poverty Monitoring Technical Note 32 (September), World Bank, Washington, DC.

Asher, Sam, Paul Novosad, and Charlie Rafkin. 2024. "Intergenerational Mobility in India: New Measures and Estimates across Time and Social Groups." *American Economic Journal: Applied Economics* 16 (2): 66–98.

Barnett, Andy, Bruce Yandle, and George Naufal. 2013. "Regulation, Trust, and Cronyism in Middle Eastern Societies: The Simple Economics of 'Wasta.'" *Journal of Socio-Economics* 44 (June): 41–46.

Baum-Snow, Nathaniel, and Byron F. Lutz. 2011. "School Desegregation, School Choice, and Changes in Residential Location Patterns by Race." *American Economic Review* 101 (7): 3019–46.

Bayer, Patrick, Stephen L. Ross, and Giorgio Topa. 2008. "Place of Work and Place of Residence: Informal Hiring Networks and Labor Market Outcomes." *Journal of Political Economy* 116 (6): 1150–96.

Beaman, Lori A., Niall Keleher, and Jeremy Magruder. 2018. "Do Job Networks Disadvantage Women? Evidence from a Recruitment Experiment in Malawi." *Journal of Labor Economics* 36 (1): 121–57.

Beaman, Lori A., and Jeremy Magruder. 2012. "Who Gets the Job Referral? Evidence from a Social Networks Experiment." *American Economic Review* 102 (7): 3574–93.

Becker, Gary Stanley, Scott Duke Kominers, Kevin M. Murphy, and Jörg L. Spenkuch. 2018. "A Theory of Intergenerational Mobility." *Journal of Political Economy* 126 (S1): S7–S25.

Bell, Alexander M., Raj Chetty, Xavier Jaravel, Neviana Petkova, and John Van Reenen. 2019. "Who Becomes an Inventor in America? The Importance of Exposure to Innovation." *Quarterly Journal of Economics* 134 (2): 647–713.

Bianchi, Nicola, and Michela Giorcelli. 2020. "Scientific Education and Innovation: From Technical Diplomas to University Stem Degrees." *Journal of the European Economic Association* 18 (5): 2608–46.

Blanchflower, David G., and Andrew J. Oswald. 1998. "What Makes an Entrepreneur?" *Journal of Labor Economics* 16 (1): 26–60.

Bloom, Nicholas, Aprajit Mahajan, David J. McKenzie, and John Roberts. 2010. "Why Do Firms in Developing Countries Have Low Productivity?" *American Economic Review* 100 (2): 619–23.

Britto, Diogo G. C., Alexandre de Andrade Fonseca, Paolo Pinotti, Breno Sampaio, and Lucas Warwar. 2022. "Intergenerational Mobility in the Land of Inequality." CESifo Working Paper 10004, Munich Society for the Promotion of Economic Research, Center for Economic Studies, Ludwig Maximilian University and Ifo Institute for Economic Research, Munich.

Bryan, Gharad T., and Melanie Morten. 2019. "The Aggregate Productivity Effects of Internal Migration: Evidence from Indonesia." *Journal of Political Economy* 127 (5): 2229–68.

Caria, Stefano, Simon Franklin, and Marc Josef Witte. 2022. "Searching with Friends." *Journal of Labor Economics* 41 (4): 887–922.

Chetty, Raj, and Nathaniel Hendren. 2018. "The Impacts of Neighborhoods on Intergenerational Mobility I: Childhood Exposure Effects." *Quarterly Journal of Economics* 133 (3): 1107–62.

Chetty, Raj, Nathaniel Hendren, and Lawrence F. Katz. 2016. "The Effects of Exposure to Better Neighborhoods on Children: New Evidence from the Moving to Opportunity Experiment." *American Economic Review* 106 (4): 855–902.

Chetty, Raj, Nathaniel Hendren, Patrick Kline, and Emmanuel Saez. 2014. "Where Is the Land of Opportunity? The Geography of Intergenerational Mobility in the United States." *Quarterly Journal of Economics* 129 (4): 1553–623.

Chetty, Raj, Matthew O. Jackson, Theresa Kuchler, Johannes Stroebel, Nathaniel Hendren, Robert B. Fluegge, Sara Gong, et al. 2022. "Social Capital I: Measurement and Associations with Economic Mobility." *Nature* 608 (7921): 108–21.

Chiplunkar, Gaurav, and Pinelopi Koujianou Goldberg. 2021. "Aggregate Implications of Barriers to Female Entrepreneurship." NBER Working Paper 28486 (February), National Bureau of Economic Research, Cambridge, MA.

Chyn, Eric. 2018. "Moved to Opportunity: The Long-Run Effects of Public Housing Demolition on Children." *American Economic Review* 108 (10): 3028–56.

Chyn, Eric, and Lawrence F. Katz. 2021. "Neighborhoods Matter: Assessing the Evidence for Place Effects." *Journal of Economic Perspectives* 35 (4): 197–222.

Cirera, Xavier, Diego Comin, and Marcio Cruz. 2022. *Bridging the Technological Divide: Technology Adoption by Firms in Developing Countries*. Washington, DC: World Bank.

Coco, Giuseppe, and Raffaele Lagravinese. 2014. "Cronyism and Education Performance." *Economic Modelling* 38 (February): 443–50.

D'Aoust, Olivia Severine, Virgilio Galdo, and Elena Ivanova Ianchovichina. 2023. "Territorial Productivity

Differences and Dynamics within Latin American Countries." Policy Research Working Paper 10480, World Bank, Washington, DC.

Demirgüç-Kunt, Asli, Leora Klapper, Dorothe Singer, and Saniya Ansar. 2022. *The Global Findex Database 2021: Financial Inclusion, Digital Payments, and Resilience in the Age of COVID-19*. Washington, DC: World Bank.

Deng, Jingyuan, Nelly Youssef Elmallakh, Luca Flabbi, and Roberta V. Gatti. 2023. "Returns to Education in the Marriage Market: Bride Price and School Reform in Egypt." Policy Research Working Paper 10288, World Bank, Washington, DC.

de Ree, Joppe, Karthik Muralidharan, Menno Prassad Pradhan, and F. Halsey Rogers. 2018. "Double for Nothing? Experimental Evidence on an Unconditional Teacher Salary Increase in Indonesia." *Quarterly Journal of Economics* 133 (2): 993–1039.

Deutscher, Nathan. 2020. "Place, Peers, and the Teenage Years: Long-Run Neighborhood Effects in Australia." *American Economic Journal: Applied Economics* 12 (2): 220–49.

Emran, M. Shahe, Hanchen Jiang, and Forhad J. Shilpi. 2021. "Gender Bias and Intergenerational Educational Mobility: Theory and Evidence from China and India." Policy Research Working Paper 9250, World Bank, Washington, DC.

Emran, M. Shahe, and Forhad J. Shilpi. 2015. "Gender, Geography, and Generations: Intergenerational Educational Mobility in Post-Reform India." *World Development* 72 (August): 362–80.

Evans, David S., and Boyan Jovanovic. 1989. "An Estimated Model of Entrepreneurial Choice under Liquidity Constraints." *Journal of Political Economy* 97 (4): 808–27.

Evans, David S., and Linda S. Leighton. 1989. "Some Empirical Aspects of Entrepreneurship." *American Economic Review* 79 (3): 519–35.

García, Jorge Luis, James J. Heckman, and Victor Ronda. 2023. "The Lasting Effects of Early-Childhood Education on Promoting the Skills and Social Mobility of Disadvantaged African Americans and Their Children." *Journal of Political Economy* 131 (6): 1477–506.

Gatti, Roberta V., Diego F. Angel-Urdinola, Joana Silva, and András Bodor. 2014. *Striving for Better Jobs: The Challenge of Informality in the Middle East and North Africa*. Directions in Development: Human Development. Washington, DC: World Bank.

Glaeser, Edward L. 2011. "Cities, Productivity, and Quality of Life." *Science* 333 (6042): 592–94.

Goldberg, Pinelope, Somik Lall, Meet Mehta, Michael Peters, and Aishwarya Ratan. 2024. "Gender Growth Gaps across Indian States." EGC Discussion Paper 1108, EliScholar, Economic Growth Center, Yale University, New Haven, CT.

Gottlieb, Charles, Markus Poschke, and Michael Tueting. 2024. "Skill Supply, Firm Size and Economic Development." Background paper prepared for *World Development Report 2024*, World Bank, Washington, DC.

Granovetter, Mark S. 1973. "The Strength of Weak Ties." *American Journal of Sociology* 78 (6): 1360–80.

Grover, Arti, Somik Vinay Lall, and William F. Maloney. 2022. *Place, Productivity, and Prosperity: Revisiting Spatially Targeted Policies for Regional Development*. Washington, DC: World Bank.

Hammond, Alicia, Eliana Rubiano Matulevich, Kathleen Beegle, and Sai Krishna Kumaraswamy. 2020. *The Equality Equation: Advancing the Participation of Women and Girls in STEM*. Washington, DC: World Bank.

Hellerstein, Judith K., Mark J. Kutzbach, and David Neumark. 2019. "Labor Market Networks and Recovery from Mass Layoffs: Evidence from the Great Recession Period." *Journal of Urban Economics* 113 (September): 103192.

Hellerstein, Judith K., Melissa McInerney, and David Neumark. 2011. "Neighbors and Coworkers: The Importance of Residential Labor Market Networks." *Journal of Labor Economics* 29 (4): 659–95.

Hsieh, Chang-Tai, Erik Hurst, Charles I. Jones, and Peter J. Klenow. 2019. "The Allocation of Talent and U.S. Economic Growth." *Econometrica* 87 (5): 1439–74.

IFC (International Finance Corporation). 2017. "MSME Finance Gap: Assessment of the Shortfalls and Opportunities in Financing Micro, Small and Medium Enterprises in Emerging Markets." IFC, Washington, DC.

Jackson, Matthew O. 2021. "Inequality's Economic and Social Roots: The Role of Social Networks and Homophily." *SSRN Electronic Journal*, vol. 25. https://papers.ssrn.com/sol3/papers.cfm?abstract_id=3795626.

Krishna, Anirudh. 2013. "Stuck in Place: Investigating Social Mobility in 14 Bangalore Slums." *Journal of Development Studies* 49 (7): 1010–28.

Laliberté, Jean-William. 2021. "Long-Term Contextual Effects in Education: Schools and Neighborhoods." *American Economic Journal: Economic Policy* 13 (2): 336–77.

Lall, Somik Vinay, J. Vernon Henderson, and Anthony J. Venables. 2017. *Africa's Cities: Opening Doors to the World*. With Juliana Aguilar, Ana Aguilera, Sarah Antos, Paolo Avner, Olivia Severine D'Aoust, Chyi-Yun Huang, Patricia Jones, Nancy Lozano Gracia, and Shohei Nakamura. Washington, DC: World Bank.

Lall, Somik Vinay, Jon Kher Kaw, Forhad J. Shilpi, and Sally Beth Murray. 2023. *Vibrant Cities: On the Bedrock of Stability, Prosperity, and Sustainability*. Washington, DC: World Bank.

Lucas, Robert E. B., Jr. 2009. "Ideas and Growth." *Economica* 76 (301): 1–19.

Lucas, Robert E. B., Jr., and Benjamin Moll. 2014. "Knowledge Growth and the Allocation of Time." *Journal of Political Economy* 122 (1): 1–51.

Mani, Anandi, and Emma Riley. 2021. "Social Networks as Levers of Mobility." In *Social Mobility in Developing Countries: Concepts, Methods, and Determinants*, edited by Vegard Iversen, Anirudh Krishna, and Kunal Sen, 424–47. UNU-WIDER Studies in Development Economics. Helsinki: United Nations University–World Institute for Development Economics Research; New York: Oxford University Press.

Marx, Benjamin, Thomas Stoker, and Tavneet Suri. 2013. "The Economics of Slums in the Developing World." *Journal of Economic Perspectives* 27 (4): 187–210.

Monteiro, Joana, and Rudi Rocha. 2017. "Drug Battles and School Achievement: Evidence from Rio de Janeiro's

Favelas." *Review of Economics and Statistics* 99 (2): 213–28.

Nakamura, Emi, Jósef Sigurdsson, and Jón Steinsson. 2022. "The Gift of Moving: Intergenerational Consequences of a Mobility Shock." *Review of Economic Studies* 89 (3): 1557–92.

Narayan, Ambar, Roy van der Weide, Alexandru Cojocaru, Christoph Lakner, Silvia Redaelli, Daniel Gerszon Mahler, Rakesh Gupta N. Ramasubbaiah, and Stefan Thewissen. 2018. *Fair Progress? Economic Mobility across Generations around the World.* Equity and Development Series. Washington, DC: World Bank.

Neidhöfer, Guido, Matías Ciaschi, and Leonardo Gasparini. 2021. "Intergenerational Mobility in Education in Latin America." CAF Working Paper 2021/14 (December 14), Corporación Andina de Fomento (Development Bank of Latin America), Caracas, República Bolivariana de Venezuela.

Nicodemo, Catia, and Gustavo Adolfo García. 2015. "Job Search Channels, Neighborhood Effects, and Wages Inequality in Developing Countries: The Colombian Case." *Developing Economies* 53 (2): 75–99.

Park, Hogeun, Nancy Lozano Gracia, Giuseppe Rossitti, and Olivia Severine D'Aoust. 2022. "A Global Review of Intra-Urban Spatial Inequality." World Bank, Washington, DC.

Pennings, Steven Michael. 2022. "A Gender Employment Gap Index (GEGI): A Simple Measure of the Economic Gains from Closing Gender Employment Gaps, with an Application to the Pacific Islands." Policy Research Working Paper 9942, World Bank, Washington, DC.

Perla, Jesse, and Christopher Tonetti. 2014. "Equilibrium Imitation and Growth." *Journal of Political Economy* 122 (1): 52–76.

Perlman, Janice E. 2006. "The Metamorphosis of Marginality: Four Generations in the Favelas of Rio de Janeiro." *Annals of the American Academy of Political and Social Science* 606 (July): 154–77.

Perlman, Janice E. 2010. *Favela: Four Decades of Living on the Edge in Rio de Janeiro.* New York: Oxford University Press.

Rains, Emily, and Anirudh Krishna. 2020. "Precarious Gains: Social Mobility and Volatility in Urban Slums." *World Development* 132 (August): 105001.

Rothstein, Richard. 2017. *The Color of Law: A Forgotten History of How Our Government Segregated America.* New York: Liveright.

Schady, Norbert R., Alaka Holla, Shwetlena Sabarwal, Joana Silva, and Andres Yi Chang. 2023. *Collapse and Recovery: How the COVID-19 Pandemic Eroded Human Capital and What to Do about It.* Washington, DC: World Bank.

Schneider, Ben Ross. 2022. "Teacher Unions, Political Machines, and the Thorny Politics of Education Reform in Latin America." *Politics and Society* 50 (1): 84–116.

Selod, Harris, and Forhad J. Shilpi. 2021. "Rural-Urban Migration in Developing Countries: Lessons from the Literature." *Regional Science and Urban Economics* 91 (November): 103713.

Stone, Samuel Z. 1990. *The Heritage of the Conquistadors: Ruling Classes in Central America from the Conquest to the Sandinistas.* Foreword by Richard E. Greenleaf. Lincoln: University of Nebraska Press.

Suryadarma, Daniel. 2012. "How Corruption Diminishes the Effectiveness of Public Spending on Education in Indonesia." *Bulletin of Indonesian Economic Studies* 48 (1): 85–100.

Toivanen, Otto, and Lotta Väänänen. 2016. "Education and Invention." *Review of Economics and Statistics* 98 (2): 382–96.

Tombe, Trevor, and Xiaodong Zhu. 2019. "Trade, Migration, and Productivity: A Quantitative Analysis of China." *American Economic Review* 109 (5): 1843–72.

Topa, Giorgio, and Yves Zenou. 2015. "Neighborhood and Network Effects." In *Handbook of Regional and Urban Economics,* vol. 5, edited by Gilles Duranton, J. Vernon Henderson, and William C. Strange, 561–624. Oxford, UK: Elsevier.

Turok, Ivan, and Jackie Borel-Saladin. 2018. "The Theory and Reality of Urban Slums: Pathways-Out-of-Poverty or Cul-de-Sacs?" *Urban Studies* 55 (4): 767–89.

WEF (World Economic Forum). 2020. *The Global Social Mobility Report 2020: Equality, Opportunity and a New Economic Imperative.* Insight Report (January). Geneva: WEF.

Wong, Mark Tsun On. 2019. "Intergenerational Family Support for 'Generation Rent': The Family Home for Socially Disengaged Young People." *Housing Studies* 34 (1): 1–23.

World Bank. 2018. *World Development Report 2018: Learning to Realize Education's Promise.* Washington, DC: World Bank.

World Bank. 2024. *Women, Business and the Law 2024.* Washington, DC: World Bank.

Zingales, Luigi. 2014. *A Capitalism for the People: Recapturing the Lost Genius of American Prosperity.* New York: Basic Books.

Ziraba, Abdhalah Kasiira, Catherine Kyobutungi, and Eliya Msiyaphazi Zulu. 2011. "Fatal Injuries in the Slums of Nairobi and Their Risk Factors: Results from a Matched Case-Control Study." *Journal of Urban Health* 88 (Supplement 2): 256–65.

6 Destruction

Key messages

- When a crisis strikes, such as that surrounding global energy, middle-income countries should seize the opportunity to instigate the needed restructuring and reallocation. For example, the global energy and climate crises have spurred rapid progress in the development and deployment of low-carbon technologies.
- In middle-income countries, the rate of adoption of key clean energy technologies is growing more rapidly than in high-income countries, but levels of adoption by firms and households remain significantly lower, particularly for solar energy, wind energy, and electric vehicles.
- Incumbents in high-carbon industries, which tend to be state-owned enterprises in middle-income countries, erect barriers to the entry of low-carbon technology because they have the strongest incentive to maintain the status quo and limit competition from low-carbon energy providers.
- Middle-income countries run the risk of becoming stranded nations—not because of anything inherent in the scaling up of low-carbon technologies and the winding down of fossil fuels, but because of (1) outdated policies and rules of thumb that limit the growth of value-creating enterprises and the exit of unproductive ones; (2) limited improvements in human capital and the mobility of workers; and (3) a refusal to let go of state control of productive assets that are being decommissioned ahead of time.

Destruction: To be expected, managed, and mitigated

The Republic of Korea's financial crisis in 1997–98 had paradoxical economic impacts on innovation, restructuring, and growth. Before the crisis, large family-owned industrial conglomerates, *chaebols*, enjoyed almost unrestrained market power and expansion thanks to excessive debt financing. They were then able to drive rival firms and small industries out of business by adopting predatory tactics, suppressing technological improvements, and persuading government to restrict new entry or open market policies. Therefore, the crisis, although triggered by external events, was largely a product of internal problems related to a weak system of corporate governance, a dysfunctional financial system, and poor labor relations.[1]

The crisis triggered major reforms and a comprehensive restructuring of the financial sector and the *chaebols*. Nearly 500 nonviable financial institutions closed, including two-thirds of commercial banks, and 15 of the 30 top conglomerates went bankrupt. The collapse of many *chaebols* made room for venture capital–backed firms, which led to the rapid growth of the information and communication technology (ICT) sector. The ICT boom—spurred by new technologies such as mobile phones, thin film transistor liquid crystal displays, and broadband and wireless internet—kick-started an unusually swift recovery in 1999, with economic growth of 10.3 percent. The reforms and restructuring led to long-term innovation-led growth and contributed to Korea's transition to high-income status. Overall, then, it took a crisis to lay bare the need for economic reforms and drive the reallocation of economic activity toward more productive, more innovative firms.

The destruction of outdated arrangements—enterprises, jobs, technologies, private contracts, policies, and public institutions—is essential to create value through investment and reallocation, infusion, and innovation. But in many countries these destructive forces are weak during boom times, with crises playing a disproportionate role in driving the process of resource reallocation.[2,3] In some cases, downturns can serve as times of cleansing in which older, less-productive firms die, making way for newer, more productive firms. As Joseph A. Schumpeter (1942, 113), writing in the aftermath of the Great Depression, argued about crises:

> They are but temporary. They are the means to reconstruct each time the economic system on a more efficient plan. But they inflict losses while they last, drive firms into the bankruptcy court, throw people out of employment, before the ground is clear and the way paved for new achievement of the kind which has created modern civilization and made the greatness of this country.

One of Schumpeter's key observations is that the process of creating new industries does not go forward without sweeping away the existing order. For example, over the last 30 years in the United States, on average nearly 16 percent of jobs in the private sector have been destroyed each year.[4] Literature on firm exit—stemming from seminal work by Hopenhayn (1992)—reveals that the exit of low-productivity firms contributes substantially to raising aggregate productivity. For example, the Great Depression (1929–39) ushered in a permanent structural change toward mass production and automation in the motor vehicle industry through the exit of smaller, less productive plants and the need for surviving plants to innovate—a process that likely would have taken much longer without the crisis.[5]

Financial crises also spur readjustments of new technologies. For example, the financial crisis of 2007 accelerated skill-biased technological change.[6] More recently, during the COVID-19 crisis economic activity was reallocated toward more productive firms, with reallocation effects higher than before the pandemic.[7]

In the context of energy, the oil price shocks in the 1980s played a major role in accelerating investments in energy efficiency and the development of cleaner energy technologies.[8] One impact of the oil price shocks was an increase in the relative cost of fossil fuels. Another was new policy support for less energy-intensive activities. More recently, the global financial crisis of 2007–09 coincided with a significant increase in the uptake of renewables.[9] Renewable energy use grew rapidly in the United States, China, and Germany in part because of the stimulus programs governments enacted to address the crisis.

This chapter focuses on the process of creative destruction being accelerated today by two crises—the climate crisis and the 2022–23 global energy crisis triggered by the Russian Federation's invasion of Ukraine. In this context, this chapter explores three questions:

- *How is the energy crisis building momentum for change?* The global energy crisis spurred rapid progress in the development and deployment of low-carbon technologies. It also triggered reshaping of the climate policy landscape in 2022 and 2023. Developed nations such as the United States and European Union (EU) member states introduced a wide variety of incentives for producing and deploying low-carbon technologies. In September 2023, the leaders of the Group of Twenty (G20) agreed to triple renewable energy capacity by 2030. Although fossil fuels have shaped the world's economy and economic geography for over a century, low-carbon technologies favor new trends: urban agglomerations and new spatial clusters; the use of highly skilled workers to develop, modify, adapt, apply, and maintain new technologies; and the entry of younger firms in the private sector. Entrants are instigators of change.

- *Who are the antagonists blocking creative destruction in energy markets?* Incumbents may resist change. Many incumbents in the energy market have the strongest incentive to maintain the status quo and limit competition from low-carbon energy providers. High-carbon firms tend to lobby against pro-environmental regulations.[10] Power purchase agreements (PPAs) with long time horizons and inflexible terms that create "lock-ins" impede change. These agreements often lock in polluting assets, resulting in significant inertia in energy systems.
- *Do middle-income countries run the risk of becoming stranded nations?* Yes, they do. But stranding is not driven by anything inherent in the scaling up of low-carbon technologies and the winding down of fossil fuels. It is the result of outdated policies and rules of thumb that limit the growth of value-creating enterprises and the exit of unproductive ones; limited improvements in human capital and mobility of workers; and not relinquishing state control of productive assets now being decommissioned ahead of time. To be sure, workers displaced from the transition will need targeted and time-bound support, but it is not a panacea for avoiding difficult reforms.

The climate and energy crises could trigger restructuring and reallocation

Disruptions are accelerating the diffusion of innovative lower-carbon technologies

Today, two crises—the climate crisis and the global energy crisis—are combining to drive rapid progress in low-carbon technologies (box 6.1). Four technologies—solar panels, wind turbines, lithium-ion batteries, and electrolyzers used for green hydrogen—have been shown to follow "learning curves," as formalized by Wright's Law: costs fall as a power function of cumulative deployment due to the positive effects of learning by doing or increasing returns to scale in the unit's production.[11] Since the first commercial use of solar panels in 1958, their costs have fallen by more than three orders of magnitude. This technology is therefore in a category that has been characterized by exponential rather than linear growth, along with computer processing power, Ford's Model T cars in the 1900s, and DNA sequencing. Figure 6.1 compares the cost trajectories of solar and wind power with other technologies that have undergone rapid cost declines. Critically, this pattern is in sharp contrast to that of fossil fuels, whose prices have stayed broadly constant when adjusted for inflation over the last century.

Diffusion of these technologies, although slow for many decades, recently accelerated. Analysis of 700 million online job postings from 35 predominantly advanced economies reveals that after very modest growth beginning in 2014, the share of jobs related to low-carbon technologies increased by more than 50 percent from 2021 to 2022 (figure 6.2, panel a).[12] Growth was rapid in three-quarters of the countries studied in Asia, Europe, and North America, but stronger in Europe. Driving this growth were electric vehicles (EVs), solar energy, insulation, EV charging, heat pumps, and wind energy. In 2022, openings related to low-carbon technologies grew rapidly in almost every industry,

> **Box 6.1 The diffusion of low-carbon technologies as defined and measured in this chapter**
>
> This chapter defines low-carbon technologies in line with the Y02 classification of patents related to "climate change mitigation technologies" adopted by the European Patent Office. Low-carbon technologies are defined as "technologies or applications which can be considered as countering the effects of climate change." This classification has seven main categories: energy, greenhouse gas capture, buildings, industry (including agriculture), transport, waste management, and wastewater management. Some examples of the technologies included under these categories are:
>
> - *Upstream energy supply technologies:* renewable energy, combustion technologies with the potential to mitigate carbon emissions, energy storage technologies, decentralized energy, efficient electrical power generation technologies, and smart grids.
> - *Downstream end-user technologies:* energy-efficient lighting, energy-efficient heating, energy-efficient appliances, heat pumps, electric vehicles, electric vehicle charging, hybrid vehicles; technologies related to processing of metals and minerals and lowering emissions in agriculture (such as solar water pumping and greenhouses); and technologies related to solid waste management, biopackaging, and bioplastics.
>
> Detailed microdata on the adoption of these granular technologies across a wide range of countries, regions, industries, and firms are not yet readily available. In the absence of such data, this chapter relies on a growing literature that takes advantage of real-time data sources and uses text analysis to infer the spread of new technologies through their footprint in the demand for new technology-related tasks or skills in online job postings.[a] Where possible, the chapter also complements these measures with country-level measures of specific technologies and data on energy intensity and carbon intensity at the country and industry levels. Finally, it also incorporates recent granular firm-level data on green technology adoption from the World Bank's Firm-level Adoption of Technology (FAT) survey.[b]
>
> a. See, for example, Acemoglu et al. (2022); Goldfarb, Taska, and Teodoridis (2023).
> b. Cirera, Comin, and Cruz (2022).

but were particularly pronounced in manufacturing, electricity, heat supply, and construction. Mentions of low-carbon technologies in the shareholder meetings of the world's largest firms also doubled in 2022 (figure 6.2, panel b).

Countries have responded to high energy prices and energy security stemming from the invasion of Ukraine with energy conservation measures, fuel switching, and accelerated deployment of cleaner energy technologies. The energy intensity of the gross domestic product (GDP) is now 3.5 percent below levels before the pandemic in 2019—a rate of decline considerably higher than the 2 percent decline three years after the onset of the 2008 financial crisis. Emissions from natural gas also fell by 1.6 percent in 2022.

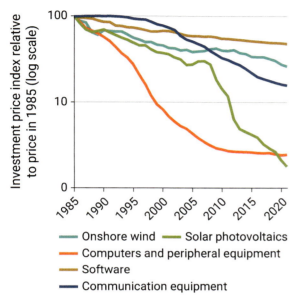

Figure 6.1 Learning by doing in the manufacture of key low-carbon technologies has resulted in rapid cost declines

Sources: WDR 2024 team elaboration from Arkolakis and Walsh (2023); FRED: Software (Federal Reserve Economic Data: Software) (database), Federal Reserve Bank of St. Louis, St. Louis, https://fred.stlouisfed.org/tags/series?t=software; IRENA (2023); Prices and Output for Information and Communication Technologies (dashboard), Bureau of Economic Analysis, Suitland, MD, https://www.bea.gov/prices-and-output-information-and-communication-technologies; Solar (photovoltaic) panel prices (grapher), Our World in Data, Global Change Data Lab and Oxford Martin Program on Global Development, University of Oxford, Oxford, UK, https://ourworldindata.org/grapher/solar-pv-prices.

Note: The figure compares the price of investment for the three sectors with the fastest declines according to data from the Bureau of Economic Analysis with that for onshore wind and solar photovoltaics, with 1985 normalized to 1.

In light of policy changes, the International Energy Agency (IEA) revised its forecast for renewable capacity additions for 2023 and 2024, raising it by 38 percent from its expectations before the war, in December 2021. Countries more dependent on imports of natural gas before the war were more exposed to the price shock and increased hiring for jobs related to low-carbon technologies.[13]

The global energy crisis also spurred a reshaping of the climate policy landscape in 2022 and 2023. The United States saw a historic shift in climate policy with passage of the Inflation Reduction Act (IRA) in late 2022, which introduced a wide variety of incentives for producing and deploying low-carbon technologies.[14] The IRA could have large impacts on power sector investments and electricity prices, lowering retail electricity rates and resulting in negative prices in some wholesale markets.[15] It could also significantly hasten the adoption of renewable energy in the United States, increasing renewable penetration by about 13 percent by 2030, and it could spur adoption in other countries as the higher US investment drives capital prices lower.[16] The European Union also made substantial shifts in climate policy in 2022 and early 2023. These included the REPowerEU strategy to end the bloc's reliance on Russian fossil fuels through lower fossil fuel use; the Green Deal Industrial Plan, which aims to boost low-carbon manufacturing and industry in Europe; and an increase in the bloc's binding renewable energy target from 32 percent to 43 percent. China has also pushed its scale-up of renewables and is now on track to meet its 2030 renewable energy generation target five years ahead of time, by 2025.[17]

This acceleration of the clean energy transition is driving the emergence of new spatial clusters and jobs (map 6.1). Evidence extending the work of Bastos et al. (2023) to analyze 1 billion online job postings across 86 countries over the last decade reveals that in 2022 alone 3.3 million new job openings were related to low-carbon technologies—just under 2 percent of jobs posted online in 2022.[18] In absolute terms, new openings have been highest in the United States, Europe, and China (figure 6.3, panel a). The new spatial clusters emerging in terms of low-carbon technology jobs are Catalonia and Madrid in Spain, home to major solar industries; Guangzhou, Beijing, Shanghai, Suzhou, and Shenzhen in China, home to China's largest EV and clean energy manufacturing hubs; Rhône-Alpes and Île-de-France (the Paris region), home to France's largest clean energy clusters; and California, the clean energy pioneer in the United States.[19]

Figure 6.2 The diffusion of low-carbon technologies is rapidly accelerating

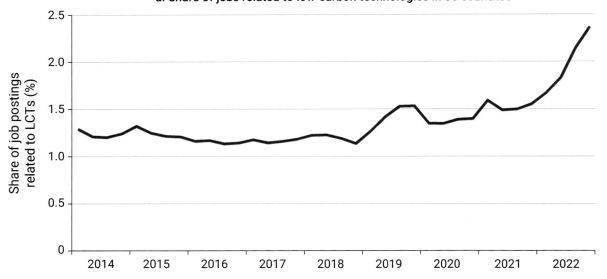

a. Share of jobs related to low-carbon technologies in 35 countries

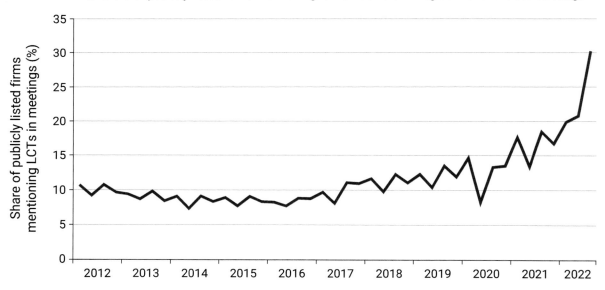

b. Share of publicly listed firms mentioning low-carbon technologies in shareholder meetings

Source: Bastos et al. 2023.

Note: Panel a displays the share of online job postings in 35 countries that mention low-carbon technologies (LCTs) as defined by the Y02 classification of patents adopted by the European Patent Office. See Classification of Patents: Climate Change Mitigation Technologies (dashboard), European Patent Office, Munich, https://www.epo.org/en/news-events/in-focus/classification/climate-change. Panel b displays the share of shareholder meeting transcripts from publicly listed firms that mention these technologies.

Map 6.1 In 2022, one-third of online job postings related to low-carbon technologies were in middle-income countries

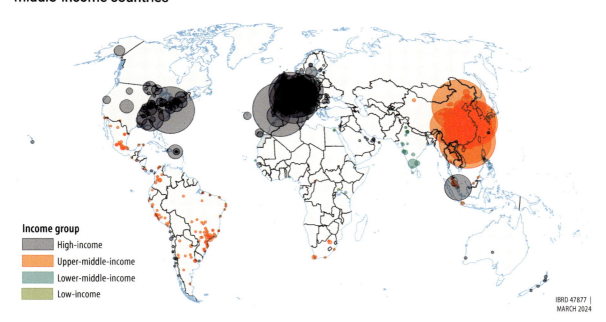

Source: WDR 2024 team analysis extending Bastos et al. (2023) to 86 countries.

Innovation is also driving the creation of start-ups and capital flows (figure 6.3, panels b and c). In 2021, about 1,500 new clean energy start-ups were listed on Crunchbase, drawing on IEA data covering 40 countries, and about one-fourth of the start-ups were in middle-income countries.[20] Of these, more than half were in China and one-third in India, although growth has been most rapid in India, with a tripling of start-up creation over the last decade. Globally, total clean energy financing passed US$1 trillion for the first time in 2022.[21]

These shifts are triggering a reallocation of economic activity across countries, regions, industries, occupations, and firms. Just as fossil fuels have shaped the geopolitical map over the last two centuries, the clean energy transformation will alter the economic geography of manufacturing and global trade and the landscape of international trade policy. Access to fossil fuels has fundamentally shaped the world's economic geography for nearly a century, with heavy industry close to coal beds and petrochemical plants near petroleum fields. The trade in fossil fuels has been a driving component of global trade and geopolitics for decades, with fuel exports accounting for 11.7 percent of total merchandise exports globally in 2019. However, this picture is starting to change—and more rapidly than had been imagined as the following shifts occur:

- *Shifts between countries and between regions within countries.* Low-carbon technologies and fossil fuels tend to be produced in different countries, and low-carbon technologies favor countries where manufacturing capabilities are already in place. Even within some countries, a spatial reallocation of production and jobs is under way. In China, for example, although fossil fuel jobs have been highly concentrated in the inland provinces highly reliant on coal mining, low-carbon technology jobs are growing in the manufacturing hubs on the east coast.[22] Spatial disparities

DESTRUCTION | 141

will be altered and potentially intensified because the geographical determinants of low-carbon energy sources differ from those of fossil fuel–based economies, and technological innovation is likely to occur most rapidly in centers of research and agglomeration.[23]

- *Shifts between industries.* Because low-carbon technologies are generally being mass manufactured, the low-carbon transition is

Figure 6.3 Low-carbon innovation is driving the emergence of new spatial clusters, start-ups, and financing

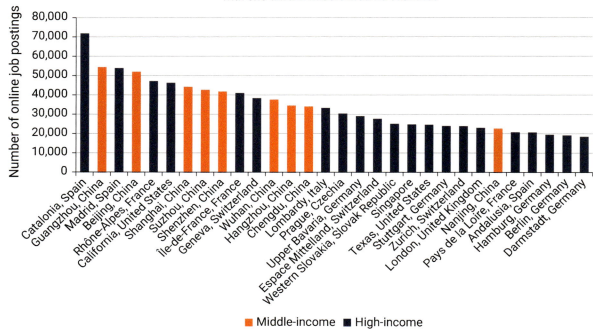

a. Online job postings related to low-carbon technologies in 2022, by city, state, region, or country

3.3 million online job openings were related to low-carbon technologies in 2022, with one-third in middle-income countries

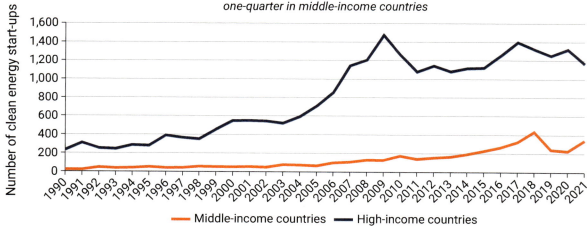

b. Creation of clean energy start-ups

1,506 clean energy start-ups were listed on Crunchbase in 2021, one-quarter in middle-income countries

(Figure continues next page)

Figure 6.3 Low-carbon innovation is driving the emergence of new spatial clusters, start-ups, and financing *(continued)*

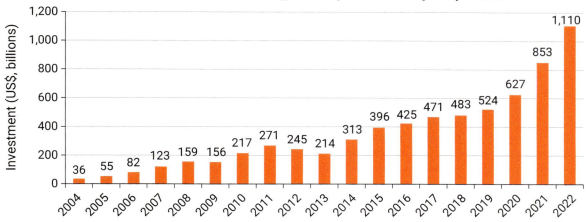

Sources: Panel a: WDR 2024 team analysis extending Bastos et al. (2023) to 86 countries. Panel b: Data and Statistics (dashboard), International Energy Agency, Paris, https://www.iea.org/data-and-statistics. Panel c: 2022 data from BloombergNEF (dashboard), Bloomberg, New York, https://about.bnef.com/.

Note: Panel a displays the number of online job postings by city, state, region, or country that mention low-carbon technologies as defined by the Y02 classification of patents adopted by the European Patent Office. See Classification of Patents: Climate Change Mitigation Technologies (dashboard), European Patent Office, Munich, https://www.epo.org/en/news-events/in-focus/classification/climate-change. Panel b displays the number of new clean energy start-ups by year for middle- and high-income countries. Panel c displays the value of clean energy financing by year globally.

driving a reallocation of economic activity across industries from extractives to manufacturing and ancillary services. Jobs are most likely to be in the manufacturing, construction, and sales industries, but low-carbon technology jobs are growing rapidly in the high-skilled white-collar industries able to develop, modify, adapt, apply, and maintain new technologies.

- *Shifts between occupations.* The manufacture of low-carbon technologies is more skill-intensive than that for the high-carbon alternatives,[24] resulting in a reallocation of economic activity between occupations and skill types. Jobs are also more likely to be filled by younger, college-educated white-collar workers, whereas high-carbon jobs are more likely to be occupied by older blue-collar workers.[25]

- *Shifts between firms.* Low-carbon technologies are more likely to be adopted by new entrants, exporters, private firms, and firms that use research and development (R&D) more intensively.[26] Low-carbon technology job postings are also highly concentrated in multinational firms and their supply chains.[27] By contrast, high-carbon jobs are more likely to be in older firms and state-owned enterprises.

The energy transition is also shaping a new global trade and industrial policy landscape, which is disrupting the last three decades of trade policy coordination. After decades of such coordination, which yielded significant growth dividends, the world's major economies now have divergent climate and trade policy approaches. The IRA in the United States, the Net-Zero Industry Act in the

European Union,[28] and the growing number of similar policies globally increasingly include local content requirements and other reshoring efforts to support local industries. Although the previous waves of middle-income countries transitioned to high-income status against the backdrop of trade policy coordination, today's middle-income countries will need to navigate a more complex landscape in which key trade rules have not yet been agreed on.

Productive incumbents and new entrants are driving the diffusion of cleaner technologies

Diffusion of upstream clean energy technologies in middle-income countries

As the costs of low-carbon technologies decline, growth using cleaner energy sources and energy efficiency technologies is for the first time a possibility in today's middle-income countries. Currently, these countries' rate of adoption of key low-carbon energy technologies is, in fact, growing more rapidly than for that of high-income countries, but levels of adoption remain significantly lower. In levels, middle-income countries are still lagging on the deployment of three key low-carbon energy technologies—solar energy, wind energy, and EVs—compared with high-income countries (figure 6.4). In 2021, the average share of electricity generated from wind and solar power in middle-income countries was about half of that in high-income countries (respectively, 4.1 percent versus 9.5 percent for wind and 2.7 percent versus 5.3 percent for solar). The uptake of EVs in middle-income countries also remains about half as much as that in high-income countries (measured as number of EVs per million inhabitants). But today in middle-income countries, the average growth rates of key clean energy technologies have overtaken those of high-income countries.[29]

Research for this Report found that after controlling for income, countries with higher rates of deployment of solar and wind energy have more favorable renewable energy policies and a more favorable regulatory environment (captured by a higher value on the Regulatory Indicators for Sustainable Energy, or RISE, Index); higher carbon pricing (as measured using the net effective carbon rate of the Organisation for Economic Co-operation and Development, OECD); and lower fossil fuel reserves.[30] Countries with higher solar potential (measured using the World Bank PVOUT Index) also have higher solar deployment rates.[31]

Diffusion of downstream low-carbon energy technologies in middle-income countries

Adoption of low-carbon technologies by firms and households in middle-income countries remains far more limited than in high-income countries. In 2021, the emissions intensity of energy consumption in middle-income countries was 49 percent higher than that in high-income countries, while energy consumption per unit of GDP was 2.5 times higher. Measures of downstream technology adoption across a wide range of countries are not readily available, but emissions intensity within narrowly defined industries can serve as a proxy for technology adoption.[32] On average, of 63 middle-income countries, two-thirds (41) have higher carbon intensity across industries—in terms of direct emissions that are owned or controlled by a company (Scope 1 emissions)—than the high-income country average, while about one-third (22) have lower carbon intensity.

Firms in middle-income countries vary widely in their adoption of low-carbon technologies, even within narrowly defined industries. Firms' overall management practices and technological sophistication, skill intensity, and international orientation are correlated with their adoption of low-carbon technologies and energy-saving practices. In Argentina, for example, firms' capacity to adopt more advanced low-carbon technologies has been shown to be correlated with their share of skilled workers.[33] Exporters usually have lower emissions intensity relative to nonexporters.[34] Foreign-owned firms generally have better environmental performance, as has been shown for Côte d'Ivoire, Mexico, and República Bolivariana de Venezuela.[35]

Figure 6.4 The rate of adoption of clean energy technologies is growing more rapidly in middle-income countries than in high-income countries, but the level of adoption is lower

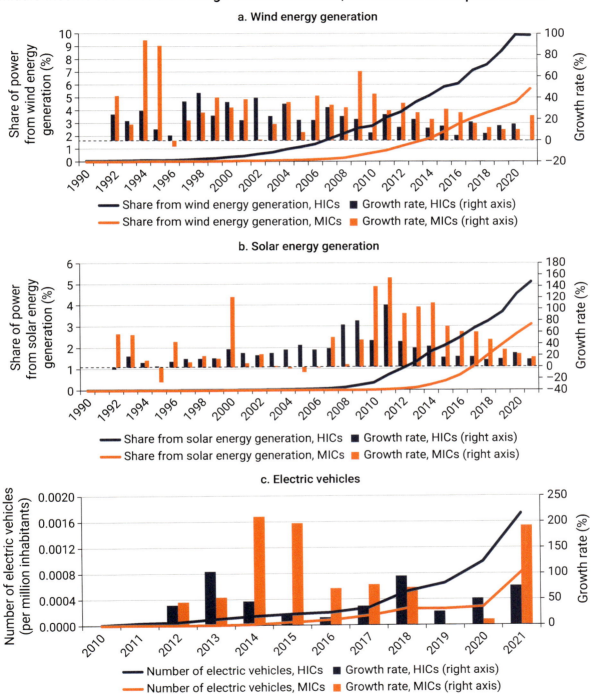

Source: WDR 2024 team analysis using data from Statistics Data (portal), International Renewable Energy Agency, Abu Dhabi, United Arab Emirates, https://www.irena.org/Data.

Note: Comparing middle- and high-income countries, panels a and b display the shares and growth rates of wind energy and solar energy, respectively, in electricity generation, and panel c the number of battery electric vehicles per million inhabitants. HICs = high-income countries; MICs = middle-income countries.

DESTRUCTION | 145

Production of low-carbon technologies is concentrated in a few middle-income countries

Substantial manufacturing or innovation in low-carbon energy technologies is occurring in only a handful of middle-income countries with competitive manufacturing sectors. In terms of production, only one middle-income country—China—is competitive in all three key low-carbon technologies in terms of breadth (across the full value chain from raw materials, processed materials, subcomponents, to the end product of the supply chain) and depth (a high average market share) (figure 6.5). By contrast, other middle-income countries have either depth or breadth and typically only in one product. For example, countries with well-established manufacturing sectors such as India and Türkiye show a high breadth of export competitiveness in the production of wind turbines. Middle-income countries with large mineral deposits (such as Brazil and Russia) have high depth in the export of critical minerals for EVs.

Patenting for low-carbon technologies is also highly concentrated in just a handful of countries, with China in the lead, according to data from the International Renewable Energy Agency (IRENA). Over the last two decades, China has filed the largest number of such patents, followed by the United States, Japan, Korea, and Germany. Such patenting has been very limited in other middle-income countries, with the second-highest middle-income country, Brazil, filing only 2 percent as many patents as China over the last 20 years.

Costa Rica and China are global front-runners in terms of job creation related to low-carbon technologies. In 2022, Costa Rica accounted for about 8 percent of all online job postings related to low-carbon technologies and China for 5 percent—just below the global maximum of 8 percent for Denmark (figure 6.6). Five other countries have exceeded the high-income country average: Brazil, Georgia, Senegal, South Africa, and the Dominican Republic. In terms of emerging spatial clusters in 2022, 28 of the 30 cities with the largest number of new online job postings related to low-carbon technologies were in China. Only Bangalore and São Paolo were the other middle-income country cities in the top 30. These sectors and jobs are clustered both within and across countries. For middle-income countries to successfully seize the opportunities of the green economy, the right policy mix, financing, regulatory environment, and infrastructure need to be in place.

Incumbent state-owned enterprises, legacy policies, and path dependence—all block creative destruction

Incumbents in high-carbon industries erect barriers to entry of low-carbon technologies

The low-carbon transition will create winners and losers—and the losses are more concentrated than the gains, resulting in a political economy prone to inertia. Although 80 percent of the global population lives in a country that imports fossil fuel, fossil fuel revenues are highly concentrated. In 18 countries, fuel exports account for more than 50 percent of total merchandise exports; seven countries generate 90 percent or more of their export earnings from fossil fuel exports.[36] Fossil fuel resources are more concentrated than renewable resources.[37] Within countries, the losses to fossil fuel companies are also highly concentrated. Studies have shown that the concentrated nature of the losses from the low-carbon transition, compared with the distributed nature of the gains, makes the clean energy transition particularly prone to obstructionism by entrenched interests.[38] Moreover, the incentives for lobbying are asymmetric. Incumbents, as a tightly defined group of actors, have a greater incentive to mobilize, and they face lower coordination costs. Smaller firms and individuals, by contrast, are more dispersed and face higher coordination costs. This results in political inertia, as has been evident from the persistent difficulty in phasing out fossil fuel subsidies globally.[39]

Incentives, both explicit and implicit, that favor higher-carbon industries and production processes over lower-carbon ones are higher in

Figure 6.5 Clean energy technology value chains are still dominated by high-income countries and China

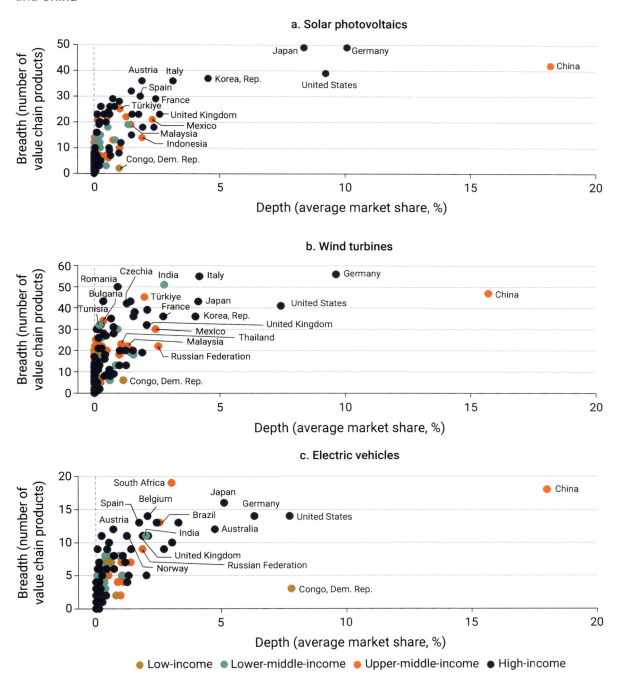

Source: Rosenow and Mealy 2024.
Note: Each panel measures countries' competitive dominance across traded products in a given supply chain in terms of two key measures. *Breadth* represents a country's export competitiveness across the raw materials, processed materials, subcomponents, and end products of the supply chain. *Depth* measures a country's export competitiveness in terms of its average market share across supply chain products. The sample includes countries whose total number of value chain products with a revealed comparative advantage exceeds 1.

DESTRUCTION | 147

Figure 6.6 Costa Rica and China are the global front-runners in jobs related to low-carbon technologies

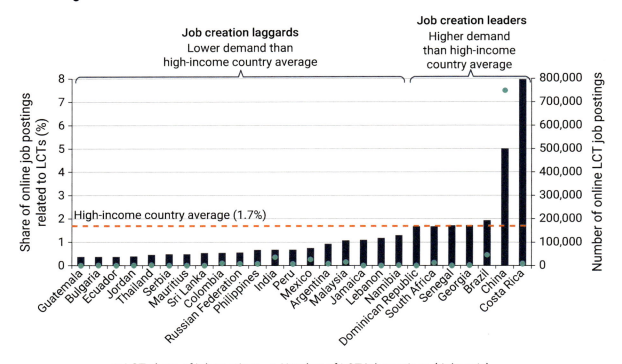

Source: WDR 2024 team analysis extending Bastos et al. (2023).
Note: The figure displays the share of online job postings of middle-income countries in 2022 that mention low-carbon technologies (LCTs) as defined by the classification of patents related to "climate change mitigation technologies" adopted by the European Patent Office. It also displays the total number of low-carbon technology postings in 2022. See Classification of Patents: Climate Change Mitigation Technologies (dashboard), European Patent Office, Munich, https://www.epo.org/en/news-events/in-focus/classification/climate-change.

middle-income countries than in high-income countries. Middle-income countries, particularly energy exporters, have significantly lower carbon prices.[40] Consumer fossil fuel subsidies in middle-income countries totaled over US$800 billion in 2022, of a global total of US$900 billion.[41] Estimates of explicit consumer and producer fossil fuel subsidies in 2022 from the International Monetary Fund (IMF) also show that middle-income countries account for 65 percent of the total.[42] Fossil fuel subsidies have a sizable fiscal cost and exacerbate air pollution, contributing directly to premature deaths.[43]

Middle-income countries also score lower on the RISE Index, particularly on the components of providing incentives and regulatory support for renewable energy and planning for the expansion of renewable energy. In addition, middle-income countries generally provide highly polluting industries with higher corporate tax incentives. Such incentives are particularly high in the Middle East and North Africa, as measured by the World Bank's Global Corporate Income Tax Incentives Database.

Incentives that support incumbent firms and energy sources, as well as major barriers to entry in power markets, also severely limit private innovation in middle-income countries. Over the last 35 years, many countries have introduced competitive markets in parts of the electricity system to reduce costs and improve reliability. In many middle-income countries, however, power markets remain a monopoly: a state-owned entity operating under a vertically integrated utility. This state-owned entity carries out all functions in the electricity sector, including generation, transmission, distribution, and retail supply. Such an arrangement has generally hindered competition, and in many countries it has resulted in the inefficient use of resources. In addition, in many middle-income countries the first generators dispatched are often not those with the lower marginal prices (that is, power dispatch often does not follow merit order), serving as a barrier to the penetration of renewables with rapidly declining costs. Generally, the shift to more competitive market structures has lowered costs and enabled more innovation and penetration of renewables.[44] In addition, the fact that energy supply technologies tend to be big, complex, expensive, and slow to develop and that new entrants must sell into entrenched markets dominated by incumbents severely limits incentives for private innovation.[45]

Power purchase agreements with long time horizons and inflexible terms that create "lock-ins" also impede change in energy systems. PPAs are widely used to procure power by establishing a contract between a seller of power and a buyer, often a utility. If well-structured, PPAs offer certainty for buyers as well as sellers, protecting them from volatility in energy prices by locking in the price buyers pay for electricity for decades to come. This kind of long-term certainty offers sellers a steady source of revenue and improves the chances of securing low-cost financing. However, by their very nature, when used to generate power in emissions-intensive ways, such as coal-fired power, these agreements lock in polluting assets, often for decades at a time, resulting in significant inertia in energy systems. Against the backdrop of the rapidly declining costs of clean energy technologies, inflexible PPAs with "take or pay" clauses are also resulting in economically—and environmentally—suboptimal energy systems choices.

High-carbon inertia curtails innovation, slows planning, and locks in behavior

A wide body of literature has now demonstrated that patents for low-carbon technologies "build on the shoulders" of earlier developments. Thus patenting is path-dependent, meaning that innovations are more likely to follow existing innovations, which can impede innovations in new technologies at an early stage.[46] This literature has generally pointed out the need for initial subsidies to jump-start the innovation process and correct for the positive externalities that result in underinvestment in R&D on low-carbon technologies, as well as the need for carbon pricing to correct for the negative externality of carbon emissions.

Inertia in keeping up with, and planning for, exponential progress in low-carbon technologies has also slowed the changes needed in energy systems. The rapid technical progress in a range of low-carbon technologies described earlier has generally outpaced the expectations of leading agencies and energy-economy models. For example, for many years the IEA forecasted linear growth in the supplies of solar under its business-as-usual scenarios, even as supplies continued to rise exponentially. Not only the IEA but historically most energy-economy models have underestimated the deployment rates for renewable energy technologies and overestimated their costs, as outlined by Grubb et al. (2021) and Way et al. (2022). The reason is that most national energy-economy models and large-scale global integrated assessment models label energy technology cost developments as exogenous. However, energy systems investments are often large and indivisible (lumpy)—that is, they are not easily divided or sold in parts—and they are made over long time horizons, often spanning multiple decades. Thus such downside forecast inaccuracy has deterred investments in low-carbon technologies and resulted in inertia in planning.

Studies have found that peer effects and social learning are important factors in decision-making related to climate change.[47] Preferences on technology adoption or social change are not cast in stone, but they change in response to decisions made by peers. The result is inertia in adoption initially and then rapid adoption later once a critical mass of peers adopts the technology. Similarly, the production of low-carbon technologies is subject to external economies of scale, which lead to lower production and operating costs for all companies in the industry. These, in turn, can increase profitability and competitiveness. However, these cost reductions do not occur until a sufficient number of industry players or scale is reached—meaning costs are higher for first movers.

Legacy transmission networks built to serve large fossil fuel plants slow diffusion of low-carbon energy

Because of the market structure of electricity generation and transmission, the deployment of clean energy technologies is more challenging and more complex than that for other technologies. Variable renewable energy sources provide energy only at certain times of the day or in certain seasons. Such intermittency poses challenges for their integration into power systems, particularly before electricity storage is fully developed. Integration also requires new approaches to demand-side management. The scale-up of the electrification of transport and buildings, which will increase the demand for electricity, also depends on the reliability of the power system. Scale-up requires accurate forecasting and forward planning. All these aspects of the energy transition create barriers and necessitate strong systemwide coordination and institutional capacity.

Legacy transmission networks built to serve large fossil fuel plants, along with outdated regulations, also create barriers to entry in middle-income countries. Typically, legacy networks have been designed for traditional energy sources for which generation can be located close to the source of demand (map 6.2). However, the renewable generation capacity for wind and solar must be built at the decentralized sites where these natural resources are found. Thus networks to transmit power are critical for the scale-up of

Map 6.2 Limited or outdated electricity transmission networks serve as barriers to the entry of renewable sources

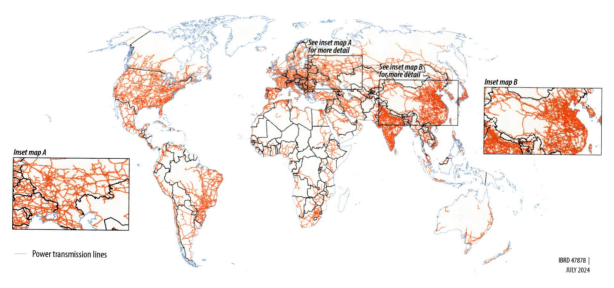

Source: Arkolakis and Walsh 2023.
Note: The map displays electricity transmission networks in 2023. The two insets focus on areas of particular interest due to the geographic disparities in coverage of transmission networks in these regions.

variable renewable energy. Because electricity transmission has elements of a public good that often result in its underprovision, transmission networks in many countries are not keeping pace with the ambitions of governments or the plans of firms. This inertia in transmission networks serves as a major barrier to the energy transition in many middle-income countries. In addition, outdated regulations related to the siting of renewables or permitting for rooftop solar also create inertia, hindering diffusion.

Destruction without creation: The risks of becoming stranded nations

Preservation worsens obsolescence; dynamic firms and mobile people are needed

The low-carbon transition poses a major risk of accelerating the obsolescence of capital, skills, and industries. It is a form of directed technical change away from carbon-intensive production processes.[48] In perfectly competitive markets, the associated reallocation of labor and capital would have minimal transition costs because workers and capital would smoothly and quickly adjust by switching jobs, moving to areas with growing demand, and supporting expansion of greener firms. In practice, however, search complications, costs to acquire human capital, or ties to particular geographic areas may give rise to significant transition costs.[49] Higher social, occupational, and geographic mobility facilitates the rapid movement of people out of declining industries and into expanding ones, which in many countries requires a move to another geographic location. Likewise, dynamic enterprises and low barriers to entry can lower transition costs within countries.

Meanwhile, fossil fuel resources that cannot be burned and fossil fuel infrastructure no longer used risk becoming "stranded assets." Stocks of unburnable carbon (such as coal reserves) could become stranded resources if their future value becomes lower than their current expected value.[50] This disconnect could lead to overly high investment in and maintenance of infrastructure that supports, and is supported by, the burning of fossil fuels, which later becomes stranded capital. In middle-income countries, coal-fired power plants are the most exposed to the risk of becoming stranded and may have to be retired 10–30 years earlier than they did in the past.[51] Several expectations influence whether assets become stranded. They include expectations about the implementation of climate policies, about technological progress, and about legal action against high emitters. Stranding could occur based on today's projections of fossil fuel production solely due to the current rate of technological change, which is faster than expected.[52] The extent of stranding will depend on how policy choices today shape expectations about the future, along with efforts today to facilitate the reallocation of resources from sunsetting industries to growing ones. Efforts by countries, industries, or firms to preserve sunsetting industries longer than is economically viable rather than reallocating resources to expanding ones risk increasing transition risks and obsolescence.

Overvalued assets also pose the risk of a carbon bubble in financial markets. The scale of the fossil fuel industry is large enough to potentially trigger broader financial crises. The exposure to correlated risks within and across portfolios, with many potentially stranded assets at risk of being devalued simultaneously, alongside the underexposure to assets in low-carbon technologies with potentially higher returns, also pose systemic risks that could affect the financial system as a whole.[53] If undermanaged, this instability could result in policy swinging away from transition to protecting the financial system more broadly. Ensuring an orderly transition and clarity in direction is necessary to limit the potential of this crisis.[54]

These financial risks are heightened in countries with more vulnerable financial systems. Countries more dependent on resource revenues would be particularly exposed, limiting their capacity to respond to the shock. The degree to which sectors are linked within the economy is also associated with the exposure of the financial system, with greater links acting to potentially multiply the effects of an initial shock, creating ripples through the wider economy, and exposing financial systems to further pressures.[55]

Countries with rich reserves of critical green minerals will also need to ensure they avoid repeating the mistakes of past natural resource booms and contracting "Dutch disease" or a green "resource curse."[56] The transition is also expected to significantly increase the demand for minerals that are critical inputs in low-carbon technologies such as lithium, cobalt, copper, and rare essential earths. This demand could present countries with large reserves of such minerals, such as Chile, the Democratic Republic of Congo, and Namibia, with a potential economic opportunity. However, critical minerals are often located in regions characterized by poor labor and environmental standards and considerable political fragility and corruption. Thus these increases in demand could contribute to a proliferation of problematic mining practices and conflict. The failure of many hydrocarbon exporters to use export revenue to diversify their economies, which now renders them vulnerable to the transition, should serve as a cautionary tale to mineral exporters. To avoid another resource curse, revenue from a higher demand for minerals could be used to support investment in education, infrastructure, and the development of economic sectors that are higher in value added.

Infusion of global technologies and diversification will be crucial for middle-income countries

Andres et al. (2023) have compiled a list of traded "brown products," whose use is likely to decline if the world is to mitigate climate change.[57] They then explore which countries are most at risk of seeing their productive capabilities "stranded." They find that, on average, brown products tend to be less complex than green products. Although countries that export technologically sophisticated brown products, such as internal combustion engine vehicles, could find it relatively easy to transition, those with exports highly concentrated in a few low-complexity brown products (such as commodities) have fewer opportunities for diversification. Of the top 10 countries facing the greatest risk of such "brown lock-ins," as measured by an index constructed by these authors, six are middle-income countries. Panel a of figure 6.7 displays the 10 middle-income countries most exposed: Iraq, Libya, Angola, Equatorial Guinea, Azerbaijan, Nigeria, Algeria, Turkmenistan, Timor-Leste, and Gabon.

Middle-income countries with a high degree of specialization of physical, institutional, and human capital in declining sectors that cannot be easily transitioned to new opportunities face the highest risks. The production of some carbon-intensive products is similar to the production of green ones—for example, there is a high degree of overlap in the manufacture of internal combustion engine (ICE) vehicles and electric vehicles. In general, the risk of brown lock-ins is negatively and significantly associated with the ease of transitioning to green or overall non-brown products. This risk is displayed in panel b of figure 6.7, which shows the correlation between the Brown Lock-in Index and the Transition Outlook, also constructed by Andres et al. (2023) to measure a country's ease of transitioning from brown to green products.

Workers with obsolete occupations and skills will need support to avoid stranding

The energy transition will lower the demand for workers who extract and refine coal, natural gas, and oil. Employment in these activities tends to be disproportionately occupied by workers without a college education.[58] Workers at legacy suppliers of electricity, such as the coal-fired power plants that are now being retired, will also be affected. At risk as well are those employed in energy-intensive manufacturing industries such as basic chemicals, nonmetallic minerals, and primary metals, and in industries like ICE

Figure 6.7 Most of the countries currently "locked in" to declining brown industries are middle-income countries

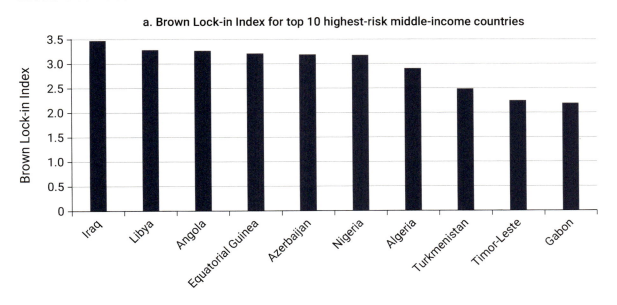

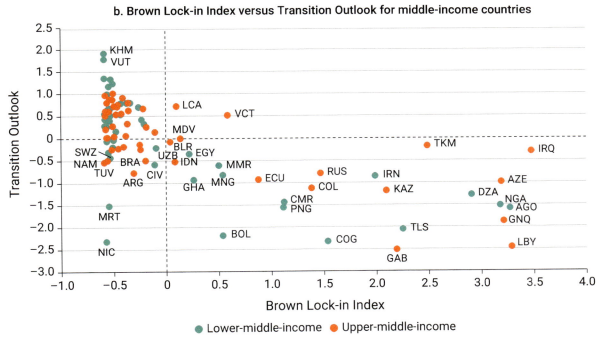

Source: WDR 2024 team analysis based on Andres et al. (2023).

Note: Panel a displays the Brown Lock-in Index for the 10 middle-income countries with the highest index values. See BLI (Brown Lock-in Index) (dashboard), Green Transition Navigator, London School of Economics and Political Science, London, https://green-transition-navigator.org/. Panel b displays the correlation between the Brown Lock-in Index and the Transition Outlook for all middle-income countries. The Brown Lock-in Index measures the risk that a country will be locked in to carbon-intensive industries. A higher index value indicates greater risk. The Transition Outlook measures a country's ease of transitioning from brown to green products. A higher value indicates greater ease of transitioning. See Green Transition Navigator (dashboard), London School of Economics and Political Science, London, https://green-transition-navigator.org/. For country abbreviations, see International Organization for Standardization (ISO), https://www.iso.org/obp/ui/#search.

vehicle manufacturing. Park et al. (2023) explore fossil fuel jobs in China and how their economic geography compares with that of low-carbon technology jobs. In China, fossil fuel jobs are concentrated around Shanxi and in the north of China, whereas low-carbon technology jobs are concentrated in the cities on the east coast and particularly in the south, demonstrating the challenge for workers to transition (map 6.3).

Recent research on job transitions has demonstrated the challenge of transitioning workers out of high-carbon jobs.[59] Using microdata representing more than 130 million online work profiles, Curtis, O'Kane, and Park (2023) explore transitions away from carbon-intensive production technologies. They find that in 2021 only 0.7 percent of workers who transitioned out of a carbon-intensive job found work in a green job. Conversely, the vast majority of workers obtaining green jobs do not come from carbon-intensive industries, but from a wide range of other industries and occupations (such as sales manager, software developer, and

Map 6.3 Low-carbon technology jobs in China are growing in manufacturing hubs on the southeast coast, whereas fossil fuel jobs are close to coal mines

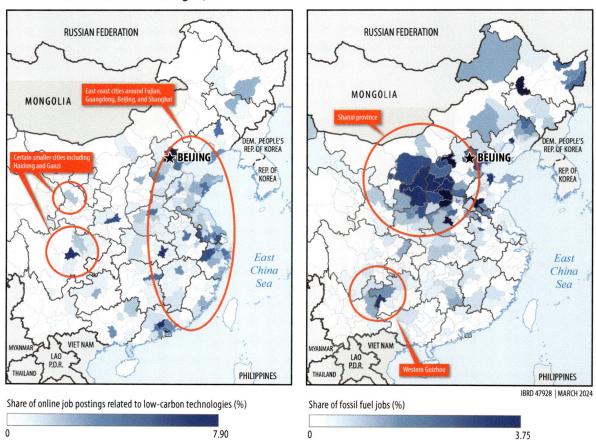

Source: Park et al. 2023.

Note: In panel b, the share of fossil fuel jobs in 2019 is based on data from China Statistical Database, National Bureau of Statistics of China, Beijing, https://www.stats.gov.cn/english/.

marketing manager). On average, 20 percent of transitions out of carbon-intensive jobs are into other carbon-intensive jobs, whereas transitions into manufacturing are the most common, accounting for more than 25 percent of all transitions out of carbon-intensive jobs. Although in some US states, such as California, the rates of transition from dirty to green jobs are relatively high, in others, such as West Virginia, the rates of green transitions are low even though these states have a high density of existing carbon-intensive jobs.

In conclusion, middle-income countries will need to amplify the forces of creation, weaken the forces of preservation, and manage the forces of destruction to advance technological progress. The chapters that follow focus on policies that these countries can implement to help them achieve these goals.

Notes

1. Krueger and Yoo (2002).
2. Davis and Haltiwanger (1990).
3. Crises do not always benefit reallocation and have also been shown to have "sullying" effects, leading to the exit of otherwise productive firms or high-quality jobs, with long-lasting scarring effects (Haltiwanger et al. 2021).
4. Haltiwanger et al. (2021).
5. Bresnahan and Raff (1991).
6. Hershbein and Kahn (2018).
7. Bruhn, Demirgüç-Kunt, and Singer (2021).
8. Peters et al. (2012).
9. UNEP (2009).
10. Kwon, Lowry, and Verardo (2023).
11. Way et al. (2022).
12. Bastos et al. (2023).
13. Bastos et al. (2023).
14. Climate and low-carbon competitiveness are also now covered in a wide number of new US policies, including the CHIPS and Science Act of 2022 and Infrastructure Investment and Jobs Act of 2021.
15. Bistline et al. (2023).
16. Arkolakis and Walsh (2023).
17. Jones (2023); Xue (2024).
18. This is similar to the IEA's finding that clean energy jobs now account for about 2 percent of all jobs globally (IEA and IFC 2023).
19. Several smaller cities and those in middle-income countries are experiencing sizable job creation from low-carbon technologies. For example, 5 percent of online job postings in 2022 in Rio de Janeiro were by low-carbon technologies, while in small provincial cities in China, such as Ningde, home to one of China's largest battery manufacturing clusters, 8 percent of all online job postings were related to low-carbon technologies.
20. Crunchbase is a US-based company that provides information about start-ups using data sourced from investors and community contributors, such as start-ups themselves. Although it includes companies in more than 200 countries, it may underrepresent start-ups in emerging markets that are funded only domestically and do not have a global presence. Thus they do not choose to list themselves and are not disclosed by investors. For more information, see Dalle, den Besten, and Menon (2017).
21. See BloombergNEF (dashboard), Bloomberg, New York, https://about.bnef.com/.
22. Park et al. (2023).
23. Bridge et al. (2013).
24. See, for example, Saussay et al. (2023).
25. Curtis, O'Kane, and Park (2023).
26. Cirera, Comin, and Cruz (2024).
27. Bastos et al. (2023).
28. "Net zero" refers to the balance between the amount of greenhouse gas produced and the amount removed from the atmosphere. It can be achieved through a combination of emissions reduction and removal.
29. In the five years before the COVID-19 pandemic (2015–19), the growth rates in the share of electricity generated from solar and wind energy were higher in middle-income countries than in high-income countries. The average growth rate in middle-income countries was about 13 percent for wind and 44 percent for solar, compared with 11 percent and 16 percent, respectively, for high-income countries. The average growth rate of EVs per capita in middle-income countries over the five years preceding the COVID-19 pandemic was in line with that of high-income countries, but in 2021 it was more than twice as high in middle-income countries than in high-income countries.
30. See OECD (2023); RISE (Regulatory Indicators for Sustainable Energy), Data Catalogue, World Bank, Washington, DC, https://datacatalog.worldbank.org/search/dataset/0040447/World---Regulatory-Indicators-for-Sustainable-Energy.
31. PVOUT (Photovoltaic Power Potential) (dashboard), Data Catalogue, World Bank, Washington, DC, https://datacatalog.worldbank.org/search/dataset/0038641.
32. This emissions intensity could also reflect the composition of products produced within these industries, so it is an imperfect proxy.
33. Albornoz et al. (2009).
34. See, for example, Holladay (2016); Richter and Schiersch (2017).
35. Eskeland and Harrison (2003).
36. Volz et al. (2021).
37. Overland, Juraev, and Vakulchuk (2022).
38. See, for example, Kwon, Lowry, and Verardo (2023); Srivastav and Rafaty 2022; Stokes (2020).
39. Skovgaard and van Asselt (2018).
40. Agnolucci et al. (2023); Agnolucci, Gencer, and Heine (2024).

41. IEA (2023).
42. Black et al. (2023). It is much more difficult to define the tax benchmark. As a result, individual country data should not be compared or aggregated, and caution should be applied when comparing producer subsidies across countries.
43. Damania et al. (2023).
44. See IFC (2023); Welch-Phillips and Goldenberg (2022).
45. Grubb et al. (2021).
46. See, for example, Acemoglu et al. (2012, 2016); Aghion et al. (2016); Grubb et al. (2021).
47. See, for example, Dechezlepretre et al. (2022); Talevi et al. (2022).
48. Curtis, O'Kane, and Park (2023). Directed technical change refers to technological progress steered by policy choices or other factors in a certain direction and so affects factors of production differently, as first defined in Acemoglu et al. (2012).
49. See, for example, Manning (2021).
50. Caldecott et al. (2021).
51. Fofrich et al. (2020).
52. Mercure et al. (2019).
53. Caldecott et al. (2021).
54. Daumas (2024).
55. Hiebert and Monin (2023).
56. The "resource curse" is the phenomenon in which countries with an abundance of natural resources (such as fossil fuels and certain minerals) have less economic growth, less democracy, or worse development outcomes than countries with fewer natural resources.
57. Brown products are based on traditional convention production styles, whereas green products are sensitive to the environment, emphasizing zero waste and net zero carbon.
58. Jacobsen and Parker (2016); Raimi (2021).
59. Curtis, O'Kane, and Park (2023).

References

Acemoglu, Daron, Philippe Aghion, Leonardo Bursztyn, and David Hémous. 2012. "The Environment and Directed Technical Change." *American Economic Review* 102 (1): 131–66.

Acemoglu, Daron, Ufuk Akcigit, Douglas Hanley, and William Kerr. 2016. "Transition to Clean Technology." *Journal of Political Economy* 124 (1): 52–104.

Acemoglu, Daron, David H. Autor, Jonathon Hazell, and Pascual Restrepo. 2022. "Artificial Intelligence and Jobs: Evidence from Online Vacancies." *Journal of Labor Economics* 40 (S1): S293–S340.

Aghion, Philippe, Antoine Dechezleprêtre, David Hémous, Ralf Martin, and John Van Reenen. 2016. "Carbon Taxes, Path Dependency, and Directed Technical Change: Evidence from the Auto Industry." *Journal of Political Economy* 124 (1): 1–51.

Agnolucci, Paolo, Carolyn Fischer, Dirk Heine, Mariza Montes de Oca Leon, Joseph Pryor, Kathleen Patroni, and Stéphane Hallegatte. 2023. "Measuring Total Carbon Pricing." *World Bank Research Observer*. https://doi.org/10.1093/wbro/lkad009.

Agnolucci, Paolo, Defne Gencer, and Dirk Heine. 2024. "Total Carbon Pricing for Energy Consumption: The Importance of Energy Taxes and Subsidies. Energy Subsidy Reform in Action Series." ESMAP Technical Report. Washington, DC: World Bank.

Albornoz, Facundo, Matthew A. Cole, Robert J. R. Elliott, and Marco G. Ercolani. 2009. "In Search of Environmental Spillovers." *World Economy* 32 (1): 136–63.

Andres, Pia, Penny Mealy, Nils Handler, and Samuel Fankhauser. 2023. "Stranded Nations? Transition Risks and Opportunities towards a Clean Economy." *Environmental Research Letters* 18 (4): 045004.

Arkolakis, Costas, and Conor Walsh. 2023. "Clean Growth." NBER Working Paper 31615 (August), National Bureau of Economic Research, Cambridge, MA.

Bastos, Paulo, Jacob Greenspon, Katherine Stapleton, and Daria Taglioni. 2023. "Did the 2022 Global Energy Crisis Accelerate the Diffusion of Low-Carbon Technologies?" Working paper, Development Research Group, World Bank, Washington, DC.

Bistline, John, Geoffrey Blanford, Maxwell Brown, Dallas Burtraw, Maya Domeshek, Jamil Farbes, Allen Fawcett, et al. 2023. "Emissions and Energy Impacts of the Inflation Reduction Act." *Science* 380 (6652): 1324–27.

Black, Simon, Antung A. Liu, Ian Parry, and Nate Vernon. 2023. "IMF Fossil Fuel Subsidies Data: 2023 Update." IMF Working Paper 169, International Monetary Fund, Washington, DC.

Bresnahan, Timothy F., and Daniel M. G. Raff. 1991. "Intra-Industry Heterogeneity and the Great Depression: The American Motor Vehicles Industry, 1929–1935." *Journal of Economic History* 51 (2): 317–31.

Bridge, Gavin, Stefan Bouzarovski, Michael Bradshaw, and Nick Eyre. 2013. "Geographies of Energy Transition: Space, Place and the Low-Carbon Economy." *Energy Policy* 53 (February): 331–40.

Bruhn, Miriam, Asli Demirgüç-Kunt, and Dorothe Singer. 2021. "Competition and Firm Recovery Post-COVID-19." Policy Research Working Paper 9851, World Bank, Washington, DC.

Caldecott, Ben, Alex Clark, Krister Koskelo, Ellie Mulholland, and Conor Hickey. 2021. "Stranded Assets: Environmental Drivers, Societal Challenges, and Supervisory Responses." *Annual Review of Environment and Resources* 46 (October): 417–47.

Cirera, Xavier, Diego A. Comin, and Marcio Cruz. 2022. *Bridging the Technological Divide: Technology Adoption by Firms in Developing Countries*. Washington, DC: World Bank.

Cirera, Xavier, Diego A. Comin, and Marcio Cruz. 2024. "Anatomy of Technology and Tasks in the Establishment." NBER Working Paper 32281 (March), National Bureau of Economic Research, Cambridge, MA.

Curtis, E. Mark, Layla O'Kane, and R. Jisung Park. 2023. "Workers and the Green-Energy Transition: Evidence from 300 Million Job Transitions." NBER Working Paper 31539 (August), National Bureau of Economic Research, Cambridge, MA.

Dalle, Jean-Michel, Matthijs den Besten, and Carlo Menon. 2017. "Using Crunchbase for Economic and Managerial Research." OECD Science, Technology, and Industry Working Paper 2017/08, Organisation for Economic Co-operation and Development, Paris.

Damania, Richard, Esteban Balseca, Charlotte de Fontaubert, Joshua Gill, Kichan Kim, Jun Rentschler, Jason Russ, and Esha Zaveri. 2023. *Detox Development: Repurposing Environmentally Harmful Subsidies.* Washington, DC: World Bank.

Daumas, Louis. 2024. "Financial Stability, Stranded Assets and the Low-Carbon Transition—A Critical Review of the Theoretical and Applied Literatures." *Journal of Economic Surveys* 38 (3): 601–716.

Davis, Steven J., and John C. Haltiwanger. 1990. "Gross Job Creation and Destruction: Microeconomic Evidence and Macroeconomic Implications." In *NBER Macroeconomics Annual 1990*, vol. 5, edited by Olivier Jean Blanchard and Stanley Fischer, 123–86. Cambridge, MA: National Bureau of Economic Research; Cambridge, MA: MIT Press.

Dechezleprêtre, Antoine, Adrien Fabre, Tobias Kruse, Bluebery Planterose, Ana Sanchez Chico, and Stefanie Stantcheva. 2022. "Fighting Climate Change: International Attitudes toward Climate Policies." NBER Working Paper 30265 (July), National Bureau of Economic Research, Cambridge, MA.

Eskeland, Gunnar S., and Ann E. Harrison. 2003. "Moving to Greener Pastures? Multinationals and the Pollution Haven Hypothesis." *Journal of Development Economics* 70 (1): 1–23.

Fofrich, Robert, Dan Tong, Katherine Calvin, Harmen Sytze De Boer, Johannes Emmerling, Oliver Fricko, Shinichiro Fujimori, Gunnar Luderer, Joeri Rogelj, and Steven J. Davis. 2020. "Early Retirement of Power Plants in Climate Mitigation Scenarios." *Environmental Research Letters* 15 (9): 094064.

Goldfarb, Avi, Bledi Taska, and Florenta Teodoridis. 2023. "Could Machine Learning Be a General Purpose Technology? A Comparison of Emerging Technologies Using Data from Online Job Postings." *Research Policy* 52 (1): 104653.

Grubb, Michael, Paul Drummond, Alexandra Poncia, Will McDowall, David Popp, Sascha Samadi, Cristina Penasco, et al. 2021. "Induced Innovation in Energy Technologies and Systems: A Review of Evidence and Potential Implications for CO_2 Mitigation." *Environmental Research Letters* 16 (4): 043007.

Haltiwanger, John C., Henry R. Hyatt, Erika McEntarfer, and Matthew Staiger. 2021. "Cyclical Worker Flows: Cleansing vs. Sullying." NBER Working Paper 28802 (May), National Bureau of Economic Research, Cambridge, MA.

Hershbein, Brad, and Lisa B. Kahn. 2018. "Do Recessions Accelerate Routine-Biased Technological Change? Evidence from Vacancy Postings." *American Economic Review* 108 (7): 1737–72.

Hiebert, Paul, and Pierre Monin. 2023. "Climate-Related Systemic Risks and Macroprudential Policy." INSPIRE Policy Briefing Paper 14 (August), London School of Economics and Political Science, London.

Holladay, J. Scott. 2016. "Exporters and the Environment." *Canadian Journal of Economics* 49 (1): 147–72.

Hopenhayn, Hugo A. 1992. "Entry, Exit, and Firm Dynamics in Long-Run Equilibrium." *Econometrica* 60 (5): 1127–50.

IEA (International Energy Agency). 2023. *Fossil Fuels Consumption Subsidies 2022.* Paris: IEA.

IEA (International Energy Agency) and IFC (International Finance Corporation). 2023. *Scaling Up Private Finance for Clean Energy in Emerging and Developing Economies.* Paris: IEA.

IFC (International Finance Corporation). 2023. "Power Markets for Development." IFC, Washington, DC.

IRENA (International Renewable Energy Agency). 2023. *Renewable Power Generation Costs in 2022.* Abu Dhabi, United Arab Emirates: IRENA.

Jacobsen, Grant D., and Dominic P. Parker. 2016. "The Economic Aftermath of Resource Booms: Evidence from Boomtowns in the American West." *Economic Journal* 126 (593): 1092–128.

Jones, Florence. 2023. "China to 'Shatter' Renewable Installation Targets by 2030." https://www.power-technology.com/news/china-shatter-renewable-installation-target/.

Krueger, Anne O., and Junghoo Yoo. 2002. "Chaebol Capitalism and the Currency-Financial Crisis in Korea." In *Preventing Currency Crises in Emerging Markets*, edited by Sebastian Edwards and Jeffrey A. Frankel, 601–62. National Bureau of Economic Research Conference Report. Cambridge, MA: National Bureau of Economic Research; Chicago: University of Chicago Press.

Kwon, Sungjoung, Michelle Lowry, and Michela Verardo. 2023. "Firms' Transition to Green: Innovation versus Lobbying." ECGI Finance Working Paper 921/2023, European Corporate Governance Institute, Brussels.

Manning, Alan. 2021. "Monopsony in Labor Markets: A Review." *ILR Review* 74 (1): 3–26.

Mercure, Jean-François, Florian Knobloch, Hector Pollitt, Leonidas L. Paroussos, Silviu Serban Scrieciu, and Richard Lewney. 2019. "Modelling Innovation and the Macroeconomics of Low-Carbon Transitions: Theory, Perspectives and Practical Use." *Climate Policy* 19 (8): 1019–37.

OECD (Organisation for Economic Co-operation and Development). 2023. "Effective Carbon Rates 2023: Pricing Greenhouse Gas Emissions through Taxes and Emissions Trading." OECD Series on Carbon Pricing and Energy Taxation. OECD, Paris.

Overland, Indra, Javlon Juraev, and Roman Vakulchuk. 2022. "Are Renewable Energy Sources More Evenly Distributed than Fossil Fuels?" *Renewable Energy* 200 (November): 379–86.

Park, Geunyong, Ande Shen, Katherine Stapleton, and Zhenxuan Wang. 2023. "The Economic Geography of Low-Carbon Technology Jobs in China." Policy Report (August), World Bank, Washington, DC.

Peters, Glen P., Gregg Marland, Corinne Le Quéré, Thomas Boden, Josep G. Canadell, and Michael R. Raupach. 2012. "Rapid Growth in CO_2 Emissions after the 2008–2009 Global Financial Crisis." *Nature Climate Change* 2: 2–4.

Raimi, Daniel. 2021. "Mapping County-Level Exposure and Vulnerability to the US Energy Transition." RFF Working Paper 21-36 (December), Resources for the Future, Washington, DC.

Richter, Philipp M., and Alexander Schiersch. 2017. "CO_2 Emission Intensity and Exporting: Evidence from Firm-Level Data." *European Economic Review* 98 (September): 373–91.

Rosenow, Samuel, and Penny Mealy. 2024. "Turning Risks into Reward: Diversifying the Global Value Chains of Decarbonization Technologies." Policy Research Working Paper 10696, World Bank, Washington, DC.

Saussay, Aurélien, Misato Sato, Francesco Vona, and Layla O'Kane. 2023. "Who's Fit for the Low-Carbon Transition? Emerging Skills and Wage Gaps in Job Ad Data." Centre for Climate Change Economics and Policy Working Paper 406, Grantham Research Institute on Climate Change and the Environment Working Paper 381, London School of Economics and Political Science, London.

Schumpeter, Joseph Alois. 1942. *Capitalism, Socialism and Democracy*. New York: Harper and Brothers.

Skovgaard, Jakob, and Harro van Asselt, eds. 2018. *The Politics of Fossil Fuel Subsidies and Their Reform*. New York: Cambridge University Press.

Srivastav, Sugandha, and Ryan Rafaty. 2022. "Political Strategies to Overcome Climate Policy Obstructionism." *Perspectives on Politics* 21 (2): 640–50.

Stokes, Leah Cardamore. 2020. *Short Circuiting Policy: Interest Groups and the Battle over Clean Energy and Climate Policy in the American States*. Studies in Postwar American Political Development. New York: Oxford University Press.

Talevi, Marta, Subhrendu K. Pattanayak, Ipsita Das, Jessica J. Lewis, and Ashok K. Singha. 2022. "Speaking from Experience: Preferences for Cooking with Biogas in Rural India." *Energy Economics* 107 (March): 105796.

UNEP (United Nations Environment Programme). 2009. "The Global Financial Crisis and Its Impact on Renewable Energy Finance." Division of Technology, Industry, and Economics, UNEP, Nairobi, Kenya.

Volz, Ulrich, Emanuele Campiglio, Etienne Espagne, Jean-François Mercure, William Oman, Hector Pollitt, Gregor Semieniuk, and Romain Svartzman. 2021. "Transboundary Climate-Related Risks: Analysing the Impacts of a Decarbonisation of the Global Economy on International Trade, Finance, and Money." Paper prepared for the 9th IMF Statistical Forum, "Measuring Climate Change: The Economic and Financial Dimensions," Washington, DC, November 17–18, 2021.

Way, Rupert, Matthew C. Ives, Penny Mealy, and J. Doyne Farmer. 2022. "Empirically Grounded Technology Forecasts and the Energy Transition." *Joule* 6 (9): 2057–82.

Welch-Phillips, Ian, and Cara Goldenberg. 2022. "Market Structures: Global Energy Transformation Guide, Electricity." RMI Innovation Center, Rocky Mountain Institute, Basalt, CO.

Xue, Yujie. 2024. "China to Meet Its 2030 Renewable Energy Target by End of This Year: State-Owned Researcher." *South China Morning Post*, July 1, 2024. https://www.scmp.com/business/china-business/article/3268707/china-meet-its-2030-renewable-energy-target-end-year-state-owned-researcher?campaign=3268707&module=perpetual_scroll_0&pgtype=article.

Part 3
Making Miracles

Part 2 of this Report describes how the forces of creation—the protagonist of economic growth—are weak in middle-income countries. Many large incumbents do not innovate or infuse global technologies, and many entrants do not disrupt. By contrast, the forces of preservation—the antagonist to creation—are strong in middle-income countries. Incumbent firms and social elites often preserve the status quo. Meanwhile, the forces of destruction—which are often needed to remove the obstacles to creation—are held back by the forces of preservation. Together, the forces of creation, preservation, and destruction are unbalanced in middle-income countries struggling with slower growth.

Part 3 of this Report examines how middle-income countries can accelerate growth by balancing these three forces, which entails the following:

- *Disciplining incumbency (chapter 7).* Middle-income countries will need to weaken the forces of preservation that protect incumbents from healthy competition. Contestable markets—and the policies that enable them—give incumbent firms the incentives to compete and upgrade their capabilities because their products and processes could be replaced by producers from other countries. This effort also entails opening access to energy markets and other sectors now dominated by favored entities, especially state-owned enterprises. In addition, middle-income countries will need to strengthen the capacity of competition agencies to identify and rein in firms that abuse their incumbency advantage. Instituting progressive tax policies to discipline incumbent elites while still incentivizing innovation will be needed as well.
- *Rewarding merit (chapter 8).* To strengthen the forces of creation, middle-income countries should reward merit activities—those with positive externalities; that is, those with positive effects on general well-being. This entails redesigning policies to focus on assessing the value added of firms in jobs, exports, technology infusion, and innovation instead of designing policies that simply focus on the size of firms. Middle-income countries will also need to design social policies that avoid targeting the distribution of incomes and instead focus on allocating talent and human capital more efficiently by ensuring that all those who have talent and display acquired ability have access to education, employment, and business opportunities. Furthermore, energy policies will need to shift from targeting the distribution of energy sources to supporting

activities that reduce emissions and local air pollution.
- *Capitalizing on crises (chapter 9).* The destructions of outdated arrangements—essential for creation—are often weak during boom times. Crises play an important role in reallocating resources and making room for new arrangements—in enterprises, jobs, technologies, policies, and public institutions. For example, the energy crisis and the climate crisis are driving rapid technological progress and the deployment of low-carbon technologies. Middle-income countries have an opportunity to infuse global technologies and produce green intermediates for global markets. Crises can also foreshadow social change. In the Republic of Korea, the government adopted comprehensive welfare reforms following the 1997–98 financial crisis, guaranteeing free access to public health care, an old-age pension, and expanded unemployment insurance for all citizens—particularly women, who bear a disproportionate burden of caregiving.

The development strategies outlined in chapters 7, 8, and 9 must be tailored to the transitions needed for a middle-income country to achieve high-income status. For each transition, middle-income countries must, to escape being trapped in slower growth, adapt their institutions to balance the forces of creation, preservation, and destruction—the key dynamic for any country aspiring to combine investment with infusion and innovation. Balancing these forces will require policy makers to make miracles. But only a handful of countries have succeeded. It will require implementing difficult and painstaking reforms, but the payoff will be significant.

7 Disciplining Incumbency

Key messages

- By promoting contestable markets, middle-income countries can strike a balance between supporting incumbents and ensuring that they do not abuse their market power.
- Middle-income countries will need to update their *institutional arrangements* that favor incumbents, including by retracting the government's direct involvement in productive enterprises, challenging state-owned incumbents in the electricity industry, and weakening the norms that discriminate against women and other marginalized groups.
- Middle-income countries can encourage incumbents to strengthen creation through policies that enhance trade openness, support upgrading firm capabilities, and incentivize the free movement of ideas and people, including highly skilled talent.
- Middle-income countries can ensure the effectiveness of competition authorities to rein in errant incumbents and use fiscal policy to make elites contestable.

Balancing incumbents' innovation and abuse of dominance

Part 2 of this Report highlighted that incumbent firms, especially market leaders, can be the vanguards of technical progress. But they can also use their incumbency advantage to block other firms from entering the market and competing, thereby resisting progress. In designing policies to facilitate investment alongside infusion and innovation, middle-income countries will need to strike a balance between supporting the growth of market leaders and ensuring that these firms do not abuse the market power that comes with their larger scale in their market. For example, in Italy labor productivity has stagnated for more than two decades. Recent research has highlighted how incumbents use their dominance to hold back progress.[1] Market leaders tend to bolster political connections by hiring more local politicians as they gain larger market shares; at the same time, they reduce their efforts to innovate (figure 7.1).

Figure 7.1 In Italy, market leaders increase their political connections while reducing innovation

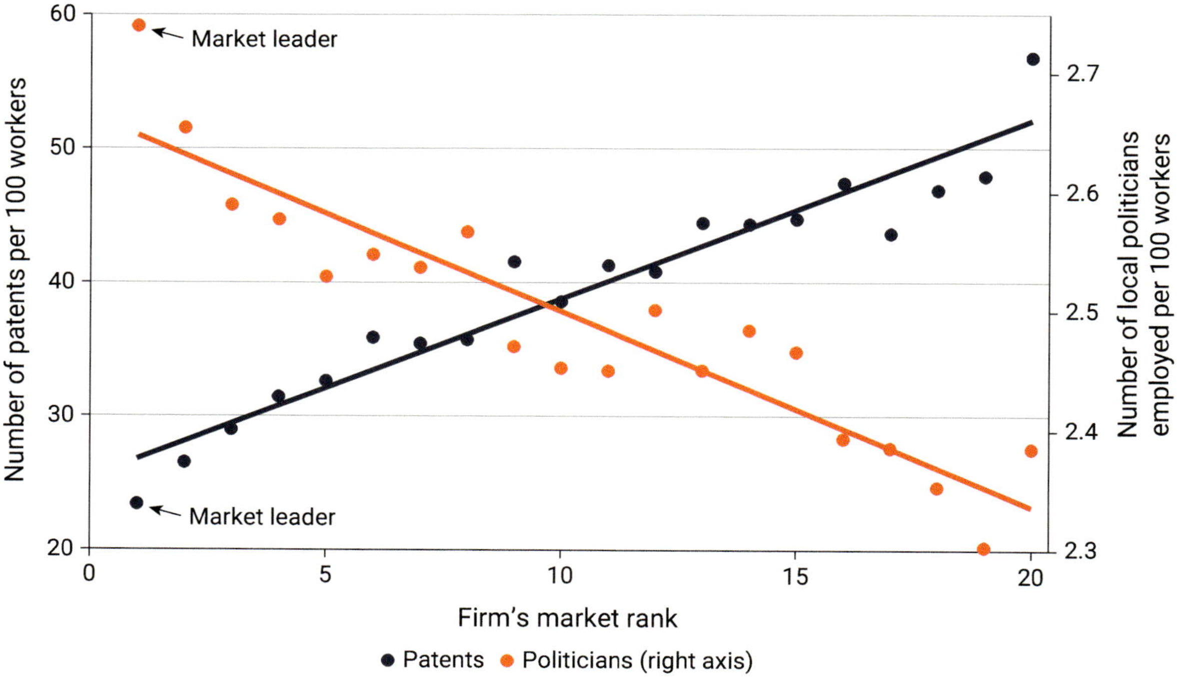

Source: Akcigit, Baslandze, and Lotti 2023.

Note: The x-axis shows the top 20 firms in a market ranked by employment share, with the rank of 1 indicating the highest employment share ("market leader"). The assessment covers markets defined at the six-digit industry level for 20 regions in Italy from 1993 to 2014. The dark blue line is the line of best fit for patents per 100 workers. The orange line is the line of best fit for the number of local politicians employed per 100 workers. "Six-digit" refers to ATECO (Classification of Economic Activity) (database), Italian National Institute of Statistics, Rome, https://www.istat.it/en/classification/ateco-classification-of-economic-activity-2007/.

The challenges of incumbency extend beyond firms. The economic elite has grown rapidly in many middle-income countries. In 2004, only 20 percent of the billionaires in the *Forbes* list were from emerging markets.[2] By 2014, this share had risen to 43 percent and by 2023 to 48 percent. China ranks second in the number of billionaires (496) after the United States (735). The recent surge of billionaire wealth in emerging markets can be traced to the creation and management of new companies. Some company founders and executives are likened to superstar billionaires by creating popular products known by millions or introducing innovative production methods that expand consumer choices and reduce prices. Examples include Jack Ma (Alibaba) and Narayana Murthy (Infosys). Many in the economic elite have amassed their fortunes through their innovative work—a reward for their ability, grit, risk-taking, and ingenuity. But others have inherited wealth or thrived in environments where business regulations, government patronage, and limited international competition have protected them.[3]

Dominant incumbents can block the policy reforms needed to promote social mobility and talent development. In early 2013, Mexican president Enrique Peña Nieto tried to take on one of the world's most powerful teacher unions, the National Union of Workers in Education (Sindicato Nacional de Trabajadores de la Educación, SNTE). The union was so large and powerful that it operated as a political machine.

Hundreds of members held administrative positions in the education system (including at the highest levels), and the union exercised control locally over hiring decisions and, in some states, over teacher payroll.[4] Reforming teachers' career paths and replacing underperforming teachers with those needed to promote children's achievement were enormous challenges under those circumstances.

State-owned enterprises (SOEs) are the dominant incumbents in fossil fuel power generation. As a result, they block entry of new players in renewables using their outsize market share, control of the grid, and influence on regulation.

Contestable markets—and the policies that enable them—are vital for middle-income countries to discipline incumbents. Contestability means that incumbents feel pressure to compete and upgrade because their existing products and processes can be displaced by technologically sophisticated producers within their own country or from other countries. Such contestability is central to creative destruction. Contestability is fostered by three sets of policies: (1) *institutions* that weaken the forces of preservation; (2) *incentives* that strengthen the forces of creation; and (3) *interventions* that target errant incumbents to destroy harmful arrangements (figure 7.2).

Figure 7.2 Promoting contestability through institutions, incentives, and interventions

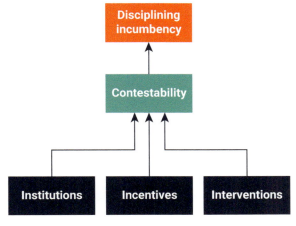

Source: WDR 2024 team.

Targeted interventions, often focusing on specific firms or individuals, are used as instruments of first resort by policy makers. But these instruments end up being ineffective and can hinder innovation if not designed with care. Policy makers should recalibrate their strategies by first strengthening the institutions that weaken the forces of preservation and then aligning the incentives to strengthen forces of creation. Targeted interventions are effective when they follow institutions and incentives.

Updating institutions to weaken the forces of preservation

Institutions—formal rules and informal norms—are often well intentioned when they are designed in their specific contexts. But they may end up persisting beyond their usefulness, protecting the status quo. Such persistence hurts the economic prospects of middle-income countries that need to rapidly change their growth model by adding *infusion* and *innovation* to *investment*. Institutional arrangements that favor incumbents will then need updating.

Retracting protection of incumbents, including state-owned enterprises

In middle-income countries, institutional inertia protects incumbents, strengthening the forces of preservation. Turnover, especially among market leaders, is low. In many middle-income countries, a small number of companies dominate markets, a survey suggest (figure 7.3).

Policy makers will need to retract government's direct involvement in productive enterprise, while removing outdated regulations that favor and protect incumbents. Often, incumbents are protected by licenses that limit the number of market participants or directly restrict market entry. Standards and minimum firm sizes can further protect incumbent interests. These dangers should be weighed against benefits, such as the incentives to improve quality that

Figure 7.3 In many middle-income countries, markets are dominated by a few business groups, as a survey suggests

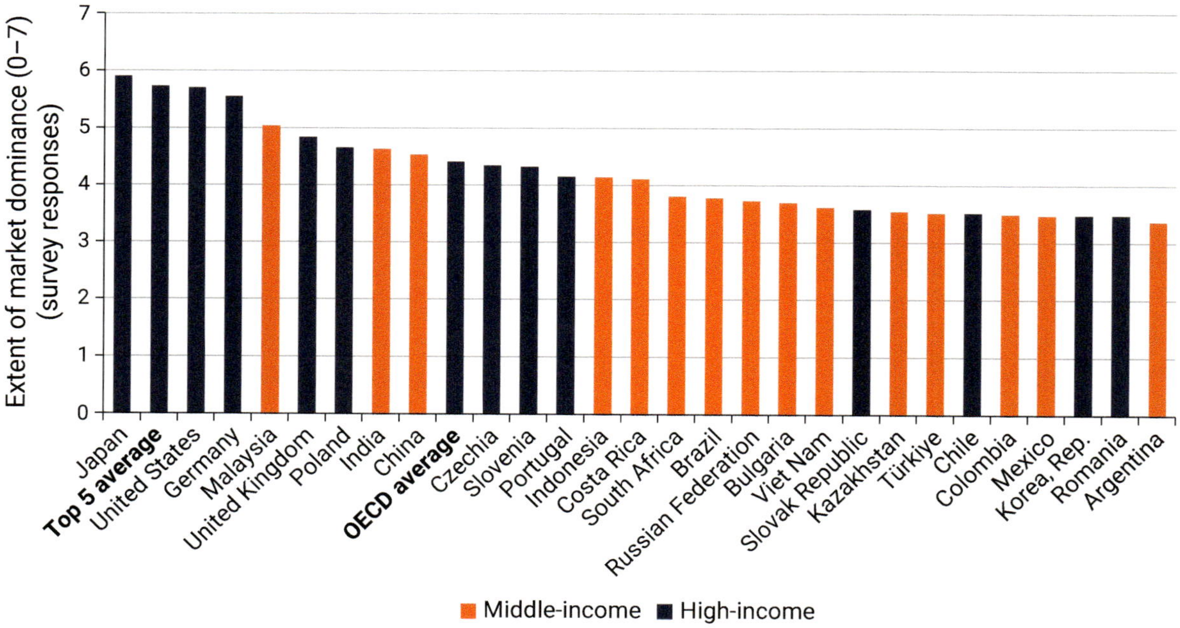

Source: WDR 2024 team based on Schwab (2019).
Note: The survey question: "In your country, how do you characterize corporate activity?" [1 = dominated by a few business groups; 7 = spread among many firms]. OECD = Organisation for Economic Co-operation and Development.

standards provide.[5] For example, the standard connector (SC), a fiber-optic connector developed by Tyco Electronics (now known as TE Connectivity Ltd) used in data networking and telecommunications, has become the dominant international standard. How? By joining national standardization organizations in many countries, the company influenced the standard-making process, with the result that European and international standards refer to the SC connector. Tyco thus gained a significant global market share, earning an additional US$50–$100 million in profits between 1995 and 2004.[6]

India's License Raj—a system of central controls introduced in 1951 regulating entry and production activity in the registered manufacturing sector—is another example. The system favored incumbents and stifled Indian entrepreneurs for more than four decades. Its dismantlement during the 1980s and 1990s amplified entry and business dynamism, and the effects were most prominent in states with labor market institutions that favored employers.[7]

Often, dominant incumbents in local markets lobby local authorities to erect ad hoc entry barriers. In Italy, such local entry regulations in the retail market increased price margins by 8 percent and reduced the productivity of incumbent firms by 3 percent in the early 2000s.[8] In Peru, when the national competition agency (Indecopi) strengthened its powers to dismantle local and sector-specific regulatory and administrative entry barriers in 2013, productivity increased significantly, including for firms operating in downstream sectors or in the same municipality.[9]

Product market regulations (PMRs), intentionally or inadvertently, protect incumbents and constrain competition (figure 7.4). These regulations include regulatory barriers to firm entry and competition in a broad range of key policy areas,

164 | WORLD DEVELOPMENT REPORT 2024

Figure 7.4 In middle-income countries, restrictive product market regulations are pervasive

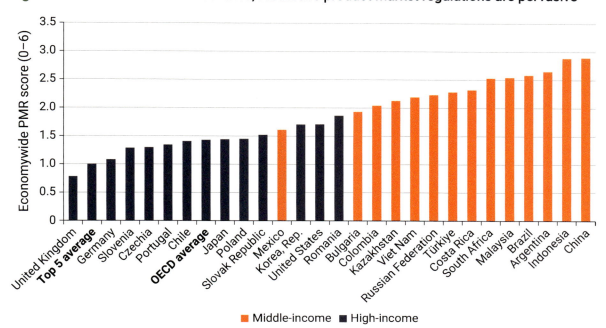

Source: WDR 2024 team based on 2018 data from PMR Database (OECD-WBG Product Market Regulation Database) (dashboard), Data Catalogue, World Bank, Washington, DC, https://prosperitydata360.worldbank.org/en/dataset/OECDWBG+PMR; PMR Indicators (Indicators of Product Market Regulation) (dashboard), Organisation for Economic Co-operation and Development, Paris, https://www.oecd.org/en/topics/sub-issues/product-market-regulation.html#:~:text=The%20PMR%20economy%2Dwide%20indicators,existing%20regulations%2C%20and%20foreign%20trade.

Note: The economywide Product Market Regulation (PMR) indicators measure the regulatory barriers to firm entry and competition in a broad range of cross-sector policy areas, as well as in specific services and network sectors. The PMR indicators range from 0 to 6. A lower value indicates that a regulatory regime is friendlier to competition. OECD = Organisation for Economic Co-operation and Development.

ranging from licensing and public procurement to governance of SOEs, price controls, evaluation of new and existing regulations, and foreign trade. They also include restrictive regulations in key network and services sectors (figure 7.5). Regulations tend to become less restrictive as country incomes rise.

Regulatory restrictions in critical input sectors can lead to adverse effects that constrain firm performance, job creation, and productivity in downstream industries. Anticompetitive regulations in key upstream sectors such as energy, transport, and communications, as well as professional services such as legal and accounting, hinder productivity growth and export performance in manufacturing firms.[10] This effect is more pronounced in sectors heavily reliant on these inputs and those closer to the productivity frontier. Reforms in services sectors can positively influence the productivity of manufacturing firms, emphasizing the importance of regulatory reform in enhancing overall economic performance.

Public ownership and its weak governance are significant entry barriers. Businesses of the state (BOSs)—enterprises with majority or minority state shareholdings—act as powerful incumbents in many middle-income countries. Several middle-income countries score much higher than the Organisation for Economic Co-operation and Development (OECD) average on the presence and weak governance of SOEs in the economy (figure 7.6). Recent research presented in the World Bank's *The Business of the State* report[11]

Figure 7.5 In middle-income countries, both economywide and sectoral input and product market regulations are more restrictive than in high-income countries

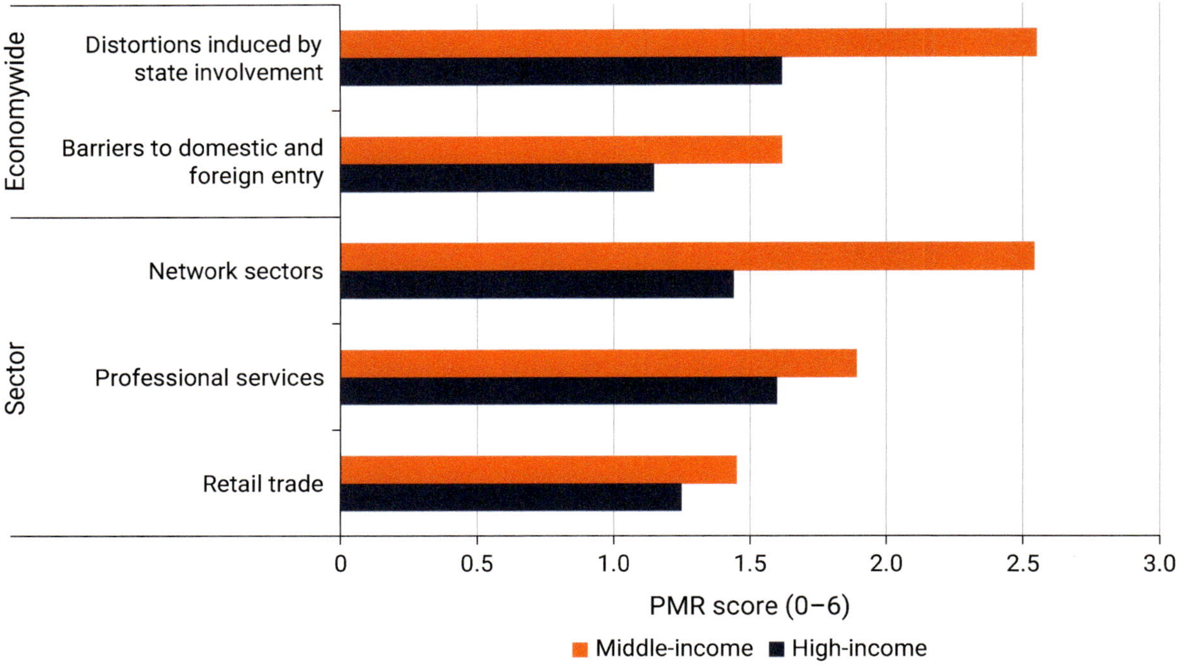

Source: WDR 2024 team based on data from PMR Database (OECD-WBG Product Market Regulation Database) (dashboard), Data Catalogue, World Bank, Washington, DC, https://prosperitydata360.worldbank.org/en/dataset/OECDWBG+PMR; PMR Indicators (Indicators of Product Market Regulation) (dashboard), Organisation for Economic Co-operation and Development, Paris, https://www.oecd.org/en/topics/sub-issues/product-market-regulation.html#:~:text=The%20PMR%20economy%2Dwide%20indicators,existing%20regulations%2C%20and%20foreign%20trade.

Note: The economywide Product Market Regulation (PMR) indicators measure the regulatory barriers to firm entry and competition in a broad range of cross-sector policy areas, as well as in specific services and network sectors. The sector PMR indicators measure the regulatory barriers to firm entry and competition at the level of individual sectors, with a focus on network industries, professional services, and retail distribution. The PMR indicators range from 0 to 6. A lower value indicates that a regulatory regime is friendlier to competition. The figure includes data for 38 high-income countries and 22 middle-income countries.

reveals that a doubling of states' market share in a given sector is associated with 5–35 percent lower entry (figure 7.7, panel a). BOSs' operational and financial performance lags behind that of their private peers, and they, on average, have lower labor productivity, profitability, and return on investments, while operating with higher levels of debt vis-à-vis private counterparts.[12] Advantages such as subsidies, exclusion from competition laws, preferential access to finance, restrictions on foreign direct investment (FDI), and import bans in sectors dominated by SOEs are more prevalent in lower-middle-income countries compared to upper-middle-income countries (figure 7.7, panel b). Mechanisms to improve SOE governance and efficiency are still limited in many countries, including separation of ownership from regulation, as well as transparent and reliable information on performance-based measures.

Challenging state-owned incumbents in the electricity industry

Disciplining the incumbency advantage of public ownership is most pressing in the electricity industry. Although the cost of lower-carbon

Figure 7.6 The BRICS and large middle-income countries have a significant presence of publicly owned enterprises and governance frameworks that stifle competition

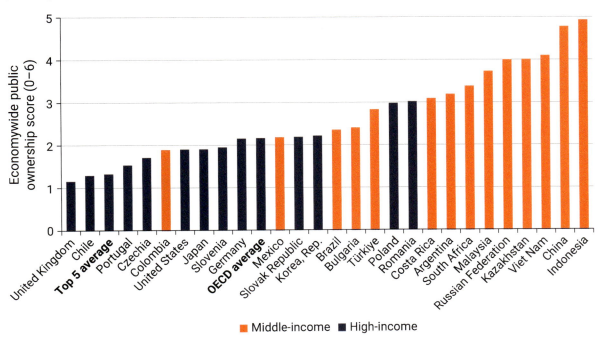

Source: WDR 2024 team based on 2018 data from PMR Database (OECD-WBG Product Market Regulation Database) (dashboard), Data Catalogue, World Bank, Washington, DC, https://prosperitydata360.worldbank.org/en/dataset/OECDWBG +PMR; PMR Indicators (Indicators of Product Market Regulation) (dashboard), Organisation for Economic Co-operation and Development, Paris, https://www.oecd.org/en/topics/sub-issues/product-market-regulation.html#:~:text=The%20PMR %20economy%2Dwide%20indicators,existing%20regulations%2C%20and%20foreign%20trade.

Note: The BRICS nations are Brazil, the Russian Federation, India, China, and South Africa. The public ownership indicator shows the extent of the presence of state-owned enterprises (SOEs) in the economy and their governance. A higher score indicates higher presence of SOEs with weaker governance of SOEs. OECD = Organisation for Economic Co-operation and Development.

energy is declining rapidly, private providers in many countries face major barriers to entry. SOEs dominate fossil fuel power generation, mainly in coal-fueled power plants, where they account for 84 percent of total installed capacity (figure 7.8). By contrast, the private sector owns about an equal share (80 percent) of the installed capacity of renewable energy.

Historically, the electricity industry was considered to be a "natural monopoly" with one dominant firm due to economies of scale in transmission and distribution (networks) and the need to coordinate generation with the grid. Arguments related to economies of scale became obsolete when smaller co-generators and gas-fired power plants became competitive with larger, utility-owned power plants. Arguments calling for economies of scope no longer hold because advances in communication technology have reduced coordination costs, enabling competition in bulk (wholesale) power markets and then in retail sales. The retail choice is similar to how consumers choose a cell phone plan; consumers can buy electricity from any supplier just as they would purchase mobile phone services from a telecom provider.[13] However, as of 2020 in 125 developing countries 60 percent of consumers still relied on a public distribution utility for electricity.

In South Africa, the vertically integrated power company Eskom dominates the power

Figure 7.7 A state presence has important effects on firm entry, market concentration, and preferential treatment

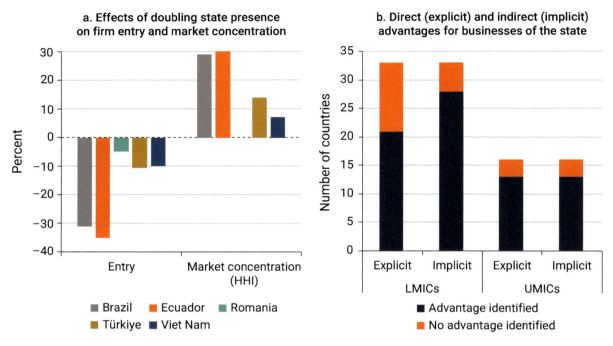

Source: World Bank 2023a.

Note: Panel a: Entry is based on the rate of entry of new firms in Romania and Türkiye and on the share of revenue accounted for by young firms (less than five years old) in Brazil, Ecuador, and Viet Nam. Market concentration is captured by the Herfindahl-Hirschman Index (HHI) (Herfindahl 1950; Hirschman 1964). For the World Bank Global Businesses of the State Database, see Dall'Olio et al. (2022). Panel b: Direct (explicit) advantages are legal provisions that explicitly favor a group of market players such as state-owned enterprises. These typically involve taxes, public debt, public procurement conditions, state support, and exemptions to legal frameworks. Indirect (implicit) advantages are regulations and enforcement conditions that exist at the product, sector, or economywide level but that, in practice, unlevel the playing field in favor of a group of players. These typically involve import restrictions, bans on licenses, price or quota regulation, and poor antitrust enforcement. Businesses of the state are enterprises with majority or minority state shareholdings. The figure is based on a sample of 58 World Bank Country Private Sector Diagnostics, including 33 for lower-middle-income countries (LMICs) and 16 for upper-middle-income countries (UMICs).

market with a 90 percent market share. In Poland, four companies—Polska Grupa Energetyczna (PGE), Tauron Polska Energia, Energa, and Enea—control nearly three-fourths of the market share in electricity production, with PGE holding 40 percent. Poland's transmission grid is owned and operated by state-owned Polskie Sieci Elektroenergetyczne.[14] SOEs use their dominant position to thwart entrants and protect their markets by blocking technological change.

SOEs are also significant investors in energy, contributing 36 percent of global energy investment. In low- and middle-income countries, SOEs are the largest providers of energy finance—accounting for 60 percent of energy investment (figure 7.9). A concern is that SOEs account for 50 percent of fossil fuel power investment globally, notably due to expanding coal plants in India and South Africa and gas plants in the Middle East and North Africa.

SOEs can block entry of new market players using their outsize market share and control of the grid. To compete for customers, rival firms need access to the grid controlled by a large incumbent. Thus access pricing becomes important. Access prices are set by the sectoral regulator.

Figure 7.8 State-owned enterprises dominate coal power generation, while the private sector leads in modern renewable energy

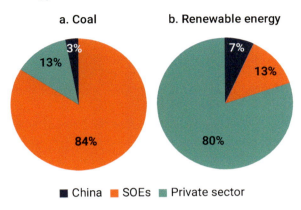

Source: Vagliasindi (2023) based on analysis of power plant data for countries, including Pakistan, Poland, South Africa, and Türkiye.
Note: The figures for the private sector and state-owned enterprise (SOE) shares of coal and renewable energy are the average shares of total installed capacity across the set of countries included in the analysis, excluding ownership by China, which is shown separately in dark blue.

Figure 7.9 In low- and middle-income countries, state-owned enterprises are the largest investors in fossil fuel energy generation

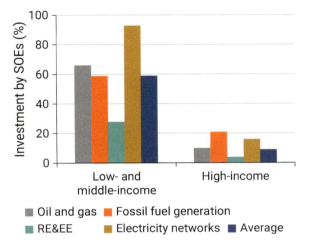

Source: Vagliasindi (2023) based on IEA (2020).
Note: The figure shows the percentage share of investment by state-owned enterprises (SOEs) by fuel type. RE&EE = renewable energy and energy efficiency.

To set a fair access price, the regulator may need the incumbent utility to reveal information about its cost function. The incumbent has an incentive to overstate the cost of supplying the input to its competitors in order to raise the access price and try to eliminate the competition—that is, "foreclose" the downstream market. Concerns about anticompetitive foreclosure—through high prices, discriminatory conditions, and low quality of service—are an important incentive for regulation of access in network industries such as energy supply and telecommunications that rely on networks to transmit and distribute their services (network industries).

Incumbents can collude to block new entrants. Price collusion and other forms of collusion in wholesale markets are frequent in small power systems and illiquid markets and are difficult to detect in advance by sectoral regulators and after the fact by competition agencies. Various market analyses are employed to capture the strategic aspects of competition in this industry and avoid focusing only on simplistic concentration measures. These include examining

- *The incentives of producers.* In the near term, it is likely that electricity markets will feature a diverse set of firms, including publicly owned utilities, unregulated generation companies, and traditional vertically integrated regulated utilities. Each type of firm is likely to respond differently to a given competitive environment.
- *The price responsiveness (elasticity) of demand.* In markets in which customers can easily choose not to consume a product or to consume a substitute instead, producers cannot raise their prices far above costs without significantly reducing sales. Conversely, a producer that knows that buyers find its product essential can profitably raise prices to very high levels.
- *The potential for expansion of output by competitors and potential competitors.* Just

as a producer with very price-responsive customers cannot exercise much market power, neither can a producer faced with many price-responsive competitors. Transmission capacity in a region and available competitive generation capacity are the main factors determining the potential for short-term competitive entry or output expansion.

Incumbents can be disciplined using less restrictive PMRs. Ex ante rules on access to essential infrastructure and open wholesale and retail electricity markets can enable entry by private providers, avoiding cases of "curtailment," respecting the merit order (chapter 8), and encouraging entry through global competition.

Weakening patriarchal gender norms

Norms that discriminate against women perpetuate the hold of men (the incumbents) in the workplace. In the labor market, women remain an underused resource, particularly in the Middle East and North Africa and in South Asia, where female labor force participation is only half the level expected given these regions' income levels. However, some factors have contributed to an ongoing rise in female labor force participation: an increase in the kinds of jobs requiring brains rather than brawn (such as professional positions); the increase in part-time jobs; the adoption of labor-saving household technologies; the growing number of educated women; the availability of contraceptives; the elimination of policies that punished married women; and the decline in social stigma against women working outside the home.[15] In the United States, for example, the gender gap in labor force participation has nearly been eliminated. Countries with strong preferences for male children, such as China, Japan, and the Republic of Korea, have experienced similar increases in female labor force participation as their economies have grown.

Equal treatment of women in the law is associated with higher female labor force participation, smaller gender wage gaps, and more successful careers for women as employees and entrepreneurs.[16] However, women still lack basic legal rights in many countries related to running a business, such as to sign a contract, register a business, and open a bank account. In Papua New Guinea, social norms that hinder female labor force participation and productivity are estimated to cost the economy about 0.5 percent of the gross domestic product (GDP) a year.[17] Legal reforms that grant better property and inheritance rights also improve women's social and economic outcomes. For example, in India the 2005 Hindu Succession (Amendment) Act, which increased a daughter's share of land inheritance from 8 percent to 16 percent,[18] led to an increase in women's education rates, labor force participation, entrepreneurship, and autonomy within their marriages.[19] The starting point to bringing more women into the labor force is implementing institutional reforms that grant women rights to property ownership, inheritance, and other basic rights to access economic opportunities.

Social norms shape personal attitudes toward women's participation in the labor force. The likelihood of a wife being employed increases if her husband's mother worked during his childhood.[20] Parents also have a major impact on their children's attitudes toward gender (even more than their peers), with mothers exerting more influence than fathers.[21] But personal attitudes tend to be more progressive than collective social expectations, leading to misconceptions about social norms themselves.[22]

Broad-based education and information interventions can help address both personal attitudes and misperceptions about social attitudes. For example, a study in India found that two years of classroom discussions about gender equality led to improved attitudes toward gender equality among teenage boys and girls.[23] An intervention that encouraged teenage girls to question restrictive social norms in India combined with connecting girls to changemakers in the wider community reduced school dropout rates and early marriage and improved mental health.[24] In China, the Spring Bud Project, initiated in 1989, promotes equitable, inclusive, and quality education (primary to the higher education level) for girls by means of subsidies for those from low-income families, large-scale advocacy and awareness-raising, and skills building for adolescent girls, including digital competencies for income generation and employment.[25] In Viet Nam, early exposure to female classmates led to more egalitarian gender attitudes in adulthood—even more so for men who grew up in conservative households.[26]

The misperception about support for gender norms is widespread across the world: many people think social support for working women is much lower than it is.[27] For example, in Saudi Arabia misperceptions about gender norms restrict women's basic rights to work outside of the home, and yet most Saudi men privately support women working but underestimate the extent to which others share this view. Correcting this misperception can lead to a significant increase in female labor force participation.[28] Saudi Arabia has experienced an unprecedented surge in female labor force participation since 2017 as a result of changing regulations and shifting social norms, the implementation of sound structural reforms, and effective government communications. Saudi Arabia's success in increasing female labor force participation from 17.4 percent in 2017 to 36 percent in 2023 may contain important lessons for other countries and regions.

In Bangladesh, the robust growth of the garment manufacturing industry has generated more than 5 million jobs, amounting to 60 percent of female employment, one-quarter of industrial employment, and three-quarters of the country's export earnings in recent years. Employment in the garment industry has enabled migrant women from rural areas to earn cash for their families back home and has had far-reaching positive effects on the welfare and empowerment of women in rural and urban areas.

Role models, including women who challenge traditional behavior, can change the behavior and aspirations of other women. Their actions have led to an increase in female participation in political positions in local village councils (*panchayats*) and assemblies in India, which, in turn, has increased female labor force participation.[29] The rise in the number of female entrepreneurs has also boosted female labor force participation and the number of women in higher management positions.[30] In addition, educating the public about the costs and benefits of working is an important way in which female labor force participation and other modern practices can spread through society.[31]

Bringing women into labor markets will mean providing them with support services such as child and elderly care, safety in the workplace, and transport. Both men and women in Indonesia also cite harassment in public transport and commuting, as well as in the workplace, as important factors in women not wanting to work.[32] For women, difficulty in finding childcare is the primary reason given for not working. A review of 22 studies across low- and middle-income countries reveals that increasing access to and reducing the cost of childcare can improve maternal labor market outcomes, including employment, hours worked, income, productivity, and job type.[33] Governments can use various options that range from free state-provided care to offering providers and parents financial subsidies, tax incentives, or other forms of support. The challenge of accessing affordable childcare disproportionately affects poor families. Childcare subsidies in low-income countries can help make childcare more affordable. However, such targeted policies are not very common in lower-middle-income and upper-middle-income countries, where only 9 percent and 41 percent of countries, respectively, have a law that establishes some form of financial support for families for childcare services, compared with 80 percent of high-income countries.[34]

In countries where women lack equal economic and social rights, support for them will increase their chances of contributing to the labor market, including through gender-based affirmative action policies in education or employment (box 7.1). Upskilling and training programs are more effective when complemented with other interventions that address social, family, and logistical constraints that women can face, such as household and childcare responsibilities.

> **Box 7.1** A digital tool helps female entrepreneurs obtain capital and training in rural Mexico
>
> To improve opportunities for indigenous rural women in some of Mexico's southeastern states, a local nongovernmental organization, Pro Mujer, partnered with Google to help women access capital and entrepreneurship training. In February 2023, they launched a joint initiative, "Women: Force of the Southeast," which includes an online platform to provide female entrepreneurs with free, customized online training. By means of hybrid sessions, participating entrepreneurs learn how to use social media to sell their products, prepare a budget, handle their finances, and communicate effectively. The platform also offers small loans with minimum requirements and no collateral requirements, as well as other financial services. In this region of Mexico, where about 80 percent of women live in poverty, digital technologies offer the promise of boosting skills, entrepreneurship, and incomes. The program is expected to benefit 6,000 women through small loans and about 2,000 women through entrepreneurship and financial literacy training.
>
> *Sources:* Google 2023; Pro Mujer 2023.

Incentives for incumbents to strengthen creation

Openness in goods and product markets is critical for firms in middle-income countries seeking to absorb and infuse global knowledge. And yet openness to trade and foreign investment works two ways. Although openness provides firms with access to larger markets, international value chains, technology, and know-how, it also exposes domestic firms to competition with international firms closer to the technology frontier. Firms can either scale up or be eased out.

Upgrading by trading

A key part of contestability is trade openness. Because the firms in middle-income countries most able to adopt global technologies are often large incumbents (see chapter 4), these incumbents will be more likely to compete by enhancing products and processes to the extent that markets are globally connected.[35]

Knowledge acquired from the global economy holds the key to the economic catch-up of middle-income countries. Countries that have experienced sustained high growth have rapidly absorbed know-how (knowledge that is not easily transmittable), technology, and, more generally, knowledge from the rest of the world.[36] Middle-income countries far from the knowledge frontier should act quickly and furiously to infuse knowledge. The World Bank Productivity Project highlights that roughly half of overall productivity growth is driven by incumbent firms adopting new technologies, products, and processes.[37] Yet middle-income countries face an "innovation paradox"—returns on infusion are believed to be high in middle-income countries, and yet firms in these countries appear to invest little.[38]

The incentives for and ability of middle-income country firms to absorb knowledge can be enhanced by government policies that support upgrading the capabilities of firms. For this, industrial policy will need to connect global and local firms and support adoption of modern

Figure 7.10 Foreign technology licensing is limited among middle-income country firms

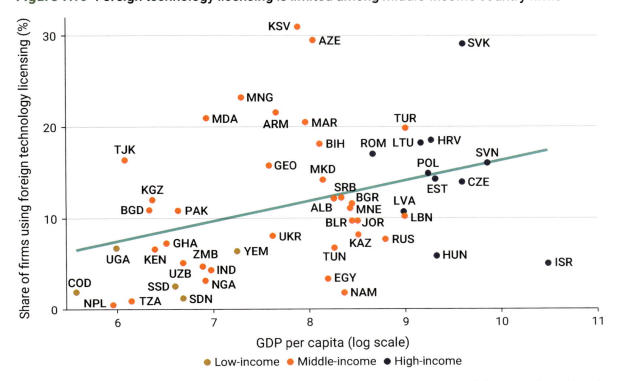

Source: Cirera and Maloney (2017) based on data from WBES (World Bank Enterprise Surveys) (dashboard), World Bank, Washington, DC, https://www.enterprisesurveys.org/en/enterprisesurveys.
Note: For country abbreviations (except KSV, here representing Kosovo), see International Organization for Standardization (ISO), https://www.iso.org/obp/ui/#search. GDP = gross domestic product.

organizational models. Because knowledge is often embodied in machinery and equipment, for many countries purchasing equipment from a foreign-owned company is an important way to acquire knowledge. In fact, 45 percent of firms in Asia and 29 percent in Africa, on average, are doing so.[39] Technology licensing is also important for infusion, as seen in Korea (see chapter 2). However, licensing increases with proximity to the technology frontier, with most firms unable to license foreign technologies, possibly reflecting weak human capabilities in using these technologies (chapter 8), as well as weak institutions protecting intellectual property. Less than 10 percent of firms in middle-income countries such as the Arab Republic of Egypt, India, and Tunisia use licensed technology. And even in other countries that are more economically advanced, such as Croatia and Türkiye, only 20 percent of firms engage in licensing (figure 7.10). Of considerable concern is that rising geopolitical tensions and protectionism can potentially worsen the diffusion of knowledge to middle-income countries.[40]

In view of the positive effects associated with deploying advanced technologies, a government can help firms by using industrial policy to make it easier for them to license technologies. Countries can use infusion incentives, such as Korea's temporary subsidies for the adoption of foreign technology,[41] while pursuing more general policies such as investing in upgrading domestic skills (chapter 8) and protecting intellectual property. Market contestability also promotes faster foreign technology adoption at a lower cost to consumers.[42]

Government policies to open markets and facilitate economic integration can also help domestic firms connect with multinational corporations

DISCIPLINING INCUMBENCY | **173**

(MNCs), thereby introducing a country's firms to foreign production techniques, overseas markets, and international supply chains. The gains from such connections are evident in Poland. After Poland joined the European Union, the benefits to direct suppliers in sectors that use research and development (R&D) more intensively spread to the broader economy through positive vertical spillovers, while positive horizontal spillovers were boosted as domestic firms accumulated intangible assets such as licenses and patents.[43] In Costa Rica, domestic firms increased productivity by 4 percent and expanded their workforce by 26 percent within four years of joining an MNC supply chain. Supplying MNCs also led to improvements in domestic firms' production processes, supported by capacity building from the MNCs.[44]

Domestic rules can encourage sharing technology with MNCs, such as licensing agreements and the ability of local suppliers to acquire competitive or licensed technologies (box 7.2).

Local conditions and institutions also matter, such as national innovation systems and training programs, access to financing, and contestable domestic markets. For example, the success of Norwegian FDI for salmon farming in Chile stemmed in large part from the favorable local business conditions.[45]

Increased participation in global value chains also promotes diversification and sophistication and magnifies the gains of traditional trade. Exporting transmits knowledge back to the domestic economy through value chain links and learning by exporting.[46] And long-term supply relationships between exporters and foreign buyers can promote upgrading in product quality and management practices.[47] However, mixed results have emerged from promoting specific industries or sectors through tax breaks, direct subsidies, import tariff exemptions, cheap credit, dedicated infrastructure, or the bundling of all of these in export zones.[48]

Box 7.2 Technology for market access

Quid pro quo policies mandate that multinational firms entering the domestic market establish direct partnerships with local firms through joint ventures. The objective is to amplify the positive spillovers from multinational firms to domestic ones, solidify their connections, and facilitate knowledge transfers. Despite the potential, little is known about the impacts of such policies.

Two recent studies have examined a policy implemented in 1978 in China that required international automakers wishing to enter the Chinese market to establish joint ventures with domestic firms for production facilities.[a] The policy facilitated the transmission of knowledge between foreign and domestic firms through workers. The research indicates that the likelihood of workers transitioning from a joint venture to a domestic firm was 18 percentage points higher than a benchmark in which worker movements were random. Domestic firms affiliated with multinationals through a joint venture shared, on average, 12 common suppliers, or nearly seven more than the suppliers shared between unaffiliated domestic firms and multinationals. The enhanced network explains about 65 percent of knowledge spillover via joint venturing. Finally, this policy contributed to an enhancement in product quality, measured as a 3.8 percent reduction in defects per car model for affiliated domestic firms.

a. Bai et al. (2022); Zuniga (2024).

Improving firms' capabilities—including through exporter training, country promotion, and market research—has been shown to increase exports by reducing fixed costs and enabling firms to initiate exports, explore new international markets, or introduce new products.[49] Openness to trade also matters. For example, in Pakistan increases in upstream markets' tariff duties reduced the productivity of firms in the downstream markets.[50] In Peru, firms that were helped to enhance their capabilities in the early 2000s experienced a 17 percent higher export growth rate than firms that did not participate. The higher rate was driven primarily by expansion in the number of countries served and the variety of products traded.[51] Direct support programs to encourage the integration of small firms with large ones have been shown to increase the export capabilities of small firms (box 7.3). But to ensure that the benefits are durable, complementary measures to facilitate technology absorption are also needed.[52]

The integration of economic principles in industrial policy design and implementation is essential for infusion for three reasons. First, assessing the need for industrial policy to address identified market failures, as well as the opportunity costs of state support, is important. Second, ensuring that design and implementation foster contestability and merit will mitigate the risks

Box 7.3 Supplier development programs to connect small firms with large firms

Chile's Supplier Development Program establishes two-way connections between potential suppliers that are small and medium enterprises (SMEs) and their large firm customers. In such connections, SMEs benefit from higher sales and employment, resulting in a lower likelihood of exit, while large buying firms enjoy higher sales and bolster their export capabilities. The program provides the government with a subsidy to execute projects sponsored by large firms, on the condition that SMEs act as suppliers for these larger companies. The program also subsidizes activities to enhance SMEs' technical capabilities, such as providing professional advice and facilitating technology transfers. In the agribusiness sector, supplier firms saw a 16 percent increase in sales and an 8 percent increase in employment within one year after the program was approved. And the large firm customers enjoyed a 19 percent increase in sales and a 3 percent gain in the probability of becoming an exporter.[a]

In the early 2000s, Costa Rica's new PROPYME program began promoting innovation among Costa Rican SMEs by facilitating their connections with research units. These units were associated with local or foreign universities or private research centers with no university affiliation. Together, they collaborate on projects geared toward technology development, innovation, growth of human capital, or technology transfer. In addition to fostering these partnerships, the government is financing up to 80 percent of the projects' total cost. PROPYME resulted in a substantial 19 percentage point increase in labor demand and a 9.6 percentage point boost in the probability of SMEs engaging in exporting.[b]

Source: Zuniga 2024.
a. Arráiz, Henríquez, and Stucchi (2011).
b. Monge-González, Hewitt, and Torres-Carballo (2015).

of market distortions and favoritism. And, third, monitoring and evaluating the direct intended impact, as well as market and spillover effects, will maximize effectiveness. The European Union uses these principles in its state aid control framework, and they are now being used and implemented in different ways in various countries, including Chile, Colombia, Moldova, and the Philippines.

Upgrading to ward off foreign competitors

Trade openness improves access to larger markets, international value chains, technology, and know-how. But it also exposes domestic firms to competition from international firms closer to the technology frontier. Such competition forces domestic leaders to upgrade to "escape" competition and puts pressure on laggards to quit, especially when domestic markets are threatened by imports. Such competition can induce a reallocation of resources toward firms that are more productive.[53] It can also incentivize innovation by well-positioned incumbents[54] and upgrading of product quality, including by introducing greater variety.[55]

China's accession to the World Trade Organization (WTO) is a clear and compelling example of how market leaders in different countries have responded to competition in domestic markets. China's overall exports grew from US$62 billion in 1990 to US$1.2 trillion in 2007, a staggering average increase of about 20 percent a year. China entered the WTO in 2001. By 2009, it had become the world's largest exporter and by 2010 the second-largest economy in the world. How have firms responded to rising competition? In 12 European countries, imports from China increased the innovative activity of European firms that survived the competition, while reducing employment and lowering overall chances of firm survival.[56] In heavily exposed sectors, low-tech firms suffered declines in jobs and survival rates, while high-tech ones remained relatively safe. In Argentina, there was a positive association between competition and technology upgrading.[57] In Peru, higher exposure to foreign competition translated into higher value, quantity, and product shares of high-quality exports.[58]

Evidence from Chile and Mexico highlight the following:

- *In Chile*, as imports of Chinese products rose at an average pace of 27 percent each year from 2001 to 2007, Chilean firms that were market leaders increased their product innovation by 15 percent and product quality by 22 percent. The laggards scaled back their process innovation by 11 percent and product innovation by 13 percent.[59]
- *In Mexico*, firms making a "peripheral" product (one of small importance in the firm's total sales) were more likely to pull it off the market if it faced strong competition. However, products that were core to a firm's business (those with large shares of total output) were less vulnerable.[60] Larger plants and "core" products benefited from expanded access to cheaper imported intermediates, helping firms improve the competitiveness of core products. Furthermore, Mexican firms that faced competition from Chinese imports used existing information technologies to increase productivity, while firms that did not face competition as intense did not, even if they acquired the same technology.[61]

Learning by moving

Connecting with the world by means of trade is a basic requirement for incentivizing incumbents to upgrade, thereby sustaining growth at the middle-income level. But so is the free movement of ideas and people. Together, the movement of ideas, along with goods, services, capital, and people, are critical for advancing technology diffusion.[62]

Middle-income countries should not restrict the movement of their highly skilled individuals. Their emigration can be an opportunity for the origin country rather than a loss. The extent to which this can happen depends on how strongly emigrants remain connected to the origin countries—or even return—and on emigrants' ability to accumulate knowledge about modern production processes and technologies in their destination countries (box 7.4). This is particularly relevant in conflict-affected countries such as Ukraine that have experienced a large outflow of highly skilled individuals. Origin countries can also create a conducive environment for knowledge transfer involving the diaspora by creating conditions such as political stability, institutional quality, and a favorable investment climate.[63] In addition, origin countries can leverage immigrants' earnings for economic growth by enabling a safe, efficient flow of remittances.

Some countries have adopted measures to facilitate engagement with their diaspora and foster collaboration on R&D. For example, in 2019 the Academy of Sciences of Albania created NanoAlb, a virtual center to coordinate nanoscience and nanotechnology research in institutions located in Albania as well as Israel, Italy, Kosovo, Montenegro, North Macedonia, Spain, the United Kingdom, and the United States.[64] By engaging the Albanian diaspora in those countries, NanoAlb is able to deliver a variety of products, engage in R&D activities, and offer classes in applications of nanotechnology. The center also disseminates knowledge to society at large and provides educational activities for young students.

Convincing highly skilled emigrants to return home has been a priority for countries such as China, where the Thousand Talents program brings back researchers for permanent employment or short-term visits.[65] However, policies to bring such migrants back can have mixed results. R&D workers are highly mobile and respond to monetary incentives as well as research support and the proximity of other researchers.[66] Reducing the tax rates for returning R&D workers may lead to an increase in the number of inventors through both the retention of domestic inventors and the immigration of foreign inventors, although it may also reduce knowledge spillovers and productivity in the countries from which they are returning.[67] Regardless of the specific policies used, turning brain drain into brain gain remains an imperative in countries' talent agendas.

Box 7.4 Turning brain drain into brain gain

A highly skilled migrant who moves to a high-income country but cannot find a job—or must work as a cab driver—cannot gain new skills, whereas one who works using his or her skills (as a manager, professional, or technician) is more likely to do so. Figure B7.4.1 measures the potential of origin countries to realize gains from knowledge spillovers from their diaspora. To quantify this potential for each origin country, the figure measures the extent to which tertiary-educated workers migrate to high-income countries and the share of tertiary-educated migrants who succeed by working in "good" occupations in the destination country. Countries in the upper right of the figure have the greatest potential because their diaspora is large and successful. To leverage this potential, they should promote knowledge exchange and connections between the diaspora and local industry leaders and investors. Other countries send fewer highly skilled emigrants to advanced countries (lower values on the x-axis), or their migrants are less successful (lower values on the y-axis). Although these features can complicate knowledge transfers, a small number of skilled and successful emigrants may nevertheless be sufficient to transmit ideas or knowledge back to their sending communities.

(Box continues next page)

Box 7.4 Turning brain drain into brain gain (continued)

Figure B7.4.1 Some countries are strongly positioned to benefit from knowledge spillovers from their diaspora

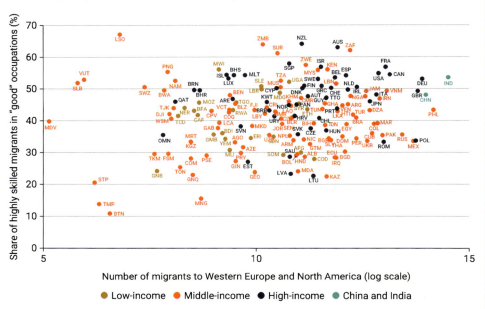

Sources: WDR 2024 team calculations; DIOC (Database on Immigrants in OECD and Non-OECD Countries), reference years 2010/11, Organisation for Economic Co-operation and Development, Paris, https://www.oecd.org/els/mig/dioc.htm.

Note: DIOC 2010/11 provides data on migration flows by skill and current occupation and covers migration flows from 200 origins to 34 OECD country destinations. Each scatter point in the figure represents an origin (or birth) country. For each birth country, the x-axis shows the number of tertiary-educated migrants who now live in destination countries in Western Europe or North America (log scale). The y-axis shows the share of these tertiary-educated migrants who work as a manager, professional, or technician in their destination country. These occupations are labeled "good." They represent the top three one-digit International Standard Classification of Occupations (ISCO) codes. The sample is restricted to persons at least 15 years old. Tertiary education is defined as a completed tertiary education. The analysis includes the following 15 high-income Western European and North American countries as destination countries: AUT (Austria), BEL (Belgium), CAN (Canada), DNK (Denmark), FRA (France), DEU (Germany), IRL (Ireland), ITA (Italy), NLD (Netherlands), NOR (Norway), ESP (Spain), SWE (Sweden), CHE (Switzerland), GBR (United Kingdom), and USA (United States). For country abbreviations, see International Organization for Standardization (ISO), https://www.iso.org/obp/ui/#search. OECD = Organisation for Economic Co-operation and Development.

Interventions to correct errant behavior by incumbents

Governments can also discipline incumbents through targeted interventions. In countries where competition laws are in place (typically rules against abuse of dominance and anticompetitive agreements, as well as merger controls), competition authorities monitor, discourage, and punish anticompetitive behavior by firms and prevent mergers that could harm competition.

According to the World Bank Anti-Cartel Enforcement Database, competition authorities in 34 middle-income countries sanctioned 406 cartels from 2017 to 2022.[68] These cartels cover a diverse set of markets, including manufacturing, construction, wholesale and retail trade, and transportation and storage. In middle-income countries in Latin America, elimination of anticompetitive practices has increased innovation and productivity (box 7.5).

For competition rules to be effective, threats of enforcement must be credible. A few middle-income countries (such as Brazil, Egypt, Mexico, and South Africa) have successfully decided cases about cartels and abuse of dominance involving digital platforms, as per the Global Digital Antitrust Database.[69] And yet the staffing and budget limits of competition authorities in many middle-income countries reduce their capacity

---

Box 7.5 Tackling anticompetitive practices increases incumbents' innovation incentives

Economic cartels are prevalent across various economies affecting many markets. Unlike other forms of anticompetitive practices, such as abuses of dominance in which efficiencies could counterbalance some of the negative effects, cartels in middle-income countries constitute the most harmful anticompetitive practices. Failure to address cartel activity limits productivity growth.[a] Anticompetitive agreements weaken efficiency incentives, and the presence of cartels can cut the growth of labor productivity by as much as 20–30 percentage points when compared with that for industries without cartels.[b] Evidence from a 40-year-old cartel in the United States suggests that sectoral output declined by 22 percent over the counterfactual.

Cartels also harm export competitiveness by raising the cost of inputs, with negative implications for the development of both domestic and international value chains, thereby diminishing the benefits of trade liberalization. Among countries in the Pacific Alliance (which have the lowest trade barriers in Latin America), at least 67 cartels operate in tradable sectors, and one-third of them have been in place for more than five years.[c]

Cartels and abuse of dominance have been associated with lower wages in Mexico and lower incumbent productivity or innovation efforts in Chile, Colombia, and Uruguay. In Mexico, after antitrust sanctions were put in place wages grew by 1.4 percentage points a year and productivity rose by 2.4 percentage points a year.[d] In Colombia, following sanctions on a sugar cartel and a separate intervention to sanction abuse of dominance, sales and value added in the affected market increased, while markups fell (figure B7.5.1). Furthermore, the leading firms increased efforts to raise productivity as they dealt with growing competition in the market after price-fixing behavior was curtailed (figure B7.5.2).[e]

(Box continues next page)

Box 7.5 Tackling anticompetitive practices increases incumbents' innovation incentives *(continued)*

Figure B7.5.1 In Colombia, after a cartel is sanctioned, market outcomes improve through the entry and growth of previously lagging firms

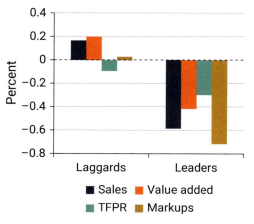

Source: Sampi, Urrutia Arrieta, and Vostroknutova 2022.

Note: The figure shows the changes in various market outcome variables after a cartel is sanctioned for previously lagging firms and leading firms in the unaffected market. TFPR = total factor productivity ratio.

Figure B7.5.2 In Colombia, after an abuse of dominance case, positive market outcomes are driven by improvements in leading firms

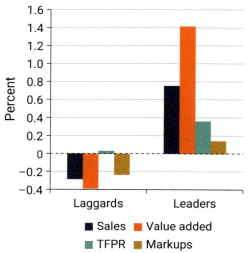

Source: Sampi, Urrutia Arrieta, and Vostroknutova 2022.

Note: The figure shows the changes in various market outcome variables after an abuse of dominance case for previously lagging firms and leading firms in affected markets. TFPR = total factor productivity ratio.

Sources: Bridgman, Qi, and Schmitz 2009; OECD 2014; Petit, Kemp, and van Sinderen 2015; Reed et al. 2022; Sampi, Urrutia Arreita, and Vostroknutova 2022; Vostroknutova et al. 2024; World Bank 2021.

a. Petit, Kemp, and van Sinderen (2015).
b. OECD (2014).
c. World Bank (2021).
d. Reed et al. (2022).
e. Sampi, Urrutia Arrieta, and Vostroknutova (2022).

to act (figure 7.11). According to another sample, in those countries more than two-thirds of competition authorities have annual budgets of less than US$5 million, while the average number of staff per million inhabitants in high-income countries is more than 70 percent higher than in middle-income countries.[70] Upper-middle-income countries, in particular, should invest in building independent and accountable competition authorities that are adequately funded and staffed.

Competition authorities should also have the power to advocate the elimination of regulatory restrictions of competition that can ultimately facilitate anticompetitive practices. Competition laws that do not exclude certain firms (such as businesses of the state) or specific sectors[71] are also essential.

The challenges with competition are even more pronounced in partially contestable markets and natural monopolies. For example, to ensure efficient pricing, controls are needed for

Figure 7.11 Competition authorities in middle-income countries need more capacity to deal with sophisticated policy problems

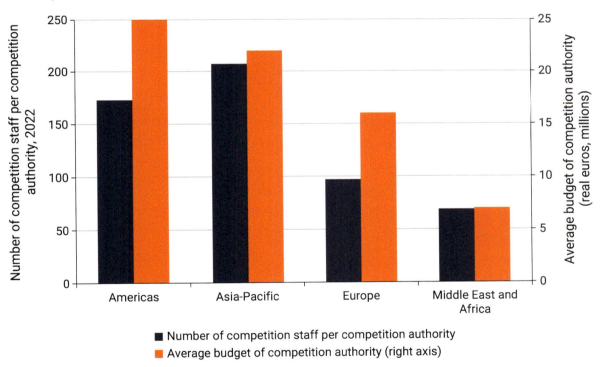

Source: OECD Competition Statistics Survey data (OECD 2024).
Note: OECD Competition Trends cover 77 OECD and non-OECD jurisdictions. For a list of countries included in each region shown in the figure, see OECD Competition Statistics (OECD CompStats) Survey 2024 (web page), Organisation for Economic Co-operation and Development, Paris, https://survey.oecd.org/index.php?r=survey/index&sid=371986&lang=en; OECD Competition Trends (portal), Organisation for Economic Co-operation and Development, Paris, https://www.oecd.org/fr/corruption/oecd-competition-trends.htm.

final services and products in the case of natural monopolies and only for essential inputs in the case of partially contestable markets. By contrast, price controls can completely undermine market signals in competitive markets.

As economies (or sectors) move closer to the technology frontier, competition agencies will need to consider a possible trade-off between innovation incentives and market power.[72] When market power reduces the incentive to innovate, firms may resort to anticompetitive behavior, necessitating the intervention of antitrust policies. Here, competition and innovation policies will have to be coordinated to achieve the optimal outcomes for innovation.[73] Again, for the sake of coordination, competition authorities must have adequate independence, budget, capacity, and technical sophistication.

For upper-middle-income countries shifting to innovation, a special concern should be the containment of *killer acquisitions*—that is, when incumbents acquire innovative firms specifically to kill future competing products and technologies.[74] Not all acquisitions are deadly: many young entrepreneurs try deliberately to be acquired by an incumbent, producing complementary innovations that an incumbent can scale up. Antitrust agencies must use a risk-based approach to carefully examine the effects of risky acquisitions on corporate innovation and future competition.

Even if competition authorities use counterfactuals to anticipate the potential effects of a deal, building such scenarios in rapidly evolving markets such as digital ones may result in errors. Thus distinguishing good concentration from bad is hard.[75] In these instances, a dynamic, forward-looking perspective is essential, building on credible data. Authorities should consider the future potential of the acquired firms, recognizing the possibility that these start-ups will grow rapidly and become tomorrow's superstar firms.

While strengthening competition authorities and regulatory institutions to discipline incumbent firms, a government should also use fiscal policy and support coalition building to make elites contestable. A society's wealthiest members often use their social and political power to slow creation and preserve the systems that benefit them. Meanwhile, wealth is frequently inherited or acquired through rent-seeking, which does not create and add value to the economy. Instead, it manipulates the social and political conditions of economic activity to distribute wealth upward.

By adopting a progressive income taxation system, countries can compress the after-tax income distribution, reduce inequality, and promote social mobility.[76] Tax rates that are too high, however, can dampen incentives to undertake high-return, high-risk innovation activities. For example, in response to higher income taxes, innovators or entrepreneurs can reduce their efforts, evade taxes, or migrate to lower-tax localities. Inventors prefer to locate in the same places as other inventors in their specific domain.[77]

Countries can use inheritance or estate taxes to reduce wealth inequality while financing social protection programs. Progressive inheritance taxes can motivate charitable giving by allowing tax deductions for donations by wealthy individuals—and others—just as progressive income taxes often do. Charitable giving has gained momentum in some middle-income countries, including the BRICs (Brazil, Russia, India, China). And yet in terms of gifts per donor, Asia and Latin America rank the lowest (about US$200,000).

Overall, policy makers in middle-income countries, like those in advanced economies, must strike a fine balance in disciplining economic elites without getting rid of the geese that could lay the golden eggs. What is critical is finding the optimal tax rate that will balance disincentive effects with steps to lower inequality. Governments can also offset some of the disincentive effects of progressive taxation by supporting an enabling innovation environment, with universities, high-quality infrastructure, urban amenities, and direct incentives for innovation (R&D subsidies).

Notes

1. Akcigit, Baslandze, and Lotti (2023).
2. *Emerging markets* are defined here as countries or territories that have a billionaire but are not one of the high-income member countries of the Organisation for Economic Co-operation and Development (OECD). They are mostly middle-income countries. The data for 2004 and 2014 are from Freund (2016).
3. A study indicates that as of 2014 a substantial share of the extremely wealthy individuals in developing nations had amassed their wealth through inheritance (29 percent), resource exploitation, or preferential government ties and monopolies (16 percent), rather than through genuine productive investments (Freund 2016). More recent data are not available.
4. Schneider (2022).
5. Arayavechkit, Jooste, and Urrutia Arrieta (2022).
6. de Vries 2006; Dixit and Gill (2024).
7. Aghion et al. (2008).
8. Schivardi and Viviano (2011).
9. Schiffbauer, Sampi, and Coronado (2022).
10. Dauda and Drozd (2020).
11. World Bank (2023a).
12. Sanchez Navarro (2024). On average, BOSs are less productive in terms of revenue per worker, have lower profit margins, and for every dollar in assets in a BOS firm, the return is lower than the median private peer in the same industry.
13. Ellig (2020).
14. For details, see Vagliasindi (2023) and World Bank (2023a).
15. Goldin (2006, 2014, 2021); Goldin and Katz (2002).
16. Hyland et al. (2021).
17. Piontkivsky and Nikijuluw (2023).
18. Deininger, Goyal, and Nagarajan (2013).
19. Deininger et al. (2019); Heath and Tan (2020); Naaraayanan (2022); Roy (2008).
20. Fernández, Fogli, and Olivetti (2004). See also World Bank (2011, 2018, 2024).
21. Dhar, Jain, and Jayachandran (2019).
22. World Bank (2022a, 2022b).
23. Dhar, Jain, and Jayachandran (2022).
24. Andrew et al. (2022).
25. For more information, see https://www.unesco.org/en/articles/unesco-laureate-china-children-and-teenagers-fund-helps-disadvantaged-girls-thrive-through-education.
26. Garcia-Brazales (2021).
27. Bursztyn et al. (2023).
28. Bursztyn, González, and Yanagizawa-Drott (2020).
29. Beaman et al. (2012); Priyanka (2020).
30. Chiplunkar and Goldberg (2021).
31. Fernández (2013).
32. Cameron, Contreras Suarez, and Tseng (2023).
33. Halim, Perova, and Reynolds (2021).
34. World Bank (2024).
35. Aghion et al. (2001, 2005); Akcigit, Alp, and Peters (2021).
36. Commission on Growth and Development (2008).
37. For more information on the World Bank Productivity Project, see https://www.worldbank.org/en/topic/competitiveness/brief/the-world-bank-productivity-project.
38. Cirera and Maloney (2017).
39. Cirera and Maloney (2017).
40. Melitz and Redding (2021); World Bank (2023b); and discussion in chapter 3.
41. Choi and Shim (2023).
42. Phumpiu Chang and Castillo (2024).
43. Kolasa (2008).
44. Jordaan, Douw, and Qiang (2020).
45. Fløysand and Barton (2014).
46. Akcigit and Melitz (2022); World Bank (2020).
47. Verhoogen (2023).
48. Commission on Growth and Development (2008); Defever, Riaño, and Varela (2020); Defever et al. (2020); Lovo and Varela (2023).
49. Lederman, Olarreaga, and Payton (2006).
50. Varela et al. (2022).
51. Volpe Martincus and Carballo (2008).
52. Cadot et al. (2015).
53. Melitz and Redding (2021).
54. Aghion et al. (2022).
55. Verhoogen (2023).
56. Bloom, Draca, and Van Reenen (2016).
57. Bustos (2011).
58. Medina (2022).
59. Cusolito, Garcia-Marin, and Maloney (2023).
60. Iacovone, Rauch, and Winters (2013).
61. Iacovone, Pereira López, and Schiffbauer (2023).
62. Buera and Oberfield (2020); Coe and Helpman (1995); Coe, Helpman, and Hoffmaister (1997); Eaton and Kortum (2001); Hsieh et al. (2019); Rachapalli (2021).
63. World Bank (2023c).
64. See García-Sanchez and Crawley (2024).
65. See Shi, Liu, and Wang (2023) and references therein.
66. Akcigit, Baslandze, and Stantcheva (2016).
67. Prato (2023).
68. Although the Anti-Cartel Enforcement Database covers a much broader time period and 75 countries, complete data for middle-income countries are available only for 34 countries between 2017 and 2022. For more information on the database, see World Bank (2021).
69. World Bank (2021).
70. These data are based on a sample of 43 high-income countries and 52 middle-income countries and on public information for 2021 or the latest year available (Begazo and Licetti 2024). Statistics on budget exclude Cambodia, Kuwait, and Nigeria, which only publish staff information.
71. Begazo and Licetti (2024).
72. Cheng (2021); Gal et al. (2019).
73. Aghion et al. (2001, 2009).
74. Cunningham, Ederer, and Ma (2021).
75. Syverson (2019).
76. Diamond and Saez (2011).
77. Akcigit et al. (2022).

References

Aghion, Philippe, Antonin Bergeaud, Matthieu Lequien, Marc Melitz, and Thomas Zuber. 2022. "Opposing Firm-Level Responses to the China Shock: Horizontal Competition versus Vertical Relationships?" NBER Working Paper 29196, National Bureau of Economic Research, Cambridge, MA.

Aghion, Philippe, Nick Bloom, Richard Blundell, Rachel Griffith, and Peter Howitt. 2005. "Competition and Innovation: An Inverted-U Relationship." *Quarterly Journal of Economics* 120 (2): 701–28.

Aghion, Philippe, Richard Blundell, Rachel Griffith, Peter Howitt, and Susanne Prantl. 2009. "The Effects of Entry on Incumbent Innovation and Productivity." *Review of Economics and Statistics* 91 (1): 20–32.

Aghion, Philippe, Robin Burgess, Stephen J. Redding, and Fabrizio Zilibotti. 2008. "The Unequal Effects of Liberalization: Evidence from Dismantling the License Raj in India." *American Economic Review* 98 (4): 1397–412.

Aghion, Philippe, Christopher Harris, Peter Howitt, and John Vickers. 2001. "Competition, Imitation and Growth with Step-by-Step Innovation." *Review of Economic Studies* 68 (3): 467–92.

Akcigit, Ufuk, Harun Alp, and Michael Peters. 2021. "Lack of Selection and Limits to Delegation: Firm Dynamics in Developing Countries." *American Economic Review* 111 (1): 231–75.

Akcigit, Ufuk, Salomé Baslandze, and Francesca Lotti. 2023. "Connecting to Power: Political Connections, Innovation, and Firm Dynamics." *Econometrica* 91 (2): 529–64.

Akcigit, Ufuk, Salomé Baslandze, and Stefanie Stantcheva. 2016. "Taxation and the International Mobility of Inventors." *American Economic Review* 106 (10): 2930–81.

Akcigit, Ufuk, John Grigsby, Tom Nicholas, and Stefanie Stantcheva. 2022. "Taxation and Innovation in the 20th Century." *Quarterly Journal of Economics* 137 (1): 329–85.

Akcigit, Ufuk, and Marc J. Melitz. 2022. "International Trade and Innovation." In *Handbook of International Economics: International Trade*, vol. 5, edited by Gina Gopinath, Elhanan Helpman, and Kenneth Rogoff, 377–404. Handbooks in Economics Series. Amsterdam: North-Holland, Elsevier.

Andrew, Alison, Sonya Krutikova, Gabriela Smarrelli, and Hemlata Verma. 2022. "Gender Norms, Violence and Adolescent Girls' Trajectories: Evidence from a Field Experiment in India." IFS Working Paper W22/41, Institute for Fiscal Studies, London.

Arayavechkit, Tanida, Charl Jooste, and Ana Urrutia Arrieta. 2022. "How Regulation and Enforcement of Competition Affects ICT Productivity: Evidence from Matched Regulatory-Production Surveys in Peru's ICT Sector." Policy Research Working Paper 10151, World Bank, Washington, DC.

Arráiz, Irani, Francisca Henríquez, and Rodolfo Stucchi. 2011. "Impact of the Chilean Supplier Development Program on the Performance of SMEs and Their Large Firm Customers." OVE Working Paper OVE/WP–04/11 (May), Office of Evaluation and Oversight, Inter-American Development Bank, Washington, DC.

Bai, Jie, Panle Jia Barwick, Shengmao Cao, and Shanjun Li. 2022. "Quid Pro Quo, Knowledge Spillover, and Industrial Quality Upgrading: Evidence from the Chinese Auto Industry." NBER Working Paper 27644 rev. (November), National Bureau of Economic Research, Cambridge, MA.

Beaman, Lori A., Esther Duflo, Rohini Pande, and Petia Topalova. 2012. "Female Leadership Raises Aspirations and Educational Attainment for Girls: A Policy Experiment in India." *Science* 335 (6068): 582–86.

Begazo, Tania Priscilla, and Martha Martínez Licetti. 2024. *Market Institutions: Beyond Competition Authorities and the Need for a Broader Institutional Ecosystem.* Washington, DC: World Bank.

Bloom, Nicholas, Mirko Draca, and John Van Reenen. 2016. "Trade Induced Technical Change? The Impact of Chinese Imports on Innovation, IT and Productivity." *Review of Economic Studies* 83 (1): 87–117.

Bridgman, Benjamin, Shi Qi, and James A. Schmitz, Jr. 2009. "The Economic Performance of Cartels: Evidence from the New Deal U.S. Sugar Manufacturing Cartel 1934–74." Research Department Staff Report 437 (November), Federal Reserve Bank of Minneapolis, Minneapolis.

Buera, Francisco Javier, and Ezra Oberfield. 2020. "The Global Diffusion of Ideas." *Econometrica* 88 (1): 83–114.

Bursztyn, Leonardo, Alexander W. Cappelen, Bertil Tungodden, Alessandra Voena, and David H. Yanagizawa-Drott. 2023. "How Are Gender Norms Perceived?" NBER Working Paper 31049 (March), National Bureau of Economic Research, Cambridge, MA.

Bursztyn, Leonardo, Alessandra L. González, and David Yanagizawa-Drott. 2020. "Misperceived Social Norms: Women Working Outside the Home in Saudi Arabia." *American Economic Review* 110 (10): 2997–3029.

Bustos, Paula. 2011. "Trade Liberalization, Exports, and Technology Upgrading: Evidence on the Impact of MERCOSUR on Argentinian Firms." *American Economic Review* 101 (1): 304–40.

Cadot, Olivier, Alan Asprilla, Julien Gourdon, Christian Knebel, and Ralf Peters. 2015. "Deep Regional Integration and Non-Tariff Measures: A Methodology for Data Analysis." Policy Issues in International Trade and Commodities Research Studies Series 69, United Nations Conference on Trade and Development, Geneva.

Cameron, Lisa, Diana Contreras Suarez, and Yi-Ping Tseng. 2023. "Women's Transitions in the Labour Market as a Result of Childbearing: The Challenges of Formal Sector Employment in Indonesia." IZA Discussion Paper Series 16136, Institute of Labor Economics (IZA), Bonn, Germany.

Cheng, Thomas K. 2021. *The Patent-Competition Interface in Developing Countries.* Oxford, UK: Oxford University Press.

Chiplunkar, Gaurav, and Pinelopi Koujianou Goldberg. 2021. "Aggregate Implications of Barriers to Female Entrepreneurship." NBER Working Paper 28486 (February), National Bureau of Economic Research, Cambridge, MA.

Choi, Jaedo, and Younghun Shim. 2023. "Technology Adoption and Late Industrialization." STEG Working Paper WP033 rev. (September), Structural Transformation and Economic Growth, Centre for Economic Policy Research, London.

Cirera, Xavier, and William F. Maloney. 2017. *The Innovation Paradox: Developing-Country Capabilities and the Unrealized Promise of Technological Catch-Up.* Washington, DC: World Bank.

Coe, David T., and Elhanan Helpman. 1995. "International R&D Spillovers." *European Economic Review* 39 (5): 859–87.

Coe, David T., Elhanan Helpman, and Alexander W. Hoffmaister. 1997. "North-South R&D Spillovers." *Economic Journal* 107 (440): 134–49.

Commission on Growth and Development. 2008. *The Growth Report: Strategies for Sustained Growth and Inclusive Development.* Washington, DC: World Bank. https://openknowledge.worldbank.org/handle/10986/6507.

Cunningham, Colleen, Florian Ederer, and Song Ma. 2021. "Killer Acquisitions." *Journal of Political Economy* 129 (3): 649–702.

Cusolito, Ana Paula, Alvaro Garcia-Marin, and William F. Maloney. 2023. "Proximity to the Frontier, Markups, and the Response of Innovation to Foreign Competition: Evidence from Matched Production-Innovation Surveys in Chile." *American Economic Review: Insights* 5 (1): 35–54.

Dall'Olio, Andrea, Tanja Goodwin, Martha Martinez Licetti, Ana Cristina Alonso Soria, Maciej Drozd, Jan Orlowski, Fausto Patiño Peña, and Dennis Sanchez-Navarro. 2022. "Are All State-Owned Enterprises Equal? A Taxonomy of Economic Activities to Assess SOE Presence in the Economy." Policy Research Working Paper 10262, World Bank, Washington, DC.

Dauda, Seidu, and Maciej Drozd. 2020. *Barriers to Competition in Product Market Regulation: New Insights on Emerging Market and Developing Economies.* Washington, DC: World Bank.

Defever, Fabrice, José-Daniel Reyes, Alejandro Riaño, and Gonzalo J. Varela. 2020. "All These Worlds Are Yours, Except India: The Effectiveness of Cash Subsidies to Export in Nepal." *European Economic Review* 128 (September): 103494.

Defever, Fabrice, Alejandro Riaño, and Gonzalo J. Varela. 2020. "Evaluating the Impact of Export Finance Support on Firm-Level Export Performance: Evidence from Pakistan." CESifo Working Paper 8519 (August), Munich Society for the Promotion of Economic Research, Center for Economic Studies, Ludwig Maximilian University and Ifo Institute for Economic Research, Munich.

Deininger, Klaus W., Aparajita Goyal, and Hari K. Nagarajan. 2013. "Women's Inheritance Rights and Intergenerational Transmission of Resources in India." *Journal of Human Resources* 48 (1): 114–41.

Deininger, Klaus W., Songqing Jin, Hari K. Nagarajan, and Fang Xia. 2019. "Inheritance Law Reform, Empowerment, and Human Capital Accumulation: Second-Generation Effects from India." *Journal of Development Studies* 55 (12): 2549–71.

de Vries, Henk J. 2006. "Standards for Business: How Companies Benefit from Participation in International Standards Setting." In *International Standardization as a Strategic Tool: Commended Papers from the IEC Centenary Challenge 2006*, 130–41. Geneva: International Electrotechnical Commission.

Dhar, Diva, Tarun Jain, and Seema Jayachandran. 2019. "Intergenerational Transmission of Gender Attitudes: Evidence from India." *Journal of Development Studies* 55 (12): 2572–92.

Dhar, Diva, Tarun Jain, and Seema Jayachandran. 2022. "Reshaping Adolescents' Gender Attitudes: Evidence from a School-Based Experiment in India." *American Economic Review* 112 (3): 899–927.

Diamond, Peter, and Emmanuel Saez. 2011. "The Case for a Progressive Tax: From Basic Research to Policy Recommendations." *Journal of Economic Perspectives* 25 (4): 165–90.

Dixit, Siddharth, and Indermit S. Gill. 2024. "AI, the New Wingman of Development." Background paper prepared for *World Development Report 2024*, World Bank, Washington, DC.

Eaton, Jonathan, and Samuel Kortum. 2001. "Technology, Trade, and Growth: A Unified Framework." *European Economic Review* 45 (4–6): 742–55.

Ellig, Jerry. 2020. "Retail Electric Competition and Natural Monopoly: The Shocking Truth." In *Regulation and Economic Opportunity: Blueprints for Reform*, edited by Adam Hoffer and Todd Nesbit, 277–302. Logan, UT: Center for Growth and Opportunity, Utah State University.

Fernández, Raquel. 2013. "Cultural Change as Learning: The Evolution of Female Labor Force Participation over a Century." *American Economic Review* 103 (1): 472–500.

Fernández, Raquel, Alessandra Fogli, and Claudia Olivetti. 2004. "Mothers and Sons: Preference Formation and Female Labor Force Dynamics." *Quarterly Journal of Economics* 119 (4): 1249–99.

Fløysand, Arnt, and Jonathan R. Barton. 2014. "Foreign Direct Investment, Local Development, and Poverty Reduction: The Sustainability of the Salmon Industry in Southern Chile." In *Alternative Development: Unravelling Marginalization, Voicing Change*, edited by Cathrine Brun, Piers Blaikie, and Michael Jones, 55–71. Farnham, UK: Ashgate Publishing.

Freund, Caroline L. 2016. *Rich People Poor Countries: The Rise of Emerging-Market Tycoons and Their Mega Firms.* Assisted by Sarah Oliver. Washington, DC: Peterson Institute for International Economics.

Gal, Peter, Giuseppe Nicoletti, Theodore Renault, Stéphane Sorbe, and Christina Timilioti. 2019. "Digitalisation and Productivity: In Search of the Holy Grail; Firm-Level Empirical Evidence from EU Countries." OECD Economics Department Working Paper 1533 (February 6), Organisation for Economic Co-operation and Development, Paris.

Garcia-Brazales, Javier. 2021. "Changing Gender Attitudes: The Long-Run Effects of Early Exposure to Female Classmates." Paper presented at the virtual 33rd Annual Conference of the European Association of

Labour Economists, Department of Economics and Management Marco Fanno, University of Padua, Padua, Italy, September 16–18, 2021.

García-Sanchez, Cristobal, and Edward Crawley. 2024. "Accelerating Innovation for Development: How Universities Leverage Knowledge Exchange to Boost Economic Growth in Middle-Income Countries." Background paper prepared for *World Development Report 2024*, World Bank, Washington, DC.

Goldin, Claudia. 2006. "The Quiet Revolution that Transformed Women's Employment, Education, and Family." *American Economic Review* 96 (2): 1–21.

Goldin, Claudia. 2014. "A Grand Gender Convergence: Its Last Chapter." *American Economic Review* 104 (4): 1091–119.

Goldin, Claudia. 2021. *Career and Family: Women's Century-Long Journey toward Equity*. Princeton, NJ: Princeton University Press.

Goldin, Claudia, and Lawrence F. Katz. 2002. "The Power of the Pill: Oral Contraceptives and Women's Career and Marriage Decisions." *Journal of Political Economy* 110 (4): 730–70.

Google. 2023. "Unidos por el Bienestar Económico de las Mujeres del Sureste Mexicano." February 21, 2023, blog. https://blog.google/intl/es-419/unidos-por-el-bienestar-economico-de-las-mujeres-del-sureste-mexicano/.

Halim, Daniel, Elizaveta Perova, and Sarah Reynolds. 2021. "Childcare and Mothers' Labor Market Outcomes in Lower- and Middle-Income Countries." Policy Research Working Paper 9828, World Bank, Washington, DC.

Heath, Rachel, and Xu Tan. 2020. "Intrahousehold Bargaining, Female Autonomy, and Labor Supply: Theory and Evidence from India." *Journal of the European Economic Association* 18 (4): 1928–68.

Herfindahl, Orris C. 1950. "Concentration in the U.S. Steel Industry." PhD dissertation, Columbia University, New York.

Hirschman, Albert O. 1964. "The Paternity of an Index." *American Economic Review* 54 (5): 761–62.

Hsieh, Chang-Tai, Erik Hurst, Charles I. Jones, and Peter J. Klenow. 2019. "The Allocation of Talent and U.S. Economic Growth." *Econometrica* 87 (5): 1439–74.

Hyland, Marie Caitriona, Nona Karalashvili, Silvia Muzi, and Domenico Viganola. 2021. "Female-Owned Firms during the COVID-19 Crisis." Global Indicators Brief 2 (July 29), World Bank, Washington, DC.

Iacovone, Leonardo, Mariana De La Paz Pereira López, and Marc Tobias Schiffbauer. 2023. "Competition Makes IT Better: Evidence on When Firms Use IT More Effectively." *Research Policy* 52 (8): 104786.

Iacovone, Leonardo, Ferdinand Rauch, and L. Alan Winters. 2013. "Trade as an Engine of Creative Destruction: Mexican Experience with Chinese Competition." *Journal of International Economics* 89 (2): 379–92.

IEA (International Energy Agency). 2020. *World Energy Investment 2020*. July. Paris: IEA.

Jordaan, Jacob Arie, Willem Douw, and Christine Zhenwei Qiang. 2020. "Multinational Corporation Affiliates, Backward Linkages, and Productivity Spillovers in Developing and Emerging Economies: Evidence and Policy Making." Policy Research Working Paper 9364, World Bank, Washington, DC.

Kolasa, Marcin. 2008. "How Does FDI Inflow Affect Productivity of Domestic Firms? The Role of Horizontal and Vertical Spillovers, Absorptive Capacity and Competition." *Journal of International Trade and Economic Development* 17 (1): 155–73.

Lederman, Daniel, Marcelo Olarreaga, and Lucy Payton. 2006. "Export Promotion Agencies: What Works and What Doesn't." Policy Research Working Paper 4044, World Bank, Washington, DC.

Lovo, Stefania, and Gonzalo J. Varela. 2023. "Internationally Linked Firms, Integration Reforms and Productivity: Evidence from Pakistan." Policy Research Working Paper 9349, World Bank, Washington, DC.

Medina, Pamela. 2022. "Import Competition, Quality Upgrading, and Exporting: Evidence from the Peruvian Apparel Industry." *Review of Economics and Statistics*. Published ahead of print, July 26, 2022. https://doi.org/10.1162/rest_a_01221.

Melitz, Marc J., and Stephen J. Redding. 2021. "Trade and Innovation." NBER Working Paper 28945 (June), National Bureau of Economic Research, Cambridge, MA.

Monge-González, Ricardo, John Hewitt, and Federico Torres-Carballo. 2015. "Do Multinationals Help or Hinder Local Firms? Evidence from the Costa Rican ICT Sector." CAATEC Working Paper, Comisión Asesora en Alta Tecnología, San José, Costa Rica.

Naaraayanan, Sankararama Lakshmi. 2022. "Women's Inheritance Rights and Entrepreneurship Gender Gap." Paper presented at the Indian School of Business–National Bureau of Economic Research conference, "Economic Policy and the Indian Economy," Indian School of Business, Hyderabad, India, December 17–18, 2022.

OECD (Organisation for Economic Co-operation and Development). 2014. "Factsheet on How Competition Policy Affects Macro-Economic Outcomes." October, OECD, Paris.

OECD (Organisation for Economic Co-operation and Development). 2024. *OECD Competition Trends 2024*. Paris: OECD Publishing. https://doi.org/10.1787/e69018f9-en.

Petit, Lilian T. D., Ron G. M. Kemp, and Jarig van Sinderen. 2015. "Cartels and Productivity Growth: An Empirical Investigation of the Impact of Cartels on Productivity in the Netherlands." *Journal of Competition Law and Economics* 11 (2): 501–25.

Phumpiu Chang, Paul, and Jose Castillo. 2024. "Shaping Market Dynamics: The Role of Competition Policy in Fostering Contestability and Technological Adoption in the Mobile Telecommunications Sector in Middle-Income Countries." Background paper prepared for *World Development Report 2024*, World Bank, Washington, DC.

Piontkivsky, Ruslan, and Ruth Nikijuluw. 2023. "Papua New Guinea Country Economic Memorandum: Pathways to Faster and More Inclusive Growth." World Bank, Washington, DC.

Prato, Marta. 2023. "The Global Race for Talent: Brain Drain, Knowledge Transfer, and Economic Growth." Working Paper, Ettore Bocconi Department of Economics, Bocconi University, Milan.

Priyanka, Sadia. 2020. "Do Female Politicians Matter for Female Labor Market Outcomes? Evidence from State Legislative Elections in India." *Labour Economics* 64 (June): 101822.

Pro Mujer. 2023. "Pro Mujer and Google Join Forces to Impact the Lives of Thousands of Indigenous Women in Southeast Mexico." *Pro Mujer* (blog), February 23, 2023. https://promujer.org/en/blog/with-support-from-the-ministry-of-economy-pro-mujer-and-google-join-forces-to-impact-the-lives-of-thousands-of-indigenous-women-in-southeast-mexico/.

Rachapalli, Swapnika. 2021. "Learning between Buyers and Sellers along the Global Value Chain." Paper presented at the Cowles Foundation for Research in Economics virtual 2021 Conference on International Trade, Yale University, New Haven, CT, June 7, 2021.

Reed, Tristan, Mariana De La Paz Pereira López, Ana Francisca Urrutia Arrieta, and Leonardo Iacovone. 2022. "Cartels, Antitrust Enforcement, and Industry Performance: Evidence from Mexico." Policy Research Working Paper 10269, World Bank, Washington, DC.

Roy, Sanchari. 2008. "Female Empowerment through Inheritance Rights: Evidence from India." Paper presented at the Second Riccardo Faini Doctoral Conference on Development Economics, University of Milan, Milan, September 7–9, 2008. https://www.dagliano.unimi.it/media/roy.pdf.

Sampi, James, Ana Francisca Urrutia Arrieta, and Ekaterina Vostroknutova. 2022. "Antitrust Enforcement, Markups, and Productivity in South America." World Bank, Washington, DC.

Sanchez Navarro, Dennis. 2024. "What Happens When the State Is Bossing around Markets? An Analysis of the Performance Differentials between Businesses of the State (BOS) and Private-Owned Enterprises (POEs)." Policy Research Working Paper 10820, World Bank, Washington, DC.

Schiffbauer, Marc Tobias, James Sampi, and Javier Coronado. 2022. "Competition and Productivity: Evidence from Peruvian Municipalities." *Review of Economics and Statistics*. Published ahead of print, November 15, 2022. https://doi.org/10.1162/rest_a_01257.

Schivardi, Fabiano, and Eliana Viviano. 2011. "Entry Barriers in Retail Trade." *Economic Journal* 121 (551): 145–70.

Schneider, Ben Ross. 2022. "Teacher Unions, Political Machines, and the Thorny Politics of Education Reform in Latin America." *Politics and Society* 50 (1): 84–116.

Schwab, Klaus, ed. 2019. *Insight Report: The Global Competitiveness Report 2019*. Geneva: World Economic Forum. http://www3.weforum.org/docs/WEF_TheGlobalCompetitivenessReport2019.pdf.

Shi, Dongbo, Weichen Liu, and Yanbo Wang. 2023. "Has China's Young Thousand Talents Program Been Successful in Recruiting and Nurturing Top-Caliber Scientists?" *Science* 379 (6627): 62–65.

Syverson, Chad. 2019. "Macroeconomics and Market Power: Context, Implications, and Open Questions." *Journal of Economic Perspectives* 33 (3): 23–43.

Vagliasindi, Maria. 2023. "The Role of SOEs in Climate Change." Background paper prepared for *The Business of the State*, World Bank, Washington, DC.

Varela, Gonzalo, Zehra Aslam, Andreas Eberhard, Aroub Farooq, Veronica Michel Gutierrez, Alen Mulabdic, Rafay Khan, et al. 2022. "From Swimming in Sand to High and Sustainable Growth: Pakistan's Country Economic Memorandum." World Bank, Washington, DC. https://documents1.worldbank.org/curated/en/099820410112267354/pdf/P1749040fc80a70ca0b6f70f7860c4a1034.pdf.

Verhoogen, Eric A. 2023. "Firm-Level Upgrading in Developing Countries." *Journal of Economic Literature* 61 (4): 1410–64.

Volpe Martincus, Christian, and Jerónimo Carballo. 2008. "Is Export Promotion Effective in Developing Countries? Firm-Level Evidence on the Intensive and the Extensive Margins of Exports." *Journal of International Economics* 76 (1): 89–106.

Vostroknutova, Ekaterina, James Sampi, Charl Jooste, and Jorge Thompson Araujo. 2024. *Competition and Productivity in Latin America and the Caribbean*. Washington, DC: World Bank.

World Bank. 2011. *World Development Report 2012: Gender Equality and Development*. Washington, DC: World Bank.

World Bank. 2018. *Women Economic Empowerment Study*. May. Washington, DC: World Bank.

World Bank. 2020. *World Development Report 2020: Trading for Development in the Age of Global Value Chains*. Washington, DC: World Bank.

World Bank. 2021. "Fixing Markets, Not Prices: Policy Options to Tackle Economic Cartels in Latin America and the Caribbean." World Bank, Washington, DC.

World Bank. 2022a. *Poverty and Shared Prosperity 2022: Correcting Course*. Washington, DC: World Bank.

World Bank. 2022b. *Reshaping Norms: A New Way Forward*. South Asia Economic Focus (April). Washington, DC: World Bank.

World Bank. 2023a. *The Business of the State*. Washington, DC: World Bank.

World Bank. 2023b. "Protectionism Is Failing to Achieve Its Goals and Threatens the Future of Critical Industries." *Feature Story*, August 29, 2023. https://www.worldbank.org/en/news/feature/2023/08/29/protectionism-is-failing-to-achieve-its-goals-and-threatens-the-future-of-critical-industries.

World Bank. 2023c. *World Development Report 2023: Migrants, Refugees, and Societies*. Washington, DC: World Bank.

World Bank. 2024. *Women, Business and the Law 2024*. Washington, DC: World Bank.

Zuniga, Maria Pluvia. 2024. "The Impact and Effectiveness of Innovation Policy: Evidence from Middle-Income Countries." Background paper prepared for *World Development Report 2024*, World Bank, Washington, DC.

8 Rewarding Merit

Key messages
- Middle-income countries can allocate talent and human capital more efficiently by opening up education, employment, and business opportunities to all who have talent and display acquired ability. Economic development policies should not target an ideal income distribution but pay attention to enhancing mobility.
- Middle-income countries should avoid solely targeting firms for support by size. Instead, they could also assess the value that firms add to the economy through jobs, exports, technology infusion, and innovation. Countries' policies should target support to those firms that display the most potential for growth, while letting go of unproductive firms, modernizing organizational models to manage firms, and connecting entrepreneurs with money (financing opportunities), mentors, and markets.
- Middle-income countries will need to adopt policies that support the diffusion of lower-carbon energy technologies, incentivize the efficient use of energy, and consider the social and ecological costs of greenhouse gas emissions. They should consider all options for decoupling their growing economies from the growth of these emissions.

Moving forward by promoting merit activities

To strengthen the forces of creation, middle-income countries will need to shift their policies and institutions toward promoting merit activities—that is, those with positive effects on general well-being and that aid in the efficient use of talent, capital, and energy.

Specifically, middle-income countries should put three considerations at the center of economic policy making: the *economic and social mobility of people;* the *value added by firms;* and the *greenhouse gases (GHGs) emitted by the economy*.

- *The economic and social mobility of people*. Governments should adopt policies that will enable an economy to allocate talent and human capital more efficiently—in particular, by opening up education, employment, and business opportunities to all those who have talent and display acquired ability. Because advancing the sophistication of an economy can increase income inequality, economic development policies should not target an ideal income distribution. Instead, by rewarding talent and effort, policies can generate both higher social and economic mobility, which leads to faster growth.[1] However, perceptions of mobility matter. When perceptions of the opportunities for future mobility are high, social tolerance of inequality is also high, and vice versa.[2]

- *The value added by firms.* A similar principle applies to firms. Dynamic, productive young firms should be able to expand, and less productive firms should be able to contract and exit, thereby enhancing value added across the economy through efficient resource utilization. Policies should not target firms for support by size, but instead should assess the value that firms add to the economy through jobs, exports, technology infusion, and innovation.
- *The GHG emissions of an economy.* A similar principle also applies to energy. Government policies should aid in the diffusion of lower-carbon energy technologies, encourage the efficient use of energy, and consider the social and ecological costs of GHG emissions. Because today's middle-income countries account for two-thirds of global GHG emissions and all new emissions growth, they will need to consider all options to decouple their growing economies from higher GHG emissions.

The economic and social mobility of people

The introduction of global technologies must go hand in hand with a search for the technical workers and specialized professionals needed for firms to adopt technologies, along with competent managers to run firms. Meanwhile, more engineers are needed to build and maintain infrastructure, teachers to educate students, doctors to treat patients, and highly qualified men and women to run governments. Chapter 5 highlighted that middle-income countries face two related challenges. First, talent is scarce in those countries because they do not accumulate human capital. Second, middle-income countries are not as effective as high-income countries in allocating talent to tasks. Middle-income countries must then focus on improving social mobility—going beyond narrowly focusing on inequality. In doing so, these countries will need to revise how they reward talent by upgrading their talent pool, selecting efficient learners, expanding occupation choices and rewards, and nurturing scientific inquiry and enhancing research capabilities, and installing a socially responsible safety net to protect those who may lose their livelihoods in the creative destruction process.

Upgrading the talent pool

Support high-quality secondary and higher education

Countries that transitioned from middle- to high-income status in recent decades sought to accumulate human capital, which begins with developing foundational skills. As a result, their upper-secondary enrollment and graduation rates, as well as their tertiary education enrollment rates, steadily increased (figure 8.1). Countries that did not transition to high-income status have attained levels of tertiary education that are close to the levels achieved by countries at the time of their transition, but enrollment in and completion of upper-secondary education have lagged for a wider swath of the population.[3] For significant shares of the population in countries that have not transitioned to high-income status, education stops in the early teen years, or earlier, especially for girls and members of minorities. Unless these countries secure foundational skills, their talent pipeline will remain weak.

How should countries allocate education spending between foundational and advanced skills? In setting priorities, countries may want to consider the principle of progressive

Figure 8.1 Middle-income countries that transitioned to high-income status first focused on foundational skills

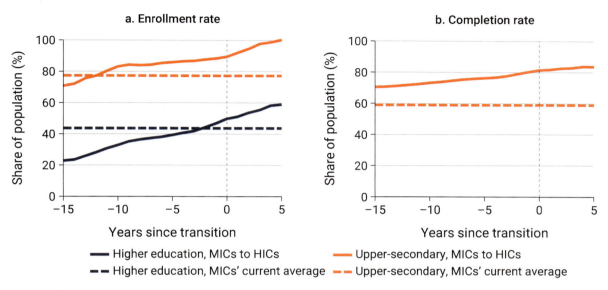

Source: WDR 2024 team calculations based on data of UIS.Stat (dashboard), Institute for Statistics, United Nations Educational, Scientific, and Cultural Organization, Montreal, http://data.uis.unesco.org/.

Note: Solid lines show averages for countries that were middle-income countries in the early 1990s and transitioned to high-income status any time before 2019 (23 countries for enrollment rates and 15 countries for completion rates). Dashed lines indicate the current average for middle-income countries that have not yet transitioned. Gross enrollment rate is the ratio of total enrollment, regardless of age, to the population of the official age group for the education level. Completion rate is the percentage of individuals three to five years older than the theoretical age of completion of the level's last grade who have completed the level's last grade. For countries that have transitioned, data are for 1981–2022 for enrollment rates and 1990–2021 for completion rates. The number of years since graduation is computed as the calendar year minus transition year. For countries not yet transitioned, data are for the most recent year available. HICs = high-income countries; MICs = middle-income countries.

universalism, which advocates investing progressively in higher education as quality for all is reached at lower educational levels.[4] The "universal" component advocates high-quality education for all. The "progressive" component recognizes that efforts and resources are limited and prioritizes the early years of a child's life, as well as outreach to disadvantaged students who face the greatest learning hurdles. The Republic of Korea adopted this approach. In the 1950s, it enforced compulsory education and devoted nearly 80 percent of its education budget to primary education, thereby increasing enrollment rates from about 40 percent to 90 percent in 10 years. Korea then shifted its efforts and spending to secondary education and attained equally rapid success. Only later did it invest substantially in tertiary education. Throughout this period, Korea focused not only on enrollment but also on learning—for all.[5] Because its efforts to improve foundational skills were focused and deliberate, Korea was able to pivot to advanced skills in a relatively short period of time. An emphasis on foundational skills for all was key to the success of school reforms in other countries as well (box 8.1).

Strengthening foundational skills does not always require more money, but it does require efficient spending. In fact, countries that spend more do not necessarily have better learning outcomes.[6]

REWARDING MERIT | 191

Box 8.1 Developing foundational skills: Learning from Finland and Chile

The successful reforms implemented by countries that graduated from middle- to high-income status have shared three elements.[a] First, they broadened access to foundational skills to create a large, deep talent pool of high school graduates. Second, they relied on student assessments to collect information on learning and evaluate progress toward achieving policy goals. Third, education reforms were part of a deliberate long-term growth strategy.

Finland. In the early 1970s, Finland replaced its two-track school system (students were divided into two tracks, general secondary and vocational, after the first four years of education) with a nine-year comprehensive school system (all students followed the same national curriculum until age 16 and then chose a track). In addition, teacher training became more selective and rigorous. Finally, curricula setting went from highly centralized to more decentralized.[b] These reforms broadened the talent pool, which may have helped weaken the relationship between parental income and, for example, the likelihood of becoming an inventor.[c] Reforms also targeted higher education, making access more equitable and holding institutions accountable for their contributions to the economy.

Chile. Since the 1980s, students in Chile have had access to universal vouchers to attend private schools. In 2008, a reform was enacted to raise the voucher amount for disadvantaged students, provide additional funding to schools with large shares of such students, and create an accountability system for schools receiving vouchers. Critically, a test-based assessment system was created in the 1980s and is still being used to gauge results. The opening of private universities was encouraged, new sources of student funding became available through scholarships and loans, and the supply of short-cycle higher education programs grew rapidly.[d] Against the backdrop of these reforms, the share of high school students scoring above minimum proficiency levels in the worldwide assessment, the Programme for International Student Assessment (PISA), rose from 53 percent to 68 percent between 2000 and 2018, and net enrollment rates in higher education have grown from less than 5 percent to about 45 percent since 1970. Furthermore, college access has become more equitable for men and women and for students from different socioeconomic backgrounds.[e] However, the share of disadvantaged students among top performers in the high school math exit exam has barely changed over the past five decades, suggesting that, although many disadvantaged students have gained access to college, their elementary and high schools are not yet preparing them for admission to Chile's top universities.

a. See, for example, Aghion et al. (2023) and Pekkarinen, Uusitalo, and Pekkala Kerr (2009) for Finland; World Bank (2021) for Ireland; Lee, Jeong, and Hong (2014) for the Republic of Korea; Guyon, Maurin, and McNally (2012) for Northern Ireland; and Jakubowski et al. (2016) for Poland.
b. Pekkarinen, Uusitalo, and Pekkala Kerr (2009); Saavedra-Chanduví, Alasuutari, and Gutiérrez Bernal (2018).
c. Aghion et al. (2023).
d. Aguirre (2021); Fontaine and Urzúa (2018); Murnane et al. (2017); Solis (2017); Vegas (2018).
e. Gallegos, Barrios-Fernández, and Neilson (2024).

A comparison across 46 countries of 150 interventions in early childhood and primary and secondary education reveals that some of the most cost-effective programs deliver the equivalent of three additional years of high-quality schooling (comparable with that of the highest-performing education systems) for just US$100 per child.[7] The three most cost-effective interventions are targeted information campaigns about the benefits, costs, and quality of schooling; interventions to target teaching instruction by learning level rather than grade; and improved pedagogy through structured lesson plans providing student materials, teacher professional development, and monitoring.[8] Other policies—such as early childhood development and merit-based scholarships—are costlier and yet are still highly effective.

Develop advanced skills

To build a pool of talent with advanced skills, middle-income countries must substantially upgrade their higher education systems. These systems need to be aware of the skills in demand or they run the risk of producing unemployable graduates whose skills are not relevant to the labor market. In Latin America and the Caribbean, shorter-term higher education programs that interact more with employers and help students in their job search contribute more to students' labor market outcomes than other such "short-cycle" programs.[9] Although short-cycle programs pursue such connections more often than bachelor's programs,[10] the connections are equally important for both.

Lack of experience often holds back university graduates from finding jobs. Education models that incorporate work experience attempt to break this cycle and facilitate the school-to-work transition. Examples include dual training programs, apprenticeships, co-operative education, and integrated curricula. In Ecuador, Corporación Formados provides students with dual training based on the German model to produce not only technical workers in manufacturing but also middle managers (who, according to firms, are undertrained), as well as sales and banking specialists.[11] The co-op model alternates between terms of classroom-based instruction and terms of paid work, and it relies on partnerships between institutions and employers. Institutions in middle-income countries offering co-ops include the Universidade de São Paulo in Brazil, Nelson Mandela University in South Africa, and TOBB University of Economics and Technology in Türkiye.[12] The integrated curriculum model is exemplified by Indonesia's Merdeka Belajar (Emancipated Learning) initiative. Educational authorities oversee large-scale curriculum coordination among universities, firms, and other institutions, which allows students to spend up to a third of their time in work settings inside or outside the country. Universities also train practitioners who are interested in learning how to teach and pair them with mentors.[13]

Countries can use public *funding* for higher education to pursue country-level strategic goals and promote equitable access to higher education. Expanding the base of science, technology, engineering, and mathematics (STEM) graduates may be one such strategic goal. China, for example, has dramatically expanded its tertiary-educated population over the last few decades by means of policies at home and training overseas, as well as its base of STEM graduates.[14] Targeted scholarships can increase student interest in STEM careers, including the life sciences, physical sciences, engineering, mathematics, computer science, and the health sciences. When coupled with information and mentoring interventions, they are particularly effective at attracting females to STEM fields.[15] To promote equitable access to higher education, some countries provide need-based financial aid—such as Brazil's ProUni and South Africa's National Student Financial Aid Scheme (NSFAS); unsubsidized student loans—such as those provided by Tanzania's Higher Education Students' Loan Board (HESLB); and subsidized student loans—such as Malaysia's Student Loan Fund Corporation (PTPTN).

Countries can provide incentives to align the attainment and use of actual skills in the workplace and entrepreneurship. For example, short-term technical and vocational education and training (TVET) programs depend for their success on connecting to employers,[16] and offering incentives to industry can help.[17] In Finland, institutions sign student performance contracts with the government and are held accountable for their outcomes. The government of Denmark also signs performance contracts with universities. The country relies on local advisory councils formed by representatives of governments, institutions, and enterprises for short-term programs and training. Councils periodically discuss local skill needs and decide how many programs are needed to address them, closing programs as needed. Denmark also has a well-developed system to forecast skills, as well as an information system that provides data on job opportunities for hundreds of occupations by region.[18]

Selecting efficient learners

Some institutions and programs—particularly those teaching highly advanced material—may require advanced academic readiness and establish selective, merit-based admission criteria. Countries need an effective mechanism to identify, select, and promote talent and ability. Efficient learners with "merit" can be identified using the test scores of higher education entrance exams (or high school exit exams), sometimes in combination with other criteria.

Entrance exams are a standardized, comparable way to evaluate students from different backgrounds, especially when used nationally. On the one hand, exams are a transparent and simple way to sort students across institutions and programs. In 2005, for example, the country of Georgia established a university entrance exam because its previous admission system—inherited from the Soviet era—was obscure, prone to corruption, and widely perceived as inequitable.[19] Entrance exams also establish clear rules for the selection of students across institutions and majors, and they are the backbone of the increasingly popular centralized admission systems used in many countries (box 8.2). On the other hand, entrance exams can perpetuate the very inequities they seek to eliminate. Because students with more educated parents and from higher-income households enjoy access to higher-quality basic education,[20] they score higher on university entrance exams and therefore appear to have more "merit" than others. Students are more likely to confuse an actual "aristocracy of privilege" with an imagined "aristocracy of talent."[21]

Unless all students develop foundational skills and receive excellent basic education, merit-based schemes can detract from—rather than promote—social mobility. Furthermore, entrance exams are not perfect measures of student preparation or the potential for advanced training. As a result, institutions may reject applicants who would perform well if they were admitted.

A more holistic approach to selection may be needed. In principle, "merit" could be defined in broader terms than just exam scores. For example, institutions could reserve a share of their classroom seats for students from disadvantaged minorities, who would also be chosen based on merit—as in Brazil. They may also choose to admit the top share of students from every high school—as in the Top Ten Percent Program in the US state of Texas and similar programs in California and Florida. All these variants, however, have their own trade-offs. More important, capacity at highly selective institutions is limited. The challenge is to build tertiary education systems that provide high-quality opportunities at *all* institutions, not only the most selective ones. In the United States, many institutions—not only top-ranked universities where merit-based admission is most prevalent—promote social mobility.[22] Although countries may want to adopt merit-based admission to some higher education institutions, the emphasis should be on ensuring high-quality education at *all* institutions and educational levels in order to build a broad, deep talent pool.

Box 8.2 Promoting better student choices with digital tools

Countries have increasingly adopted centralized choice and admission systems (CCAS) for primary, secondary, and higher education. CCAS can enhance students' decision-making by providing information about the available choices and helping students use it. Currently, 57 developing countries rely on such mechanisms. Chatbots powered by artificial intelligence have helped students gain admission to higher-quality colleges than they would have attended otherwise in cities such as Bogotá and Palmira (Colombia), Recife (Brazil), Tacna (Peru), and various cities across Chile.[a]

Digital tools are particularly powerful when combined with administrative data. For example, trackers can use administrative data on graduates to follow them through higher education and beyond. In Chile, an online portal reports the average labor market outcomes for every higher education program in the country,[b] allowing prospective students to identify programs with high returns.

Although necessary for good decision-making, information alone is not sufficient because disadvantaged students often need help to interpret or utilize information. Advice and counseling—including through chatbots—can further enhance student decision-making.[c]

Source: Neilson 2024.
a. Arteaga et al. (2022).
b. See Subsecretaría de Educación Superior (Subsecretariat of Higher Education) (portal), Ministry of Education, Santiago, Chile, https://www.mifuturo.cl/.
c. For more on information-related interventions for higher education, see Ferreyra et al. (2021).

Leverage digital technologies

Digital technologies—such as the internet, mobile phones, social media, and web-based information systems—have a large capacity to promote both social mobility and talent development. The internet, for example, allows individuals to find information, which makes them more productive; email allows for the exchange of ideas, which leads to knowledge diffusion; smartphones can be used for mobile banking, which promotes entrepreneurship; and data systems provide government with a wealth of information that can be used to efficiently target interventions.

In selecting students for higher education programs, merit-based selection requires standardized measures of merit such as test scores. Higher-income parents typically have the means to invest in tutoring services for their children, ensuring a critical advantage for them to improve their test scores. To level the playing field and give students from more disadvantaged backgrounds opportunities, countries can leverage digital technologies to deliver instructional materials to many more students online (box 8.3).

Expanding occupation choice and rewards

Climbing the economic and social ladder may not be possible when individuals cannot gain access to jobs or realize their entrepreneurial potential on the basis of merit. In many countries, attending an elite school is not sufficient to secure a top job because connections—not merit—determine recruitment (see chapter 5). Although combating

> **Box 8.3 Improving students' test scores by using online studying assistance from the Khan Academy**
>
> In 2004, Sal Khan, a Bangladeshi American, began tutoring his cousin Nadia in mathematics using a phone and Yahoo Doodle. As Nadia improved her performance in mathematics, word of Khan's service spread, and he began tutoring a handful of his cousins and family members. In 2006, lacking the time for one-on-one tutoring, he began recording videos and posting them on YouTube, offering them to everyone to watch at their own pace. In 2008, this initiative turned into the Khan Academy. It has since produced more than 8,000 video lessons on a wide range of academic subjects, including mathematics, sciences, literature, and computer science, as well as supplementary practice exercises and materials for educators. The learning materials, all provided free of charge, are available in many different languages. Today, they are a supplement to in-class learning, giving teachers more time to focus on individual students' needs.
>
> In July 2017, the Khan Academy became the official practice partner for the College Board's Advanced Placement courses. Students who study for the college entrance exam, the SAT, for at least 20 hours via the Khan Academy increase their scores, on average, by 115 points (of a possible 1,600).
>
> *Source:* Khan Academy (website), Mountain View, CA, https://www.khanacademy.org/.

such discriminatory practices is a necessary first step, it is not sufficient because it does not address the inherent information asymmetry between job candidates and employers. Job candidates rely on social networks to learn about job openings and employers' characteristics. Meanwhile, employers rely on these networks to ascertain workers' skills and trustworthiness. This is particularly true in countries with a high degree of informality and limited information about labor markets.

To address these issues, countries need institutions that can serve as reliable, timely conduits of information. Online job portals—proliferating quickly across middle-income countries—are a cost-effective mechanism to communicate job openings to job-seekers. But information on job opportunities needs to be combined with credible certifications of skills. In South Africa, a job matching program provided candidates with information about job openings and a credible assessment of their own skills. Giving job-seekers this assessment to share with firms increased employment and earnings and enabled them to better align their beliefs about their job performance and their search strategies.[23]

Although lack of information creates unrealistic expectations for many job-seekers about the type of work and wages they can find, some interventions can help.[24] In Ethiopia, a job fair experiment that brought firms and job-seekers together allowed firms to advertise openings more widely and job-seekers to apply for more positions. It also improved employment outcomes for less-educated job-seekers.[25] In South Africa, young job-seekers who live far from the city centers where jobs are located overestimated their employment prospects and underestimated actual commuting costs. By increasing their access and exposure to the broader labor market job-seekers were able to adjust their expectations and accept jobs closer to home.[26]

Giving job-seekers access to "better" networks—those of more influential individuals—can also boost their opportunities.[27] Mentoring improves outcomes mostly by teaching mentees about entry-level jobs and labor market dynamics.[28]

A mentoring program in Uganda that assisted vocational students during their school-to-work transitions increased their employment prospects three months after graduation, and their earnings were higher one year later.

Nurturing scientific inquiry and enhancing research capabilities

The process of nurturing innovation can start early. Identifying high-potential, high-performing students—advanced learners—in the early school grades and inculcating in them a mindset for scientific inquiry is crucial. In India, Atal Tinkering Labs, with the sponsorship of the government, sets up in schools physical laboratories that are equipped with scientific kits and apparatuses for use by students between the sixth and twelfth grades. The opportunity to "tinker" and learn by doing is intended to sow the seeds of a scientific mindset and an entrepreneurial spirit from an early age.[29] Between 2016 and mid-2022, the program funded 9,600 spaces in 34 states and Union Territories.

Mechanisms to identify advanced learners are also important. Testing plays an important role. Instead of using a single absolute measure such as the student's place in the national distribution of test scores, teachers can identify students with the greatest potential or the best performers in every classroom or school. In fact, they can do so repeatedly and not just in one high-stakes test, which leads to a larger, more equitable talent pool.[30] Advanced learners can be offered opportunities—such as participating in advanced classes or attending selective schools—that match their interests and abilities without necessarily hurting other students' outcomes.[31]

Developed countries such as Finland, France, Japan, the Netherlands, Spain, the United Kingdom, and the United States provide special publicly backed programs for advanced learners. Developing countries such as Colombia and Mexico have followed suit.[32] Programs vary in format. In the United States, many schools and school districts run a broad array of programs for advanced learners,[33] whereas in Israel, the National Mentoring Program matches advanced learners in 10th and 11th grades with top professionals in students' areas of interest to collaborate on a project of mutual interest.[34] In a similar vein, exposing young children—particularly those from disadvantaged backgrounds—to inventors and scientists can widen this pipeline. In the United States, several private initiatives bring children together with inventors; in Spain, workshop initiatives bring children and scientists together.[35]

Building and expanding high-quality universities that can train top talent and contribute to innovation requires an efficient system of public funding for research, as well as fluid university-industry connections to promote the exchange of knowledge. Public spending on research and development (R&D) is lower in middle-income countries—0.3 percent of the gross domestic product (GDP) of the median middle-income country—than in high-income countries—1.4 percent of GDP in the median high-income country.[36] Thus it is more efficient for middle-income countries to focus their public funding on a few strategic areas of research such as STEM, health, and the energy transition, with funds allocated in a competitive fashion. For example, the Pakistan Science Foundation gives competitive research grants to scientists, engineers, technologists, innovators, academics, and entrepreneurs who need support to build on their initial research findings and develop new products, prototypes, and pilot-scale production in nanotechnology, material science, and artificial intelligence.[37]

There are many examples of partnerships aimed at expanding countries' research and educational capacities. In Argentina, the Instituto Balseiro is a highly selective public institution that trains undergraduate and graduate students in physics, nuclear engineering, and other STEM fields by means of a partnership between Cuyo National University and the National Atomic Energy Commission.[38] Admitted students receive full scholarships and have access to state-of-the-art labs and highly personalized training, which allows them to pursue highly successful careers, both domestically and abroad. In Israel, several higher education institutions—such as the

Technion and the Weizmann Institute—have had a strong STEM orientation since their inception. In 2013, Israel's eight universities produced more patents than the country's firms, military labs, and private labs combined.[39] Partnerships with world-class universities can serve as a strategy to develop a research base. The Egypt-Japan University of Science and Technology (E-JUST) offers graduate courses on electronics and communications, mechatronics and robotics, energy and environment, computer science, industrial science and manufacturing, chemicals and petrochemicals, and materials science.[40] The Indonesian Biodiversity Research Center (IBRC) was created in 2010 by Udayana University, Diponegoro University, the State University of Papua, the University of California at Los Angeles, and the Smithsonian Institution to promote biodiversity research and build educational and scientific capacity in Indonesia.[41]

Governments can also provide tax incentives to companies that collaborate with universities, such as a generous tax deduction, as in Sri Lanka.[42] Establishing a regulatory framework for knowledge exchange is key, particularly in relation to the intellectual property produced by universities with public resources.[43] Universities, in turn, typically establish technology transfer offices (TTOs) to promote university-based innovation and entrepreneurship. In 2003, the State University of Campinas (Unicamp) established Brazil's first TTO, Inova; four years later, Unicamp was the second most frequent patent applicant in Brazil.[44] Governments can also provide land and infrastructure close to universities to attract firms, usually in science and technology parks and incubators. The significant additional advantages of government support through universities include funding projects that are near the knowledge frontier, promoting the design of more industry-relevant education, fostering the development of an entrepreneurship ecosystem, facilitating workforce development, aiding in technology commercialization, and mitigating the risks of corruption through mechanisms such as peer review, whistleblower protection, and public disclosure of information. Furthermore, universities can enhance oversight and monitoring processes, adding robustness to the governance framework.

One outcome of university-industry collaboration is venture creation by university faculty, staff, students, and postdoctoral students, with private investors serving as venture capitalists. For example, the Tshimologong Digital Innovation Project in Johannesburg, South Africa, is a product of collaboration between the University of the Witwatersrand, the province of Gauteng, and firms such as IBM, Cisco, Microsoft, and Telkom.[45] Tshimologong ("place of new beginnings"), located in an inner-city neighborhood of Johannesburg, is close to a major research university and urban infrastructure and is accessible not only to students from the university but also to disadvantaged youth who enjoy free training in computer programming, cybersecurity, and digital animation through the program's Digital Skills Academy. The project has created more than 105 start-ups and seeks to inspire additional university-based incubators in Africa.

Universities can also partner with local companies to provide services. In Manizales, Colombia, for example, the Universidad Nacional de Colombia and Universidad Autónoma de Manizales are participating in a partnership, Innvestiga, to encourage innovation and productivity enhancement among local firms. It gathers scientists and engineers from these institutions and supports the needs of small and medium enterprises (SMEs) by generating solutions in materials science and processes and providing services such as research, prototyping, and lab tests.[46]

The value added by firms

An economy that is functioning well allocates factors of production to the most productive firms. In developing countries, the reallocation of factors of production has been an important driver of productivity growth, accounting for about 25 percent of the growth in efficiency.[47] The ability of middle-income countries to catch up will depend on how well they attract and adopt leading technologies and facilitate reallocation of resources toward growing, productive firms and industries. Countries at lower levels of development have more opportunities for potentially productivity-enhancing reallocation as workers move from less valuable and less productive activities toward more productive ones (figure 8.2). Evidence from 21 European countries reveals that countries that experience the highest growth in terms of increases in GDP per capita are those with the highest job reallocation rates.

Business dynamism is characterized by an up-or-out dynamic; entrants exit at disproportionally high rates, but those that survive grow quickly, on average. The most successful firms mature and grow larger, displacing less productive firms. Potentially high-productivity firms must decide whether to invest in the managerial and technical capabilities or the R&D required to raise efficiency and product quality. Distortions in the operating environment have a substantial impact on firms' decisions.[48] The benefits of reallocating resources through potentially high-productivity firms not only helps the firms themselves, but also boosts job and output growth and creates positive spillovers for other businesses along the value chain.[49]

Policies in many middle-income countries, however, are not compatible with rewarding merit activities. Such policies thus need to be revisited and upgraded.

Moving away from coddling small firms or vilifying large firms

Subsidies to SMEs are widespread in middle-income countries. Governments may enact such subsidies hoping small firms will grow, creating more jobs and growth. Many subsidies seek to reduce small producers' operating costs through special credit terms and tax exemptions. But the same distortions also reduce the incentives for a productive firm to expand, deterring it from scaling up production.

Many firms in middle-income countries remain small even when long-established; they simply do not aspire to grow.[50] The abundance of small firms in middle-income countries does not solely mirror the challenges they face. Instead, it indicates a deficiency in competition, originating from larger firms that would have displaced them in the market if they had expanded.[51] Blanket support for small firms can curtail the exit of unproductive small businesses, perpetuate smallness, crowd out other firms, and misallocate resources.[52] In Sri Lanka and Viet Nam, the provision of targeted subsidized loans and financial assistance reduced total factor productivity (TFP)—a measure of the efficient allocation of resources.[53] In Mexico, policies to support SMEs have been associated with talent misallocation and reduced labor productivity.[54] A long-running program in Japan documents that SME support programs reduce incentives for SME growth, thereby reducing job creation.[55]

Ideally, government support would help SMEs grow into larger, more productive companies that pay higher wages and adapt knowledge instead of perpetually supporting small firms. To help SMEs grow, support programs must identify firms with genuine constraints to expansion and productivity growth and alleviate specific constraints. Improved data and information, along with analytic capability, are necessary to identify firm-specific constraints.

And yet enforcement of tax codes often tends to lump firms together by size. Even where tax codes do not create explicit provisions based on firm size, middle-income countries may be creating a practical subsidy to SMEs through size-dependent tax enforcement: governments with weak tax collection capacity may concentrate enforcement on larger firms.[56] In Türkiye, enterprises with 50 or more workers must comply with labor and safety laws that include establishing a health and safety board and hiring physicians and other health staff and setting up a health unit.[57] In fact, between 1994 and 2014 more than 70 countries created special enforcement units for large taxpayers, in addition to the 18 countries that already had such units in 1994 (figure 8.3).[58] This development is part of a growing trend of taxpayer segmentation, recommended by international institutions.

Figure 8.2 Countries at lower levels of development have more opportunities for potentially productivity-enhancing job reallocation

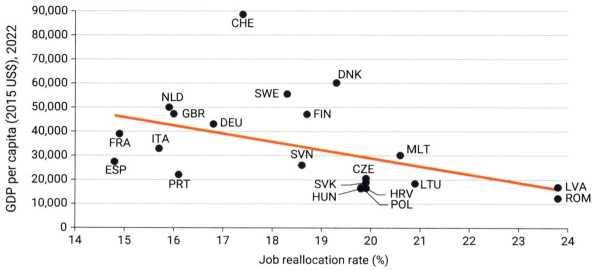

a. Job reallocation rate and GDP per capita

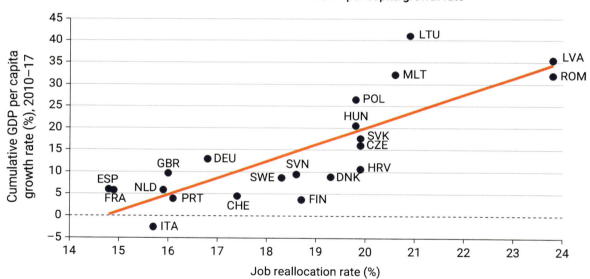

b. Job reallocation rate and GDP per capita growth rate

Source: WDR 2024 team using the 9th Vintage CompNet Dataset (dashboard), Competitiveness Research Network, Halle Institute for Economic Research, Halle, Germany, https://www.comp-net.org/data/9th-vintage/.

Note: Small firms with fewer than 20 employees are excluded to allow consistency across countries and sectors. The unit of analysis is the legal unit (firm). Entrants and exiters are excluded from the analysis. Data on gross domestic product (GDP) per capita are from National Accounts (dashboard), Organisation for Economic Co-operation and Development, Paris, https://www.oecd.org/sdd/na/; WDI (World Development Indicators) (Data Catalog), World Bank, Washington, DC, https://datacatalog.worldbank.org/search/dataset/0037712. GDP per capita growth is computed as the growth rate between 2010 and 2017 because the job reallocation rate is computed over 2010–17. Twenty-one European countries are included. The diagonal line indicates linear fitted values. For country abbreviations, see International Organization for Standardization (ISO), https://www.iso.org/obp/ui/#search.

Figure 8.3 The number of countries creating special enforcement units for large taxpayers has increased

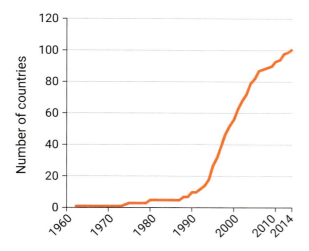

Source: Bachas, Fattal Jaef, and Jensen 2019.
Note: The figure includes data collected by Bachas, Fattal Jaef, and Jensen (2019) for all 113 countries with more than 1 million inhabitants.

Research has revealed that if firms were to comply with size-dependent tax policies, in 140 countries employment growth would drop by 25 percent. Conversely, removing size-dependent taxation would lead to TFP gains of about 1 percent, on average, and up to 2.3 percent for more distorted economies.[59] For example, in Mexico eliminating distortions created by size-dependent taxation policies favoring small firms could boost output by 9 percent.[60] In Chile, China, and India, reductions in distortions helped these economies close the gap between actual and potential productivity by 10 percent. Figure 8.4 illustrates the value of the actual level of manufacturing TFP in each country relative to the potential level if resources were allocated efficiently—that is, if the economy was on the production possibilities frontier. More important, reforms of size-dependent policies increase the return to skills and encourages technology adoption and productivity in the longer term.

Letting go of unproductive firms

Letting inefficient firms and business models fail is a core principle of creative destruction. Literature on firm exit—stemming from seminal work by Hopenhayn (1992)—shows that the exit of less productive firms contributes substantially to raising aggregate productivity. In many countries, during periods of trade liberalization the exit of the least productive firms has boosted growth.[61]

In middle-income countries, however, bureaucratic frictions prolong the survival of zombie firms—inefficient, debt-ridden companies that crowd out investment by productive firms.[62] Reforms to bankruptcy laws can prevent unproductive incumbents from turning into zombie firms and should focus on enabling failed businesses to exit swiftly and predictably and on allowing viable businesses to restructure.[63]

More generally, the shedding of outdated arrangements—enterprises, jobs, technologies, private contracts, policies, and public institutions—is essential for reallocation, innovation, and growth. Economic downturns sometimes create a much-needed opportunity for older, less productive firms to make way for newer, more productive ones. A key Schumpeterian insight is that the creation of new industries does not go forward without sweeping away past realities.[64]

Modernizing organizational models to manage firms

As barriers to growth are removed and resources are better allocated toward firms that add value, firms will need to make some strategic decisions. Firm owners aspiring to expand must delegate managerial tasks to professionals. Delegation necessitates strong legal institutions to establish and enforce contracts between owners and managers. These contracts should give managers incentives to work hard and should hold them accountable for any wrongdoing. Such arrangements encourage firms to increase their investments in expansion. As productive firms expand, creative destruction eliminates unproductive

Figure 8.4 Improvements in allocative efficiency in Chile, China, and India have been driven by reducing productivity-dependent distortions

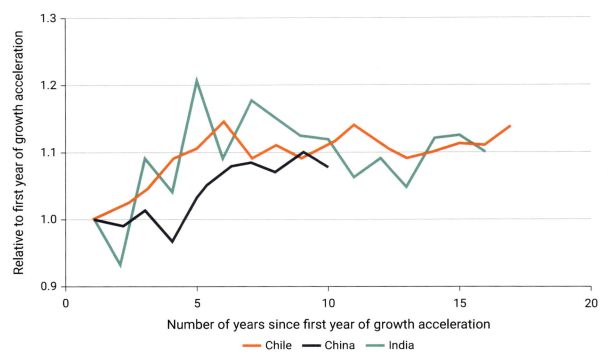

Source: WDR 2024 team based on the methodology in Hsieh and Klenow (2009).
Note: The first year in each country's growth acceleration covered by the firm-level data is 1980 in Chile, 1998 in China, and 2000 in India. Each line in the figure illustrates the evolution of the gap between observed total factor productivity (TFP) in a country relative to the potential TFP if resources had been allocated efficiently across firms, normalized by the gap observed at the beginning of the sample in 1998.

firms, driving up market compensation for managers within those expanding firms. The opportunity to earn more, in turn, encourages capable young individuals to invest in accumulating human capital to ensure a brighter future and enhances opportunities for everyone.

Capable professional managers can make sound decisions in their daily operations, think strategically, and manage human resources efficiently.[65] In small firms, good management practices include keeping separate household and business accounts and monitoring inventories. In larger firms, they include rewarding good employees, setting production targets, deciding on product varieties, and monitoring performance. The impacts of better management are critical not only to individual firms but also to countries.[66] Managerial quality accounts, on average, for about one-third of the gap in TFP between the country at the lead of the technology frontier, the United States, and other countries.[67] In fact, Spain's rapid growth from an economic backwater in Europe to a developed nation was backed by technology adoption and improving managerial capabilities (box 8.4).

Box 8.4 Catching up by opening up and modernizing firms: The Spanish growth miracle

Spain grew rapidly between 1950 and 1980, becoming a high-income economy in the late 1970s. Over those three decades, its output per capita increased from 27 percent to 57 percent of that of the United States. How did Spain achieve rapid catch-up? Political stability, a necessary condition, helped. But economic policies remained unreformed, state-owned enterprises remained a significant part of the economy, and rent-seeking by incumbents remained rampant. Spain's auto industry—which is one of the world's largest car exporters, the country's largest export sector, and one of the country's largest employers—offers three notable lessons.

First, although the domestic market for cars remained protected, Spain opened up to foreign direct investment to attract large investment in a new plant by Ford. The authorities reduced the local content requirement but set a minimum size of production, established an export ratio, and capped the number of cars that Ford could sell domestically. Overall, incentives were aligned to learn from global technology and organizational structures. The venture was disciplined by the need to export in global markets.[a]

Second, addressing complementary bottlenecks also helped.[b] Ford was able to export its large production of cars because the port of Valencia operated smoothly. The port was capitalized enough to respond to the demands placed on it.

Third, technology adoption and a greater focus on management techniques proceeded rapidly, and efficiency gains quickly materialized, supported by a well-trained cadre of local professionals and entrepreneurs who were ready to adopt and adapt the new technology to the realities of Spain.

Eventually, the opening up of Spain's economy helped speed up the "creative destruction" that is central to structural transformation.

Source: Based on Calvo-González (2021).
a. There are significant parallels with the operation of Korean *chaebols* as conduits for technology diffusion.
b. See Cusolito and Maloney (2018).

Improving general education is the first step toward promoting managerial skills, as discussed earlier in this chapter. In emerging economies, firms with more educated owners tend to have better business practices,[68] and more educated entrepreneurs start firms that are larger and grow faster.[69]

A second step—which can provide benefits sooner—involves training and information interventions. Training can be provided in a formal classroom or by means of in-firm consulting. Classroom-based training is the most popular method among small firms.[70] In-firm consulting yields high benefits to larger firms, such as in Colombia, India, and several other countries.[71] Consultants diagnose management practices and provide recommendations accordingly. Positive effects can emerge within one year and tend to last for several years—although they sometimes disappear when the manager who adopted them leaves the firm. These interventions are highly effective, but they are also relatively costly. The costs can be reduced by providing group-based consulting.[72]

Entrepreneurs in middle-income countries often rely on family and social networks to maintain business relationships and run their enterprises, but this practice hampers their ability to grow. Even for large publicly traded firms, how a firm is controlled can be traced back to the country's legal origins.[73] The share of family-controlled firms is highest in countries that have adhered to the French civil law system, followed by countries that have adopted the German civil law system and civil law countries in Scandinavia.[74] Shareholder protection rights—provisions of corporate law that allow shareholders to take legal action against managers who abuse their position—are systematically linked to dispersed patterns of ownership, which can lead to better management. In the absence of solid shareholder protection, family control and management of a firm offer protection against abuse by management.[75] However, in family firms with lower-quality governance, management quality is substantially lower.[76]

Even among publicly listed corporations, family control is more likely in countries where organized labor is more powerful and collective dispute-resolution mechanisms are stronger. After all, it is easier to collude when corporate control is concentrated in the hands of families and organized labor.[77] Management quality also varies with labor regulations and organization. In the United States, stronger union power weakens the ability of managers to use desirable performance incentives.[78] Across countries, people management practices are weaker in those with more restrictive labor regulations. Revising laws and regulations related to corporate governance may be necessary to support entrepreneurship and good management.

Connecting entrepreneurs with money, mentors, and markets

Entrepreneurs in middle-income countries are the main protagonists of Schumpeterian growth through creative destruction, but these entrepreneurs are often disconnected from finance, as well as from networks of other entrepreneurs who can mentor them and help them access markets. Information asymmetries and lack of collateral hobble their potential. For this and other reasons, there is a paradox of low entrepreneurship amid great opportunity in emerging economies:

> Like any investor, an entrepreneur is fundamentally placing a bet, comparing an entrepreneurial project with an expected range of returns and risks against other alternatives, such as "safe" salaried work, which is the opportunity cost of entrepreneurship. This implies both a process of managing risk and a process of learning—about the investment, about running a firm, and about evaluating and managing risk.[79]

Approaches aimed at supporting entrepreneurship in developing countries are hampered by a "missing middle." On the one hand, there has been a drive in development policy to focus on informal businesses or microentrepreneurs oriented toward survival.[80] On the other hand, there has been a fascination with high-tech entrepreneurs in a handful of hot spots.[81] What is missing is a clear-eyed assessment of the barriers facing growth-oriented entrepreneurs in middle-income countries—the protagonists of Schumpeterian growth. Three barriers are paramount: money, mentors, and markets.

Money. Lack of targeted finance is a fundamental reason why many opportunities in middle-income countries do not lead to more growth-oriented entrepreneurship. Improving access to finance is not only about extending credit; it is also about backing a money-making idea implemented by capable founders and managers. But it is difficult to gauge these dimensions. For example, a study of a large business plan competition in Nigeria found that even after an initial screening, expert judges, machine learning models, and economic models had very low abilities to predict which firms would grow the fastest over the next three years.[82] Female founders of firms face particular biases and obstacles. In general, project evaluators place a lower value on the competence or leadership potential of women than of men, and investors inquire more about risks when dealing with female founders than with men.[83]

Information asymmetries and lack of collateral are especially constraining for entrepreneurs with new ideas, regardless of whether those ideas are imitative or innovative. Equity markets can be instrumental in supporting innovative activities, especially in private firms, which typically face larger financing gaps than publicly listed firms.[84] However, private markets for equity financing lack depth and access in emerging economies (figure 8.5). Private equity markets also make it easier for entrepreneurs to cash in on their investments and move on to a new project, should they choose to do so. Often, entrepreneurial ventures do not perform as planned, but the costs of exiting are very high, and the entrepreneur is held responsible for the entire downside risk of a failed endeavor, leading to reputational and financial downfalls.[85] This is a great disincentive to risk-taking.

Mentors. Although money is important, entrepreneurial success is not all about the money. Most entrepreneurs need to be connected with networks of entrepreneurs—those at their stage as well as successful ones—to fully assess whether they and their ideas are fit for entrepreneurship. Data reveal that start-ups collaborating with seasoned venture capitalists tend to exhibit superior performance.[86] Accelerator programs are a relatively recent addition to the variety of programs that direct knowledge, social, and financial capital to promising people and ideas.[87] They provide training and technical assistance, along with mentorship and networking support, and offer certification, thereby reducing information asymmetries between entrepreneurs and investors.[88]

Y Combinator, launched in 2005, is widely regarded as the first accelerator program.[89] Its website stated: "You can't make people something they're not, but the right conditions can bring out the best in them. And since most people have way more potential than they realize, they're often surprised by what they're capable of."[90] A highly competitive process allows founders to join a three-month program of capability assessment and upgrading in which their ideas are pitched to investors. After the program's inception, 5,000 US-based start-ups accelerated between 2005 and 2015 raised nearly US$20 billion in venture capital.[91]

Accelerators have made their way into emerging markets, helping entrepreneurs access early-stage investment. But beyond investments, accelerators are "schools for entrepreneurs" that give competitively selected participants opportunities to build their capabilities—including through business training, networking, and mentoring—and sometimes supply funding.[92]

Researchers associated with the Global Accelerator Learning Initiative (GALI) compiled information on 2,455 ventures that applied to 43 accelerator programs between 2013 and 2015, about half in high-income countries and half in emerging markets.[93] After one year, participating ventures report higher revenue and employee growth, as well as higher equity and debt investment growth, compared with ventures rejected from the application pool. Surprisingly, the major gains for accelerated ventures in emerging markets are in leveraging debt, not equity. Furthermore, emerging market entrepreneurs rarely indicate that connections made during a program help grow their networks. They also tend to place more emphasis on business skill development. However, program managers in emerging markets report difficulties in recruiting mentors and advisers.[94]

Markets. In middle-income countries, creative destruction is amplified by better connections between opportunity and entrepreneurship. Governments can help create and sustain contestable markets by weakening the forces of preservation, and they can work with investors and growth-oriented entrepreneurs to nurture infusion and innovation.

Figure 8.5 In emerging market and developing economies, few companies are funded through venture capital or private equity

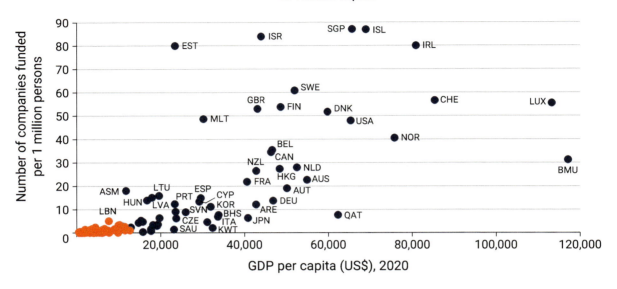

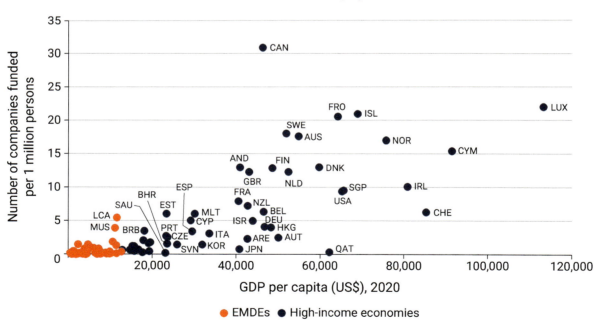

Source: Didier and Chelva 2023.

Note: The figure displays the number of companies funded through venture capital (panel a) and private equity (panel b) investments from deals concluded during 2018–19. Economies are classified according to the World Bank's income classification as of June 2020 (Serajuddin and Hamadeh 2020). For country abbreviations, see International Organization for Standardization (ISO), https://www.iso.org/obp/ui/#search. EMDEs = emerging market and developing economies; GDP = gross domestic product.

Reducing an economy's greenhouse gas emissions

In middle-income countries, emissions drive the impact of development on global climate change. Policy debates in middle- and high-income countries should be concerned primarily with decoupling GDP growth from emissions growth in all ways feasible. One important consideration is arrangements that lock middle-income countries into particular types of production, such as long-term investments in coal and other fossil fuels. To the extent that so-called lock-in effects are preventing progress toward actually meeting global environmental goals, all efforts should be directed toward reducing the path dependence from the specific energy source, while better protecting natural resources, including forests (box 8.5).

Policies and technologies to mitigate carbon emissions will vary among middle- and high-income countries, depending on their economic structures, resource endowments, and institutional and technical capabilities. A good starting point is fiscal policies. These can be surgically sharp if designed with care. The discussion that follows first examines economywide fiscal policies, then turns to sectoral policies, and finally explores the options for scaling up renewable technologies.

Economywide fiscal policies

Regarding energy, the ultimate impact of growth on global greenhouse gas emissions will depend on the carbon intensity of GDP, reflecting both GDP's energy mix and energy intensity. Fiscal policies can influence both dimensions.

Carbon pricing is an essential policy for mitigating emissions,[95] while helping to raise public revenue in an efficient and less distortive way than the alternatives. It signals to markets the social cost of emitting GHGs, creating financial incentives to abate emissions, reduce fossil fuel consumption, and innovate low-carbon products and processes. Some economists believe that carbon taxation is the most efficient instrument for reducing emissions in a growth-friendly way. On January 16, 2019, 43 of the world's most prominent economists, including 27 Nobel Laureates, issued a statement published in the *Wall Street Journal* (2019) arguing that a carbon tax in the

---

Box 8.5 Productivity growth can slow deforestation in Brazil

Brazil's Amazon region provides the world with immense ecosystem services. Estimates peg the services to be worth, at a minimum, US$317 billion a year, US$210 billion of which is accounted for by carbon dioxide (storage) alone.[a] Deforestation is among Brazil's leading sources of greenhouse gas emissions and a major threat to biodiversity.[b] In fact, ecosystem collapse in the Amazon stemming from deforestation and climate change ranks among the most catastrophic tipping points for the planet.[c] In response, Brazil has made much progress in protecting the Amazon, improving forest and land governance by means of, for example, the Action Plan for the Prevention and Control of Deforestation in the Legal Amazon, first launched in 2004 and most recently reinvigorated in 2023.

And yet Brazil's growth model also matters for the Amazon. The fact that it remains anchored in factor accumulation and land accumulation is synonymous with agricultural frontier expansion and deforestation. To overcome the middle-income trap Brazil will have to raise productivity—and growing through productivity rather than factor expansion would also slow deforestation.[d] Indeed, there is a strong relationship between Brazilian productivity and the change in forest cover in the country's Amazon (figure B8.5.1).

(Box continues next page)

Box 8.5 Productivity growth can slow deforestation in Brazil *(continued)*

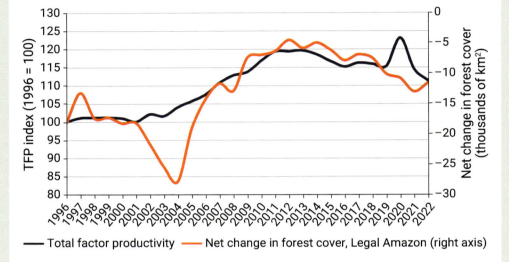

Figure B8.5.1 Amazon deforestation falls when Brazilian productivity rises

Source: WDR 2024 team extending Ferreira Filho, De Souza, and Hanusch (2022).
Note: Legal Amazon is the largest sociogeographic division in Brazil, containing all nine states in the Amazon basin. km² = square kilometer; TFP = total factor productivity.

a. Hanusch (2023).
b. World Bank (2023a).
c. Lenton et al. (2023).
d. Ferreira Filho, De Souza, and Hanusch (2022); Hanusch (2023).

United States "offers the most cost-effective lever to reduce carbon emissions at the scale and speed that [are] necessary." Others have proposed a strategic combination of temporary research subsidies and carbon taxes that could steer technological advancements toward more environmentally sustainable solutions.[96]

Direct carbon pricing instruments include carbon pricing signals sent through carbon taxes and emissions trading systems (ETSs). According to the World Bank's *State and Trends of Carbon Pricing 2023* report, these schemes currently cover a relatively limited portion of global carbon emissions, but the greater a program's scope, the more effective it can be.[97] The report points out that the number of countries that have adopted direct carbon pricing schemes through ETSs or carbon taxes is limited.[98] Perhaps more important, so is the coverage of such programs. With the introduction of the ETS in China in 2021, the share of global carbon dioxide (CO_2) emissions from fossil fuels covered by direct carbon pricing schemes rose to about 31 percent (amounting to about one-quarter of global GHG emissions). Along with their coverage, average carbon prices have been rising over the last few years. The carbon price in the European Union (EU) through the EU ETS rose sharply from 2019 to 2021. Nevertheless, the carbon prices prevailing in most jurisdictions and their estimated global average remain quite modest.

Because the overall carbon price signal is not confined to direct carbon pricing, the concept of the total carbon price (TCP) has been introduced—a metric intended to assess the price signal resulting from a combination of direct and indirect carbon pricing instruments, including energy excise taxes and fuel subsidies.[99] Illustrative TCP calculations carried out using the best available global data sets relying on annual data for 142 countries covering the last 30 years find that indirect carbon pricing instruments play a much more prominent role in sending price signals on carbon emissions. Among indirect carbon pricing instruments, an analysis of illustrative TCP calculations finds that energy taxes, in particular, send the strongest price signal. These taxes cover a significant share of global emissions and send much higher carbon price signals than their direct counterparts. By contrast, energy subsidies send strong signals in the opposite direction, undermining the positive signals sent from direct and indirect instruments, as illustrated in figure 8.6.[100]

Removing inefficient fossil fuel subsidies is an integral part of the policy mix to reduce carbon emissions. This market distortion discourages the adoption of clean energy because regulated prices or taxes favor fossil fuels. After a noticeable dip in 2020 stemming from the COVID-19 pandemic, global fossil fuel subsidies for 2022 doubled from the previous year to an all-time high of US$1 trillion, as indicated by preliminary estimates.[101] According to a global tracking effort, at least 60 countries increased (or even reintroduced) general fuel price subsidies (as opposed to targeted compensation), and at least 98 countries announced energy-related measures, including subsidies for fuel, electricity, transport, and electric vehicles, as well as price controls for fuel.[102]

Figure 8.6 Indirect carbon pricing such as energy taxes is the strongest price signal

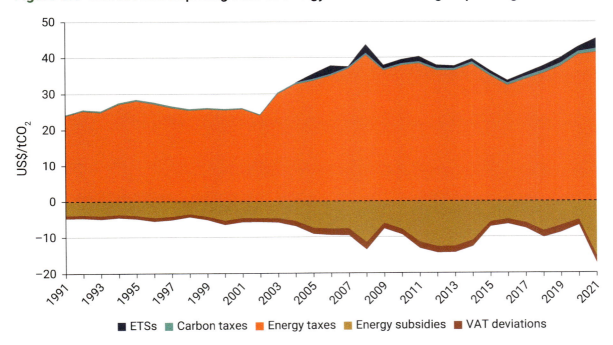

Source: Agnolucci, Gencer, and Heine 2024.
Note: The figure presents illustrative calculations for the global aggregate total carbon price using the best available global data. The figure covers 142 countries. ETSs = emissions trading systems; tCO_2 = metric tons of carbon dioxide; VAT = value added tax.

Well-designed taxes can be a starting point to incentivize citizens and businesses to make cleaner choices, thereby reducing climate damage and air pollution. Taxes also raise much-needed revenue, which can be used to fund vital government services and support vulnerable groups in adjusting to higher energy prices, including by introducing or strengthening social safety nets.

Policy makers, however, face strong resistance from industrial and residential consumers to removing subsidies and raising the social cost of carbon. Often, resistance comes from interest groups representing specific sectors concerned about bearing the brunt of the economic and job losses associated with the loss of those rents. Indeed, the literature simulating the impact of removing subsidies finds that reductions in GDP and welfare will occur in countries in the short term. In China, models indicate the GDP could decline by up to 3.8 percent.[103] In the Islamic Republic of Iran, GDP could decrease by 2.2 percent and welfare by 5.2 percent, and the non-energy price index could increase by 26 percent.[104] However, those short-term effects are reversed in the long term, leading to a substantial increase in GDP and welfare, particularly when subsidy reforms are accompanied by complementary policies such as cash transfers and other productive activities (including electrification, public transport, and investment in education and health).

Complementary sectoral policies

Countries such as Germany and Spain have used feed-in tariffs (FiTs) to support the deployment of new clean energy technologies, but as technologies mature, competitive bidding through auctions in middle-income countries (including Brazil, India, and South Africa) have been more cost-efficient in procuring renewable capacity (for example, by achieving lower prices per unit of electricity, as assigned in the power purchase agreements).[105] FiTs guarantee a fixed price for the electricity produced by renewable energy sources. However, they may result in overpayment to producers if the cost of renewable energy technologies falls over time. Auctions create a competitive market for renewable energy and allow policy makers to manage the quantity and the quality of renewable energy projects by setting the volume, technology, and the criteria for the bids. Auctions can also foster innovation and diversification of renewable energy sources by creating different categories or segments for the bids. Auctions have led to low utility-scale prices for solar photovoltaics (PV) in middle-income countries (figure 8.7).

Technology adoption and deployment are aided by scale. In Europe, the companies most diversified in renewables are the largest firms—they have a lower risk because of their size advantage. Those companies able to obtain the cheapest capital to replace energy from the Russian Federation by means of additional renewable generation are those already most invested in renewables.

Raw materials are a significant element of the cost structure of many technologies, and any disruption in supply can increase the cost of capital. For lithium-ion batteries, technology advancement and economies of scale have reduced overall costs by 90 percent over the last decade. However, if both lithium and nickel prices were to double at the same time, it would offset all the anticipated cost reductions associated with a doubling of battery production capacity. For electricity networks, copper and aluminum currently represent about 20 percent of total grid investment costs. Higher prices arising from a tight supply could constrain the level of grid investment.

The most efficient way to scale up the deployment of low-carbon energy is to respect *merit order*: the sequence followed by grid operators selling power to the market. The starting point is set by the cheapest offer (made by the power station with the lowest running costs), which determines the wholesale market prices. Any provider that can offer renewable energy at zero marginal cost—that is, with insignificant operating costs—should have priority in meeting demand. When the merit order functions as designed, it shifts prices along the supply curve, which energy economists accordingly call the "merit order curve."[106]

The design and enforcement of effective regulations are vital in ensuring that the merit order is respected. Clear, transparent rules on

Figure 8.7 In some middle-income countries, the prices of renewable energy through competitive auctions have reached record lows

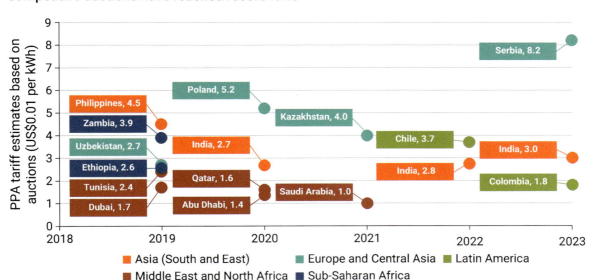

Source: WDR 2024 team based on results of auctions reported in *PV magazine*, http://www.pv-magazine.com.
Note: The emirates of Abu Dhabi and Dubai are shown separately. kWh = kilowatt-hour; PPA = power purchase agreement.

interconnection will be needed to ensure entry by low-carbon energy providers and respect of the merit order. Allegations of abuse of dominance are common in wholesale electricity markets, which are more susceptible to the exercise of market power. This abuse includes both physical withholding (not offering available capacity to the market that could be profitably produced at the market price) and economic withholding (offering available capacity at a price that does not reflect its marginal cost—including the opportunity cost). Both cases of withholding make the merit order curve steeper and shifts its intersection with the demand curve, resulting in a higher price. Customers are then worse off while producers benefit.

Worldwide, promising regulatory initiatives are under way. In the European Union, regulators began investigating 109 cases of abuse of wholesale energy market integrity and transparency in 2021. Box 8.6 describes successful cases in detecting abuse of dominance in the Bulgarian and German wholesale markets. In Mexico, the Federal Economic Competition Commission (COFECE) issued a public report in 2021 about improving the regulation of Clean Energy Certificates, an instrument that provides incentives for generating electricity using clean technologies under the framework of the Electricity Industry Law and the Energy Transition Law.

In Colombia, the Superintendence of Industry and Commerce (SIC) developed an advocacy initiative in the energy sector in 2019 encouraging competitive bidding through renewable energy auctions. For example, SIC recommended arranging subsequent rounds of auctions (tenders), instead of a single tender, to enable the participation of companies that were still preparing to enter the market and would only be able to provide renewable energy sources after the initial date indicated in the first auction model.

Box 8.6 Correcting abuses of dominance in electricity markets

Liberalizing and opening up a sector that historically has been governed by the state and state-controlled actors are challenges that go far beyond updating the regulatory framework, as witnessed in Germany and Bulgaria.

Bulgaria. In 2019, the Bulgarian Commission for Protection of Competition (BCPC) fined the National Electricity Company EAD (NEK) for abuse of dominance. NEK is part of Bulgarian Energy Holding, which owns 80 percent of all hydropower plants in Bulgaria. It is historically the last-resort supplier and the coordinator of special balancing energy groups.[a] BCPC found that NEK abused its dominant position in the balancing market of electricity producers from renewable energy sources at preferential prices in two ways.[b] First, it unilaterally altered the forecasted hourly electricity production schedules submitted by renewable energy producers. NEK submitted a different schedule, usually unilaterally providing for less production (that is, without informing the respective producer). These changes made it practically impossible for the renewable producers to meet the amounts set by NEK. Second, the BCPC found that unilaterally the renewable energy supply producers were financially burdened by the artificially increased imbalances.[c]

Germany. In May 2021, the German Federal Network Agency (Bundesnetzagentur) imposed fines of €200,000 on Energi Danmark A/S and €175,000 on Optimax Energy GmbH for manipulation of the wholesale electricity market. The penalties were the outcomes of investigations opened in September 2020 after significant imbalances were observed in the system in June 2019. The Bundesnetzagentur's analysis of trading activities indicated market manipulation involved sales of electricity that was not available. The companies placed offers to sell electricity on the intraday market shortly before the electricity was due to be supplied without intending to supply it. Their incentive to do so stemmed from the difference between the unusually high intraday price and the lower expected imbalance price in the balancing market.[d] The practice distorted market signals at a time when transmission system operators had to make full use of balancing energy and take other measures to ensure the stability of the German system. The practice not only allowed the companies to realize unjustified profits but also threatened system stability.[e]

Source: Mateina and Grunova 2020.

a. A balancing group is a group of participants on the free market, both consumers and producers which optimize their electricity costs by netting their counter hourly deviations (imbalances) and reducing the overall deviation between the projected and reported electricity consumption. A special balancing group includes only participants of the regulated market.
b. See Decision No. 833/18.07.2019.
c. Mateina and Grunova (2020).
d. Balancing services are reactive short-term means of leveling out frequency deviations in the power grid. These services (sometimes also called control reserve) are one of many ancillary services that system operators must provide for a secure power supply.
e. See Bundesnetzagentur (2021).

In many middle-income countries, policies need to be revisited and upgraded to reward merit activities. But this will require a change in mindset. Policy makers should think in terms of adding value (merit): economic, social, and environmental. That requires changes in policies to enhance value added across the economy through the efficient resource utilization of talent, capital, and energy. All these efforts will help middle-income countries escape the middle-income trap.

Notes

1. World Bank (2018).
2. Graham (2013).
3. China is an exception. By 1990, China and India were similar in terms of their gross domestic product (GDP) per capita, upper-secondary completion rate, and tertiary enrollment rate. Today, China surpasses India in all three indicators. A comprehensive study of educational upgrading in Brazil, China, India, and Indonesia starting with the 1950 cohorts finds that, although China followed a strategy of progressive universalism, India did not (Schady, Isaacs, and Parra 2024).
4. Education Commission (2016).
5. As the focus on basic education declined, so did its budget share. But because the country was growing, the absolute amount of resources spent on basic education did not decline.
6. Angrist et al. (2023); World Bank (2018).
7. Angrist et al. (2020). This comparison includes only those reforms that have been rigorously evaluated.
8. These findings are also consistent with the "Smart Buys" recommendations of the GEEAP (2023). In addition, Angrist et al. (2023) conduct a cost-benefit analysis for two interventions—structured pedagogy and teaching at the right level—and find that, if applied to 90 percent of the nearly 470 million students in low-income and lower-middle-income countries, they would cost on average US$18 per student and yield US$65 in benefits for every dollar spent. Overall, they would increase spending by a mere 6 percent and yet raise learning by 120 percent. See also Dixit and Gill (2024).
9. Dinarte-Díaz et al. (2023); Ferreyra et al. (2021).
10. Paredes (2024).
11. *La Hora* (2022).
12. In the United States, the co-op model was first implemented at the University of Cincinnati and Northeastern University. Today, additional institutions include Georgia Tech, Purdue, and Drexel.
13. Garcia and Crawley (2024).
14. China's number of science and engineering (S&E) graduates grew from 225 per million population in 2000 to 1,057 in 2014, and the number of PhD S&E graduates increased from 5.6 per million population in 2000 to 23 in 2014. The source of these figures is WDR 2024 team calculations based on World Bank (2020).
15. For example, Kitchen, Sonnert, and Sadler (2018) find that in the United States the National Science Foundation's STEM Talent Expansion Program increased high school students' interest in a STEM career. In addition, Kitchen, Sonnert, and Sadler (2020) show that campus visits, including meetings with STEM professors, significantly increased the likelihood of college students expressing STEM career aspirations. Mentoring and information interventions are among the most effective ways to boost the interest of female students in STEM (Muñoz-Boudet et al. 2017).
16. World Bank, UNESCO, and ILO (2023).
17. In their review of job training programs, Carranza and McKenzie (2023) note the importance of design issues, given that the returns to most TVET programs are modest. They highlight the success of Colombia's Jóvenes en Acción program and of others led by nongovernmental organizations. The scalability and general equilibrium effects of these programs remain to be seen.
18. Material on Finland is drawn from Nieminen and Kaukonen (2001). Information on Denmark is from Cedefop (2023), Peters et al. (2010), and the sources cited therein.
19. See, for example, Gorgodze and Chakhaia (2021).
20. World Bank (2018).
21. Khanna and Szonyi (2022).
22. Chetty et al. (2020).
23. Carranza et al. (2022).
24. Abebe et al. (2021); Alfonsi, Namubiru, and Spaziani (2022); Bandiera et al. (2022); Groh et al. (2015); Kelley, Ksoll, and Magruder (2023).
25. Abebe et al. (2021).
26. Banerjee and Sequeira (2023).
27. Chetty et al. (2022a, 2022b).
28. Alfonsi, Namubiru, and Spaziani (2022).
29. Khanna (2023).
30. Thomas B. Fordham Institute (2023).
31. Card and Giuliano (2016) documented large achievement gains for students who are tracked in separate "gifted/high achiever" classrooms. Benefits were overwhelmingly concentrated among minority participants without negative spillovers to the students who were left behind. Van Reenen (2021) reviews other evidence for the United States.
32. Rutigliano and Quarshie (2021); Tirri and Kuusisto (2013).
33. For a full discussion on advanced learners in the United States, see Thomas B. Fordham Institute (2023).
34. Zorman, Rachmel, and Bashan (2016).
35. See Baeza (2020) for Spain and Invention Programs (portal), Kid Museum, Bethesda, MD, https://kid-museum.org/invention-programs/ and NIHF (2022) for the United States.
36. WDR 2024 team calculations based on OECD (2021). Data are available for eight middle-income countries and 30 high-income countries.

37. For a description of Pakistan's Competitive Research Program, see https://psf.gov.pk/crp.aspx.
38. See About Us, Instituto Balseiro, San Carlos de Bariloche, Argentina, https://www.ib.edu.ar/english_version/about_us.php.
39. Drori and Netivi (2013).
40. Bond et al. (2012).
41. Shetty et al. (2014).
42. The deduction is 300 percent. The company reduces taxable income by three times the amount of R&D expenditure (Mendes 2015).
43. Brazil, China, Malaysia, the Philippines, and South Africa, as well as other member countries of the Organisation for Economic Co-operation and Development (OECD), have followed the United States in allowing a university, research institute, small firm, or nonprofit institution to claim ownership of an invention funded with public resources. For evidence on the effectiveness of providing scientists with greater ownership of innovations, see Hvide and Jones (2018) for Norway and Lach and Schankerman (2008) for the United States following the Bayh-Dole Act.
44. For example, see Bueno (2009).
45. Garcia and Crawley (2024).
46. Garcia and Crawley (2024).
47. Cusolito and Maloney (2018).
48. Cusolito and Maloney (2018).
49. Grover, Medvedev, and Olafsen (2019).
50. Eslava and Haltiwanger (2020); Hsieh and Olken (2014).
51. Akcigit, Alp, and Peters (2021).
52. Bertoni, Colombo, and Quas (2023); Kersten et al. (2017).
53. Aivazian and Santor (2008); Vu and Tran (2021).
54. López and Torres (2020).
55. Tsuruta (2020).
56. Bachas, Fattal Jaef, and Jensen (2019); see discussion in chapter 4.
57. Akcigit et al. (2023).
58. Bachas, Fattal Jaef, and Jensen (2019).
59. Bachas, Fattal Jaef, and Jensen (2019).
60. López and Torres (2020).
61. Melitz (2003).
62. Didier and Cusolito (2024).
63. McGowan and Andrews (2016).
64. Schumpeter (1942).
65. McKenzie et al. (2023); Scur et al. (2021).
66. Bloom and Van Reenen (2010); McKenzie and Woodruff (2017).
67. Bloom, Sadun, and Van Reenen (2016).
68. McKenzie and Woodruff (2017).
69. Queiró (2022).
70. McKenzie et al. (2023).
71. Back, Parboteeah, and Nam (2014); Bloom et al. (2013, 2020); Bruhn, Karlan, and Schoar (2018); Giorcelli (2019); Higuchi, Nam, and Sonobe (2015); Karlan, Knight, and Udry (2015).
72. Iacovone, Maloney, and McKenzie (2022).
73. Glaeser and Shleifer (2002); La Porta et al. (1998).
74. Aminadav and Papaioannou (2020); La Porta et al. (1999).
75. La Porta et al. (1997, 1999).
76. Scur et al. (2021).
77. Pagano and Volpin (2005).
78. Bloom et al. (2019).
79. Cusolito and Maloney (2018, 79).
80. Naudé (2011).
81. Aldrich and Ruef (2018).
82. McKenzie and Sansone (2019).
83. Miller et al. (2018).
84. Didier and Cusolito (2024).
85. Cusolito and Maloney (2018).
86. Akcigit et al. (2022).
87. Lall, Chen, and Roberts (2020).
88. Kim and Wagman (2014); Plummer, Allison, and Connelly (2016). For more on the highly successful accelerator program of Y Combinator, widely regarded as the first, see Hathaway (2016).
89. Hathaway (2016).
90. See https://www.ycombinator.com/about.
91. Hathaway (2016).
92. Gonzalez-Uribe and Hmaddi (2022).
93. Roberts et al. (2017).
94. Roberts et al. (2017).
95. Stern (2022).
96. See Acemoglu et al. (2012, 2016).
97. World Bank (2023b).
98. World Bank (2023b).
99. Agnolucci et al. (2023); Agnolucci, Gencer, and Heine (2024). TCP components labeled as "energy taxes" and "energy subsidies" are based on "net" computed values, as proxies for actual values of energy taxes and subsidies, due to data limitations. Energy taxes and subsidies are estimated based on the "price gap" between retail prices and supply costs for a particular energy carrier, used in a specific sector in a jurisdiction in a given year. The net energy taxes and subsidies are then aggregated across sectors, fuels, and countries to yield a global value, as illustrated in figure 8.6. More details on this methodology are discussed in Agnolucci, Gencer, and Heine (2024).
100. Agnolucci, Gencer, and Heine (2024).
101. IEA (2023).
102. Gentilini et al. (2022).
103. Lin and Li (2012).
104. Shahmoradi, Haqiqi, and Zahedi (2011).
105. Becker and Fischer (2013); Cozzi (2012); Eberhard and Kåberger (2016).
106. Acemoglu, Kakhbod, and Ozdaglar (2017).

References

Abebe, Girum, Stefano Caria, Marcel Fafchamps, Paolo Falco, Simon Franklin, Simon Quinn, and Forhad Shilpi. 2021. "Matching Frictions and Distorted Beliefs: Evidence from a Job Fair Experiment." G²LM|LIC Working Paper 49 (March), Gender, Growth, and Labour Markets in Low-Income Countries Programme, Institute of Labor Economics, Bonn, Germany.

Acemoglu, Daron, Philippe Aghion, Leonardo Bursztyn, and David Hémous. 2012. "The Environment and Directed Technical Change." *American Economic Review* 102 (1): 131–66.

Acemoglu, Daron, Ufuk Akcigit, Douglas Hanley, and William Kerr. 2016. "Transition to Clean Technology." *Journal of Political Economy* 124 (1): 52–104.

Acemoglu, Daron, Ali Kakhbod, and Asuman Ozdaglar. 2017. "Competition in Electricity Markets with Renewable Energy Sources." *Energy Journal* 38 (1): 137–55.

Aghion, Philippe, Ufuk Akcigit, Ari Hyytinen, and Otto Toivanen. 2023. "2022 Klein Lecture: Parental Education and Invention: The Finnish Enigma." *International Economic Review* 64 (2): 453–90.

Agnolucci, Paolo, Carolyn Fischer, Dirk Heine, Mariza Montes de Oca Leon, Joseph Dixon Callisto Pryor, Kathleen Patroni, and Stéphane Hallegatte. 2023. "Measuring Total Carbon Pricing." Policy Research Working Paper 10486, World Bank, Washington, DC.

Agnolucci, Paolo, Defne Gencer, and Dirk Heine. 2024. "Total Carbon Pricing for Energy Consumption: The Importance of Energy Taxes and Subsidies." ESMAP Technical Report, Energy Subsidy Reform in Action Series, World Bank, Washington, DC.

Aguirre, Josefa. 2021. "Long-Term Effects of Grants and Loans for Vocational Education." *Journal of Public Economics* 204 (December): 104539.

Aivazian, Varouj Aram, and Eric Santor. 2008. "Financial Constraints and Investment: Assessing the Impact of a World Bank Credit Program on Small and Medium Enterprises in Sri Lanka." *Canadian Journal of Economics* 41 (2): 475–500.

Akcigit, Ufuk, Yusuf Emre Akgündüz, Harun Alp, Seyit Mumin Cilasun, and Jose M. Quintero. 2023. "Good Firms, Bad Policies: The Dynamics of Informality and Industry Policy in Shaping Economic Growth." University of Chicago Working Paper, University of Chicago, Chicago.

Akcigit, Ufuk, Harun Alp, and Michael Peters. 2021. "Lack of Selection and Limits to Delegation: Firm Dynamics in Developing Countries." *American Economic Review* 111 (1): 231–75.

Akcigit, Ufuk, Emin Dinlersoz, Jeremy Greenwood, and Veronika Penciakova. 2022. "Synergizing Ventures." *Journal of Economic Dynamics and Control* 143 (October): 104427.

Aldrich, Howard E., and Martin Ruef. 2018. "Unicorns, Gazelles, and Other Distractions on the Way to Understanding Real Entrepreneurship in America." *Academy of Management Perspectives* 32 (4): 458–72.

Alfonsi, Livia, Mary Namubiru, and Sara Spaziani. 2022. "Meet Your Future: Experimental Evidence on the Labor Market Effects of Mentors." Paper presented at the virtual 17th Institute of Labor Economics and 4th Institute of Labor Economics/Center for Research in Economics and Statistics Conference, Labor Market Policy Evaluation, October 6–7, 2022. https://conference.iza.org/conference_files/EVAL_2022/alfonsi_l24410.pdf.

Aminadav, Gur, and Elias Papaioannou. 2020. "Corporate Control around the World." *Journal of Finance* 75 (3): 1191–246.

Angrist, Noam, Elisabetta Aurino, Harry A. Patrinos, George Psacharopoulos, Emiliana Vegas, Ralph Nordjo, and Brad Wong. 2023. "Improving Learning in Low- and Lower-Middle-Income Countries." *Journal of Benefit-Cost Analysis* 14 (S1): 55–80.

Angrist, Noam, David K. Evans, Deon Filmer, Rachel Glennerster, F. Halsey Rogers, and Shwetlena Sabarwal. 2020. "How to Improve Education Outcomes Most Efficiently? A Comparison of 150 Interventions Using the New Learning-Adjusted Years of Schooling Metric." Policy Research Working Paper 9450, World Bank, Washington, DC.

Arteaga, Felipe, Adam J. Kapor, Christopher A. Neilson, and Seth D. Zimmerman. 2022. "Smart Matching Platforms and Heterogeneous Beliefs in Centralized School Choice." *Quarterly Journal of Economics* 137 (3): 1791–848.

Bachas, Pierre, Roberto N. Fattal Jaef, and Anders Jensen. 2019. "Size-Dependent Tax Enforcement and Compliance: Global Evidence and Aggregate Implications." *Journal of Development Economics* 140 (September): 203–22.

Back, Yujin, K. Praveen Parboteeah, and Dae-il Nam. 2014. "Innovation in Emerging Markets: The Role of Management Consulting Firms." *Journal of International Management* 20 (4): 390–405.

Baeza, Cristóbal. 2020. "Female Role Models for the Scientists of the Future." *Gender Equality* (blog), January 27, 2020. https://www.bbva.com/en/sustainability/female-role-models-for-the-scientists-of-the-future/.

Bandiera, Oriana, Ahmed Elsayed, Anton Heil, and Andrea Smurra. 2022. "Presidential Address 2022: Economic Development and the Organisation of Labour, Evidence from the Jobs of the World Project." *Journal of the European Economic Association* 20 (6): 2226–70.

Banerjee, Abhijit Vinayak, and Sandra Sequeira. 2023. "Learning by Searching: Spatial Mismatches and Imperfect Information in Southern Labor Markets." *Journal of Development Economics* 164 (September): 103111.

Becker, Bastian, and Doris Fischer. 2013. "Promoting Renewable Electricity Generation in Emerging Economies." *Energy Policy* 56 (May): 446–55.

Bertoni, Fabio, Massimo G. Colombo, and Anita Quas. 2023. "The Long-Term Effects of Loan Guarantees on SME Performance." *Journal of Corporate Finance* 80 (June): 102408.

Bloom, Nicholas, Erik Brynjolfsson, Lucia Foster, Ron Jarmin, Megha Patnaik, Itay Saporta-Eksten, and John Michael Van Reenen. 2019. "What Drives Differences in Management Practices?" *American Economic Review* 109 (5): 1648–83.

Bloom, Nicholas, Benn Eifert, Aprajit Mahajan, David J. McKenzie, and John Roberts. 2013. "Does Management Matter? Evidence from India." *Quarterly Journal of Economics* 128 (1): 1–51.

Bloom, Nicholas, Aprajit Mahajan, David McKenzie, and John Roberts. 2020. "Do Management Interventions Last? Evidence from India." *American Economic Journal: Applied Economics* 12 (2): 198–219.

Bloom, Nicholas, Raffaella Sadun, and John Michael Van Reenen. 2016. "Management as a Technology?" NBER Working Paper 22327 (June), National Bureau of Economic Research, Cambridge, MA.

Bloom, Nicholas, and John Michael Van Reenen. 2010. "Why Do Management Practices Differ across Firms and Countries?" *Journal of Economic Perspectives* 24 (1): 203–24.

Bond, Michael, Heba Maram, Asmaa Soliman, and Riham Khattab. 2012. *Science and Innovation in Egypt*. London: Royal Society. https://royalsociety.org/~/media/policy/projects/atlas-islamic-world/atlas-egypt-report.pdf.

Bruhn, Miriam, Dean S. Karlan, and Antoinette Schoar. 2018. "The Impact of Consulting Services on Small and Medium Enterprises: Evidence from a Randomized Trial in Mexico." *Journal of Political Economy* 126 (2): 635–87.

Bueno, Rachel. 2009. "The Inova Success Story: Technology Transfer in Brazil." *WIPO Magazine* 6 (December): 24–25.

Bundesnetzagentur. 2021. "Fines for Manipulation of Wholesale Energy Market." Press Release, October 5, 2021. https://www.bundesnetzagentur.de/SharedDocs/Pressemitteilungen/EN/2021/20211005_BussgeldMarktmanipulation.html.

Calvo-González, Oscar. 2021. *Unexpected Prosperity: How Spain Escaped the Middle Income Trap*. Oxford, UK: Oxford University Press.

Card, David E., and Laura Giuliano. 2016. "Can Tracking Raise the Test Scores of High-Ability Minority Students?" *American Economic Review* 106 (10): 2783–816.

Carranza, Eliana, Robert Garlick, Kate Orkin, and Neil Rankin. 2022. "Job Search and Hiring with Limited Information about Workseekers' Skills." *American Economic Review* 112 (11): 3547–83.

Carranza, Eliana, and David J. McKenzie. 2023. "Job Training and Job Search Assistance Policies in Developing Countries." Policy Research Working Paper 10576, World Bank, Washington, DC.

Cedefop (European Centre for the Development of Vocational Training). 2023. "Skills Anticipation in Denmark (2022 Update)." Data Insights (March 21), Skills Anticipation in Countries Series, Cedefop, Thessaloniki, Greece. https://www.cedefop.europa.eu/en/data-insights/skills-anticipation-denmark.

Chetty, Raj, John N. Friedman, Emmanuel Saez, Nicholas Turner, and Danny Yagan. 2020. "Income Segregation and Intergenerational Mobility across Colleges in the United States." *Quarterly Journal of Economics* 135 (3): 1567–633.

Chetty, Raj, Matthew O. Jackson, Theresa Kuchler, Johannes Stroebel, Nathaniel Hendren, Robert B. Fluegge, Sara Gong, et al. 2022a. "Social Capital I: Measurement and Associations with Economic Mobility." *Nature* 608 (7921): 108–21.

Chetty, Raj, Matthew O. Jackson, Theresa Kuchler, Johannes Stroebel, Nathaniel Hendren, Robert B. Fluegge, Sara Gong, et al. 2022b. "Social Capital II: Determinants of Economic Connectedness." *Nature* 608 (7921): 122–34.

Cozzi, Paolo. 2012. "Assessing Reverse Auctions as a Policy Tool for Renewable Energy Deployment." Report 007 (May), Energy, Climate, and Innovation Program, Center for International Environment and Resource Policy, Tufts University, Medford, MA.

Cusolito, Ana Paula, and William F. Maloney. 2018. *Productivity Revisited: Shifting Paradigms in Analysis and Policy*. Washington, DC: World Bank.

Didier, Tatiana, and Beulah Chelva. 2023. "Private Equity Markets in EMDEs." World Bank, Washington, DC.

Didier, Tatiana, and Ana Paula Cusolito. 2024. *Unleashing Productivity through Firm Financing*. Washington, DC: World Bank.

Dinarte-Díaz, Lelys, María Marta Ferreyra, Sergio Urzúa, and Marina Bassi. 2023. "What Makes a Program Good? Evidence from Short-Cycle Higher Education Programs in Five Developing Countries." *World Development* 169 (September): 106294.

Dixit, Siddharth, and Indermit S. Gill. 2024. "AI, the New Wingman of Development." Background paper prepared for *World Development Report 2024*, World Bank, Washington, DC.

Drori, Gili S., and Avida Netivi. 2013. "STEM in Israel: The Educational Foundation of 'Start-Up Nation.'" Securing Australia's Future Series, Australian Council of Learned Academies, Melbourne.

Eberhard, Anton, and Tomas Kåberger. 2016. "Renewable Energy Auctions in South Africa Outshine Feed-In Tariffs." *Energy Science and Engineering* 4 (3): 190–93.

Education Commission. 2016. *The Learning Generation: Investing in Education for a Changing World*. New York: International Commission on Financing Global Education Opportunity.

Eslava, Marcela, and John C. Haltiwanger. 2020. "The Life-Cycle Growth of Plants: The Role of Productivity, Demand and Wedges." NBER Working Paper 27184 (May), National Bureau of Economic Research, Cambridge, MA.

Ferreira Filho, Joaquim Bento De Souza, and Marek Hanusch. 2022. "A Macroeconomic Perspective of Structural Deforestation in Brazil's Legal Amazon." Policy Research Working Paper 10162, World Bank, Washington, DC.

Ferreyra, María Marta, Lelys Dinarte Díaz, Sergio Urzúa, and Marina Bassi. 2021. *The Fast Track to New Skills: Short-Cycle Higher Education Programs in Latin America and the Caribbean*. Washington, DC: World Bank.

Fontaine, Arturo, and Sergio Urzúa. 2018. *Educación con patines*. Santiago, Chile: Ediciones El Mercurio.

Gallegos, Sebastian, Andres Barrios-Fernández, and Christopher A. Neilson. 2024. "Closing Gaps in Higher Education Opportunities for Underrepresented Students over the Past Five Decades in Chile." Background paper prepared for *World Development Report 2024*, World Bank, Washington, DC.

Garcia, Cristobal, and Edward Crawley. 2024. "Accelerating Innovation for Development: How Universities Leverage Knowledge Exchange to Boost Economic Growth in Middle-Income Countries." Background paper prepared for *World Development Report 2024*, World Bank, Washington, DC.

GEEAP (Global Education Evidence Advisory Panel). 2023. "Cost-Effective Approaches to Improve Global Learning: What Does Recent Evidence Tell Us Are 'Smart Buys' for Improving Learning in Low- and Middle-Income Countries?" May, GEEAP, World Bank, Washington, DC. https://documents1.worldbank.org/curated/en/099420106132331608/pdf/IDU0977f73d7022b1047770980c0c5a14598eef8.pdf.

Gentilini, Ugo, Mohamed Almenfi, Hrishikesh T. M. M. Iyengar, Yuko Okamura, John Austin Downes, Pamela Dale, Michael Weber, et al. 2022. *Social Protection and Jobs Responses to COVID-19: A Real-Time Review of Country Measures*. Living Paper Version 16 (February 2, 2022). Washington, DC: World Bank. http://hdl.handle.net/10986/37186.

Giorcelli, Michela. 2019. "The Long-Term Effects of Management and Technology Transfers." *American Economic Review* 109 (1): 121–52.

Glaeser, Edward L., and Andrei Shleifer. 2002. "Legal Origins." *Quarterly Journal of Economics* 117 (4): 1193–229.

Gonzalez-Uribe, Juanita, and Ouafaa Hmaddi. 2022. "The Multi-Dimensional Impacts of Business Accelerators: What Does the Research Tell Us?" June, London School of Economics and Political Science, London.

Gorgodze, Sophia, and Lela Chakhaia. 2021. "The Uses and Misuses of Centralised High Stakes Examinations: Assessment Policy and Practice in Georgia." *Assessment in Education: Principles, Policy, and Practice* 28 (3): 322–42.

Graham, Carol L. 2013. "Pursuing Happiness: Social Mobility and Well-Being." *Commentary* (blog), October 24, 2013. https://www.brookings.edu/articles/pursuing-happiness-social-mobility-and-well-being/.

Groh, Matthew, David J. McKenzie, Nour Shammout, and Tara Vishwanath. 2015. "Testing the Importance of Search Frictions and Matching through a Randomized Experiment in Jordan." *IZA Journal of Labor Economics* 4 (1): 7.

Grover, Arti, Denis Medvedev, and Ellen Olafsen. 2019. *High-Growth Firms: Facts, Fiction, and Policy Options for Emerging Economies*. Washington, DC: World Bank.

Guyon, Nina, Eric Maurin, and Sandra McNally. 2012. "The Effect of Tracking Students by Ability into Different Schools." *Journal of Human Resources* 47 (3): 684–721.

Hanusch, Marek. 2023. *A Balancing Act for Brazil's Amazonian States: An Economic Memorandum*. Washington, DC: World Bank.

Hathaway, Ian. 2016. "What Startup Accelerators Really Do." *Entrepreneurship* (blog), March 1, 2016. https://hbr.org/2016/03/what-startup-accelerators-really-do.

Higuchi, Yuki, Vu Hoang Nam, and Tetsushi Sonobe. 2015. "Sustained Impacts of *Kaizen* Training." *Journal of Economic Behavior and Organization* 120 (December): 189–206.

Hopenhayn, Hugo A. 1992. "Entry, Exit, and Firm Dynamics in Long-Run Equilibrium." *Econometrica* 60 (5): 1127–50.

Hsieh, Chang-Tai, and Peter J. Klenow. 2009. "Misallocation and Manufacturing TFP in China and India." *Quarterly Journal of Economics* 124 (November): 1403–48.

Hsieh, Chang-Tai, and Benjamin A. Olken. 2014. "The Missing 'Missing Middle'." *Journal of Economic Perspectives* 28 (3): 89–108.

Hvide, Hans K., and Benjamin F. Jones. 2018. "University Innovation and the Professor's Privilege." *American Economic Review* 108 (7): 1860–98.

Iacovone, Leonardo, William F. Maloney, and David J. McKenzie. 2022. "Improving Management with Individual and Group-Based Consulting: Results from a Randomized Experiment in Colombia." *Review of Economic Studies* 89 (1): 346–71.

IEA (International Energy Agency). 2023. "Fossil Fuels Consumption Subsidies 2022." February, IEA, Paris. https://www.iea.org/reports/fossil-fuels-consumption-subsidies-2022.

Jakubowski, Maciej, Harry Anthony Patrinos, Emilio Ernesto Porta, and Jerzy Wiśniewski. 2016. "The Effects of Delaying Tracking in Secondary School: Evidence from the 1999 Education Reform in Poland." *Education Economics* 24 (6): 557–72.

Karlan, Dean S., Ryan Knight, and Christopher R. Udry. 2015. "Consulting and Capital Experiments with Microenterprise Tailors in Ghana." *Journal of Economic Behavior and Organization* 118 (October): 281–302.

Kelley, Erin Munro, Christopher Ksoll, and Jeremy Magruder. 2023. "How Do Online Job Portals Affect Employment and Job Search? Evidence from India." Working paper, Department of Economics, University of California–Berkeley, Berkeley, CA.

Kersten, Renate, Job Harms, Kellie Liket, and Karen Maas. 2017. "Small Firms, Large Impact? A Systematic Review of the SME Finance Literature." *World Development* 97 (September): 330–48.

Khanna, Tarun. 2023. "Science-Based Entrepreneurship in India: A Policy Glass (as Yet) Quarter-Full." *India Policy Forum 2022*, vol. 19, edited by Poonam Gupta, Pravin Krishna, and Karthik Muralidharan, 1–53. New Delhi: Academic Foundation.

Khanna, Tarun, and Michael Szonyi, eds. 2022. *Making Meritocracy: Lessons from China and India, from Antiquity to the Present*. New York: Oxford University Press.

Kim, Jin-Hyuk, and Liad Wagman. 2014. "Portfolio Size and Information Disclosure: An Analysis of Startup Accelerators." *Journal of Corporate Finance* 29 (December): 520–34.

Kitchen, Joseph A., Gerhard Sonnert, and Philip M. Sadler. 2018. "The Impact of College- and University-Run High School Summer Programs on Students' End of High School STEM Career Aspirations." *Science Education* 102 (3): 529–47.

Kitchen, Joseph Allen, Gerhard Sonnert, and Philip Sadler. 2020. "Campus Visits: Impact of a College Outreach Strategy on Student STEM Aspirations." *Journal of Student Affairs Research and Practice* 57 (3): 266–81.

Lach, Saul, and Mark Schankerman. 2008. "Incentives and Invention in Universities." *RAND Journal of Economics* 39 (2): 403–33.

La Hora. 2022. "Hay una desconexión entre lo que las empresas necesitan y lo que se está formando en el sistema educativo" [There's a disconnect between what enterprises need and what the education system provides]. *País*, November 29, 2022. https://www.lahora.com.ec/pais/hay-una-desconexion-entre-lo-que-las-empresas-necesitan-y-lo-que-se-esta-formando-en-el-sistema-educativo/.

Lall, Saurabh A., Li-Wei Chen, and Peter W. Roberts. 2020. "Are We Accelerating Equity Investment into Impact-Oriented Ventures?" *World Development* 131 (July): 104952.

La Porta, Rafael, Florencio López-de-Silanes, Andrei Shleifer, and Robert W. Vishny. 1997. "Legal Determinants of External Finance." *Journal of Finance* 52 (3): 1131–50.

La Porta, Rafael, Florencio López-de-Silanes, Andrei Shleifer, and Robert W. Vishny. 1998. "Law and Finance." *Journal of Political Economy* 106 (6): 1113–55.

La Porta, Rafael, Florencio López-de-Silanes, Andrei Shleifer, and Robert W. Vishny. 1999. "Investor Protection: Origins, Consequences, and Reform." NBER Working Paper 7428 (December), National Bureau of Economic Research, Cambridge, MA.

Lee, Ju-Ho, Hyeok Jeong, and Song-Chang Hong. 2014. "Is Korea Number One in Human Capital Accumulation? Education Bubble Formation and Its Labor Market Evidence." KDI School Working Paper 14-03 (August), KDI School of Public Policy and Management, Seoul, Republic of Korea.

Lenton, Timothy M., David I. Armstrong McKay, Sina Loriani, Jesse F. Abrams, Steven J. Lade, Jonathan F. Donges, Manjana Milkoreit, et al. 2023. *The Global Tipping Points Report 2023*. Exeter, UK: University of Exeter.

Lin, Boqiang, and Aijun Li. 2012. "Impacts of Removing Fossil Fuel Subsidies on China: How Large and How to Mitigate?" *Energy* 44 (1): 741–49.

López, José Joaquín, and Jesica Torres. 2020. "Size-Dependent Policies, Talent Misallocation, and the Return to Skill." *Review of Economic Dynamics* 38 (October): 59–93.

Mateina, Eleonora, and Anastasiya Grunova. 2020. "The Bulgarian National Electricity Company Sanctioned for Abuse of Dominance on the Market of Balancing Energy of Renewables." *Kluwer Competition Law Blog* (blog), January 7, 2020. https://competitionlawblog.kluwercompetitionlaw.com/2020/01/07/.

McGowan, Müge Adalet, and Dan Andrews. 2016. "Insolvency Regimes and Productivity Growth: A Framework for Analysis." OECD Economics Department Working Paper 1309, Organisation for Economic Co-operation and Development, Paris.

McKenzie, David J., and Dario Sansone. 2019. "Predicting Entrepreneurial Success Is Hard: Evidence from a Business Plan Competition in Nigeria." *Journal of Development Economics* 141 (November): 102369.

McKenzie, David J., and Christopher M. Woodruff. 2017. "Business Practices in Small Firms in Developing Countries." *Management Science* 63 (9): 2967–81.

McKenzie, David J., Christopher M. Woodruff, Kjetil Bjorvatn, Miriam Bruhn, Jing Cai, Juanita Gonzalez Uribe, Simon Quinn, Tetsushi Sonobe, and Martin Valdivia, eds. 2023. "Training Entrepreneurs." *VoxDevLit* 1 (3). https://voxdev.org/sites/default/files/2023-11/Training_Entrepreneurs_Issue_3.pdf.

Melitz, Marc J. 2003. "The Impact of Trade on Intra-Industry Reallocations and Aggregate Industry Productivity." *Econometrica* 71 (6): 1695–725.

Mendes, Philip. 2015. "Integrating Intellectual Property into Innovation Policy Formulation in Sri Lanka." January, World Intellectual Property Organization, Geneva.

Miller, Amisha, Saurabh A. Lall, Markus P. Goldstein, and Joao H. C. Montalvao. 2023. "Asking Better Questions: The Effect of Changing Investment Organizations' Evaluation Practices on Gender Disparities in Funding Innovation." Policy Research Working Paper 10625, World Bank, Washington, DC.

Muñoz-Boudet, Ana María, Lourdes Rodríguez-Chamussy, Cristina Chiarella, and Isil Oral Savonitto. 2017. "Women and STEM in Europe and Central Asia." World Bank, Washington, DC.

Murnane, Richard J., Marcus R. Waldman, John B. Willett, Maria Soledad Bos, and Emiliana Vegas. 2017. "The Consequences of Educational Voucher Reform in Chile." NBER Working Paper 23550 (June), National Bureau of Economic Research, Cambridge, MA.

Naudé, Wim. 2011. "Entrepreneurship Is Not a Binding Constraint on Growth and Development in the Poorest Countries." *World Development* 39 (1): 33–44.

Neilson, Christopher A. 2024. "The Rise of Coordinated Choice and Assignment Systems in Education Markets around the World." Background paper prepared for *World Development Report 2024*, World Bank, Washington, DC.

Nieminen, Mika, and Erkki Kaukonen. 2001. *Universities and R&D Networking in a Knowledge-Based Economy: A Glance at Finnish Developments*. Sitra Report 11. Helsinki: Sitra.

NIHF (National Inventors Hall of Fame). 2022. "Behind the NIHF Scenes: Camp Invention Is for Every Kind of Kid!" NIHF, North Canton, OH. https://www.invent.org/blog/behind-nihf-scenes-camp-invention-2022-all-kids.

OECD (Organisation for Economic Co-operation and Development). 2021. "Man Enough? Measuring Masculine Norms to Promote Women's Empowerment." Social Institutions and Gender Index Series, OECD Development Centre, Paris.

Pagano, Marco, and Paolo F. Volpin. 2005. "Managers, Workers, and Corporate Control." *Journal of Finance* 60 (2): 841–68.

Paredes, Ricardo. 2024. "Duoc and the Higher Vocational Technical Education in Chile." Background paper prepared for *World Development Report 2024*, World Bank, Washington, DC.

Pekkarinen, Tuomas, Roope Uusitalo, and Sari Pekkala Kerr. 2009. "School Tracking and Intergenerational Income Mobility: Evidence from the Finnish Comprehensive School Reform." *Journal of Public Economics* 93 (7–8): 965–73.

Peters, Marjolein, Kees Meijer, Etienne van Nuland, Thijs Viertelhauzen, and Ekim Sincer. 2010.

Sector Councils on Employment and Skills at EU Level: Country Reports. March. Rotterdam: ECORYS Nederland BV.

Plummer, Lawrence A., Thomas H. Allison, and Brian L. Connelly. 2016. "Better Together? Signaling Interactions in New Venture Pursuit of Initial External Capital." *Academy of Management Journal* 59 (5): 1585–604.

Queiró, Francisco. 2022. "Entrepreneurial Human Capital and Firm Dynamics." *Review of Economic Studies* 89 (4): 2061–100.

Roberts, Peter W., Genevieve Edens, Abigayle Davidson, Edward Thomas, Cindy Chao, Kerri Heidkamp, and Jo-Hannah Yeo. 2017. "Accelerating Startups in Emerging Markets: Insights from 43 Programs." May, Aspen Network of Development Entrepreneurs, Washington, DC; Social Enterprise at Goizueta, Goizueta Business School, Emory University, Atlanta; Deloitte, London.

Rutigliano, Alexandre, and Nikita Quarshie. 2021. "Policy Approaches and Initiatives for the Inclusion of Gifted Students in OECD Countries." OECD Education Working Paper 262 (December 17), Organisation for Economic Co-operation and Development, Paris.

Saavedra-Chanduví, Jaime, Hanna Alasuutari, and Marcela Gutiérrez Bernal. 2018. "Finland's Education System: The Journey to Success." *Education for Global Development* (blog), August 14, 2018. https://blogs.worldbank.org/en/education/finland-s-education-system-journey-success.

Schady, Norbert R., Margarita Isaacs, and Diego Parra. 2024. "50 Years of Educational Upgrading in the Largest Developing Countries." World Bank, Washington, DC.

Schumpeter, Joseph Alois. 1942. *Capitalism, Socialism and Democracy.* New York: Harper and Brothers.

Scur, Daniela, Raffaella Sadun, John Michael Van Reenen, Renata Lemos, and Nicholas Bloom. 2021. "The World Management Survey at 18: Lessons and the Way Forward." *Oxford Review of Economic Policy* 37 (2): 231–58.

Serajuddin, Umar, and Nada Hamadeh. 2020. "New World Bank Country Classifications by Income Level: 2020–2021." *Data Blog* (blog), July 1, 2020. https://blogs.worldbank.org/opendata/new-world-bank-country-classifications-income-level-2020-2021.

Shahmoradi, Asghar, Iman Haqiqi, and Raziyeh Zahedi. 2011. "Impact Analysis of Energy Price Reform and Cash Subsidy Payment in Iran: CGE Approach." *Quarterly Journal of Economic Research and Policies* 19 (57): 5–30.

Shetty, Priya, Husein Akil, Trina Fizzanty, and Grace Simamora. 2014. *Indonesia: The Atlas of Islamic World Science and Innovation, Country Case Study.* London: Royal Society.

Solis, Alex. 2017. "Credit Access and College Enrollment." *Journal of Political Economy* 125 (2): 562–622.

Stern, Nicholas. 2022. "A Time for Action on Climate Change and a Time for Change in Economics." *Economic Journal* 132 (644): 1259–89.

Thomas B. Fordham Institute. 2023. "Building a Wider, More Diverse Pipeline of Advanced Learners: Final Report of the National Working Group on Advanced Education." June, Thomas B. Fordham Institute, Washington, DC.

Tirri, Kirsi, and Elina Kuusisto. 2013. "How Finland Serves Gifted and Talented Pupils." *Journal for the Education of the Gifted* 36 (1): 84–96.

Tsuruta, Daisuke. 2020. "SME Policies as a Barrier to Growth of SMEs." *Small Business Economics* 54 (4): 1067–106.

Van Reenen, John Michael. 2021. "Innovation and Human Capital Policy." NBER Working Paper 28713 (April), National Bureau of Economic Research, Cambridge, MA.

Vegas, Emiliana. 2018. "5 Lessons from Recent Educational Reforms in Chile." *Brookings Research* (blog), March 20, 2018. https://www.brookings.edu/articles/5-lessons-from-recent-educational-reforms-in-chile/.

Vu, Quang, and Tuyen Quang Tran. 2021. "Government Financial Support and Firm Productivity in Vietnam." *Finance Research Letters* 40 (May): 101667.

Wall Street Journal. 2019. "Economists' Statement on Carbon Dividends: Bipartisan Agreement on How to Combat Climate Change." *Opinion* (blog), January 16, 2019. https://www.wsj.com/articles/economists-statement-on-carbon-dividends-11547682910.

World Bank. 2018. *World Development Report 2018: Learning to Realize Education's Promise.* Washington, DC: World Bank.

World Bank. 2020. "Promoting Innovation in China: Lessons from International Good Practice." Finance, Competitiveness, and Innovation Insight: Firms, Entrepreneurship, and Innovation, World Bank, Washington, DC.

World Bank. 2021. "Ireland's Human Capital: The Contribution of Education and Skills Development to Economic Transformation." August, Building Human Capital: Lessons from Country Experiences Series, World Bank, Washington, DC.

World Bank. 2023a. *Country Climate and Development Report: Brazil.* Washington, DC: World Bank.

World Bank. 2023b. *State and Trends of Carbon Pricing 2023.* Washington, DC: World Bank.

World Bank, UNESCO (United Nations Educational, Scientific, and Cultural Organization), and ILO (International Labour Organization). 2023. *Building Better Formal TVET Systems: Principles and Practice in Low- and Middle-Income Countries.* Washington, DC: World Bank; Paris: UNESCO; Geneva: ILO.

Zorman, Rachel, Shlomit Rachmel, and Zipi Bashan. 2016. "The National Mentoring Program in Israel: Challenges and Achievements." *Gifted Education International* 32 (2): 173–84.

9 Capitalizing on Crises

Key messages

- The climate and energy crises are providing an opportunity for middle-income countries to infuse global technologies domestically and become producers of green intermediates for global markets. By doing so, they will help reduce the cost of decarbonization worldwide.
- To accelerate the diffusion of technologies, middle-income countries will need to improve their investment climate so that contestable markets will give domestic incumbents an incentive to upgrade their technology. Alongside these efforts, high-income countries will need to reduce the scope of industrial policies that protect domestic incumbents and prevent middle-income countries from accessing technologies and markets.
- Middle-income countries should assess viable investment opportunities for renewable energy technologies and the cost of capital.
- To reduce emissions intensity, middle-income countries will need to create a market for renewable technologies, take into account their own natural resource endowment, and optimize the choice of technologies.

Using crises to destroy outdated arrangements

To ensure it has the appropriate balance of investment, infusion, and innovation, a country must pursue the destruction of outdated arrangements—enterprises, jobs, technologies, private contracts, policies, and public institutions. In many countries, however, the forces of destruction are weak during boom times.

Because middle-income countries will need to recalibrate their mix of investment, infusion, and innovation, crises are, in a sense, a necessary evil because they weaken the forces of preservation that maintain the status quo. Today, the climate crisis is one of the most pressing challenges facing not only the global economy, but also humanity at large.

To effectively tackle the climate crisis, middle-income countries will need to direct investment, infusion, and innovation toward reducing greenhouse gas emissions, bringing them to net zero.[1] In support of climate action, more than 140 countries have set a net zero target, covering about 88 percent of global emissions.[2] This chapter explores what it will take for middle-income countries to capitalize on the climate crisis to overcome structural stasis and advance decarbonization both locally and globally.

Low-carbon sources of energy such as wind and solar are technologically sophisticated and benefit from increasing returns to scale in production and deployment. Thus middle-income countries have an opportunity to infuse global technologies domestically and become producers of green intermediates for global markets, thereby reducing the cost of decarbonization worldwide. To accelerate diffusion of such technologies, these countries will need to improve their investment climate so that contestable markets give domestic incumbents the incentive to upgrade. Alongside these efforts, major Group of Twenty (G20) and Organisation for Economic Co-operation and Development (OECD) countries will need to reduce the scope of industrial policies that protect domestic incumbents and prevent middle-income countries from accessing technologies and markets. Indeed, the globalization of protectionist industrial policy poses the risk of slowing down the globalization of decarbonization. Global coordination of the use of *green* industrial policy will ensure that industrial policy does not hinder the climate transition of or penalize low- and middle-income countries.

Middle-income countries could also diffuse low-carbon technologies at home by building green to meet their significant demand for infrastructure systems. For example, one-third of projected urban growth will occur in large middle-income countries such as China, India, and Nigeria by 2050, and three-quarters of the world's urban infrastructure that will exist in 30 years has not yet been built.[3] By building green, investments in middle-income countries can help reduce emissions at a lower cost than in high-income countries that would have to retrofit green.[4] But there is a challenge—despite the falling cost of green infrastructure and potential for high economic returns in middle-income countries, capital does not flow from high-income to low- and middle-income countries to undertake these infrastructure investments.

Finally, where capital costs are high, low-carbon energy may be unaffordable. Moreover, the intermittency of variable renewables and high storage costs pose risks to energy security if not managed well. Middle-income countries will need flexibility in choosing emissions-reducing strategies.

Globalizing decarbonization

Upgrade and compete through global low-carbon value chains

Izmir, Türkiye, a vibrant city of nearly 4.5 million people on the Aegean Sea, has been historically significant for more than 5,000 years. Its settlement goes back to the third millennium BCE. Now it is poised to become a significant producer and exporter of intermediate products in Europe's wind energy value chain. Thirteen factories produce towers, blades, gearboxes, and generators, and 80 percent of the production from this value chain is exported—primarily to Europe. Türkiye is increasing its competence and competitiveness in the wind turbine value chains, as well as developing capabilities in a broader range of technically sophisticated green products (so-called green complex products).

As this example suggests, middle-income countries could join global low-carbon energy value chains by supplying intermediate products, thereby reducing the cost of green energy faster than would be possible through national efforts alone. Moreover, through their participation, middle-income countries can infuse global knowledge into their own industries and subsequently increase their "economic complexity."[5]

An example is the solar photovoltaic (PV) industry (figure 9.1). From 2008 to 2020, the globalized market for PV modules saved PV installers in China US$36 billion, those in the United States

Figure 9.1 Use of globalized value chains for solar panels results in faster learning and lower global prices

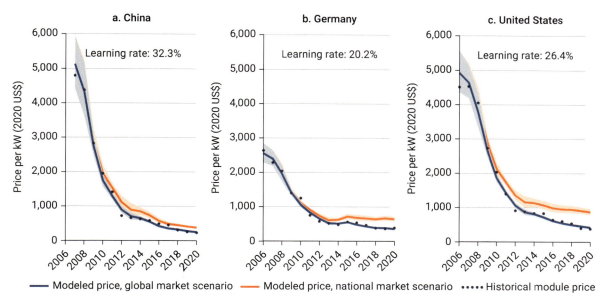

Source: Helveston, He, and Davidson 2022.
Note: The figure displays the estimated module prices for global versus national market scenarios for 2006–20. The dots represent historical module prices, and the two solid lines reflect the modeled prices using global (blue) versus national (orange) market scenarios. In each modeled curve, the learning rates are held constant by country, and the prices of silicon follow historical global trends. The global market scenario uses global capacities, and the national market scenario uses a weighted sum of national and global capacities that reflects a gradual transition to fully domestically supplied markets over a 10-year period. The shaded uncertainty bands represent 95 percent confidence intervals from the estimated learning models, which were computed using a simulation. kW = kilowatt.

US$24 billion, and those in Germany US$7 billion when compared with the cost of having domestic manufacturers supply an increasing share of installed capacity over a 10-year period.[6] China produced about 80 percent of solar PV cells and modules globally in 2023. From 2020 to 2023, China's PV module prices plummeted to US$0.15 per watt, or to more than 60 percent lower than the US price of US$0.40 cents per watt. It succeeded by *infusing* global technologies through start-ups backed by foreign finance, international collaboration among researchers, and licensing and the mass production of technologies developed in foreign labs.[7]

As highlighted in chapter 6, four technologies—solar panels, wind turbines, lithium-ion batteries, and electrolyzers used for green hydrogen—follow Wright's Law (learning curves): costs fall as a power function of cumulative deployment due to the positive effects of learning by doing or increasing returns to scale in the production of technologies.[8] By contrast, more complex technologies and those that require a greater level of customization to local environments (type 3 technologies in figure 9.2) tend to "learn" more slowly. Small "granular" technologies (type 1 and type 2 technologies in figure 9.2) can diffuse much more rapidly. Middle-income countries can create value by becoming suppliers in global value chains of type 1 and type 2 technologies.

To date, however, participation by most middle-income countries in value chains producing low-carbon energy technologies has been limited. These value chains are highly concentrated,

Figure 9.2 Middle-income countries can support global decarbonization by becoming global suppliers of "granular" (type 1 and type 2) energy technologies

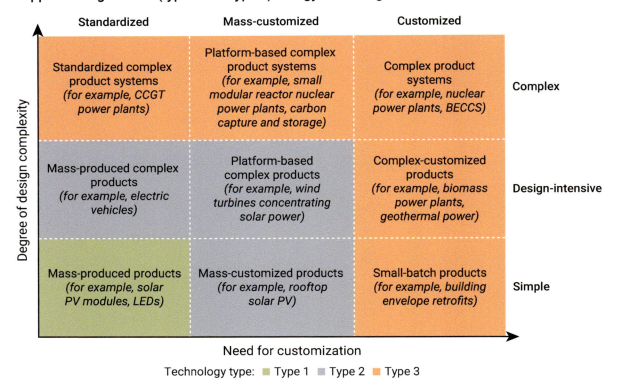

Source: Malhotra and Schmidt 2020.

Note: Type 1 technologies, such as solar photovoltaic (PV) modules and efficient light emitting diode (LED) lighting, are simple to assemble and distribute at scale (although individual components may exhibit complexity) and have rapid learning rates and scale economies. Type 2 technologies, such as wind turbines and electric vehicles, involve relatively more complex designs and move toward scalability more slowly, although they include standardized components, have the potential for scale economies and increasing replication, and have learning cycles of a few years. Type 3 technologies, such as nuclear power, require extensive customization and involve a high degree of complexity. They are susceptible to cost overruns and have limited scope for rapid learning by doing. BECCS = bioenergy with carbon capture and storage; CCGT = combined-cycle gas turbine.

as discussed in chapter 6. Many inputs into clean energy value chains are also highly concentrated. For example, the Democratic Republic of Congo supplies 74 percent of cobalt, China 68 percent of rare earth elements, and Indonesia 49 percent of nickel. Australia accounts for 47 percent of lithium mining, and Chile for 24 percent. Processing of these minerals is also highly concentrated, with China refining 90 percent of rare earth elements and 65 percent and 74 percent, respectively, of lithium and cobalt (figure 9.3).

One pathway for middle-income countries is to improve their firm capabilities and overall technological sophistication (as discussed in chapter 6). Middle-income countries tapping into manufacturing opportunities for clean energy technologies are typically those already competitive in manufacturing or exporters of high-technology products.[9] Research conducted for this Report shows that the share of online job postings for all disruptive technologies is highly correlated with the share of online job postings related to low-carbon technologies.[10] This finding suggests that countries experiencing a rapid diffusion of all emerging disruptive technologies are also witnessing a rapid diffusion of low-carbon technologies.

Figure 9.3 Extraction and processing of critical minerals for the clean energy transition remain highly concentrated in certain countries

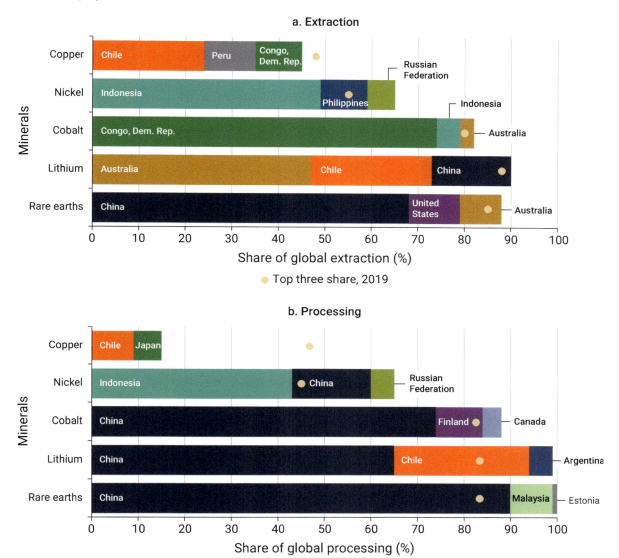

Source: IEA 2023a.

In fact, low-carbon production has been higher in countries with greater overall competitiveness.[11] The green complexity index—which measures a country's current ability to export green complex products competitively—reveals that middle-income countries currently able to competitively export a wide range of green complex products include China, Bulgaria, India, Mexico, Türkiye, Serbia, Belarus, Thailand, Bosnia and Herzegovina, and Tunisia[12] (figure 9.4, panel a). The green complexity potential index measures countries' potential to export green, technologically sophisticated

Figure 9.4 Many middle-income countries have untapped potential to manufacture green products

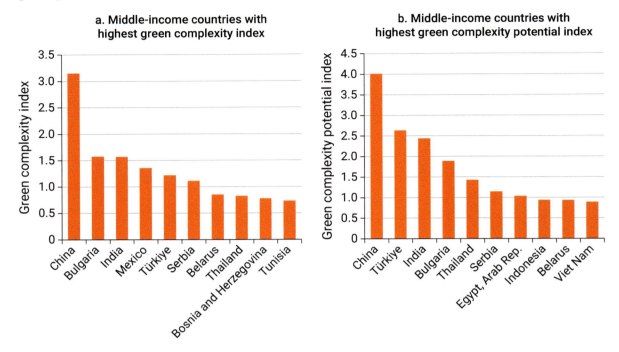

Source: WDR 2024 team based on Mealy and Teytelboym (2022).
Note: Panel a shows the green complexity index (GCI), which is aimed at capturing the extent to which countries are able to competitively export green, technologically sophisticated products. A country is considered to be *competitive* in a product if its revealed comparative advantage for this product is greater than 1. Panel b shows the green complexity potential (GCP) index. This index aggregates the information contained in each country's green adjacent possible (GAP)—which is aimed at identifying the green diversification opportunities for each country—into a single, comparable metric. The GCP index measures each country's average relatedness to green complex products in which the country is not yet competitive.

products in the future, and it reveals that many middle-income countries have untapped potential to export green complex products. China, Türkiye, India, Bulgaria, and Thailand have the highest untapped potential based on other products they are currently manufacturing (figure 9.4, panel b). Türkiye, for example, has high potential in the value chains for wind turbines and electric vehicles. Although production is growing rapidly, these industries could become even greater drivers of growth.

Only if middle-income countries are able to join low-carbon value chains can they effectively contribute to global decarbonization and realistically aspire to tilting their own markets green.

Resist uncoordinated and protectionist industrial policy

In the climate context, there is a strong case economically for countries to use industrial policies to support far-from-market low-carbon technologies. Furthermore, countries are faced with legitimate concerns about energy security and the need for politically feasible climate policies, which warrant certain unique considerations in making energy-related trade policy. Nevertheless, to ensure a successful low-carbon transition, it is essential to implement well-coordinated, balanced industrial policies that avoid protectionism and minimize market distortions.

Research using the New Industrial Policy Observer (NIPO) reveals the significant implementation of new industrial policy measures in 2023, particularly by high-income and large middle-income countries (figure 9.5, panel a).[13] For industrial policies targeting low-carbon technologies specifically, a similar pattern holds (figure 9.5, panel b). Policies in the NIPO classified as potentially trade distorting and that target low-carbon technologies have been spearheaded by a few large G20 countries. These include the European Union's Green Deal Industrial Plan, the US Inflation Reduction Act (IRA), Japan's Green Growth Strategy, and the Korean New Deal. However, green industrial policies are rapidly spreading across low- and middle-income countries. Many middle-income economies are designing and deploying state-led projects to foster green industrialization. Notably, the Arab Republic of Egypt, Kenya, Morocco, Namibia, South Africa, and Tunisia have launched initiatives to support the development of green hydrogen. This shift introduces significant challenges, often imposing a "development tax" whether or not countries engage in industrial policies. For example, policy response options for International Development Association and other low-income countries are typically limited to nontariff measures (NTMs) due to financial constraints and World Trade Organization (WTO) commitments. Subsidizing

Figure 9.5 All industrial policy implementation and green industrial policy implementation are correlated with GDP per capita

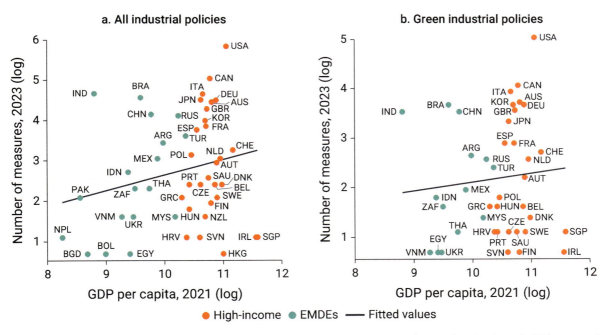

Sources: Panel a: Barattieri, Mattoo, and Taglioni 2024. Panel b: WDR 2024 team analysis replicating Barattieri, Mattoo, and Taglioni (2024) for green technologies only.

Note: The vertical axis in both panels is the log of numbers of all potentially trade distortive measures from the New Industrial Policy Observer (NIPO). The horizontal axis in both panels is gross domestic product (GDP) per capita in 2021 based on WDI (World Development Indicators) (Data Catalog), World Bank, Washington, DC, https://datacatalog.worldbank.org/search/dataset/. Panel b includes all NIPO policies classified as targeting low-carbon technologies, hydrogen, or critical minerals, according to NIPO definitions. EMDEs = emerging market and developing economies. For country abbreviations, see International Organization for Standardization (ISO), https://www.iso.org/obp/ui/#search.

their own industries can divert funds from essential public services, and NTMs can strain economies, potentially leading to impoverishing growth and a global race to the bottom.

Such policies may also risk slowing down knowledge transfer and the diffusion of low-carbon technologies. Policy makers in the world's major economies must therefore coordinate on the appropriate use of green industrial policies. Indeed, they should consider that the energy transition has outcomes that extend beyond its effects on climate, but also on technology diffusion and the economic development of middle-income countries.

To support middle-income countries as they move toward global decarbonization, policy makers will need to update global trade policy rules to clearly define the appropriate use of green subsidies, export controls, and import controls. Such reforms are already being discussed and designed at the WTO level. The Villars Framework 2.0 has also detailed various potential reforms of the WTO to bring the international trading system into harmony with a global "commitment to a sustainable future." These reforms include, among others, carefully distinguishing between subsidies that benefit sustainability and subsidies that impair it. Other possibilities include modifying existing agreements with supplementary clauses in much the same way that Articles 20 and 21 of the General Agreement on Tariffs and Trade (GATT) were used to carve out exceptions.[14] Such clauses could acknowledge that countries may need to nurture emerging domestic industries if they are to achieve a transition with energy security, but the use of subsidies should also be restricted to specific circumstances, such as the commercialization of far-from-market low-carbon technologies.

Expanding low-carbon infrastructure

To achieve the United Nations' Sustainable Development Goals (SDGs) related to infrastructure and stay on track to limit climate change to 2 degrees Celsius, low- and middle-income countries will have to undertake investments of 4.5 percent of their gross domestic product (GDP) each year.[15] Additional investments will be needed to provide safe water and sanitation, as well as reliable electricity and transport to meet the rising demand based on growing incomes.

Many of these investments can provide double dividends by enhancing living standards and mitigating greenhouse gas (GHG) emissions. For example, city developers that integrate land use and transport plans can enhance economic productivity while reducing GHG emissions.[16] Designing buildings with emissions and energy savings in mind is likely to be more cost-efficient than retrofitting, the dominant practice in high-income countries.[17] Similarly, scaling up investment in energy production and distribution, as well as transportation systems in low- and middle-income countries, can provide important benefits in structural transformation and economic productivity.[18]

Considering the development and decarbonization potential of these investments, investment opportunities in middle-income countries appear to be untapped. By leveraging multilateral resources, private capital in high-income countries could alleviate the shortage of infrastructure in low- and middle-income countries, help achieve the SDGs, and contribute to economic growth, as suggested by the World Bank and International Monetary Fund, along with regional development banks.[19]

Research conducted for this Report provides the first set of estimates on "investment potential" in renewable energy in middle-income countries by examining the expected rates of return and cost of capital.[20] Capital costs constitute the largest part of life cycle costs in renewable energy projects. In middle-income countries such as Brazil and India, the cost of capital can even account for 50 percent of the levelized cost of energy for solar PV.[21] For fossil fuel–based power generation, fuel costs and other operational costs make up the largest proportion of costs.

To assess whether investing in a renewable energy technology in a middle-income country would be an efficient use of domestic and foreign savings, this study compares a middle-income country's social rate of return on infrastructure with its social rate of return[22] on private capital and the social rate of return on foreign capital:

- If a middle-income country's infrastructure is scarce, its social rate of return on infrastructure will exceed its social rate of return on private capital—that is, its ratio is greater than 1. The vertical axis in figure 9.6 clears such a domestic hurdle, so that to the right of the axis it is economically efficient to invest in low-carbon energy infrastructure.
- If a middle-income country's infrastructure is scarce relative to that of a wealthier country, it becomes economically efficient for capital to move toward the middle-income country. Above the horizontal axis, the hurdle for foreign investment is cleared.

Figure 9.6 Countries must clear hurdles for both efficient domestic investment and foreign investment in renewable energy

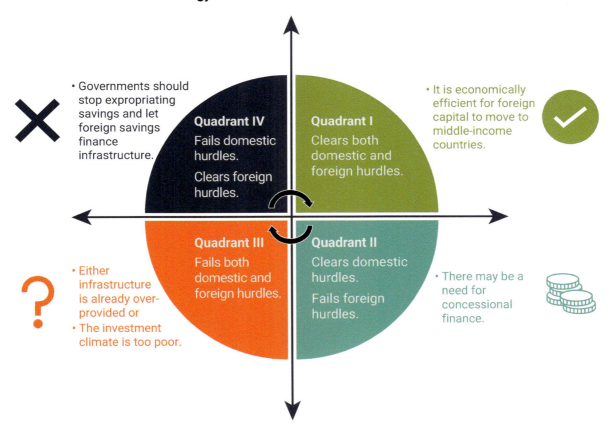

Source: Gardner and Henry 2023.
Note: For a middle-income country, the dual-hurdle framework sorts each country-infrastructure observation into one of four quadrants according to whether it clears the hurdle for both efficient domestic investment and foreign investment. The framework allows evaluating whether investing in the infrastructure of a given developing country would be an efficient use of developing country (domestic) and developed country (foreign) savings.

The unit cost of installing renewable energy and country-specific rates of return to capital are calculated using evidence from a new meta-analysis to derive the output elasticity of renewable energy together with data from the World Bank Private Participation in Infrastructure (PPI) database[23] as well as country estimates from the International Energy Agency (IEA), the International Renewable Energy Agency (IRENA), the World Bank Electricity Planning Model (EPM), and renewable energy auctions.[24] The following insights then emerge from the framework (figure 9.7):

- Quadrant I in figure 9.6 comprises countries in which the return on infrastructure clears both the domestic and foreign hurdles—that is, the minimum rate of return that an investor needs to proceed with a project. Five of 31 middle-income countries in the study pass both hurdles, including Ecuador, Jordan, and Malaysia.
- Quadrant II comprises countries in which the social rate of return on infrastructure clears the domestic hurdle but falls below the foreign hurdle. Although these countries would benefit from additional investment in renewable energy, it is not efficient for foreign savings to finance it. These countries can tap into domestic savings, and there may be a role for concessional foreign financing due to the global co-benefits in GHG reductions. This category includes 12 of 31 middle-income countries, including Brazil, Cambodia, China, Colombia, and India.
- Quadrant III comprises countries in which the social rate of return on renewable energy clears neither the domestic nor the foreign hurdle. Additional investigation is warranted for these countries. On the one hand, a country with a vibrant private investment climate (and therefore a high social rate of return on renewable energy) may be well endowed with capital in renewable energy. Thus the marginal benefit of installing another unit is not an efficient use of either local or foreign savings. On the other hand, a country may have a poor investment climate that leads to low social rates of return on private investment, even as it remains relatively undercapitalized in renewable energy.

Assess financial returns and cost of capital for renewable energy

For investments that add value in economic terms, investors—domestic or foreign—will want to know whether they can cover their cost of capital and secure sufficient revenue over an extended period to access finance on reasonable terms. Investors use the cost of capital to assess project risk. Costs vary among countries, with the spread often determining the competitiveness of renewable energy.[25] Investment risk

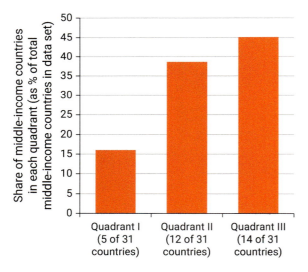

Figure 9.7 In many middle-income countries, it is economically efficient to expand renewable energy

Source: Lall and Vagliasindi 2024.
Note: The sample includes 31 middle-income countries. In quadrant I countries, the return on infrastructure clears both the domestic and the foreign hurdles. In quadrant II countries, the economic rate of return on infrastructure clears the domestic hurdle but falls below the foreign hurdle. In quadrant III countries, the economic rate of return on renewable energy clears neither the domestic nor the foreign hurdle.

also varies according to type of renewable technology.[26] Rotating equipment such as a wind turbine is prone to more wear and tear than a photoelectric system such as solar PV, thereby raising operating costs and increasing uncertainty about the costs of repairing the components of wind turbines.[27] Country-specific and technology-specific investment risks can vary over time[28] due to specific policy or cost changes in a technology or economywide variations in interest rates.[29]

Before entering long-term commitments, investors consider the level of risk in a country, such as macroeconomic stability and political uncertainties.[30] Where cash flow depends on payments from a state-owned enterprise, the credibility of the specific policy framework matters.[31]

The cost of capital for low-carbon technologies affects the investment decisions of both financial institutions and private corporations. Data on the cost of capital in 45 countries using solar PV or wind technologies reveal that the cost of capital in middle-income countries is twice that in high-income countries, averaging 3.8 percent in high-income countries, but 7.2 percent in upper-middle-income countries and more than 8.5 percent in lower-middle-income countries[32] (figure 9.8).[33] The high cost of capital has material implications for affordable energy. For example, for a representative solar PV project or onshore wind project, the total cost of electricity increases by 80 percent if the cost of capital is 10 percent rather than 2 percent.[34]

The high cost of capital in many low- and middle-income countries could increase the cost of renewables by 50 percent or more. The Energy Transition Risk and Cost of Capital Program of the Oxford Sustainable Finance Group tracks the cost of capital across equities, syndicated loans, corporate bonds, and accounting data, and it has revealed a significant variation in trends across regions.[35] In European countries, the cost of capital for low-carbon electric utilities is significantly lower than the cost for high-carbon ones. In North America, the cost of debt and equity for low-carbon electric utilities is comparable to that for high-carbon ones.

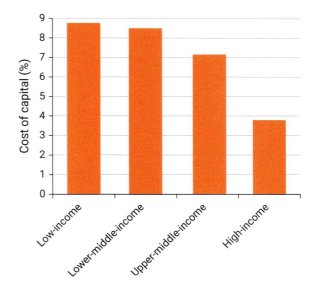

Figure 9.8 In low- and middle-income countries, the cost of capital for renewables is high

Source: IRENA 2023.
Note: Data are for 2021 and 2022.

The trends in middle-income countries such as China are the opposite: low-carbon electric utilities have a higher cost of debt than high-carbon ones. In other emerging markets, such as Latin America and Asia, utilities focused on renewables are subject to a higher cost of capital. And there is a clear divide in the cost of capital between OECD and non-OECD countries, with average cost of debt in 2021 of 3.9 percent for OECD countries compared with 4.7 percent for non-OECD countries.

Accelerating reductions in carbon emissions will require reducing the cost of capital for low-carbon technologies. Addressing technology risk, development risk, and pricing risk can help incentivize investors—utilities, banks, or other institutions—to invest in renewable projects. Derisking requires a whole-of-economy approach. It depends on licensing, policy stability, and social acceptance, along with technical, market, and regulatory risks.[36] Derisking not only makes renewable energy projects less expensive, but also reduces the amount of public finance needed to support these projects.

Decoupling economic growth and emissions

Middle-income countries aspire to grow their economies and achieve living standards closer to those of high-income countries. But economic expansion in middle-income countries could lead to a significant surge in the demand for energy if efficiency is not improved.[37] A country does not, however, need to grow at the expense of steps to reduce emissions if it can reduce both the amount of energy required to fuel its economy and the carbon emissions per unit of energy used by the economy. Growth has become less energy-intensive (figure 9.9). Most notably, the amount of energy needed to fuel the economy (per unit of GDP) is much lower for today's upper-middle-income countries than for upper-middle-income countries in the past. In other words, there is evidence that leapfrogging is advancing over time as middle-income countries move closer to the technology frontier.

Economic growth is also accompanied by structural and spatial transformations that help reduce the carbon emissions of an economy. The carbon emissions of the global economy—a combination of energy intensity (energy consumed per dollar of GDP) and carbon intensity (carbon emissions per unit of energy)—have declined globally from about 0.69 million tons of carbon dioxide (CO_2) per billion dollars of GDP in 1980 to 0.46 million tons in 2018 (figure 9.10).[38] In particular, China's drop in carbon intensity is globally material because China is the world's largest emitter.[39] More broadly, the carbon emissions per unit of GDP over time of upper-middle-income and lower-middle-income countries have declined, even when supply chain emissions are taken into account. A recent study covering 137 countries also finds that countries with higher GDP per capita have lower energy intensity. Furthermore, countries with a high level of energy intensity experience a stronger reduction in energy intensity.[40]

Past oil crises motivated high-income countries to lower energy intensity and to accelerate

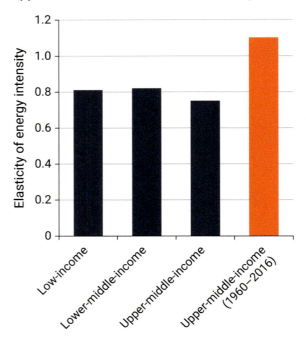

Figure 9.9 Today's upper-middle-income countries are more energy efficient than upper-middle-income countries in the past

Source: WDR 2024 team calculations based on data from Fetter (2022).

Note: Elasticity of energy intensity refers to the energy used per unit of gross domestic product (GDP). Estimates of the elasticity of energy intensity in the long run are based on a fixed effect dynamic response lag model covering 136 countries over the period 1960–2017 (34,800 observations), including log price index, two lags of end-user energy consumption, dummies for structural breaks in data series, and country-sector fixed effects. Values of the elasticity of energy intensity can be interpreted as follows: if GDP increases by 1 percent, energy consumption increases only by 0.75 percent in upper-middle-income countries that achieved upper-middle-income status as of 2017, compared with 1.1 percent in upper-middle-income countries that achieved upper-middle-income status within the period 1960–2016.

innovation and research into renewables. Those measures substantially compensated for the increase in these countries' emissions arising from a growing economy (figure 9.11). Today, a combination of reductions in carbon emissions and improvements in carbon efficiency are offsetting the increase in emissions stemming from economic and population growth. By contrast,

Figure 9.10 Carbon emissions per unit of GDP have been declining worldwide

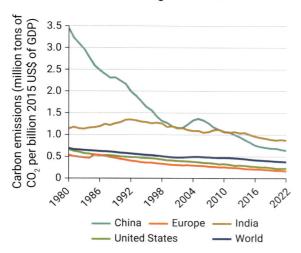

Source: WDR 2024 team analysis based on adapting from and updating Pindyck (2021). Carbon emissions data are from Energy Institute (2023). GDP data are from WDI (World Development Indicators) (Data Catalog), World Bank, Washington, DC, https://datacatalog.worldbank.org/search/dataset/0037712.

Note: Carbon emissions, the product of energy intensity and energy efficiency, are measured in million metric tons of carbon dioxide (CO_2) emissions per billion 2015 US dollars of GDP. GDP = gross domestic product.

economic growth is the key driver of emissions in middle-income countries, and those emissions more than outweigh the reductions in emissions from lowering energy intensity and improving energy efficiency. The effect of economic growth on emissions is especially strong in upper-middle-income countries. According to projections from the Network for Greening the Financial System, if middle-income countries continue their current policies, there is an 83 percent chance that even if today's high-income countries achieve their 2050 net zero goals, global emissions will exceed the remaining carbon budget required for limiting the change in global warming to less than 2 degrees Celsius by 2050.[41]

In deciding how to "decouple" emissions from a growing economy, middle-income countries will need to consider their country's concerns with energy security and access to reliable energy.

Although low-carbon and renewable energy can improve energy security by reducing price volatility through lower exposure to fuel price shocks during supply disruptions, energy from these sources cannot be produced consistently throughout the day. Because electricity systems must always be balanced—that is, ensure that the supply of electricity is meeting the demand at all times—countries will have to consider a balanced mix of energy sources in which low-carbon and renewable sources cannot provide 100 percent of the supply and to incentivize energy-intensive users to adopt energy-conserving technologies. What can these countries do to reduce energy intensity and accelerate energy efficiency?

How middle-income countries can reduce energy intensity

In 2022, middle-income countries were experiencing energy intensity (energy consumption per unit of GDP) 2.5 times higher than that in high-income countries. The first set of insights on middle-income countries' adoption of energy-saving technologies is now available through the World Bank's Firm-level Adoption of Technology (FAT) survey of seven countries—Bangladesh, Brazil, Cambodia, Chile, Ethiopia, Georgia, and India.

Adoption of energy-saving technologies varies significantly across the countries sampled for the FAT survey. For example, the primary green building certification, Leadership in Energy and Environmental Design (LEED), reflects the level of technologies used in buildings.[42] Research suggests that firms operating in green-certified buildings use 8 percent less energy than those in noncertified buildings.[43] The adoption of the LEED certification varies significantly. The highest adoption rates are in Brazil and Chile, where more than 20 percent of firms are LEED-certified. In Bangladesh, 7 percent of firms are certified, whereas less than 3 percent of firms in Georgia and 1 percent in India are LEED-certified.[44]

Scale economies matter in the adoption of energy-saving technologies. Technologies such

Figure 9.11 High-income countries have succeeded in reducing overall emissions by curbing energy intensity

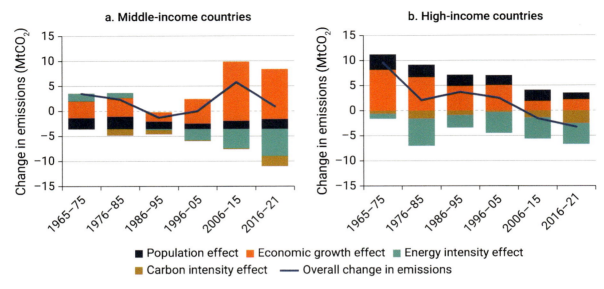

Source: WDR 2024 team analysis based on data from GCB (Global Carbon Budget) (data hub), Future Earth, Fort Collins, CO; University of Exeter, Exeter, UK, https://globalcarbonbudgetdata.org/#.

Note: Decomposition according to the Kaya identity, which states that the overall change in emissions (blue line) is the sum of four factors: population; gross domestic product (GDP) per capita (economic growth); energy intensity (energy used per unit of GDP); and carbon intensity (emissions per unit of energy consumed). The analysis is based on a global sample of 182 middle- and high-income countries and a time horizon since 1965, which allows the analysis to incorporate major crises, including the oil price shocks in the 1970s. $MtCO_2$ = million tonnes of carbon dioxide. One tonne is equal to 1,000 kilograms.

as advanced end-of-pipe treatment entail large installation costs, making adoption more likely among larger firms. Competition also matters. In Georgia, markets with a higher concentration have lower energy efficiency (concentration measured as the average price markups of the top 25 percent of firms in the markup distribution within their sector-size group and municipality). In addition, of firms with similar capital intensity, entrants are more energy-efficient than incumbents. In Argentina, for example, firms with a higher share of skilled workers are better able to adopt advanced green technologies.[45] Exporters also tend to have lower emissions intensity than nonexporters.[46] And foreign-owned firms generally perform better on environmental standards, such as in Côte d'Ivoire, Mexico, and República Bolivariana de Venezuela.[47]

Such evidence indicates that market contestability, as well as opportunities for value-adding firms to grow, is compatible with adopting energy-saving technologies. As for renewable energy, firms' adoption of energy efficiency technologies has been hampered by the high up-front costs of acquiring the technology, lack of access to accurate information about the technology and its costs and benefits, and low returns from early adoption of technologies that require a large network of users.[48] Policies that improve the efficient allocation of resources by subsidizing technology adoption, to the extent that environmental benefits are not fully captured by adopters, or ease the financing constraints that prevent technology adoption are important in decoupling emissions from economic growth.

There is reason to be optimistic that ongoing energy price increases will encourage firms and other users to reduce energy intensity. In the long term, countries spend 5–9 percent of GDP on energy, and increases in energy prices tend to be fully compensated by higher efficiency.[49] In the short term, however, price shocks may pose a cost to an economy, so complementary policies may be needed to compensate for economic and welfare impacts. Governments can help provide firms that use energy intensively with access to energy-conserving technologies and finance for adoption as part of a reform program. Proactive programs that offer a mix of information, finance, and support can encourage changes in production technology and investment in energy-saving equipment.

How middle-income countries can reduce emissions intensity

Access to reliable, affordable energy is an important consideration for growing middle-income countries, which must choose the appropriate mix of energy sources that reduce emissions while ensuring stable energy supplies. Moving across energy sources is a slow process. Despite commitments by high-income and low- and middle-income countries, fossil fuels continue to account for more than 75 percent of global energy consumption (figure 9.12). Although there has been significant growth in renewable energy in recent years—particularly wind, solar, and hydroelectric power—the relative contributions are still small.

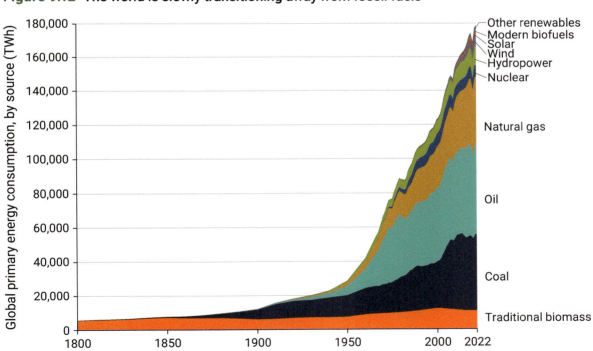

Figure 9.12 The world is slowly transitioning away from fossil fuels

Source: WDR 2024 team analysis of data from Our World in Data (dashboard), Global Change Data Lab and Oxford Martin Program on Global Development, University of Oxford, Oxford, UK, https://ourworldindata.org/; Statistical Review of World Energy (dashboard), BP, London, https://www.bp.com/en/global/corporate/energy-economics/statistical-review-of-world-energy.html.

Note: TWh = terawatt-hour. One terawatt-hour is equal to 1 trillion watt-hours, or the amount of power generated by a 1-terawatt generator running for one hour.

Create a market for technologies

To hasten the expansion of today's low-carbon technologies and support research and development (R&D) to create new technologies in the future, should government policies in middle-income countries subsidize development of specific technologies? This Report has highlighted that most middle-income countries would benefit from infusing global technologies, not innovating prematurely, before the necessary complements are in place. To promote energy efficiency, middle-income countries need a cluster of technologies that affect energy production, storage, and consumption.

Policy should be directed at creating markets for low-carbon technologies. This would include removing subsidies for fossil fuel–related technology (see chapter 8) so that low-carbon technologies can compete on a level playing field. Furthermore, middle-income countries need complementary investments in transmission infrastructure, as well as interoperability standards. As in China, demand-side "pull" may be needed to create a market for these technologies. Sectoral policies such as government feed-in tariff programs[50] were particularly significant in creating a market for renewable energy, first in Germany in the 1990s, followed by Italy, Spain, the United States, China, and India by the 2010s. Notably, as technologies have matured, feed-in tariffs have been replaced by more cost-efficient procurement methods, such as auctions (for example, in Brazil, India, South Africa, and, more recently, the Middle East and North Africa and Sub-Saharan Africa). Auctions have achieved record lowest prices per unit of electricity.

Consider resource endowment

A country's likelihood of switching from energy sources related to fossil fuels depends heavily on its resource endowment. For example, if solar radiation is not sufficiently powerful, the market value of producing such renewable energy would be low and would not justify the switch for an incumbent firm or energy company. But irradiance is not the full story in measuring the solar potential of a region—it is also influenced by temperature (the higher the temperature, the less efficient is the solar potential), the type of terrain, the extent and type of mountains and hills, and so on. Taking these factors into account, the solar potential of each location within a country can be computed—the so-called PVOUT, the ratio between energy obtained (in kilowatt-hours, kWh) and installed power (in terms of kilowatt peak, kWp). This ratio serves as an assessment of the efficiency and productivity of solar plants in each region.

To switch to a renewable energy source, a country must have the potential to create an abundant supply of that energy. Meanwhile, countries with a rich endowment of fossil fuels may find it more difficult to embrace an energy transition due to the forces of inertia and the uneven playing field from fossil fuel subsidies.

Optimize the choice of technologies

Multiple sources of low-carbon technologies offer a myriad of possibilities for alleviating the heavy reliance on fossil fuels. Among the options are emerging and next-generation technologies, including, on the supply side, carbon capture, utilization, and storage (CCUS), carbon capture and storage (CCS), green hydrogen, blue hydrogen, and carbon removal technologies (DACCS and BECCS),[51] and, on the demand side, hydrogen technologies in transport (hydrogen fuel cell trucks, aircraft) and industry (green steel). According to a comprehensive modeling exercise focusing on Europe and Central Asia, these new technologies have a critical role to play in the energy transition.[52] Their growth rates will need to replicate the rapid rates of solar and wind energy to stay in line with climate targets,[53] as most net zero modeling of these new technologies indicates. But they are not on such a trajectory now.

Although the multiple sources of low-carbon technologies offer countries options for weaning off carbon and other fossil fuels, infrastructure constraints related to generation, transmission, and storage, as well as limits on the availability of renewable resources, present challenges. Renewable energy sources depend on geographic location, climate, and weather. Thus regions have different needs for and availability of specific renewable sources. Moreover, connecting renewable sources to the electricity grid is a major issue in terms of cost and efficiency. Currently, there is a bottleneck in transmission lines because the existing transmission grids are supporting conventional energy resources. Legacy power grids that have been in place for several decades occupy the routes and land needed to set up additional power lines supporting renewable sources.

Middle-income countries may be able to partially leapfrog legacy grids located near large fossil fuel power plants in urban areas. But it may be difficult to leapfrog to a grid that is entirely powered by wind and solar plus energy storage—at least not while also expanding electricity access and driving economic growth. Even in advanced countries such as the United States, transmission lines need to increase by at least 25 percent over the next decade. Expanding distribution for power through renewable sources requires not only investments in new transmission lines, but also in renovating legacy lines to integrate them smoothly in new frameworks. As long as energy storage options remain both economically and technically limited, the appetite may increase for other technologies to maintain baseload energy supplies. Examples are natural gas and hydro technologies, as well as other technologies at different levels of maturity (ranging from geothermal to green hydrogen), along with fuels such as nuclear power. Box 9.1 discusses the role of alternate technologies as system stabilizers.

In view of the high cost of capital, the risk of intermittency, and the high storage cost for low carbon energy, middle-income countries will need flexibility in managing how they go about reducing their own emissions, while expanding energy access and maintaining security. Furthermore, to support global decarbonization, they will need to ensure coordination on the use of *green* industrial policy so that it does not limit their participation in low-carbon value chains.

Box 9.1 Technologies that can act as "stabilizers" of energy supply

Different technologies can play different roles as stabilizers of energy supply.

Hydropower. In addition to being a low-carbon source of energy, hydropower is a dispatchable and flexible technology. Hydropower with storage is currently one of the most cost-effective low-carbon solutions for integrating large-scale variable renewable energy capacity. For example, 1 megawatt of hydropower in Bhutan and Nepal can help integrate 5–6 megawatts of variable renewable energy in India and Bangladesh. There is an urgent need to scale up investment in rehabilitating and upgrading the existing hydropower installed capacity as well as restoring the current reservoir storage capacity. By 2030, more than 20 percent of the global hydropower infrastructure is expected to be more than 55 years old, the age at which major electromechanical equipment needs to be rehabilitated and upgraded. The risk-return profile and long gestation period of large hydropower projects has resulted in the limited participation of private financing in hydropower projects. Only 27 percent of the added hydropower installed capacity from 2011 to 2020 was privately owned—a rate that is even lower for large hydropower projects.

Geothermal. Geothermal power is one of the cleanest energy resources. It is also associated with some of the lowest land use of any energy technology, including other

(Box continues next page)

Box 9.1 Technologies that can act as "stabilizers" of energy supply (continued)

renewable sources. Although traditionally a baseload source of electricity, geothermal power can offer flexibility because plants can run continuously or adjust quickly to match demand and supply. Adopting appropriate pricing structures that recognize geothermal power's up-front costs can increase the flexibility in generating and dispatching geothermal power. Geothermal energy and heat pumps can also play a key role in enhancing the stability and flexibility of the grid, particularly with the rise of renewable energy sources.

Hydrogen. Hydrogen has a role to play in storing energy and providing grid flexibility, as well as serving as a fuel in sectors in which carbon emissions are hard to abate. The cost of renewable hydrogen production depends on the cost of renewable power and the capital cost of equipment—notably, electrolyzers[a]—as well as on the financing cost represented by the cost of capital. In today's best locations and under optimistic assumptions, the production cost can be as low as US$3 per kilogram, although this level cannot serve as a benchmark for low- and middle-income countries due to lower-quality renewable resources and high capital costs of equipment. For example, the cost of an electrolyzer system varies significantly, from less than US$500 per kilowatt in China to as much as US$2,000 per kilowatt elsewhere.[b] Electrolyzer costs are expected to fall rapidly in the coming years, and so future projects will benefit from large-scale electrolyzers that will be cheaper. Although the current investment in hydrogen is significantly less than that in mature renewable energy technologies such as wind and solar, hydrogen technology has seen strong inflows of early stage capital as well as high levels of national funding in recent years in Europe and the United States. Regions with abundant solar and wind endowments, especially in Africa, can provide cheap green hydrogen for both domestic use and export. Demand for green hydrogen can also reciprocally boost investments in renewables and provide a salient business case for investment in renewables while facilitating electrification in some middle-income countries.

Natural gas. The use of natural gas reduces emissions if it displaces coal and if fugitive emissions are sufficiently low. Natural gas can empower industrial development as a chemical feedstock, fertilizer component, direct energy source, and electricity provider. However, switching from coal to natural gas does not help to shift or avoid path-dependency. It can lead to a carbon lock-in—that is, a long-term reliance on the built fossil fuel infrastructure.[c] Wealth losses from stranded gas reserves could be significant. Estimates range from US$1.7 trillion to US$3.8 trillion based on climate targets that are aligned with the Paris Agreement on climate change.[d] This force for preservation is further exacerbated by the large share of government ownership of natural gas reserves—approximately 80 percent. As a result, governments may be reluctant to abandon these assets due to windfall profits and rents.

Sources: ESMAP et al. 2023; Hansen 2022.

a. An electrolyzer is a device that uses electricity to split water or other components into their constituent elements. It is a critical technology for producing low-emission hydrogen from renewable electricity.
b. ESMAP et al. (2023).
c. Melekh, Grubb, and Dixon (2024).
d. Hansen (2022).

Notes

1. Stern (2023). Pursuit of net zero is important for stabilizing global temperatures and keeping global surface temperature increases below 2 degrees Celsius.
2. See For a Livable Climate: Net-Zero Commitments Must Be Backed by Credible Action (dashboard), United Nations, New York, https://www.un.org/en/climatechange/net-zero-coalition.
3. Dasgupta (2018).
4. Glennerster and Jayachandran (2023).
5. Introduced by Hausmann et al. (2014), "economic complexity" refers to a measure of a society's productive knowledge. Prosperous societies have the knowledge to make a larger variety of more complex products. Hausmann et al. (2014) attempt to measure the amount of productive knowledge countries hold and how they can move to accumulate more of it by making more complex products.
6. Helveston, He, and Davidson (2022).
7. Green (2019).
8. Way et al. (2022).
9. Mealy and Teytelboym (2022).
10. Bloom et al. (2023).
11. Bettarelli et al. (2023).
12. Mealy and Teytelboym (2022).
13. Barattieri, Mattoo, and Taglioni (2024). Any attempt to measure industrial policies is fraught with challenges, and this database reflects only one measure of industrial policies, which may overrepresent countries that issue a relatively large quantity of legislative documents or those with greater regulatory transparency.
14. Jain et al. (2024).
15. As research conducted by Rozenberg and Fay (2019) suggests.
16. Lall et al. (2023).
17. Glennerster and Jayachandran (2023).
18. Foster et al. (2023).
19. Gardner and Henry 2023; World Bank (2015).
20. Lall and Vagliasindi (2024).
21. Schmidt, Cancella, and Pereira (2016).
22. The social rate of return refers to the extrafinancial value of an investment (such as the value of environmental or social outcomes).
23. See PPI (Private Participation in Infrastructure Database), World Bank, Washington, DC, http://ppi.worldbank.org/.
24. Using parameters from Lowe, Papageorgiou, and Pérez-Sebastián (2019).
25. Egli (2020); Mazzucato and Semieniuk (2018); Steffen and Waidelich (2022).
26. Polzin et al. (2019); Salm (2018).
27. Steffen et al. (2020).
28. Egli 2020; Mazzucato and Semieniuk (2018).
29. Egli, Steffen, and Schmidt (2018); Kirkpatrick and Bennear (2014).
30. Waissbein et al. (2013); WEF (2014).
31. Egli, Steffen, and Schmidt 2018; Estache and Steichen 2015; Lüthi and Wüstenhagen (2012).
32. IRENA (2023).
33. Estimates of the cost of capital are based on the cost of debt and the cost of equity. The cost of debt is the cost to finance a loan for a renewable energy asset. The cost of equity is the return on equity required by the project developer (IRENA 2023).
34. Iyer et al. (2015); Schmidt, Cancella, and Pereira (2016).
35. Zhou et al. (2023).
36. Noothout et al. (2016).
37. Kahn and Lall (2022). This surge in demand reflects a combination of relatively high-income elasticities and modest price elasticities—see the meta-analysis in Labandeira, Labeaga, and López-Otero (2017). This combination implies that energy demand is likely to continue growing, particularly for middle-income countries, notwithstanding efforts to enhance energy efficiency.
38. Pindyck (2021).
39. IEA (2021).
40. Deichmann et al. (2019).
41. See Scenarios Portal, Network for Greening the Financial System, Paris, https://www.ngfs.net/ngfs-scenarios-portal/.
42. The LEED certification is based on a scored rating mechanism that evaluates the environmental performance of buildings, including location, sustainable sites, water efficiency, energy efficiency and atmosphere, material selection and resources used, indoor air quality, and integrative process.
43. Qiu and Kahn (2019).
44. Cirera, Lee, and Ding (2024).
45. Albornoz et al. (2009).
46. Holladay (2016); Richter and Schiersch (2017).
47. Eskeland and Harrison (2003).
48. Bryan and Williams (2021).
49. Bashmakov (2007); Bashmakov et al. (2023).
50. A feed-in tariff is a policy tool that encourages the use of renewable energy technologies by guaranteeing customers a set price for the electricity they generate.
51. Carbon capture, utilization, and storage (CCUS) is an advanced iteration of the traditional carbon capture and storage (CCS) technology. CCS focuses mainly on the capture and sequestration of carbon dioxide to mitigate emissions, whereas CCUS takes a step further by finding practical applications for the captured carbon. DACCS is direct air capture with carbon storage. BECCS is bioenergy with carbon capture and storage.
52. World Bank and ESMAP (2024).
53. IEA (2023b).

References

Albornoz, Facundo, Matthew A. Cole, Robert J. R. Elliott, and Marco G. Ercolani. 2009. "In Search of Environmental Spillovers." *World Economy* 32 (1): 136–63.

Barattieri, Alessandro, Aaditya Mattoo, and Daria Taglioni. 2024. "Trade Effects of Industrial Policies: Are Preferential Agreements a Shield?" World Bank, Washington, DC.

Bashmakov, Igor. 2007. "Three Laws of Energy Transitions." *Energy Policy* 35 (7): 3583–94.

Bashmakov, Igor, Michael Grubb, Paul Drummond, Robert Lowe, Anna Myshak, and Ben Hinder. 2023. "'Minus 1' and Energy Costs Constants: Empirical Evidence, Theory and Policy Implications." SSRN Preprint (March 30), Social Science Research Network, Rochester, NY. https://papers.ssrn.com/sol3/papers.cfm?abstract_id=4401851.

Bettarelli, Luca, Davide Furceri, Pietro Pizzuto, and Nadia Shakoor. 2023. "Environmental Policies and Innovation in Renewable Energy." IMF Working Paper WP/23/180 (September), International Monetary Fund, Washington, DC.

Bloom, Nicholas, Tarek Alexander Hassan, Aakash Kalyani, Josh Lerner, and Ahmed Tahoun. 2023. "The Diffusion of New Technologies." NBER Working Paper 28999 rev. (November), National Bureau of Economic Research, Cambridge, MA.

Bryan, Kevin A., and Heidi L. Williams. 2021. "Innovation: Market Failures and Public Policies." Chapter 13 in *Handbook of Industrial Organization*, vol. 5, edited by Kate Ho, Ali Hortaçsu, and Alessandro Lizzeri, 281–388. Amsterdam: North-Holland.

Cirera, Xavier, Kyung Min Lee, and Yuheng Ding. 2024. "Green Technology Adoption, Energy Efficiency, and Carbon Emissions in India: A Firm Perspective." World Bank, Washington, DC.

Dasgupta, Ani. 2018. "IPCC 1.5° Report: We Need to Build and Live Differently in Cities." Commentary, Topic: Cities (blog), October 31, 2018. https://www.wri.org/insights/ipcc-15deg-report-we-need-build-and-live-differently-cities.

Deichmann, Uwe, Anna Reuter, Sebastian Vollmer, and Fan Zhang. 2019. "The Relationship between Energy Intensity and Economic Growth: New Evidence from a Multi-Country Multi-Sectorial Dataset." *World Development* 124 (December): 104664.

Egli, Florian. 2020. "Renewable Energy Investment Risk: An Investigation of Changes over Time and the Underlying Drivers." *Energy Policy* 140 (May): 111428.

Egli, Florian, Bjarne Steffen, and Tobias S. Schmidt. 2018. "A Dynamic Analysis of Financing Conditions for Renewable Energy Technologies." *Nature Energy* 3 (November): 1084–92.

Energy Institute. 2023. "Statistical Review of World Energy 2023." June, Energy Institute, London.

Eskeland, Gunnar S., and Ann E. Harrison. 2003. "Moving to Greener Pastures? Multinationals and the Pollution Haven Hypothesis." *Journal of Development Economics* 70 (1): 1–23.

ESMAP (Energy Sector Management Assistance Program), OECD (Organisation for Economic Co-operation and Development), GIF (Global Infrastructure Facility), and Hydrogen Council. 2023. "Scaling Hydrogen Financing for Development." ESMAP Paper, World Bank, Washington, DC.

Estache, Antonio, and Anne-Sophie Steichen. 2015. "Is Belgium Overshooting in Its Policy Support to Cut the Cost of Capital of Renewable Sources of Energy?" *Reflets et Perspectives de la Vie Économique* 54 (1–45): 33–45.

Fetter, T. Robert. 2022. "Energy Transitions and Technology Change: 'Leapfrogging' Reconsidered." *Resource and Energy Economics* 70: 101327.

Foster, Vivien, Nisan Gorgulu, Dhruv Jain, Stéphane Straub, and Maria Vagliasindi. 2023. "The Impact of Infrastructure on Development Outcomes: A Meta-Analysis." Policy Research Working Paper 10350, World Bank, Washington, DC.

Gardner, Camille, and Peter Blair Henry. 2023. "The Global Infrastructure Gap: Potential, Perils, and a Framework for Distinction." *Journal of Economic Literature* 61 (4): 1318–58.

Glennerster, Rachel, and Seema Jayachandran. 2023. "Think Globally, Act Globally: Opportunities to Mitigate Greenhouse Gas Emissions in Low- and Middle-Income Countries." *Journal of Economic Perspectives* 37 (3): 111–36.

Green, Martin A. 2019. "How Did Solar Cells Get So Cheap?" *Joule* 3 (3): 631–33.

Hansen, Tyler A. 2022. "Stranded Assets and Reduced Profits: Analyzing the Economic Underpinnings of the Fossil Fuel Industry's Resistance to Climate Stabilization." *Renewable and Sustainable Energy Reviews* 158 (April): 112144.

Hausmann, Ricardo, César A. Hidalgo, Sebastián Bustos, Michele Coscia, Alexander James Gaspar Simoes, and Muhammed A. Yildirim. 2014. *The Atlas of Economic Complexity: Mapping Paths to Prosperity*. Cambridge, MA: MIT Press.

Helveston, John Paul, Gang He, and Michael R. Davidson. 2022. "Quantifying the Cost Savings of Global Solar Photovoltaic Supply Chains." *Nature* 612 (7938): 83–87.

Holladay, J. Scott. 2016. "Exporters and the Environment." *Canadian Journal of Economics* 49 (1): 147–72.

IEA (International Energy Agency). 2021. "An Energy Sector Roadmap to Carbon Neutrality in China." IEA, Paris.

IEA (International Energy Agency). 2023a. "Critical Minerals Market Review 2023." IEA, Paris.

IEA (International Energy Agency). 2023b. *World Energy Outlook 2023*. Paris: IEA.

IRENA (International Renewable Energy Agency). 2023. "The Cost of Financing for Renewable Power." IRENA, Abu Dhabi, United Arab Emirates.

Iyer, Gokul C., Leon E. Clarke, James A. Edmonds, Brian P. Flannery, Nathan E. Hultman, Haewon C. McJeon, and David G. Victor. 2015. "Improved Representation of Investment Decisions in Assessments of CO_2 Mitigation." *Nature Climate Change* 5 (March): 436–40.

Jain, Gautam, Chris Bataille, Noah Kaufman, and Sagatom Saha. 2024. "Resuscitating WTO for the Energy Transition: Why, How, and Who." Background paper prepared for *World Development Report 2024,* World Bank, Washington, DC.

Kahn, Matthew E., and Somik Vinay Lall. 2022. "Will the Developing World's Growing Middle Class Support Low-Carbon Policies?" NBER Working Paper 30238 (July), National Bureau of Economic Research, Cambridge, MA.

Kirkpatrick, A. Justin, and Lori S. Bennear. 2014. "Promoting Clean Energy Investment: An Empirical Analysis of Property Assessed Clean Energy." *Journal of Environmental Economics and Management* 68 (2): 357–75.

Labandeira, Xavier, José M. Labeaga, and Xiral López-Otero. 2017. "A Meta-Analysis on the Price Elasticity of Energy Demand." *Energy Policy* 102 (March): 549–68.

Lall, Somik Vinay, Jon Kher Kaw, Forhad J. Shilpi, and Sally Beth Murray. 2023. *Vibrant Cities: On the Bedrock of Stability, Prosperity, and Sustainability.* Washington, DC: World Bank.

Lall, Somik Vinay, and Maria Vagliasindi. 2024. "The Green Lucas Paradox: Are There Renewable Energy Bargains in Developing Countries?" Background paper prepared for *World Development Report 2024,* World Bank, Washington, DC.

Lowe, Matt, Chris Papageorgiou, and Fidel Pérez-Sebastián. 2019. "The Public and Private Marginal Product of Capital." *Economica* 86 (342): 336–61.

Lüthi, Sonja, and Rolf Wüstenhagen. 2012. "The Price of Policy Risk: Empirical Insights from Choice Experiments with European Photovoltaic Project Developers." *Energy Economics* 34 (4): 1001–11.

Malhotra, Abhishek, and Tobias S. Schmidt. 2020. "Accelerating Low-Carbon Innovation." *Joule* 4 (11): 2259–67.

Mazzucato, Mariana, and Gregor Semieniuk. 2018. "Financing Renewable Energy: Who Is Financing What and Why It Matters." *Technological Forecasting and Social Change* 127 (February): 8–22.

Mealy, Penny, and Alexander Teytelboym. 2022. "Economic Complexity and the Green Economy." *Research Policy* 51 (8): 103948.

Melekh, Yaroslav, Michael Grubb, and James Dixon. 2024. "Energy Technologies for Low-Carbon Development in Middle-Income Countries: Assessment and Implications." Background paper prepared for *World Development Report 2024,* World Bank, Washington, DC.

Noothout, Paul, David de Jager, Lucie Tesnière, Sascha van Rooijen, Nikolaos Karypidis, Robert Brückmann, Filip Jirouš, et al. 2016. *The Impact of Risks in Renewable Energy Investments and the Role of Smart Policies: Final Report.* Karlsruhe, Germany: Fraunhofer Institute for Systems and Innovation Research.

Pindyck, Robert S. 2021. "What We Know and Don't Know about Climate Change, and Implications for Policy." *Environmental and Energy Policy and the Economy* 2 (1): 4–43.

Polzin, Friedemann, Florian Egli, Bjarne Steffen, and Tobias S. Schmidt. 2019. "How Do Policies Mobilize Private Finance for Renewable Energy? A Systematic Review with an Investor Perspective." *Applied Energy* 236 (February 15): 1249–68.

Qiu, Yueming, and Matthew E. Kahn. 2019. "Impact of Voluntary Green Certification on Building Energy Performance." *Energy Economics* 80 (May): 461–75.

Richter, Philipp M., and Alexander Schiersch. 2017. "CO_2 Emission Intensity and Exporting: Evidence from Firm-Level Data." *European Economic Review* 98 (September): 373–91.

Rozenberg, Julie, and Marianne Fay, eds. 2019. *Beyond the Gap: How Countries Can Afford the Infrastructure They Need while Protecting the Planet.* Sustainable Infrastructure Series. Washington, DC: World Bank.

Salm, Sarah. 2018. "The Investor-Specific Price of Renewable Energy Project Risk: A Choice Experiment with Incumbent Utilities and Institutional Investors." *Renewable and Sustainable Energy Reviews* 82 (Part 1): 1364–75.

Schmidt, Johannes, Rafael Cancella, and Amaro O. Pereira, Jr. 2016. "An Optimal Mix of Solar PV, Wind and Hydro Power for a Low-Carbon Electricity Supply in Brazil." *Renewable Energy* 85 (January): 137–47.

Steffen, Bjarne, Martin Beuse, Paul Tautorat, and Tobias S. Schmidt. 2020. "Experience Curves for Operations and Maintenance Costs of Renewable Energy Technologies." *Joule* 4 (2): 359–75.

Steffen, Bjarne, and Paul Waidelich. 2022. "Determinants of Cost of Capital in the Electricity Sector." *Progress in Energy* 4 (3): 033001.

Stern, Nicholas. 2023. "Harnessing Creative Destruction to the Tackling of Climate Change: Purpose, Pace, Policy." In *The Economics of Creative Destruction: New Research on Themes from Aghion and Howitt,* edited by Ufuk Akcigit and John Michael Van Reenan, 365–97. Cambridge, MA: Harvard University Press.

Waissbein, Oliver, Yannick Glemarec, Hande Bayraktar, and Tobias S. Schmidt. 2013. *Derisking Renewable Energy Investment: A Framework to Support Policymakers in Selecting Public Instruments to Promote Renewable Energy Investment in Developing Countries.* March. New York: United Nations Development Programme.

Way, Rupert, Matthew C. Ives, Penny Mealy, and J. Doyne Farmer. 2022. "Empirically Grounded Technology Forecasts and the Energy Transition." *Joule* 6 (9): 2057–82.

WEF (World Economic Forum). 2014. "Mitigation of Political and Regulatory Risk in Infrastructure Projects: Introduction and Landscape of Risk." WEF, Geneva.

World Bank. 2015. "From Billions to Trillions: MDB Contributions to Financing for Development." July, World Bank, Washington, DC.

World Bank and ESMAP (Energy Sector Management Assistance Program). 2024. "Net Zero Energy by 2060: Charting Europe and Central Asia's Journey toward Sustainable Energy Futures." World Bank, Washington, DC.

Zhou, Xiaoyan, Christian Wilson, Anthony Limburg, Gireesh Shrimali, and Ben Caldecott. 2023. "Energy Transition and the Changing Cost of Capital: 2023 Review." March, Oxford Sustainable Finance Group, Smith School of Enterprise and the Environment, University of Oxford, Oxford, UK.